Objective Writing
for Business
and Industry

Objective Writing for Business and Industry

Marcia V. Mascolini
Caryl P. Freeman

Reston Publishing Company, Inc.
A Prentice-Hall Company
Reston, Virginia

Library of Congress Cataloging in Publication Data

Mascolini, Marcia V.
    Objective writing for business and industry.

    1. Business report writing.   2. Report writing.
I. Freeman, Caryl P.   II. Title.
HF5719.M37 1983   808'.066651021   83-9565
ISBN 0-8359-5139-1

Interior design and production by Jeanne-Marie Peterson

© 1984 by Reston Publishing Company, Inc.
A Prentice-Hall Company
Reston, Virginia 22090

10   9   8   7   6   5   4   3   2   1

Printed in the United States of America

To
Gertrude M. Mascolini
and
Lorna E. Freeman

Contents

Acknowledgments

As we complete this text, we would like to thank L. M. Moskovis, who thought of using case materials in introductory writing courses before the idea was discovered by scholarly journals, and Leo Niemi, who encouraged us throughout the project. Thanks also to Emily Gillula for contributing the section on use of computer databases in preparing bibliographies and to students and business people, acknowledged throughout the text, for sharing their work with us.

Introduction

Gaining technical expertise in your field demands a major commitment of time and resources. Thus, you are probably concentrating hardest on courses directly related to your profession. However, your employer will expect you to have not only technical expertise but also the communication skills necessary to convey your knowledge to other employees or to the public. In fact, the more you know about a specialized subject area, the more others will depend on you for information. To give information, you need good communications skills— including the ability to write simply, clearly, and concisely. This book will help you to learn to write about facts, that is, to write objectively. Objective writing always has a definite purpose. It is intended for a specific audience with a particular need for the information. It focuses on gathering, analyzing, and reporting factual information. Your ability to complete these steps will enable you to accept a professional position with confidence in your writing ability.

To be successful as an objective writer, you must first sharpen your analytical skills. Today, pushing a button can bring a printout of information which might better be measured in pounds than in pages. The objective writer is responsible for sifting through these mountains of data to find pertinent information and to interpret it accurately. This book will help you develop skills which speed the process of analysis. You will start from the first day of the course to concentrate on the steps which facilitate the processes of interpreting and reporting information.

The first two chapters of the book focus your thinking on the reasons for writing—what the audience needs to know and why the audience wants to know. In chapter 3, you encounter the first common business format—a standard form. You learn how to provide complete and accurate business information quickly. Then you have some time to build your skill in writing the basic message unit—a paragraph of objective information which meets the needs of a particular audience. By chapter 7 you will have progressed to writing another common business message—instructions. Then you can share your technical expertise with others who need to learn from you.

As you learn to organize longer messages, you can work with more data to find simple solutions for your readers. Each chapter explains the kind of thinking you need to do and provides a complete example not only of the finished product but also of the thought processes that make the solution possible. You will be studying some of the classical methods of organizing information, but always in a practical context.

Chapter 14 lets you use all your knowledge to write a formal report. You can complete reports using either primary or secondary research techniques. And if you are already in the job search process, the chapter on career planning gives you information and examples of resumes and letters of application to help you find employment.

Throughout this growth process, you will appreciate some special features of this text. Using this textbook, you never have to "think of a subject to write about" because you will be working on cases. Cases are practical situations in which you have a major role as writer. Your job then is not to think of a subject but to study a situation, determine what information will be most useful to a particular audience, organize that information for quick understanding, and present it in an appropriate format. Using cases has another advantage. It will make the time you spend in class more beneficial. Because your classmates and instructor have the same information you have, you can all work together on each step of the process.

For technical help in structuring sentences, you can refer to the appendixes. Appendix A reminds you of the major elements of sentence structure and punctuation that you need for objective writing. Each section is complete in itself and contains an exercise to test your grasp of the concept. Appendix B shows a few special techniques to help you write in a style that readers will find easy to understand.

So welcome to the modern world of information processing. If you give this book careful attention, complete the exercises thoughtfully, and set aside time to think through assignments, you will complete the course with a refined ability to assess a situation quickly, analyze your audience, organize your thoughts, and write a useful, informational message.

Chapter 1

Identifying
the Audience

To the Student:
As you read chapter 1 and complete the exercises, you will be asked to
. . . define the term "audience"
. . . assess the audience's previous knowledge of a subject
. . . consider the audience's point of view
. . . assess the language an audience understands.

When you write poetry or fiction, you are your principal audience. You have an idea or impression which you try to express with a combination of words, patterned in the way you choose, to please yourself. This process is personal. If your poem or story is published, your readers may or may not agree with it or enjoy it, but you are not necessarily responsible for teaching them or for giving them pleasure.

However, when you write in a business or an organizational setting, your messages are public rather than personal. You may, in fact, address several publics in the same message. For example, the writer of a company's annual report addresses the stockholders of the company, the company's employees, and often the people in the community where the company is located. The writer's task is not to amuse or to entertain but to provide information to each audience. The memos, letters, and reports you will write are far simpler than an annual report. Yet, like the annual report, each of them is a message to the reader. Your ability to identify and assess your audience will help you make writing choices that will help to determine the quality of your message. Identifying your audience is also the first step in the pre-writing process which includes all the steps you must take before actually drafting a message.

WHO READS YOUR WRITING?

Your intended audience is the person who requests information; however, your actual audience may be a great deal broader. For example, you prepare a report at the request of your supervisor. She passes it along to the district manager. He incorporates part of it in a report of his own. Depending on the nature of the report, it may be sent to the headquarters office, or it may be returned to regional or district offices for action. Like all written work, your message becomes a sort of public property because, once it leaves your hands, it takes on an almost independent life. In one sense, your audience in a professional setting is everyone who has access to your writing. In another sense, your audience is only one person—the person who must take action or make a decision on the basis of information you provide. Before you begin to write, you should understand how much the immediate reader needs to know about the subject of your message, the reader's point of view about the subject, and what level of language the reader will understand. If your message might be of interest to other readers, you must also identify them insofar as possible so you can be sure that they, too, can understand your message.

WHAT WILL THE AUDIENCE WANT TO READ?

Readers usually know something about any subject when they start to read. After studying a subject, writers almost always know more about it than readers. The writer's responsibility is to select facts which a reader needs from a large store of information. The writer must provide sufficient information for the reader to make a decision or act on the basis of the information. The writer must also be sure to include only pertinent information which bears directly on the subject of the message. Sufficient information refers to the quantity of information. The reader must have enough information to understand your message but not so much as to become confused. Pertinent information refers to the quality of the information. The reader wants only information which is relevant to the subject of the message. Here is an example which will help you understand the concept of sufficient, pertinent information.

You have met with Michael Mercer of Jefferson's Asphalt Sealing Company to sign a contract for paving four parking lots around the plant. One of your duties is to see that employees know when the work will begin so that the contractor will not find cars in the lot when he plans to work on it. The following bulletin board notice obviously contains more information than a reader needs to know but less information than he or she needs to take appropriate action.

NOTICE

Today I had a chat with Michael Mercer, an old friend of mine who works for a really fine paving contractor. We went over all the company parking lots to see what shape they are in. Actually, they are in quite good shape, but if we fill in some holes now and reseal all the surfaces, they will remain in good shape. So, beginning on Monday, July 7, the machinery will roll into Lot B, and Mike and his crew will fill potholes, seal cracks, seal the surface, and repaint nice shiny new yellow parking lines. Then on July 10, he'll start on Parking Lot A to give it the same treatment. He'll even be working on Saturday to make things easier on us. That means he can start on Lot C on Monday, July 14, and be through with all the work by the end of that week if the weather stays good. I hope you will all cooperate while we get the parking lots repaved.

Employees at the bulletin board would laugh at such a notice. They might also wonder why "your old friend" is getting the paving contract. They will be glad to have the potholes repaired, but they will not know how "to cooperate," for the message does not ask employees to park in other lots during the paving process.

You could write a much shorter, but equally ineffective, bulletin notice:

NOTICE

Effective at 12:01 a.m., July 7, no one may park in Lot B until further notice.

The information is certainly pertinent, but it is not sufficient. Employees who regularly use Lot B will be angry that "their" lot is closed for no apparent reason. Other employees will foresee an unnecessary traffic jam in Lots A, C, and D. They will be justifiably upset. All the turmoil could be avoided with a notice that provides sufficient, pertinent information such as this one.

NOTICE

So it may be repaved, each company parking lot will be closed for a few days, beginning July 7.

Lots will be temporarily closed according to the following schedule:

Lot B   closed   12:01 a.m. July 7 −8 p.m. July 9
Lot A   closed   12:01 a.m. July 10 −8 p.m. July 12
Lot C   closed   12:01 a.m. July 14 −8 p.m. July 16
Lot D   closed   12:01 a.m. July 17 −8 p.m. July 19

Exercise A   The following article appeared in a student newspaper.

Jim Jenkens served as president of the university from 1951-1961. During his tenure in office, the university expanded greatly. Cavanaugh Hall and Edgar Science Building were erected. And through it all, President Jenkens took special pride in the landscaping around these and other campus buildings. He personally supervised the selection and planting of the many beautiful trees and shrubs on campus. In fact, students, seeing him outside planning the landscaping, used to say to each other, "Don't let Jenkens catch you walking on the grass." That story of course is an exaggeration. He wanted the whole university community to enjoy the beauty of the campus. Now we can repay President Jenkens by volunteering to work at the first Jim Jenkens Day. Volunteers will clean brush from wooded areas and paint trash containers among other tasks.

1. If the article appeared in a chapter of a book titled *History of the University*, what information should be left out?
2. If the article appeared under a newspaper column titled "Future Events," what information should be left out?
3. If the article appeared in a newspaper column titled "Volunteers Needed," what information should be added?

Messages Which Consider the Reader's Point of View

Different audiences react differently to the same object or idea because each audience has special interests, needs, and desires. All readers agree, for example, that a potato is a plant grown for its edible tubers. Yet, outside of a botany class, few readers ever think of a potato in this way. They think of it rather as it relates to their needs, as it has value in their lives. As a writer, your responsibility is to think about a subject as it relates to a particular audience.

As you address each audience, your responsibility as a writer is to anticipate and supply the kinds of information each audience wants. Dieters, shoppers, and farmers each form different audiences. The following table shows what each audience might find most interesting about potatoes.

Group	Information
1. Dieters:	A half cup of mashed potatoes, made with milk, contains 63 calories, 22 calories fewer than a half cup of canned corn. But a half cup of potato salad has 99 calories.
2. Shoppers:	Ten pounds of Idaho baking potatoes cost 43 cents more than 10 pounds of all-purpose potatoes.
3. Farmers:	Potatoes require well fertilized sandy soil to grow well. Or you may plant treated eye segments above ground in special mulch.

Exercise B   You can take any piece of equipment, event, or idea and find that different groups of people react from different viewpoints. For each item below, indicate what each audience might want to know.

1. Hospital X-ray machine
    a. X-ray technician:
    b. Patient with injured wrist:
    c. Patient's doctor:
    d. X-ray department billing clerk:
2. Breakdown of a hospital X-ray machine
    a. X-ray technician:
    b. Patient with injured wrist:
    c. Patient's doctor:
    d. Machine service representative:
3. Airport X-ray machine
    a. Machine operator:
    b. Airline passenger:
    c. Airport security guard:
4. Power failure
    a. Person stuck in an elevator:

b. Police:

c. Owner of frozen food warehouse:

d. Worker at frozen food warehouse:

5. Unemployment

a. Teenager:

b. State employment officer:

c. Social services case worker:

d. Factory owner:

Messages Which Use Language the Reader Will Understand

Your ability to identify your audience and thus to understand its viewpoint will give you some insight into the level of language you need to communicate effectively.

A starting point is to divide audiences into specialist and nonspecialist. Specialists are people with technical expertise in a certain area. They command a specialized vocabulary—terminology that a nonspecialist does not understand. Nonspecialists are people who may have an interest in a certain field but no special knowledge of the field beyond appreciation.

For example, specialists and nonspecialists alike are interested in stereo equipment, but communicating with these groups requires different vocabulary. A manufacturer might describe specifications of stereo equipment to an engineer or knowledgeable user in the following terms:

Tone Control	TREBLE: ± 12dB at 10kHz
	BASS: ± 12dB at 100Hz
Signal to Noise Ratio	PHONO: 75dB (IHF "A" Weighted, 1 watt output, 5mV input) 85dB ("A" Weighted, 10mV input)
	TAPE PLAY: 80dB (IHF "A" Weighted, 1 watt output, 0.5 input) 95dB ("A" Weighted)
Loudness	+ 9dB at 40Hz
	+ 5dB at 20kHz

This vocabulary is probably meaningless to the nonspecialist, however. A music lover with no specialized knowledge of stereo equipment might be happier with this information:

Independent bass and treble tone controls let you adjust response to suit room conditions and phono cartridge and speaker characteristics.

The loudness switch boosts bass and treble response for more natural tonality at low listening levels. This feature is a real convenience for late-night listening.

Many audiences fall somewhere between specialist and nonspecialist. They are people familiar with the common terminology of a field through reading or questioning or even comparison shopping. Thus, they will understand technical terms if the writer provides explanations like those in the following paragraphs about a stereo amplifier.

> The power amp section of this unit delivers high output with extremely low distortion: 27 watts per channel, both channels driving into 8 ohms, 20~20,000 Hz, with no more than 0.06% total harmonic distortion.
>
> These outstanding specifications mean that you'll enjoy room-filling power to satisfy your ears with your favorite music. The 0.06% distortion figure is so low that you can turn up the volume without being bothered by overloading the amplifier circuitry. So music always sounds clear, clean, and natural.

From the examples you have just read, you can see the importance of using vocabulary that an audience will understand. The technical description of stereo specifications in the first example would completely baffle the nonspecialist who would probably not bother reading to the end of the list. The specialist would derive little useful information from the second example and be bored by it. When a writer must use a single piece of writing which may be read by both specialist and nonspecialist, he or she will need to use some technical terms to be precise but will add explanatory sections so nonspecialists can expand their knowledge by reading the same material that specialists understand.

The less familiar an audience is with a field, the more information and explanation the writer has to supply. (Remember that a specialist in one field is not necessarily a specialist in another field.) You noticed in the first example that the writer can use almost a kind of shorthand, made up of numbers and abbreviations, to communicate with the specialist while in the second and third examples the explanations are in sentence form. The nonspecialist reader could look up many terms like *treble, bass, tonality, distortion,* and *amplified* in a standard dictionary.

Exercise C   1. Here is a simple recipe for strawberry shortcake. Read through the recipe and list the terms that would have to be explained to beginners in the kitchen.

½ c. flour	4 t. baking powder
2 egg yolks	¼ c. sugar
½ c. cornmeal	Filling: strawberries, sugar, cream or egg whites
½ c. butter	

Cream butter and sugar. Add egg and dry ingredients in the usual way. Bake in hot oven. Cool cake. Cut off top. Fill with crushed berries and sugar. Decorate with strawberries and cream or egg white (sweetened to taste).

2. What audiences understand each set of specifications?

WEIGHT	11 LB.	5 KG.
HEIGHT	4½ IN.	11.4 CM.
VOLUME	8 GAL.	30.3 L.

3. The following descriptions of a microcomputer would appeal to different audiences. Describe the audience who will understand each description.

ASCII keyboard

1500 bps cassette interface

8 fully buffered peripheral board connectors with interrupt and DMA priority structure

4 analog-to-digital inputs, 3 TTL inputs and 4 TTL outputs for game I/O

****

standard typewriter keyboard

accepts rapid input from tape recorder

handles more than one program at a time; yet keeps them separate

2 to 4 people can play video games

4. The following features are all listed on the specifications page in a brochure describing a new car. Which features will be understood only by specialists?

2-speed windshield wiper/washer

1.4 liter (1,397 cc.) 4-cyl. OHV engine with catalytic converter

clear window glass

flip-out rear side windows

transistorized electric ignition system with solid-state voltage regulator

recirculating ball steering

lowback front bucket seats with adjustable head restraints

full carpeting

rear-view mirror

5-speed overdrive manual all-synchromesh transmission with 3.700 final drive ratio

color coordinated 2-spoke steering wheel

independent MacPherson strut front/4-bar line rear suspension

175 SR 13 steel-belted radial white wall tires

Chapter 2

Identifying
the Subject

To the Student:

    As you read chapter 2 and complete the cases, you will be asked to

      . . . identify the subject of your writing

      . . . relate the subject to the audience

      . . . describe your subject in a single sentence.

In chapter 1, you studied methods for identifying your audience such as distinguishing between intended and actual audience; determining the kind of information the audience wants; and estimating the audience's level of understanding. Without completing this analysis carefully, you cannot go to the next stage of the pre-writing process—determining the exact subject of your writing.

WHY DO YOU DEFINE THE SUBJECT?

Writing a single sentence that describes your topic "in a nutshell" is the most important step in writing. Defining the topic accurately will help you solve two problems. First, you insure that the reader gets only the information needed to make a decision. Second, you save time.

Like most writers, you have probably had the experience of sitting down to write when you did not have a clear idea about what you had to write. You did one of two things: You stared for hours at a blank sheet of paper or you filled pages and pages with writing that missed the point. If you can formulate a single sentence to guide your writing, you start sooner and stay on the subject so you will have to write less.

HOW DO YOU DEFINE THE SUBJECT?

To make sure you direct all your energies to writing no more and no less than you need to write, you must begin with an accurate description. The process is simple. Just answer these five questions as accurately as possible in one sentence.

Why?   Give your reason for writing about this subject.

What?   Name the particular aspect of the subject you will discuss in your message.

When?   Specify the time frame for the subject.

Where?   Indicate the physical area where this message applies.

Who?   Mention the people who are part of the subject you will discuss.

Why is the first question to answer because it concerns your reasons for investigating a subject. You answer the *why* question by analyzing your audience: Why does your audience need information? Does the reader need a list of facts or does the reader need facts and a conclusion?

What refers to the kind of information the reader needs. You may list or describe or classify or define or evaluate the facts you gather to meet this need.

When refers to the time frame your report covers. If you are writing about an event that is happening now, your time frame is current. Or you may be writing about something that happened in the past; then you would cite a specific year, 1960, or a specific span of time, 1960-1970.

Where refers to a particular place—Indiana; Muskogee, Oklahoma; or Cook County. *Who* indicates the people your report involves. Sometimes you can skip the *who* category. For example, if you are writing a report on the average rainfall in Seattle, *who* is irrelevant.

Answering these questions will allow you to take a broad topic and narrow it to a workable one.

Example 1   Let us take a sample topic—fringe benefits. This topic is extremely broad. It ranges from limited medical or life insurance for which each employee pays to the free use of private airplanes and country club facilities. Because most employees have some job-related fringe benefits, writing about such a vast, vague topic is impossible. You can make the topic workable, however, by analyzing your audience and by answering the five questions: *why, what, when, where,* and *who.*

The audience for this report is the new personnel manager of your company, Peerless Plastic Products, of York, Pennsylvania. His first meeting with union officials is coming up soon. Before the meeting, he wants to know what fringe benefits Peerless Plastic Products provides. This information helps to answer the *what* question as well as the *when* and *where* questions. Because the personnel manager tells you he is meeting with union officials, you understand that he wants information about hourly employees rather than salaried employees so you also have the answer to the *who* question.

Worksheet and Solution

Here is how a worksheet for defining this subject looks:

Why: To inform Peerless Plastic Products' new personnel manager
What: List and describe fringe benefits
Where: York, Pennsylvania
When: Current
Who: Hourly employees

After you have finished the worksheet, you are ready to combine your answers into a single descriptive sentence. Using the answers on the fringe benefit worksheet, your descriptive sentence could be

This report will *list and describe the fringe benefits* the *York, Pennsylvania,* branch of Peerless Plastic Products *currently* offers *hourly employees* so *the new personnel manager will understand them.*

Notice that the italicized words in the sentence are the answers to *why,*
what, where, when, and *who* on the worksheet. However, these answers as
they appear in your descriptive sentence do not follow the order of the questions on the worksheet. The information now follows this order: *what,*
where, when, who, and *why.* Your object in writing the description is to use
all the relevant information on the worksheet in the order that results in the
most clearly written sentence. When you have finished writing the descriptive sentence, you have defined your topic and may begin gathering the
specific information you will need for the message.

Example 2   If the new personnel manager had asked you to report about the benefits for
salaried employees, your worksheet would look like this:

Why: To inform the Peerless Plastics Products' new personnel man-
           ager

What: List and describe fringe benefits

Where: York, Pennsylvania

When: Current

Who: Salaried employees

Your descriptive sentence might read

> This report will *list and describe the fringe benefits* the *York,*
> *Pennsylvania,* branch of Peerless Plastic Products *currently* of-
> fers *salaried employees so the new personnel manager will*
> *understand them.*

Example 3   But what if the personnel manager had asked, "Are the fringe benefits we
provide competitive with those offered by other firms in the area?" Now
your worksheet looks like this:

Why: To determine if Peerless Plastic Products is competitive

What: Evaluate fringe benefits paid by Peerless Plastic Products and
           other area firms

Where: York, Pennsylvania

When: Current

Who: Hourly employees

Your single sentence could be written

> This report will indicate whether the *fringe benefits* Peerless
> Plastic Products *currently* offers *hourly employees* are *competi-*
> *tive* with those offered by other companies in *York, Pennsyl-*
> *vania.*

You can see that although the general topic of each report is fringe
benefits, the descriptive sentence must change each time you report on a dif-

ferent aspect of the topic. In Examples 1 and 2, your final report would probably take the form of a detailed list. You would be very careful to list every benefit and describe it, but you would not have to make any decision about the worth or adequacy of the benefit.

In Example 3, your report might contain lists and graphs and much more information to show the benefits at Peerless and the benefits at other companies, but because of your answer to the *what* question, you will have to make a decision: "Yes, we are competitive," or "No, we are not competitive."

Cases   1. Here are some additional situations. For each, prepare a worksheet and write a single sentence to describe your final report.

a. "What's the dollar value of the benefits Peerless provides for hourly employees?"

b. "We only employ 100 hourly workers. How do our fringe benefits compare with those offered by other small manufacturers around here?"

c. "Are our fringe benefits for hourly workers up to the national average for our industry?"

d. "Please compare the fringe benefits of our salaried and hourly employees." (Hint: be sure to state the basis for comparison — actual benefits or monetary value of benefits.)

e. "How does the community perceive our overall fringe benefit package?"

2. One of the most common opening questions in a job interview is "Tell me something about yourself." Some applicants waste this valuable two or three minutes with irrelevant information, "Well, I was born in Chicago, but we moved here when I was only six."

Refer to chapter 1. Think hard about the person who might interview you for your next position. Write two or three sentences to identify the kind of company where you want a position and the exact job you want.

Now use a chapter 2 worksheet to pinpoint some important facts about yourself that will make your answer relevant to the interviewer.

a. Fill out the worksheet and then write the single sentence that will describe the way you will answer the question, "Tell me about yourself."

b. Now think of another company and a totally different job. Again, identify the company and the job and the interests of the interviewer. Complete the assignment by using the technique in chapter 2 to help you write the single sentence that will guide you to give the most appropriate answer to the question, "Tell me about yourself."

3. You have had the experience in class of being asked to write a paper about a broad topic. If the instructor did not give a specific outline, you probably wrote what you knew best and crossed your fingers. Sometimes you were lucky; sometimes, not so lucky.

Let us take a necessary but unusual item—clothing. In each class the instructor makes the same vague assignment: "For next Friday's paper, prepare two or three pages about clothing." Your plan, as a serious student, is to take two descriptive sentences to the instructor on Monday to ask, "Which of these papers would you prefer for Friday? I think both topics are interesting and appropriate for the class and would enjoy writing either paper."

Prepare two worksheets and two descriptive sentences for each situation described below.

a. Your Textiles 200 class is in the second week of a four-week unit on cotton and part-cotton fabrics. This class about consumer-oriented textiles emphasizes fibers, yarns, fabric construction, and fabric finishes as they relate to use, serviceability, and care.

b. You are a student in Institutional Management 416. The course work includes study of institutional administration, job analysis, labor policies, personnel problems, and cost control in different types of food-service institutions. You have selected fast-food restaurants for your special study.

c. You have already written papers on make-up, stage properties, and lighting in your Play Production 250 class which is an introductory course in the principles and practices of play production.

d. Men and Women in Contemporary Society 190 is a class that analyzes the roles of men and women with particular emphasis on problems and adjustment and conflict in contemporary society. You have already written papers on career aspirations and food preferences.

e. Culture and Communication 370 is a course that concentrates on the nature and role of various symbolic systems of communication, especially nonverbal, such as food, dress, art forms, use of space, mythology, and folklore. You are writing this paper in connection with a chapter in the text entitled "Superiority—East and West."

WORKSHEET

Exercise No.

Why:

What:

When:

Where:

Who:

Descriptive Sentence:

WORKSHEET

Exercise No.

Why:

What:

When:

Where:

Who:

Descriptive Sentence:

WORKSHEET

Exercise No.

Why:

What:

When:

Where:

Who:

Descriptive Sentence:

WORKSHEET

Exercise No.

Why:

What:

When:

Where:

Who:

Descriptive Sentence:

WORKSHEET

Exercise No.

Why:

What:

When:

Where:

Who:

Descriptive Sentence:

WORKSHEET

Exercise No.

Why:

What:

When:

Where:

Who:

Descriptive Sentence:

WORKSHEET

Exercise No.

Why:

What:

When:

Where:

Who:

Descriptive Sentence:

WORKSHEET

Exercise No.

Why:

What:

When:

Where:

Who:

Descriptive Sentence:

WORKSHEET

Exercise No.

Why:

What:

When:

Where:

Who:

Descriptive Sentence:

WORKSHEET

Exercise No.

Why:

What:

When:

Where:

Who:

Descriptive Sentence:

WORKSHEET

Exercise No.

Why:

What:

When:

Where:

Who:

Descriptive Sentence:

WORKSHEET

Exercise No.

Why:

What:

When:

Where:

Who:

Descriptive Sentence:

Chapter 3

Using Forms

To the Student:

As you read chapter 3 and complete the cases, you will be asked to

. . . understand the importance of forms

. . . appreciate the need to keep business records

. . . practice techniques for completing forms successfully.

Filling out forms is an aspect of daily living that almost nobody can escape. Forms supply the basic data for many different transactions. We fill out forms in conducting personal business like renting an apartment. We fill them out in applying for college admission, loans, scholarships, and jobs, and, once we get a job, in reporting on our work.

Forms come in an amazing number of varieties. Some, such as checklists, require almost no writing at all. The checker has only to mark appropriate boxes. Various standard forms require putting facts in appropriate blanks. Other forms call for written comments, remarks, or explanations of factual information.

In this chapter, we are concerned with standard forms which you, the writer, use to supply factual information and brief written comments. Although you will not have to produce whole paragraphs or even very many whole sentences, you will have to pay attention to two rules of good writing: (1) be aware of your audience and (2) give specific information.

AUDIENCE ANALYSIS

When you fill out a form, your audience, the recipient of the form, is specific. For example, when you complete an apartment inventory, a rental agent is your audience. When you apply for work, a personnel officer is your audience. On the job, you usually report to your immediate supervisor. In addressing any of these audiences, you are actually sending two messages. The visible written message contains facts. The rental agent may want to know about the condition of the rug in your apartment. A prospective employer needs to know the name of your high school. Your work supervisor is interested in the number of customers you called on during a business day. But you also send an unwritten message with each form. The invisible message contains information about you as a person. Are you neat? Can you follow directions? Are you accurate? Are your answers specific?

All of us fill out so many forms that we often do not pay enough attention to doing them well. By keeping a few helpful hints in mind, however, you can avoid many pitfalls and present yourself and your information well to your audience.

HELPFUL HINTS

Forms are usually designed to provide the reader with maximum information from a writer in a minimum of time. You can keep the time you spend on forms at a minimum if you follow these suggestions.

1. *Get organized.* Grade reports, cancelled checks, bank statements, copies of tax forms, appointment books, and expense records are among

the various kinds of documents useful for filling out different kinds of personal application forms such as those for scholarships, loans, and housing. If you keep these documents on file in one place, the information will be easy to retrieve.

2. *Review forms thoroughly.* Read forms from beginning to end before you fill them out. A thorough review of all the questions helps you avoid entering information in the wrong places.

3. *Keep accurate records.* Often forms, such as applications for credit, ask for personal history. Typical questions concern how long you have lived in a town, how long you have lived in each of your last three dwellings, and what banks you have accounts with. A look at your personal records will quickly reveal all such information, and you can be sure of recording it accurately. Once you have filled out several forms of the same kind, such as job applications, you can even plan ahead and take a list of your references' names, addresses, and telephone numbers to the employment office, for example, to insure accuracy.

Another method of insuring accuracy is to fill out forms while information is still fresh in your mind. For example, many salespeople are responsible for giving an account of the customers they called on in a day. Making accurate notes about each call insures a complete record at the end of the day.

4. *Make entries readable.* Whether you type or write by hand, the actual words on paper are the means of communication. If the words are not readable, the message is lost. Typed entries are almost always more readable than handwritten entries. Before you type a final copy of an important form, however, you may want to make a trial attempt, if feasible, on a photo- or duplicate copy to get an idea of spacing requirements. Also, if you are typing several carbon copies, you may want to check the pressure setting on your typewriter to make sure that the impression on the final copy is clear. Of course, errors must be corrected on each copy.

If you must fill in a form by hand, do the final copy in ink rather than pencil (unless instructed otherwise) because ink is easier to read and is more permanent.

5. *Fill in all the blanks.* Insure completeness of information by filling in all the blanks on forms. If a question does not apply to you, draw a line through the blank to show you have considered the question rather than skipped it. For example, many forms have a space for military service. If you have not served in the armed forces, draw a line through that space.

6. *Be consistent.* You will find on some forms that you repeat the same words or use the same information several times. If such is the case, give the answer in the same way. For example, if you attended three different schools and have to supply their addresses, abbreviate the state name the same way each time: Kingston, PA, Dallas, PA, and Wilkes-Barre, PA,

rather than Kingston, Penn., Dallas, Penna., and Wilkes-Barre, PA. Figure out the most efficient form before you start and use it throughout.

7. *Use judgment.* No form perfectly fits every single person who fills it out. You may find that you have more information than the form has space for. If such is the case, you are asked on many forms to add a sheet for additional information. Write a title on the additional sheet so that its relationship to the form itself is clear.

One standard Inventory Checklist offers the following choices:

Furniture: 1. If only limited furniture included, list on this form.
            2. If unit is rented furnished or too many items to list here:
                A. Attach list of furniture, showing condition.
                B. Tenant should sign attached furniture list.
                C. Under this "Furniture" heading on this form, tenant should write: "See list attached".

If your unit is completely furnished, your Inventory Checklist will look like this:

Furniture: 1. If only limited furniture included, list on this form.
            2. If unit is rented furnished or too many items to list here:
                A. Attach list of furniture, showing condition.
                B. Tenant should sign attached furniture list.
                C. Under this "Furniture" heading on this form, tenant should write: "See list attached".

See list attached.

Then you will start your own "attached list" on a separate page like this:

Furniture in Unit 2B Concord Arms Apartments

September 1, 198-

Item	Condition
Day bed	Fair
3-shelf bookcase	Scratched
Upholstered side chair	Poor

etc. through all furniture items.

8. *Use current forms.* Most large businesses review and revise forms on a regular schedule. When you receive an updated form, compare it to the older model so you understand what information will be added or deleted on the new form. Then throw away the outdated forms.

9. *Use the "Comments" section.* This short space often lets you point out special events or exceptions which will be important to the reader. If delivery can only be made after 3 p.m., say so. If one of your regular customers is moving the business to another state, be sure the regional sales manager knows that fact from your daily sales report.

Forms are designed to pull information together and get it organized. As you work with the cases in this chapter, you will need to read carefully. In the real world, information does not always appear in the order called for by a form. Be sure your work gives all the information the reader needs and be sure your writing is legible.

Cases   1. Fill in the form shown below using the information in the phone conversation that follows it. Be sure to fill in the form as you are reading the conversation — not after you finish reading it. When you have completed the form, answer the five questions that follow the conversation.

SERVICE CALL

Date_____Time_____ A.M. ☐
                                              P.M. ☐

Name_____

Address_____

Service Address_____

Phone _____Apt. No._____

SERVICE WANTED:

☐ Install   ☐ Repair   ☐ Deliver   ☐ Pickup

☐ Contract   ☐ Complaint   ☐ Warranty   ☐ Estimate

COMMENTS: _____

_____

_____

Product_____Make_____

Model_____Serial No._____

BILLING:

☐ C.O.D.   ☐ Charge   ☐ Repeat   ☐ Guarantee

Promised for_____Route_____

Serviceman_____Taken by_____

TOPS NO. 4100

Reprinted with permission.

You: Good morning, Ace Appliance. May I help you?

Caller: When I opened the refrigerator to fix breakfast this morning, the light didn't come on and everything seemed sort of room temperature. So I looked in the freezer and things are melting. It's just quit!

You: Have you checked to be sure the plug is in the wall socket and the other lights on that circuit are working?

Caller: Of course, I checked the fuses and the plug. The refrigerator has quit working!

You: Then you want repair service.

Caller: I certainly do!

You: You understand our service policy. There is an initial charge of $25 and an additional charge for parts and labor. All charges are payable when the service is performed.

Caller: You'll take a check, I hope.

You: You may use a charge card or a local check if you have two other pieces of identification. May I have your name and address, please?

Caller: Marilyn Jones, 221 West Elm Street.

You: The refrigerator is at this address?

Caller: Certainly!

You: Is that a single family home or an apartment?

Caller: A house.

You: What make and model is the refrigerator?

Caller: It's a Freezaire. That's why I called your company because that brand is listed in your ad. How do I know what model it is?

You: I can tell you how to find that. Take a pencil and paper to the refrigerator and open the door. On most models, you will see a white or gray sticker near the bottom of the box itself—not on the door. It will tell you the model and serial number.

Caller: Do I need the serial number too?

You: Not for a standard repair. We do need the model to be sure our service representative has the correct parts on the truck. Will you get the model for me, please?

Caller: Hold the phone. (pause) Hello. It's rather faint. This thing must be 10 years old, but it looks like Model TA254BC and Serial Number 8539.

You: Thank you. Will someone responsible be home today?

Caller: This is my day to go grocery shopping, but there's not much point unless I can put the food away, is there? When can you come?

You: Well, it depends on how long other calls take. I think the earliest time would be 11:30, and it could be as late as 2 this afternoon. May I have your phone number? Our representative will call before he arrives.

Caller: 666-7777

You: Thank you. To preserve the cold air you have, don't open your freezer again. That food will be fine, and we'll be there to-day.

Answer these questions after you have filled in the service call form.

    a. Did you use the comments line? Why or why not?

    b. Who needs the information on the form?

    c. What are the two possible ways you may give this information to the service representative?

    d. What may happen if you give incorrect or incomplete information to the service representative?

    e. Is your handwriting legible, and are the facts you put on the form correct?

2. Some companies print their own employment applications. Other companies have different forms for hourly and salaried workers. Still others buy standard forms which the printing company updates to conform to current laws. The form for Case 2 is such a "public" form. Applicants for employment ranging from part-time clerk to manager or supervisor must provide the same application information to the company.

Your instructor will probably give you special instructions for this assignment. If not, fill out the application that appears after these instructions for the next job you want to hold. Do not think ahead to "when I finish my studies"; think instead about what you can do now and in the near future. If you want to move up in your present company, fill out the application as you would to compete with outside applicants. Put the name of a real company at the top of the page. Learn enough about the company to put down a real job title after the word "position." Supply a realistic figure for "salary desired." (If you are applying for a scheduled position in a union shop, you may write "scale" in the blank.)

Look up the exact dates of your employment history. Some employers do not care, but others will use any small error as a method of eliminating your name from the list of applicants. Think about your "reason for leaving." "Got a better job" or "Returned to school" are fine; but "Hours interfered with school" sounds much better than "Lousy work schedule." Tell the truth, but put the best face you can on bad situations; "Laid off" somehow sounds better to most readers than "Fired."

The health question is now very straightforward. Employers cannot discriminate for health reasons if your health allows you to do the job. Eyeglasses are not an impairment—unless you are applying to be a deep sea diver. Likewise, a trick knee or bad back are not interesting to an employer UNLESS you are applying for a job that requires you to lift heavy objects as part of the day's work.

When you think of references, think about the job. If mathematical ability is important, think of a person who can attest to your speed and accuracy with figures. If safe driving is important, who can give you a fine recommendation about your careful driving? Can a previous employer speak well of your work habits? Students often list one or two important teachers. When you have decided who the best references are, ask them if they are willing to have you use their names. Once you have used their names on a school assignment, you may want to use them on a real application, and you MUST always ask permission BEFORE you actually use a person's name as a reference.

Remember to use a pen and to fill in every blank even if you put in a dash (−). This form does not specify "Please print," so you may write or print. Pick the writing form that is most readable.

APPLICATION FOR EMPLOYMENT

PERSONAL INFORMATION

DATE _____

NAME _____

PRESENT ADDRESS _____
                                 Street   City

_____ TELEPHONE _____
       State   Zip

HOW LONG HAVE YOU LIVED AT THIS ADDRESS? _____

PERMANENT MAILING ADDRESS _____
                                       Street   City

_____ TELEPHONE _____
       State   Zip

SOCIAL SECURITY NUMBER _____ ARE YOU 18 YEARS OLD OR OLDER? _____

ARE YOU A CITIZEN OF U.S.? _____

HAVE YOU EVER BEEN CONVICTED OF A CRIME? IF SO, WHEN, WHERE, AND NATURE OF OFFENSE? _____

_____

_____

ARE THERE ANY FELONY CHARGES PENDING AGAINST YOU? _____

EMPLOYMENT DESIRED

POSITION _____ DATE YOU CAN START _____ SALARY DESIRED _____

ARE YOU EMPLOYED NOW? _____ IF SO MAY WE INQUIRE OF YOUR PRESENT EMPLOYER? _____

EVER APPLIED TO THIS COMPANY BEFORE? _____ WHERE? _____ WHEN? _____

EDUCATION	NAME AND LOCATION OF SCHOOL	YEARS ATTENDED	DID YOU GRADUATE	SUBJECTS STUDIED
GRAMMAR SCHOOL				
HIGH SCHOOL				
COLLEGE				
TRADE, BUSINESS OR CORRESPONDENCE SCHOOL				

GENERAL

SUBJECTS OF SPECIAL STUDY OR RESEARCH WORK _____

_____

WHAT SPECIAL WORK EXPERIENCES HAVE YOU HAD? _____

_____

_____

WHAT FOREIGN LANGUAGES DO YOU SPEAK OR WRITE FLUENTLY? _____

U.S. MILITARY OR NAVAL SERVICE _____ RANK _____ PRESENT MEMBERSHIP IN NATIONAL GUARD OR RESERVES _____

(CONTINUED ON OTHER SIDE)

LAST

FIRST

MIDDLE

FORMERS EMPLOYERS (LIST BELOW LAST FOUR EMPLOYERS, STARTING WITH LAST ONE FIRST)

DATE MONTH AND YEAR	NAME AND ADDRESS OF EMPLOYER	SALARY	POSITION	REASON FOR LEAVING
FROM				
TO				
FROM				
TO				
FROM				
TO				
FROM				
TO				

REFERENCES: GIVE BELOW THE NAMES OF THREE PERSONS NOT RELATED TO YOU, WHOM YOU HAVE KNOWN AT LEAST ONE YEAR.

	NAME	ADDRESS	BUSINESS	YEARS ACQUAINTED
1				
2				
3				

HEALTH RECORD: DO YOU HAVE ANY IMPAIRMENTS PHYSICAL, MENTAL, OR MEDICAL WHICH WOULD INTERFERE WITH YOUR ABILITY TO DO THE JOB FOR WHICH YOU HAVE APPLIED? *

* Completion of this part of the application is optional and will not result in adverse treatment.

IN CASE OF EMERGENCY NOTIFY

Name	Address	Phone No.

I AUTHORIZE INVESTIGATION OF ALL STATEMENTS CONTAINED IN THIS APPLICATION. I UNDERSTAND THAT MISREPRESENTATION OR OMISSION OF FACTS CALLED FOR IS CAUSE FOR DISMISSAL. FURTHER, I UNDERSTAND AND AGREE THAT MY EMPLOYMENT IS FOR NO DEFINITE PERIOD AND MAY, REGARDLESS OF THE DATE OF PAYMENT OF MY WAGES AND SALARY, BE TERMINATED AT ANY TIME WITHOUT ANY PREVIOUS NOTICE.

DATE _____ SIGNATURE _____

DO NOT WRITE BELOW THIS LINE

INTERVIEWED BY _____ DATE _____

REMARKS:

NEATNESS		CHARACTER	
PERSONALITY		ABILITY	

HIRED	FOR DEPT.	POSITION	WILL REPORT	SALARY/ WAGES

APPROVED: 1. _____ 2. _____ 3. _____

EMPLOYMENT MANAGER · DEPT. HEAD · GENERAL MANAGER

Reprinted with permission of Doubleday Bros. & Co.

3. Use the Inventory Checklists that are printed at the end of this case, and ask a friend to help you complete this assignment.

Step 1. You and your friend will each need one Inventory Checklist to complete this part of the assignment. You should not talk to each other while you complete parts a. and b. of step 1.

    a. You should consider that you are moving out of your living quarters. Check "Termination Inventory Checklist" and fill out each item on the list that is applicable in your room or house or apartment. As you work on your list, remember that you do not want to be charged heavily for excessive damage.

    b. Do not tell your friend about part a. which you are completing. Ask your friend to check "Commencement Inventory Checklist" and to fill out each applicable item on the list as if he or she were moving into your quarters at this time. Tell your friend to remember that he or she should be careful to write down any damage for which he or she would not want to be charged when the lease is up.

Step 2. When you and your friend have each completed an Inventory Checklist, compare the lists. If your lists are the same, go to step 4. If you disagreed about the condition of some items or had other differences, go to step 3.

Step 3. Use the third Inventory Checklist for this step. Work together and re-inspect each item about which you originally disagreed. Keep your original point of view (you are moving out and your friend is moving in) but discuss each area of disagreement until you can find language that you feel is fair to both points of view. Write that new language on the third Inventory Checklist.

Step 4. Take the completed Inventory Checklists to class and be prepared for class discussion as indicated below.

    a. If your list and your friend's list were alike, read the questions in part b. below. Then suggest reasons why you and your friend avoided any disagreement.

    b. If your list and your friend's list were not alike, prepare answers for the questions below.

        1. Why did you and your friend agree about some items and disagree about others? (Do your answers have anything to do with audience or purpose?)

        2. Which items on the list provoked the most discussion? Can you suggest any reasons why these items should have caused more disagreement than others?

        3. Can you suggest changes in the form that would have made agreement easier?

        4. Why would the changes you suggest make agreement easier?

Order by Form No. ML M911 (Rev.)

Doubleday Bros. & Co., Kalamazoo, Mich.

INVENTORY CHECKLIST

To Tenant: (If this form used as commencement inventory checklist).

YOU SHOULD COMPLETE THIS CHECKLIST, NOTING THE CONDITION OF THE RENTAL PROPERTY, AND RETURN IT TO THE LANDLORD WITHIN 7 DAYS AFTER OBTAINING POSSESSION OF THE RENTAL UNIT. YOU ARE ALSO ENTITLED TO RE-QUEST AND RECEIVE A COPY OF THE LAST TERMINATION INVENTORY CHECK-LIST WHICH SHOWS WHAT CLAIMS WERE CHARGEABLE TO THE LAST PRIOR TENANTS.

This form may be used for either commencement or termination inventory checklist. This form is herewith designated as:

Check one
{ ☐ Commencement Inventory Checklist.   Date _19 _ _ _ _ _
{ ☐ Termination Inventory Checklist..   Date _19 _ _ _ _ _

Condition

Appliances (list) _

Carpeting _

Closets _

Doors _

Draperies _

Electrical Fixtures _

Paint _

Plumbing Fixtures _

Shelves _

Walls --- ------------------------
-- ------------------------
-- ------------------------
Windows --- ------------------------
-- ------------------------
-- ------------------------

Furniture: 1. If only limited furniture included, list on this form.
            2. If unit is rented furnished or too many items to list here:
                A. Attach list of furniture, showing condition.
                B. Tenant should sign attached furniture list.
                C. Under this "Furniture" heading on this form, tenant should write: "See list attached".

-- ------------------------
-- ------------------------
-- ------------------------
Other --- ------------------------
-- ------------------------
-- ------------------------
Specify defects noted --- ------------------------

The above is a complete inventory checklist of the premises commonly described as --
                                                                            Apartment Number
located at --, --------------------------------------, Michigan.
                                   Address

    Tenant moved in/out --, 19 --------.

---   ---
                     Tenant   Landlord

NOTES: If used as commencement inventory:
         1. Landlord shall furnish 2 blank copies to tenant.
         2. Unless landlord and tenant agree to complete this inventory checklist within a shorter period, the tenant shall review the checklist,
             note the condition of the property and return 1 copy of the checklist to the landlord within 7 days after receiving possession of the
             premises.
         If used as termination inventory: Landlord should complete this checklist at termination of occupancy. Show all damages claimed
         caused by tenant.

FORM NO. ML M-911 (REV.) Copyright 1973 by Doubleday Bros. & Co., Kalamazoo, Michigan STOCK FORM PRINTERS

Reprinted with permission.

Order by Form No. ML M911 (Rev.)

Doubleday Bros. & Co., Kalamazoo, Mich.

INVENTORY CHECKLIST

To Tenant: (If this form used as commencement inventory checklist).

YOU SHOULD COMPLETE THIS CHECKLIST, NOTING THE CONDITION OF THE RENTAL PROPERTY, AND RETURN IT TO THE LANDLORD WITHIN 7 DAYS AFTER OBTAINING POSSESSION OF THE RENTAL UNIT. YOU ARE ALSO ENTITLED TO RE-QUEST AND RECEIVE A COPY OF THE LAST TERMINATION INVENTORY CHECK-LIST WHICH SHOWS WHAT CLAIMS WERE CHARGEABLE TO THE LAST PRIOR TENANTS.

This form may be used for either commencement or termination inventory checklist. This form is herewith designated as:

Check one
☐ Commencement Inventory Checklist. Date _ _ _ _ _ _ _ _ _ _ _ _ _ _ _ _ _ _ _19 _ _ _ _
☐ Termination Inventory Checklist.. Date _ _ _ _ _ _ _ _ _ _ _ _ _ _ _ _ _ _ _19 _ _ _ _

Condition

Appliances (list) _

Carpeting _

Closets _

Doors _

Draperies _

Electrical Fixtures _

Paint _

Plumbing Fixtures _

Shelves _

Walls -
- -
- -
Windows -
- -
- -

Furniture: 1. If only limited furniture included, list on this form.
2. If unit is rented furnished or too many items to list here:
    A. Attach list of furniture, showing condition.
    B. Tenant should sign attached furniture list.
    C. Under this "Furniture" heading on this form, tenant should write: "See list attached".

- -
- -
- -
Other -
- -
Specify defects noted -
- -
- -

The above is a complete inventory checklist of the premises commonly described as -
Apartment Number

located at -, -, Michigan.
Address

Tenant moved in/out -, 19 - - - - - -.

-          -
                   Tenant   Landlord

NOTES: If used as commencement inventory:
1. Landlord shall furnish 2 blank copies to tenant.
2. Unless landlord and tenant agree to complete this inventory checklist within a shorter period, the tenant shall review the checklist, note the condition of the property and return 1 copy of the checklist to the landlord within 7 days after receiving possession of the premises.

If used as termination inventory: Landlord should complete this checklist at termination of occupancy. Show all damages claimed caused by tenant.

FORM NO. ML M-911 (REV.) Copyright 1973 by Doubleday Bros. & Co., Kalamazoo, Michigan STOCK FORM PRINTERS

Reprinted with permission.

Order by Form No. ML M911 (Rev.)

Doubleday Bros. & Co., Kalamazoo, Mich.

INVENTORY CHECKLIST

To Tenant: (If this form used as commencement inventory checklist).

YOU SHOULD COMPLETE THIS CHECKLIST, NOTING THE CONDITION OF THE RENTAL PROPERTY, AND RETURN IT TO THE LANDLORD WITHIN 7 DAYS AFTER OBTAINING POSSESSION OF THE RENTAL UNIT. YOU ARE ALSO ENTITLED TO RE-QUEST AND RECEIVE A COPY OF THE LAST TERMINATION INVENTORY CHECK-LIST WHICH SHOWS WHAT CLAIMS WERE CHARGEABLE TO THE LAST PRIOR TENANTS.

This form may be used for either commencement or termination inventory checklist. This form is herewith designated as:

Check one
- ☐ Commencement Inventory Checklist.   Date _____ 19 _____
- ☐ Termination Inventory Checklist..   Date _____ 19 _____
                                                                        Condition

Appliances (list) _____   _____

Carpeting _____   _____

Closets _____   _____

Doors _____   _____

Draperies _____   _____

Electrical Fixtures _____   _____

Paint _____   _____

Plumbing Fixtures _____   _____

Shelves _____   _____

Walls --- ------------------------------

--- ------------------------------

--- ------------------------------

Windows --- ------------------------------

--- ------------------------------

--- ------------------------------

Furniture: 1. If only limited furniture included, list on this form.
            2. If unit is rented furnished or too many items to list here:
                A. Attach list of furniture, showing condition.
                B. Tenant should sign attached furniture list.
                C. Under this "Furniture" heading on this form, tenant should write: "See list attached".

--- ------------------------------

--- ------------------------------

--- ------------------------------

Other --- ------------------------------

--- ------------------------------

--- ------------------------------

Specify defects noted --

The above is a complete inventory checklist of the premises commonly described as --------------------------
                                                                          Apartment Number
located at --, ------------------------------, Michigan.
                              Address
Tenant moved in/out --, 19 --------.

---   --
                 Tenant   Landlord

NOTES: If used as commencement inventory:
        1. Landlord shall furnish 2 blank copies to tenant.
        2. Unless landlord and tenant agree to complete this inventory checklist within a shorter period, the tenant shall review the checklist,
            note the condition of the property and return 1 copy of the checklist to the landlord within 7 days after receiving possession of the
            premises.
        If used as termination inventory: Landlord should complete this checklist at termination of occupancy. Show all damages claimed
        caused by tenant.
FORM NO. ML M-911 (REV.) Copyright 1973 by Doubleday Bros. & Co., Kalamazoo, Michigan STOCK FORM PRINTERS

Reprinted with permission.

4. Your home is in Muskegon, Michigan, and your sales territory is the western part of the state. Your company provides a major credit card and a major oil company credit card. The charges you make on these cards are billed directly to the company, but you also have some cash expenses each week. The company does not provide a cash advance, so you must request payment for out-of-pocket expenses each week. Use the diary notes shown below to fill out the expense report which appears on the next page.

February 1	February 2	February 3	February 4
mileage 19841-19990	end miles 20082	end miles 20153	end miles 20229
to St. Joseph	To Kalamazoo	to Grand Rapids	to Lansing
Coffee break w/ 1.80	Park .25, 1.00, .10	a.m. bellhop 1.00	a.m. bellhop 1.00
Willis Stone	Bellhop 1.00	p.m. bellhop 1.00	p.m. bellhop 3.00
Parking .65, .25	Lunch 1.89	coffees .40 , .60	taxi 3.75 + .50 tip
			Tow truck 32.50
			Lunch 2.80 + .35 tip

February 5	February 6	February 7	Memoranda
car in shop in			left car in Lansing to
Lansing + home by bus			complete repairs on
bell hop 3.00			ignition system
taxis 4.50 + .70, 5.20 + .75			Sample cases at
3.40 + .50 , 1.10 + .25			Capitol Hotel
Bus .75, .75 22.95			

SALESMAN'S EXPENSE REPORT

FOR WEEK ENDING _____

Salesman _____

NO _____

19 ___

DAY	TOWNS (MUST BE STATED)	MEALS	LODGING	TAXI	CASH TRAIN & BUS	BAGGAGE	MILE-AGE	AUTOMOBILE EXPENSE					OTHER EXPENSES EXPLAIN BELOW	EXPENSE SUMMARY
								GAS	OIL	GARAGE	WASH GREASE	REPAIRS		
SUNDAY														MEALS
MONDAY														LODGING
TUESDAY														TAXI
WEDNESDAY														CASH TRAIN & BUS
THURSDAY														BAGGAGE
FRIDAY														GASOLINE
SATURDAY														OIL
														GARAGE
													MEMO.	WASH & GREASE
														REPAIRS
TOTALS FOR THE WEEK (POST TO EXPENSE SUMMARY)														TOTAL EXPENSE

CASH SUMMARY

CASH AT START
CASH FROM FIRM
COLLECTIONS
TOTAL CASH
TOTAL EXPENSE
CASH SENT FIRM
CASH BALANCE ON HAND
DEFICIT

EXPLANATION OF AUTO REPAIRS AND OTHER EXPENSE _____

MAIL CHECK TO _____

TO REACH ME BY _____

I HEREBY CERTIFY THAT THE ABOVE EXPENDITURES REPRESENT CASH SPENT FOR LEGITIMATE COMPANY BUSINESS ONLY AND INCLUDES NO ITEMS OF A PERSONAL NATURE.

SIGNED _____ SALESMAN

APPROVAL

SALES MGR | AUDITED

FINAL | POSTED

CASHIERS MEMO

CHECK NO _____ DATE _____
AMOUNT _____
SENT TO _____
CARE OF _____

Tops—Form No. 1202 LITHO IN U.S.A.

Reprinted with permission.

Chapter 4

Planning
to Write

To the Student:
　　As you read chapter 4 and complete the exercises, you will be asked to
　　　. . . understand the importance of organization in writing
　　　. . . identify indirect and direct order
　　　. . . select an appropriate order for your audience
　　　. . . identify letter and memo formats
　　　. . . select an appropriate format for your audience.

Analyzing the audience and defining the subject are two important preliminary steps in writing. Once you have completed them and gathered the necessary facts, you are ready to organize your message.

WHY IS ORGANIZATION IMPORTANT?

Good organization is a logical arrangement of facts and ideas that allows the writer to communicate efficiently. In the process of organizing, the writer first groups similar facts and ideas together, then places these groups in the order that achieves a desirable effect. A disorganized message is a jumble of facts and ideas that does not lead to any particular point.

Good organization is important to readers because it prevents frustration. Readers like to pick up a message, read it once, and understand it completely. When you organize your writing to present a single pertinent point and to supply back-up or supporting information, your reader will be able to use your message. Effective messages produce the results a writer wants.

Equally important, good organization saves many hours of planning, writing, and rewriting. Without a good plan, most writers can waste hours "trying to get started." Sometimes, they write down every fact and idea related to the subject, then spend more time sorting and typing before the random ideas begin to resemble a message.

Planning a message to fit the audience and the topic will help you start quickly and stick to the topic. But first you must determine whether you want to organize your message in indirect order or direct order before you begin to write.

WHAT ARE INDIRECT ORDER AND DIRECT ORDER?

Indirect and direct order are the two basic ways to organize messages. Each order has advantages as well as a particular orientation.

Indirect Order

Using indirect order, the writer gives specific details first and builds up to the main idea at the end of the report. The following is a brief example of indirect order.

Detail 1:	I was tired from working overtime.
Detail 2:	I was run down from missing meals and lack of regular exercise.
Detail 3:	Several of the people I work with were ill.
Main Idea:	I caught the flu.

You can think of this structure almost as an addition problem. Detail 1 plus detail 2 plus detail 3 equals main idea, which is the sum of all three details.

Direct Order

Using direct order, the writer gives the main idea first and uses specific details to provide additional information about the main idea or to prove its accuracy. Written in direct order, the previous example looks like this:

Main Idea:	I caught the flu.
Detail 1:	I was tired from working overtime.
Detail 2:	I was run down from missing meals and lack of regular exercise.
Detail 3:	Several of the people I work with were ill.

Here, the details are added later to show the reasons for the writer's main idea. The following exercises give you an opportunity to work with both indirect and direct orders.

Exercise A   Organize the following topics, using indirect order.

1. Explain the disadvantages of car pooling.
   Detail
   Detail
   Detail
   Main Idea

2. Reprimand an employee for wasting materials.
   Detail
   Detail
   Detail
   Main Idea

3. Give reasons for requesting extra time to complete an assignment.
   Detail
   Detail
   Detail
   Main Idea

Exercise B   Organize the following topics, using direct order.

1. Explain the advantages of car pooling.
   Main Idea
   Detail
   Detail
   Detail

2. Congratulate an employee for meeting his or her production quota each week this month.
   Main Idea
   Detail
   Detail
   Detail

3. Ask a hotel to reserve a room for you when you attend a convention next month.
   Main Idea
   Detail
   Detail
   Detail

WHAT ARE THE ADVANTAGES OF EACH ORDER?

After completing these exercises, you see some of the advantages of each order. In Exercise A, you are giving an essentially negative message, one that your reader does not particularly want to hear. Indirect order is effective in these exercises because it prepares the reader to accept the main idea, especially if he or she is resistant to it.

In Exercise B, you are giving either neutral or positive information. You may suppose the reader wants to know what you have to say and is willing to accept the content. Thus, you use direct order, putting the main idea first.

WHAT ORDER SHOULD YOU SELECT?

Audience analysis, again, is a key factor in helping you decide whether to use indirect or direct order. Most business writing is in direct order. First, direct order is more efficient for the reader because the most important information is easier to find than in indirect order. Second, most business writing that you will do is part of your job. The people you will be writing to or for are familiar with the content of your message. Thus, direct order is appropriate for the majority of business messages. Here are some other ideas which will help you make a choice.

1. Consider the reader's reaction to the content of your message. As a general rule, use indirect order to convey a message that will meet with reader resistance. Use direct order for a message which your readers will probably accept.

2. Consider the reader's knowledge of the subject of your message. If your readers have little or no knowledge of the subject about which you are writing, use indirect order. Indirect order allows them to learn as they read. Your main idea, coming after you have discussed all the details, will seem appropriately placed. However, if your readers are already familiar with the subject matter, use direct order. They will want to see the main idea first. Then they may scan as much or as little of the remainder of your message for details, as they wish.

3. Follow specific directions if given. Whether your audience is an instructor or work supervisor, he or she may express a definite preference about what order to use. If that is the case, by all means follow your superior's wishes.

Exercise C Read the following list of topics carefully. Decide whether your audience will resist the message or accept it. Then choose the appropriate order in which to put your main idea and at least three supporting details. Be ready to give reasons for your choices.

1. Explain to an instructor of a previous class why you deserve a better grade than the one you received.
2. Explain the benefits of jogging to a friend.
3. Explain the advantages of a sensible diet to an overweight friend.
4. Explain the advantages of diesel-powered cars.
5. Explain why you are/are not a vegetarian.

WHAT FORMAT SHOULD YOU SELECT?

After you have decided how to organize the content of your message most effectively, you must decide upon a format to use. Format is the arrangement of your message on paper. Business people sometimes need to use report formats such as those you will study in chapter 14 in this book, but two of the most common business formats for short messages are memos and letters. The choice of format depends on whether the message is an internal communication which will stay inside the organization or an external communication which will go outside the organization.

Using Memos

Memos are the most common business format. They are used for internal communication, that is, for sending messages between offices, departments, and branches of the same organization. For example, if an employee in the dispatcher's office at Rogers Trucking Company wants to send a written message to an employee in the payroll office, the dispatcher's office employee uses the memo format. Even if the first employee works in the Ohio office of Rogers Trucking and is sending a message to someone in the company's Kentucky office, the communication is still within the organization, and the memo format is usually used.

Using Letters

Business people use letter format for external communication, to send messages outside their own organizations and to communicate with private individuals or with employees at other companies. For example, if Rogers Trucking wanted to notify an applicant of the formation of a new drivers' training class or to order supplies, it would use letter format.

HOW SHOULD YOUR MESSAGE LOOK?

You may already be familiar with the letter or memo style used by the firm that employs you. Or you may have seen a number of different styles in typewriting textbooks. Business handbooks also show several different correct styles for both memos and letters. However, you can only write one style at a time, so study the next few pages to learn simple correct styles which you can use as you write letters and memos as answers for the cases in this text.

Memos

A. Form Identification

Most companies provide a printed form which identifies itself as correct to use for inter-office communication. Some companies use their regular printed letterhead and add the word MEMO to identify the form. Some companies provide no special memo forms, and the typist will type the word MEMO in the center of the page near the top of the page.

B. Standard Memo Parts

Memos have four standard pieces of information at the top of the first page: *To, From, Subject*, and *Date*. If the company does not provide a printed form, the typist must supply these parts. These four special lines are always double spaced for easy reading.

1. The *To* line names the recipient of the message. This section may contain one or more names. These names do not need to be preceded by a courtesy title such as Mr., Miss, Mrs., or Ms. Indicating the recipient's job title and department shows courtesy and helps to direct the message to the right place.

2. The *From* line names the writer of the memo. It may also include the writer's position and department name. Again, the author does not use a courtesy title (Mr., Miss, Mrs., or Ms). The author of a typed memo often signs his or her initials in ink by the typed name to indicate that the message is authorized.

3. The *Subject* line summarizes the nature of the message. The purpose of the line is to indicate the contents of the memo in a few words. It serves as a "headline" and should focus the reader's attention on the subject of the memo.

4. The *Date* line gives the date on which the memo is sent and is an important part of the record of the transaction. If no special line calls for a date, the typist must supply the date anyway. On memos, the date may be spelled out (February 16, 1983) or, less formally, given as numbers (2/16/83).

C. Body

The body of a memo contains the message the writer wishes to send. Some companies insist that a memo be confined to one subject. Even if the writer has two messages for the same recipient, he or she should use two separate memos. If writers stick to the one-subject/one-memo rule, then readers can easily send on only the part of the message that another employee needs to see.

D. Special Notation

Att. stands for *Attachment* and indicates that the writer has sent something with the message. *Attachment* is used rather than the word *Enclosure* because the extra papers are often stapled or clipped to the memo and sent without an envelope.

(A) **INTER-OFFICE MEMORANDUM**

DATE (4) February 15, 1983

(B) {
(1) TO ___ Arliss Baylor, Supervisor, Payroll

(2) FROM Dale Frieze, Dispatcher's Office

SUBJECT Request for Automatic Payroll Deposit Forms

(3)
}

(C) { Please send me 20 automatic payroll deposit forms for
distribution to drivers and office personnel.

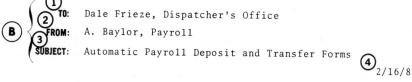

(A) **memo**

(B) {
(1) TO: Dale Frieze, Dispatcher's Office

(2) FROM: A. Baylor, Payroll

(3) SUBJECT: Automatic Payroll Deposit and Transfer Forms
}
(4) 2/16/83

(C) { Here are the automatic payroll deposit forms you requested.
I've also included 20 transfer forms for employees who may
want to change banks.

(D) Att.

Business Letters

The letter on the following page has been typed on letterhead stationery in full block style. The full block style is one of several acceptable business letter styles. It is a particularly easy style to type because all the parts of the letter begin at the left margin. The letter also shows a common business punctuation style, called mixed punctuation. This term means that you use a colon after the salutation and a comma after the complimentary closing line. This letter shows most of the standard parts of a business letter.

A. Letterhead

Business organizations use letterhead stationery for external messages. This printed part of the page contains the name, address, and often the phone number of the company sending the message. Some organizations print other information as well, such as a Telex number or cable code.

B. Date

The date appears two lines below the end of the printed letterhead. On a letter, the date is always typed in full (February 22, 1983).

C. Inside Address

This part of the letter contains the same information that appears on the envelope of the letter. In fact, in some cases, the letter is inserted in a window envelope, and the inside address also serves as the mailing address. The inside address usually begins four lines below the date. For very short letters, the inside address may be placed farther down the page (but no more than 10 lines from the date). The inside address contains from three to five lines of information. All the lines are always single spaced.

1. The recipient's courtesy title (Mr., Mrs., Miss, or Ms.), full name, and job title belong on the first line of the inside address. If the job title is so long that it makes the first line look unbalanced, it may be placed alone as the second line of the inside address:

Mr. George Thomas
Employee Communications Specialist

2. The name of the company for whom the recipient works appears on the next line. Of course, if the letter will be directed to an individual at home, the company name line is omitted.

(A) **WESTON PUBLISHING COMPANY**
2123 Willow Pass Road
Wilkes-Barre, PA 18708

(717) 832-9877   Cable: Westco

(B) April 18, 1984

(C)
Miss Ann Tunell
Engineering Department
Broadworth and Associates
P.O. Box 281
Denver, CO 80213

(D) Dear Miss Tunell:

(E)
Your promptness in reviewing the manuscript we sent you last
month helped us to meet an important deadline. Your comments
about Chapters 4 and 5 will be particularly helpful to the
author and to our staff. A check for your work is enclosed.

Melvin Claudell will be editing this text. I will let him
know that you are familiar with the work. Perhaps he will
call on you for more technical advice.

(F) Sincerely,

Max Baxter

(G) Max Baxter

(H) cc

(I) Enclosure

(J) cc Melvin Claudel, Editor

3. The street address or post office box number appears on the next line of the inside address. The writer usually finds this address on the printed letterhead of the letter he or she is answering. If the address includes a suite number or apartment number, that information goes on the line with the street address:

2409 Golden Rain Road   Apt. No. 2

4. The recipient's city, state, and zip code appear on the last line of the inside address. A comma follows the name of the city. The typist leaves one space after the comma and uses capital letters to type the U.S. Postal Service two-letter abbreviation for the name of the state. The special Postal Service state abbreviations do not require a period. The zip code is typed two to five spaces after the state abbreviation.

D. Salutation

This line appears two lines after the last line of the inside address. Although some firms are starting to experiment with new forms, most companies still begin this line with the word "Dear" followed by the recipient's courtesy title (Mr., Mrs., Miss, or Ms.) and last name. When the writer has no way to know a particular person's name, he or she may use a more impersonal term such as "Ladies and Gentlemen." Whatever salutation is used, the mixed punctuation style requires that the line end with a colon (:).

E. Body

The body of the letter begins two lines below the salutation. This part of the letter may be a few lines or several pages, depending on the length of the message. Each paragraph is typed with single spacing, but the typist leaves a blank line between paragraphs.

F. Complimentary Closing

This line appears two lines below the last line of the last paragraph of the letter. Some of the commonly used business closings are *Sincerely*, and *Cordially*. Whatever closing is used, the line ends with a comma in the mixed punctuation style.

G. Signature Lines

The writer's name is typed four lines below the complimentary closing. The four lines leave space for the writer to sign the letter in ink after it is typed. The writer usually does not use a courtesy title. Sometimes a woman writes her courtesy title in parentheses so the recipient will be able to use the correct title in an answer:

(Miss) Sally Jones

The writer's job title appears on the line following his or her name.

H. Typist's Initials

The person who types the letter for the author uses lowercase letters to type his or her initials two lines below the writer's job title. If the writer of the letter types the letter, no initials are needed.

I. Enclosure Notation

The word, *Enclosure*, or the abbreviation, *Enc.*, typed two lines below the typist's initials (or two lines below the writer's name if the writer typed the letter) indicates that the writer has put one item in the envelope in addition to the letter. If the writer sends several items in the envelope, the plural, *Enclosures*, is typed in this space. Sometimes the author will want to specify the enclosures:

Enclosures: Brochure
             Refund check

J. Carbon Copy Notation

When copies of the letter go to other people as well as to the addressee, the writer types the carbon copy notation two lines below the last typed line to tell the reader the name or names of other people who have a copy of the letter.

The letter on the following page was written by an individual to a business. The writer chose to type the letter in a modified block style. This style aligns the return address and the closing lines toward the right side of the page. The writer also uses mixed punctuation.

A personal business letter has all the parts of a business letter, but the writer must supply a return address.

A. Return Address Block

The writer types his or her street address about two inches from the top of a standard 8½" by 11" sheet of plain stationery. The city, state, and zip code are on the next line, and the date of the letter is on the third line of this block.

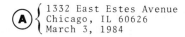

(A) { 1332 East Estes Avenue
Chicago, IL 60626
March 3, 1984

Bann Brace Company
P.O. Box 85A
Grand Central Station
New York, NY 11044

Ladies and Gentlemen:

For some years I have been purchasing your #468L
dorsal brace from Barnas Brothers on West 14th
Street in Chicago. Yesterday I went down to purchase another brace and found a hole in the ground
where the block of stores used to be. The current
phone directory does not list Barnas Brothers.

As I need to have the garment fitted, I would prefer to buy it here rather than order it directly
from you. Please send me the names of other stores
in the Chicago area where I may purchase this back
brace.

Yours truly,

Lorna Edwards

Lorna Edwards

Envelopes

All the information from the inside address must appear on the envelope.

A. Printed Return Address

Business firms usually use printed envelopes which match their letterhead so the typist need not supply a return address.

B. Recipient's Address

The typist copies the inside address on the envelope, usually line for line. The Postal Service prefers the address to be single spaced and typed in all capital letters. The address should be more than one inch from both the left and right margins of the envelope and at least ⅝ inch, but not more than three inches, from the bottom of the envelope.

A. The Return Address

Writers using plain stationery for the letter will also use an unprinted envelope. The recipient's address is typed as on a printed envelope, but the writer must type a return address in the upper left corner of the envelope.

Typing begins on the third line from the top of the envelope and two or three spaces from the edge of the envelope. Some writers use three lines, putting a name on the first line. Others prefer two lines, showing only the same return address information that they type on the letter itself.

WESTON PUBLISHING COMPANY
2123 Willow Pass Road
Wilkes-Barre, PA 18708

B ⟩ MISS ANN TUNELL
ENGINEERING DEPARTMENT
BROADWORTH AND ASSOCIATES
P.O. BOX 281
DENVER, CO   80213

A 1332 East Estes Avenue
Chicago, IL   60626

BANN BRACE COMPANY
P.O. BOX 85A
GRAND CENTRAL STATION
NEW YORK, NY   11044

63

Succeeding Pages

Most business messages are short, but some can be several pages in length. When a letter or a memo requires more than one page, the writer uses plain paper for the second and succeeding pages. Each page must be identified so that if the pages become separated, the reader or writer can put the message back in complete form.

A. Succeeding Page Heading

The easiest page heading is the block form heading. It begins one inch from the top of the page at the left margin. Line one shows the name of the recipient of the letter or memo. This line will be the same as the first line of the inside address, but the person's job title may be omitted. Line two shows the page number, and the final line tells the date of the correspondence.

Remainder of the message

Two lines after the end of the page heading, the message continues. The last page of any business message should contain at least one complete paragraph before the closing lines begin. All the closing lines of a letter or memo on a long message are the same as they are on a one-page message.

(A) { Mr. James Bannerman
Page 4
March 3, 1984

These prices include all taxes and allow conferees full
use of all hotel facilities without charge. The hotel
will only reserve 100 rooms at this special price. Therefore, I am asking several nearby motels to hold rooms for
us until July 1 in case we have an unusually large registration.

Please let me have a final copy of the program by April 1
so we can get a full set of registration materials in
the mail by May 1.

Sincerely,

Marge

Marge Falkenstein

Enclosures: 5

cc Conference Board
      Eric Worthington
      Marcia Grubbs
      Marion Palancheck
      Burton Taylor

Exercise D   You are the director of the Convention and Visitors Bureau at the Kalamazoo Chamber of Commerce. When you return from an early morning meeting, you find five items in your in-basket (see pages 69 through 72). Read them through and then complete the following exercises.

1. List the items in the order you will deal with them. Give reasons for the order you have chosen.

Order	*Item*	*Reason*
1		
2		
3		
4		
5		

2. Indicate the format you will use for each response you make. Give reasons for your choices.

Item	*Format*	*Reason*
1		
2		
3		
4		
5		

3. Show the inside address or memo heading you will use for each written response.

Item	Address or heading for written response
1	
2	
3	
4	
5	

4. Read each item closely. What facts can you infer about each person to whom you must respond?

Item	*What the writer can infer about the reader*
1	
2	
3	
4	
5	

5. Indicate whether your answer will be planned directly or indirectly. Give a reason for your decision.

Item	*Writing plan*	*Reason*
1		
2		
3		
4		
5		

FUN with FOODS

11239 Futura Ave.
Saline, MI 48176

March 18, 198-

Chamber of Commerce
978 Parkway Road
Kalamazoo, MI 49007

Gentlemen:

Your town is a ripoff! We booked a convention at the Nelson
Hotel nearly a year ago and signed a contract for prices and
services. Six months ago, we agreed to an eight percent
across-the-board increase as only fair at today's prices.
We had not printed mailing materials and merely added the
increase to registration costs.

Now that we are committed to a meeting in less than three
weeks, the hotel is asking for special surcharges on everything from rooms to coffee. I am enclosing their letter
and surcharge list. If you ever want us in your city again,
make them eat this ridiculous price increase.

Please let me know immediately what to expect. We cannot
raise prices and don't want to have to use convention time
to hold a raffle. I'm getting NO satisfaction from the
Nelson!

Sincerely,

CR Lowrenson

Clare Lowrenson
Executive Director

cp

Enclosures: 2

(your name) —
Please handle this
W. D.

69

QUICK NOTE

DATE **3/19** , 19___

TO: _Your Name_

COPY TO:_____

SUBJECT
Downtown Club Meeting

As I will be out of town on Tuesday, will you please represent us at the regular Downtown Club meeting (9 a.m. at the Nelson, Room B).

FROM _W. D. Vanden Bosch_

Reprinted with permission.

While You Were Away

FOR ___*Your Name*___

DATE ___*3/20*___ TIME ___*8:30*___ (a.m.) / p.m.

IMPORTANT MESSAGE

FROM ___*W. D. Vanden Bosch*___

OF ___*Executive Director*___

PHONE NO. ___

TELEPHONED		PLEASE CALL BACK
CALLED TO SEE YOU	X	WILL CALL AGAIN
WANTS TO SEE YOU		RETURNED YOUR CALL

MESSAGE *Needs data on number of convention bookings in January of the last three years. Can you account for increases or decreases? For lunch meeting today.*

Signed ___*yg*___

While You Were Away

FOR ___*Your Name*___

DATE ___*3/20*___ TIME ___*9*___ (a.m.) / p.m.

IMPORTANT MESSAGE

FROM ___*Sandy Slocum*___

OF ___*Chamber Newsletter*___

PHONE NO. ___

TELEPHONED	X	PLEASE CALL BACK
CALLED TO SEE YOU		WILL CALL AGAIN
WANTS TO SEE YOU		RETURNED YOUR CALL

MESSAGE *Has room for 200 words from your department if you can get them in by Friday.*

Signed ___*yg*___

71

IABC/michigan

INTERNATIONAL ASSOCIATION OF BUSINESS COMMUNICATORS

March 17, 198-

Chamber of Commerce
978 Parkway Road
Kalamazoo, MI 49007

Gentlemen:

We want to hold an area workshop in Kalamazoo on
September 21. Attendance may be as small as 50 or as
large as 200. We will need two conference rooms, lunch,
and a morning coffee tray.

As this is only a workshop, we try to keep costs
low. What facilities can you suggest that are

1. open that day and

2. adaptable to our possible size variation?

Please let me hear from you at the address shown
below by June 1 so that we can contact the facilities
and plan our publicity.

Sincerely,

Sue D. O'Ryan

Susan Dodge O'Ryan
President

668 Market Street
Three Rivers, MI 49093

formerly Michigan Communicators Association

Chapter 5

Starting to Write

To the Student:
    As you read chapter 5 and complete the exercises and cases, you will be asked to
       . . . recognize a paragraph
       . . . write the topic sentence for a paragraph
       . . . provide details, facts, and examples to explain a topic sentence
       . . . write a concluding sentence for a paragraph
       . . . write short paragraphs about one specific subject.

In analyzing your audience and in stating the subject you will write about, you have taken two important steps in the writing process. Now you are ready to put your knowledge of audience and subject together with the information you want to convey to write a paragraph.

WHAT IS A PARAGRAPH?

A paragraph is a group of related sentences which inform readers about one subject or a particular aspect of one subject. Typically, a paragraph has three main parts: (1) a topic sentence, (2) a body, and (3) a concluding sentence. Paragraphs are easy to recognize. You can signal the reader that you are beginning a paragraph in two ways. When your message is double spaced, indent the first typed line of the first sentence five spaces. When your message is single spaced, leave two lines between paragraphs. Here is what a paragraph looks like:

Indented Topic Sentence	Garden plants need different amounts of sunlight. Cucumbers, for example, are very hard to please. They like heat, moisture, well drained soil, and some shade. The gardener may provide such conditions by planting cucumbers with corn. The corn, which likes heat and sun,
Body	helps shade the cucumbers. Scattering lettuce among other, taller plants which provide shade is another example of special planting. Plant sunflowers, which like lots of sun, on the north side of a garden where they can enjoy the sun but not shade other plants. Successful garden-
Concluding Sentence	ers provide just the right amount of sunlight for each plant's needs.

HOW DO YOU WRITE A TOPIC SENTENCE?

The topic sentence states the central idea of the paragraph. Thus, the topic sentence is a general statement which covers the other, more specific ideas in the body of the paragraph. Like every other sentence, it has a subject and predicate but, because the topic sentence comes first in most paragraphs, the writing of the subject and predicate of the topic sentence deserves particular attention. This sentence is the key to the contents of the paragraph. A good topic sentence helps the writer select relevant ideas for the body of the paragraph, and it informs the reader of the writer's viewpoint.

The Subject of a Topic Sentence

Because a paragraph is a short piece of writing, it should deal with only one subject. For example:

> The *advantages* of Christmas shopping in July

is one subject that you could describe in a single paragraph. A writer wishing to discuss

> The *advantages* and *disadvantages* of Christmas shopping in July

would require two paragraphs to describe the two subjects. You must narrow the subject of the topic sentence so that you can write a convincing paragraph about it. For example, "solar energy" is a subject that is too broad to discuss in a single paragraph.

> The solar water heater installed at 2429 Heverly Drive

is a much more specific subject.

You can narrow your subject in several ways. You can take a specific part of a broad subject to write about.

Broad Subject	Narrowed Subject	Specific Subject
public transportation	the subway system	the Howard Street subway line
politics	local elections	Democratic candidate from the first ward
gardening	vegetable gardening	growing carrots
art	"The Old Masters"	Rembrandt's "Night Watch"
taxes	import/export fees	duty on shoes

You can also qualify your subject; that is, separate it from similar items in the same category by giving its particulars. For instance, a qualification of the broad topic "ski equipment" is "cross country ski equipment," a different kind of ski equipment from "downhill ski equipment." "Designer jeans" qualifies the broad topic "jeans." Of course, you can narrow these subjects even further by attaching brand names to each product.

You may also specify subjects by time, place, and size:

> The *1983* Oldsmobile
> The drought in *Kansas*
> The *50-watt* reflector light bulb
> The *24-inch* color television set

Exercise A Circle the subject and underline the words that help to narrow it in each sentence below.

1. The convenience store nearest my home has a limited stock of fresh foods.

2. College bookstores stock books for general reading as well as for college classes.

3. A landscape architect designed the formal gardens behind the new library.

4. "The axe-wielding, table-pounding executive is back in vogue," according to the *Wall Street Journal.*

5. Pink stucco houses with white trim are common in southern California but rare in cold climates.

6. The Clearwater Art Institute's summer exhibit displayed examples of the work of primitive artists.

7. Starting a new job can cause stress for the employee and for the employer.

8. Should the amateur photographer purchase a single-reflex Penkon B or a fully automatic Conkon A camera?

9. Land near the Wabash River should be saved for pasture as it may be subject to spring floods.

10. Can a monthly business publication be produced successfully when the editor lives 2,000 miles from the publication staff?

Exercise B Following the example you studied earlier, produce narrowed topics and specific subjects for each of the following broad topics.

Broad Topic	Narrowed Topic	Specific Subject
1. food		
2. snack foods		
3. hunger		
4. farming		
5. shelter		
6. housing		
7. boats		

8. books

9. music

10. data processing

The Predicate of the Topic Sentence

The other part of the topic sentence, the predicate, is a generalization about the subject. A generalization is a broad statement to which all the other statements in the paragraph apply. Generalizations may be opinions—that is, they may reflect a personal attitude or viewpoint on the subject. For example, in the sentence

> This car costs too much.

"too much" represents the writer's personal opinion about the worth of the car. Generalizations may also be factual and, with business subjects, form typical topic sentences in business writing. For example,

> Winslow Steel experienced a serious downturn last year.

is a factual statement, yet the words "serious downturn" are general enough to allow for other statements to be developed as proof.

To understand generalizations, you must distinguish between the concepts of general and specific. Whether it is an opinion or a fact, a generalization summarizes the details and examples in the body of the paragraph. Simply put, a generalization allows the writer to develop an idea beyond one or two sentences. By contrast, a specific statement allows no further development. In the sentence

> He is well educated.

"well educated" is a general opinion. If it were used as a topic sentence, the writer could develop the idea of "well educated" by mentioning such facts as successful completion of schooling, academic honors, and high scores on achievement tests. The sentence

> He graduated from Darby Central High School.

would not make a good topic sentence, however, because it is too specific. The phrase "graduated from Darby Central High School" can be proved or disproved by checking high school records, but it cannot be further developed in any meaningful way. By the same token, a factual generalization like

The QEW word processor is an efficient machine.

may be developed as a topic sentence by citing the reasons for its efficiency. The sentence

The QEW word processor costs $12,000.

could not be used as a topic sentence because it is too specific. Having mentioned its price, the writer has little else to say on the subject. Changing this topic sentence to

The QEW word processor is expensive.

does not help much either. After adding "It costs $12,000," the writer faces another dead end. Thus, before using them, you must test topic sentences to see whether you can add relevant details to explain or prove them in the body of the paragraph. If you can develop them further, you know you have made a general statement about the subject.

In contrast to generalizations which are too specific to allow further development, some generalizations are too broad. They leave the reader to guess at the particular aspect of the subject that the writer plans to develop in the paragraph. Thus, in the same way that you narrowed the subject of the topic sentence, you must also narrow the predicate so that you can focus attention on the specific aspect of the subject you plan to develop in the rest of the paragraph.

The Model 6 copier is a good machine.

is a broad generalization and therefore makes a weak topic sentence. The problem with the sentence is the vague word *good*. What does *good* mean? The reader may interpret it in many different ways. He or she may think that the writer is planning to say that the machine is easy to operate, or that it can copy from different kinds of originals, or that it is inexpensive to buy, run, or maintain. The variety of interpretations which the reader may apply to the word *good* is a sign to the writer that revision is necessary to focus the reader's attention on the particular aspect of the subject the writer plans to develop. Revising to narrow the generalization of "The Model 6 is a good machine" might result in topic sentences like the following.

The Model 6 copier requires only three steps for efficient operation.

The Model 6 copier can reproduce from several different kinds of originals.

The Model 6 costs very little to buy, run, and maintain.

Exercise C In the sentences below, mark sentences that are too specific to serve as topic sentences with an *S*. Mark sentences that are too broad to serve as topic sentences with a *B*. Write *OK* before sentences that would serve as topic sentences.

1. The XR-10 gets 40 miles per gallon in highway driving.
2. The XR-10 is a nice car.
3. The XR-10 is an expensive car.
4. The local newspaper is much more readable than it used to be.
5. The local newspaper has switched to a computer type-setting process.
6. Stamp collecting may be financially rewarding.
7. Stamp collectors learn geography while pursuing their hobby.
8. Computer games are a waste.
9. Computer games teach hand-eye coordination.
10. A typical computer game costs $25 to $35.

Refining the Topic Sentence

In completing Exercises A-C, you have practiced two necessary steps in the process of writing topic sentences—narrowing the subject and distinguishing general from specific statements. Now you need to put these skills together and add another factor: interest.

In Exercise 3 at the end of chapter 2, you thought about *clothing* as a topic for a short paper. Let us look now at some specific sentences you might use in one of those hypothetical papers. In Example A, Textiles 200, you will certainly want to talk about fabric care. Here are some sample topic sentences. Each sentence has a specific subject and is a generalization, but which ones make you want to read more of the paragraph?

1. Cotton fabric is washable.
2. There is no problem in washing cotton.
3. One nice thing about cotton fabric is its washability.
4. Soap and water will clean most cotton fabrics.
5. Cotton is nice to wash.
6. Soap advertisers wish every fabric washed as well as cotton.
7. Cotton's enduring popularity may result directly from its getting softer with each washing.

You probably checked the last two sentences as interesting, but you decided against sentence 6 because your subject is *cotton fabric*, not *soap advertisers*. What made the last sentence interesting? It goes one step beyond a statement of fact to create a complete picture in the reader's mind. The reader is ready to agree with you before you start the body of the paragraph.

Let us look at two sentences that are similar in meaning.

Clothing made of a cotton blend is particularly nice to wear in hot weather.

Clothing made of a cotton blend sheds wrinkles even on a particularly hot summer day.

Readers prefer the second sentence to the first for two reasons. First, the second sentence uses the action verb *sheds* while the first sentence uses the weak linking verb, *is*. The verb *sheds* means something. The reader can picture the action of shedding. By contrast, the verb *is* (or any other part of the verb *to be* such as *am, are, was, were, be, been, being*) evokes no picture in the reader's mind. It only signals that the writer is linking the subject *clothing* with the weak adjective, *nice*. Second, an adjective like *nice* is a problem, too, because *nice* exists only in the reader's mind. If everyone in class drew a picture of *nice*, we would have as many different pictures as artists. As you can see, "sheds wrinkles" involves the reader more than does "is nice."

Similarly, in Exercise C, chapter 2, Play Production 250, the first topic sentence to spring to mind might be

Costumes are important in planning a play.

However, *are important* has the same effect as *is nice* in the sentence about clothing; it tells the reader your feelings about costumes but nothing about the subject *costumes* itself. Two rewritten topic sentences on the subject *costumes* might read

Costumes can cost more than scenery in a well staged play.

'Clothes make the man' and nowhere more than on stage in a new play.

These sentences do a better job of appealing to the reader and of moving quickly to the detailed material of the body of the paragraph than does the sentence

Costumes are important in planning a play.

Exercise D   Study the sample below. See how a simple idea can become the beginning of several very different paragraphs.

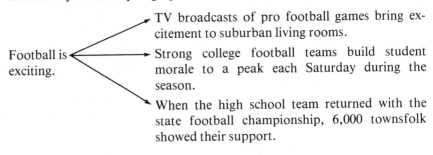

Football is exciting.

TV broadcasts of pro football games bring excitement to suburban living rooms.

Strong college football teams build student morale to a peak each Saturday during the season.

When the high school team returned with the state football championship, 6,000 townsfolk showed their support.

In this exercise, rewrite the simple topic sentence to make it interesting. Try to think of at least three different topic sentences for each idea.

1. Hamburgers are fattening.
2. Summer is hot.
3. Napoleon was a famous French general.
4. Sales are fun.
5. Swimming is good exercise.
6. My job is interesting.
7. Cows are useful animals.
8. Sewing is a nice hobby.
9. Los Angeles is a good place to vacation.
10. Now I'm going to show you how to fry potatoes.

HOW DO YOU WRITE THE BODY OF A PARAGRAPH?

The body of the paragraph supports or proves the generalization you made in the topic sentence. It is made up of sentences of fact, specific detail, and example.

Using Facts

Facts, as you have learned already, are items of information that can be verified. Using facts in writing is effective because specific information allows the reader to arrive at a clear understanding of the thought you are trying to communicate. Their use also shows the reader that you are a believable source of information.

Study Paragraphs A and B which follow.

Paragraph A	*Paragraph B*

Considering its size, Bernice paid too much for her house. The cost was too high for the space she got. The kitchen is too little. It hasn't enough cupboard space. Furthermore, she has almost no storage space outside the kitchen. Considering the size of her house, Bernice got very little for her money.	Considering its size, Bernice paid too much for her house. It cost $50,000 for 1,300 square feet of floor space. The kitchen, which measures 10' × 12', has only a narrow two-foot walkway between the appliances on one side and the sink on the other. Also, the kitchen has only four built-in cabinets. The house has no attic, and the basement, which is unfinished, only extends under half the house. She has only two 4' closets in the bedrooms and a hall closet which is 1' × 2'. Considering the size of her house, Bernice got very little for her money.

Everything Paragraph A says may be true. However, words and phrases like "paid too much," "too little," and "tiny" are all judgments. What is too high in price in the writer's judgment may seem like a bargain to the reader. What is too small to the writer may seem quite roomy to the reader. The reader may agree or disagree that Bernice was cheated, but replacing the judgments with facts in the body of the paragraph clarifies the writer's viewpoint.

Study the following sentences to focus on the differences between facts and judgments.

Fact	*Judgment*
The top 17 brands of beer at the last World's Fair all came from Europe, Japan, or Mexico.	American beer is *inferior* to foreign beer.
The average American can expect to hold 15 different jobs during his or her working life.	The average American worker changes jobs *frequently*.
Seattle averages 62 inches of rain a year.	It rains *a lot* in Seattle.

Exercise E   Rewrite the following sentences to replace judgments with facts.

1. I didn't make any money on my last job.

2. The rent on that apartment is too high.

3. Last month's sales letter was quite effective.

4. The ambulance went rapidly through traffic.

5. Cement costs more than asphalt.

6. The new rules will increase taxes.

7. The company needs larger quarters.

8. Many people applied for the new position.

9. Midtown is the place to live.

10. Selling T-shirts is a great way to make money!

Using Specific Details

Clear writing demands exactness, and one way to achieve exactness is to use specific details. Check for specific details in your writing by asking yourself whether you have answered questions like who, what, when, and where as fully as possible.

1. Did you name people?

   John Griswold, the first-shift foreman instead of "my boss"

2. Did you name things?

   The Wells-o-matic industrial vacuum instead of "the sweeper"

3. Were you specific about dates and times?

   At 8 a.m. on Monday, August 31, instead of "early yesterday morning"

4. Did you name places?

   Building 3 of the Valley Lumber Company instead of "at the lumberyard," or the Insty-Mart at 17332 North Main Street rather than "the convenience store on Main"

   A second way to incorporate specific details in your writing is to use figures.

1. Did you give exact cost figures?

   $5.95 instead of "inexpensive" or $6 per square foot or $8 an hour

2. Did you use statistics when they were available?

   9 percent of the clerical employees instead of "some" or "a few"

3. Did you give exact measurements?

   1,750 miles from New York City rather than "far away" or a 70-foot swimming pool instead of "a big pool"

4. Did you give specific times?

   5 hours' work rather than "all afternoon" or an airspeed of 650 miles an hour rather than "fast"

Exercise F   Rewrite the following sentences to incorporate specific details.

1. He bought an expensive foreign camera.

2. The truck approached the bridge too rapidly.

3. Last year we spent the summer at the shore.

4. The farmers had a good wheat crop.

5. Entry-level wages were low.

6. Several items were back ordered last month.

7. Small businesses provide more jobs than companies listed in the Fortune 500.

8. You can make better time using the interstate highway.

9. The team lost.

10. This timetable is outdated.

Using Examples

Examples are illustrations. They give the reader additional information about abstractions — words that stand for ideas rather than for people or things. "Messy" is an abstraction because the reader supplies the meaning. You cannot show the reader a pound of "messy" or a dozen of "messy." If the topic sentence is "His workbench is messy," you would use examples to allow the reader to visualize, to see in his or her mind, the same picture of the workbench that is in your mind. Thus, you would give examples in the body of the paragraph. First, of course, you would try to rewrite the general topic sentence to one that created a more specific picture for the reader. Let us try "His workbench needed cleaning."

His workbench needed cleaning. Tools were scattered everywhere. Among the tools were odd screws, nuts, bolts, and small parts from broken clocks and radios. Nails of different sizes filled every odd space. Pieces of used sandpaper littered the work area. Some of them lay in pools of old grease while others stuck to paint dripping off a half-empty gallon of marigold yellow latex paint. A crusted stirring stick had glued itself to the top of the paint can. An unwashed paint brush, its bristles stuck together, rested among dirty rags and a crumbling sponge. The clutter on his workbench made finding a specific item nearly impossible.

The paragraph about the workbench uses descriptive examples. They allow the reader to picture a scene. Another kind of example is the factual example. Specific factual examples often explain factual general statements. For instance,

Burdick, Inc., has failed in its last three attempts to take over other companies.

is a factual general statement. If you used this statement as a topic sentence, your reader might ask what companies did Burdick try to take over? Why did the attempts fail? The body of the paragraph would give specific facts detailing the names of the companies and the reasons the takeover attempts failed. A paragraph on this subject could also contain dates and place names as well as other details such as what each company manufactured. A skeleton outline would look like this:

Names of Companies	Reasons for failure of takeover attempts
Eco Labs	Outside appraiser ruled that Burdick's bid was too low.
Ronchett Inst.	Ronchett bought back stock Burdick had acquired.
Gandy Plastics	Transcomco outbid Burdick.

Exercise G   Supply informative examples for each of the following sentences.

1. My summer job had three great virtues.
2. Newcomers soon discover that this city provides a variety of entertainment.
3. Rush hour traffic requires the driver's full attention.
4. Fast food restaurants now offer a varied menu.
5. "Relaxing music" varies with the listener's mood.

HOW DO YOU WRITE A CONCLUDING SENTENCE?

The concluding sentence is the last sentence in the paragraph. Its purpose is to remind the reader of the central idea of the paragraph which was expressed in the topic sentence. Thus, one way to write a concluding sentence is to refer to the main idea stated in the topic sentence. You do not simply copy over the topic sentence, however. You use the idea of the topic sentence but find a new way to state it.

The following paragraph illustrates a restatement of the topic sentence in the concluding sentence:

> *Harry Swickert turned the Schuyler Shoe Company, a dying business, into a profitable company.* First he moved from his outmoded factory in Philadelphia to a modern facility in Stroudsburg. At the Philadelphia plant, expenses were high, work space was cramped, and the workers were unreliable. He also changed the company's product line. He created a new product called the Wilderness boot which he manufactured in addition to work boots. Then he hired Prescott and Prescott to advertise the new boot. They created several eye-catching ads such as one award winner which portrays a bride and groom in gown and tuxedo, both wearing Wilderness boots. These ads, which appeared in quality magazines, helped to increase sales by 50 percent in the last five years. *Thus, a company that was nearly bankrupt capitalized on the market for brand name equipment and is doing a flourishing business.*

If you re-read the topic sentence and the concluding sentence, you will notice that "dying business" and "profitable company" from the topic sentence become "a company that was nearly bankrupt" and "flourishing business" in the concluding sentence.

A second way to write a concluding sentence is to summarize the main points of the paragraph. A summary concluding sentence for the Schuyler Shoe Company paragraph would go like this:

> With a new factory, a new product line, and a good advertising campaign, Harry Swickert has saved Schuyler Shoe Company from bankruptcy and has turned it into a solid money maker.

Exercise H Write topic sentences and two kinds of concluding sentences for the following paragraphs.

Paragraph 1

Topic sentence:

Consumers can buy orange drink which contains 14 different chemicals but no oranges. They can also buy lemon drink made of nonnatural materials. Now a new product has come on the market. It's an apple drink which lists as its ingredients water, sugar, citric and malic acids, potassium and sodium citrates, coloring, and flavoring.

Restated concluding sentence:

Summary concluding sentence:

Paragraph 2

Topic sentence:

The fruit fly, destroyer of valuable fruit, nut, and vegetable crops, was first discovered in San Jose, a suburb of San Francisco. It made its second appearance in the fertile San Joaquin Valley. Then evidence of the fruit fly was found farther south, in Baldwin Park, a suburb of Los Angeles. The fruit fly has also traveled north. Fruit growers have found fertile fruit flies near Oakland.

Restated concluding sentence:

Summary concluding sentence:

Paragraph 3

Topic sentence:

Robert E. Alexander, president of First American Bank, says he takes occasional short vacations because he believes they rejuvenate him and allow him to be more productive when he is back on the job. While on vacation, Alexander calls his assistant every night for a five-minute report on the day's business activities. Lynn Redfern, president of Redfern Enterprises, a computer company, reports that she takes five days off three times a year to ski and scuba dive. Redfern says her vice presidents are capable managers who rarely have to contact her while she is away. Gregory West, chairman of the West Corporation, a manufacturer of office equipment, spent a week relaxing in Hawaii in January and another week traveling in Scotland and England in June. West reports that he phones his company twice a week during his vacations but doesn't have any fears about how the business is run in his absence.

Restated concluding sentence:

Summary concluding sentence:

Paragraph 4

Topic sentence:

In 1910, Eastern Ohio Normal School was founded to prepare elementary and secondary school teachers. It had 1 building, 6 instructors on its staff, and 80 students. In 1923, Eastern Ohio Normal School changed its name to Eastern Ohio State Teachers College. With 3 buildings, 28 instructors, and 640 students, it offered degrees in education and the liberal arts. In 1952, Eastern Ohio State Teachers College became Eastern Ohio College. It had 8 buildings, 128 instructors, and 6,900 students. Students could take degrees in education, the liberal arts, business, and engineering. In 1965, Eastern Ohio College became Eastern

Ohio University. It now had 10 buildings, 591 instructors, 12,800 students, and four colleges offering degrees. A branch campus opened in Claremont, Ohio, in 1967. It offers a two-year program in the liberal arts.
Restated concluding sentence:

Summary concluding sentence:

Review   A paragraph consists of a related group of sentences which inform the reader about one subject or a particular aspect of a subject. The paragraph begins with a topic sentence which presents a generalization about a specific subject. The body of the paragraph uses facts, details, and examples to help the reader understand the idea of the topic sentence. Finally, a concluding sentence reviews the paragraph.

Cases   1. Use the information below to write a paragraph. Remember to write a topic sentence and a concluding sentence. The facts you will use in the body of the paragraph are in note form. You must write them in sentence form.

Background information. You are personnel manager of the ABX Corporation. You have decided to hire Joyce Jefferson as assistant personnel manager of your company. Now you must write a paragraph stating your decision for the personnel files. In this paragraph, you describe Jefferson's qualifications for the job.

Facts about Joyce Jefferson. Education: Associate of Arts degree, secretarial administration, Maple Springs Community College, 1973; Bachelor of Business Administration degree, major in management, Eastern Ohio University, 1976; management internship, Bernhard-Belvedere, Inc., 1975. *Experience*: management trainee, Bernhard-Belvedere, 1977 (completed the course with honors); assistant manager, Bernhard-Belvedere, 1978-present. *Personal characteristics*: friendly, outgoing; works well with others; accurate about details.

2. Use all of the following facts to write one paragraph about the Wilson-Bachman Company. Remember to begin with a topic sentence and to put all information in sentence form. Make your concluding sentence a restatement of the topic sentence.

Company founders: Peter Wilson, Frank Bachman

TRANSACTIONS	NUMBER OF EMPLOYEES	PRODUCTS
bought factory--Peoria, IL (1923)	10 (1923)	bicycle parts (1923)
bought factory--Flint, MI (1929)	175 (1929)	car steering gears (1929)
sold Peoria factory (1929)	700 (1935)	automobile brakes (1935)
took over Seely Tool Company in	2,400 (1942)	drill bits (1935)
Shelby, MI (1935)		ball bearings (1935)
sold out to Peerless Tool of		airplane parts (1942)
Bradford, CT (1948)		automatic rifles (1942)
		rocket launchers (1942)

3. In Exercise B in this chapter, you might have narrowed the broad subject, *food*, to dairy products, and finally to a specific subject, *butter*. You could use the following topic sentences for a paragraph about butter:

a. Great French chefs rely on butter to produce delicately flavored sauces.

b. Although Americans think of butter as a product associated with cows, Tibetans use yak milk to make butter.

c. Medical studies in the past ten years have made butter a controversial food.

d. Operating the butter churn was a chore usually reserved for the youngsters on a farm.

Use the other specific subjects you developed in Exercise B. How many different topic sentences can you devise?

4. Choose three of the topic sentences you have just written and list the facts, details, and examples you will need to explain or support the generalization in the topic sentence.

5. Write two different concluding sentences for each of the paragraphs you outlined in Exercise 4.

6. Now select an audience and purpose (or follow your instructor's direction about audience and purpose) for one of the paragraph outlines you have completed. Fill in the *Pre-writing Checklist for Paragraphs*. Remember to make changes in your original outline to adapt it to the specific audience who will be reading the paragraph.

7. Write the paragraph.

8. Review the work you did to complete Exercise 2 in chapter 2.

a. Select a very specific job you would like to have while you are a student (you must already meet all the qualifications!).

b. With that job in mind, fill out the *Pre-writing Checklist for Paragraphs* for your answer to the question, "Tell me about yourself."

c. Type no more than 12 lines which answer the question, "Tell me about yourself."

PRE-WRITING CHECKLIST FOR PARAGRAPHS

Who is the audience for this message?

What is the purpose of the message?

What is the specific subject of the topic sentence?

What is the generalization in the topic sentence?

What key facts, details, and examples will support the topic sentence?

How will each sentence relate to the central idea of the topic sentence?

How will the concluding sentence lead the reader back to the central idea of the topic sentence?

PRE-WRITING CHECKLIST FOR PARAGRAPHS

Who is the audience for this message?

What is the purpose of the message?

What is the specific subject of the topic sentence?

What is the generalization in the topic sentence?

What key facts, details, and examples will support the topic sentence?

How will each sentence relate to the central idea of the topic sentence?

How will the concluding sentence lead the reader back to the central idea of the topic sentence?

PRE-WRITING CHECKLIST FOR PARAGRAPHS

Who is the audience for this message?

What is the purpose of the message?

What is the specific subject of the topic sentence?

What is the generalization in the topic sentence?

What key facts, details, and examples will support the topic sentence?

How will each sentence relate to the central idea of the topic sentence?

How will the concluding sentence lead the reader back to the central idea of the topic sentence?

PRE-WRITING CHECKLIST FOR PARAGRAPHS

Who is the audience for this message?

What is the purpose of the message?

What is the specific subject of the topic sentence?

What is the generalization in the topic sentence?

What key facts, details, and examples will support the topic sentence?

How will each sentence relate to the central idea of the topic sentence?

How will the concluding sentence lead the reader back to the central idea of the topic sentence?

Chapter 6

Writing Clearly

To the Student:

    As you read chapter 6 and complete the exercises and cases, you will be asked to

       . . . define unity in writing

       . . . define coherence in writing

       . . . identify special techniques to achieve coherence in writing

       . . . write unified, coherent paragraphs.

In working on the exercises in chapter 5, you have practiced writing a topic sentence, supporting or proving the topic sentence in the body of the paragraph, and ending the paragraph with a concluding sentence. Your next step is to make sure the paragraph is unified and coherent.

WHAT IS UNITY?

Unity is the process of selecting support that relates to the generalization of the viewpoint. To insure unity, you must review your first draft carefully and eliminate all sentences that do not relate to the central idea you are trying to communicate. For example, in the topic sentence, "Alice Bates is an enterprising business person," the key word to support or prove is "enterprising." Thus, if the next sentence in the paragraph is "She is 35 years old," the paragraph would lack unity because age, in itself, has nothing to do with enterprise. A 35-year-old is not necessarily more enterprising than a 25-year-old or a 45-year-old.

WHY IS UNITY IMPORTANT?

Unity is important because when you write you are a director, a manager of ideas. Your readers are the people you are directing. You want them to start at the beginning of your paragraph and move to the end without getting lost on the way. You guarantee them a smooth passage by including sentences that refer to the central idea you want them to understand. Including irrelevant sentences interrupts the readers' thought processes. When a paragraph contains irrelevant sentences, readers may become confused or bored or irritated. Any of these reactions will make them less receptive to the message.

Exercise A Circle the central idea of each topic sentence. Underline the phrases or sentences in the paragraph that do not support the central idea of the topic sentence in each of the following paragraphs.

1. One company president declared that minicomputers were raising computer consciousness in his firm. He stated, "In the past twelve months, over 100 people have had hands-on experience with small computers. These people used to use paper and pencil." As managers became more aware of the many uses for computers, they requested new specialized programs. But in this company, many projects had to wait a year or more for mainframe programming. Now managers use the minicomputers to solve unit-level problems. After using computers, the managers are at last becoming more interested in timesharing projects that utilize the mainframe. The president concluded, "People are ready to understand

the larger machines once they have experienced the power of personal computing."

2. The Milltown Inn can provide the best facilities for the annual nature association convention to be held on April 1 and 2. The hotel is centrally located in the state and easy to reach from the airport and from main highways. It can provide three meeting rooms for groups of 30-50 and a banquet room which seats 150. Furthermore, the hotel has 100 newly redecorated bedrooms which can accommodate from 1 to 4 delegates each. Delegates may order in-room breakfasts from a lengthy menu or eat in one of two spacious restaurants in the hotel. Or breakfast is available at a nearby McBurger House. For nonsession hours, the hotel provides a pool, health club, and after-hours lounge which delegates may want to patronize. Because Milltown Inn is centrally located, has adequate meeting, housing, and dining facilities, as well as facilities for individual relaxation, the nature association should select it as the center for next year's convention.

WHAT IS COHERENCE?

Coherence is the orderly arrangement of parts of the paragraph. The information in the paragraph often dictates the method of arrangement of sentences within the body of the paragraph.

Methods of Arrangement

Chronological Order – The Order of Time

Using chronological order, you tell what happened first, what happened second, what happened third, and so forth, as you see in the following example.

Last night's fire devastated the warehouse. Apparently the fire began shortly after 5 p.m. when papers and an oil-soaked rag in a trash barrel were ignited by smoldering cigarettes which were probably dumped into the barrel just before closing time. When the flames burned through the untreated cardboard sides of the barrel, the exhaust fan scattered embers and burning paper along several rows of stored paper products. Several packages smoldered until nearly 9 p.m. before their combined heat led to a general conflagration. At 9:30, a cleaning crew in the office smelled smoke and called the fire department. Before the trucks arrived, fire had spread to the chemical storage area. Several explosions sent fire balls to every area of the building, and firemen fought the blaze until dawn before declaring that the danger was past.

Spatial Order – The Order of Items in Space
With this method, you describe the arrangement of items, for example, from left to right, from top to bottom, foreground to background, clockwise and counterclockwise. The following sample paragraph is written in spatial order.

> The most efficient working method for painting a ceiling is to work repeatedly across the narrow dimension of the room and (for right-handed people) to work from left to right. Begin in a corner to paint the ceiling, working across the narrower dimension of the room. If you are left-handed, plan to work from right to left; if you are right-handed, from left to right. Use a brush or special instrument to paint a neat line where wall and ceiling meet. Then use a roller to apply paint in a strip no more than two feet wide, working toward the closest wall. When you complete one strip across the ceiling, move the ladder back across the room to apply paint next to your starting point before that paint dries. Following this work pattern will speed up application and leave few if any lap marks on a ceiling.

Order of Importance – The Order of Ideas
You arrange ideas from most important to least important or from least important to most important. The sample paragraph puts the most important reason first in the body of the paragraph.

> First National Bank should grant a three-year signature loan of $5,000 to Marion Prezeski so that she may complete her education without further delay. Although she has no collateral, she has an exemplary credit record of 10 years' duration. During that time, she has borrowed and repaid a total of $8,000 with interest. All repayments were made on time although Mrs. Prezeski has the financial responsibility of raising a child and her earnings have been restricted by her lack of education. Mrs. Prezeski's child is now in school a full day, and Mrs. Prezeski has to complete only 30 hours of courses to earn a BBA degree in accounting. With the loan, she can complete her work in one year. With the degree, her job opportunities will be such that she can easily repay the loan in the following two years.

Exercise B   1. As you can guess from the dates in the following sentences, these sentences form a paragraph organized in chronological order. Reorganize the sentences to make a coherent paragraph.

a. He invented the machine because he was behind in his correspondence and wanted to write faster.

b. But by 1874, new money and additional patents made assembly-line production of the Remington Type-writer a reality.

c. After Burt, some 50 other inventors tried their hand at making a fast typing machine.

d. The typewriter floundered for nearly 50 years from patent to production.

e. In 1867, Christopher Latham Scholes completed the first working model of a machine which was later called a "type-writer."

f. Unfortunately, his early box model — while neat and legible — was slower than handwriting.

g. The first American TYPOGRAPHER was invented by William A. Burt during the winter of 1828-1829 and patented on July 23, 1829.

h. In its early years, the typewriter developed slowly.

i. The machine underwent countless changes in the next few years and nearly disappeared altogether under a sea of red ink.

2. Rearrange the following sentences to form a coherent paragraph. Be prepared to say what order you used to form the paragraph and defend your reorganization.

a. Furthermore, keeping an unsuitable employee is unfair to him or her.

b. Discharging an unsatisfactory employee will never be pleasant, but it is sometimes necessary.

c. In another position, in another company, he or she might do very well.

d. Other workers must take time to make up for failures and untangle messes.

e. Firing people is neglected in some organizations because it is an unpleasant duty.

f. The employee is costing the company time and money which could be used to build profits.

g. If a worker is not producing after a year on the job, managers need to admit that hiring the employee was a mistake.

A coherent paragraph also provides the reader with a clear flow of ideas. The reader should be able to move from one sentence to another without asking questions such as "How did that idea get in here?" or "What is that supposed to mean?" In a well written paragraph, the reader never should have to stop to puzzle over the writing itself.

Guides to Writing Coherent Paragraphs

1. Repeat key words of the topic sentence in the body of the paragraph.

2. Use synonyms for key words.

3. Use pronouns to refer to key words.

4. Repeat sentence structures within the paragraph.

5. Use transitions to lead the reader from one idea to the next.

   a. Number ideas: *first, second, third, fourth.* This technique is especially helpful to link a series of events using chronological order or to explain a process.

   b. Signal additions of similar material with words like *another, also, in addition, additionally,* and *furthermore.*

   c. Introduce examples with words and phrases like *for example, for instance,* and *such as.*

   d. Signal contrast with words like *although, however, by contrast, in contrast to,* and *on the other hand.*

   e. Sum up ideas with *thus, therefore, finally,* and *as a result.*

WHY IS COHERENCE IMPORTANT?

Coherence is important because it makes writing smooth, allowing readers to concentrate on the information that is presented rather than on figuring out what the writer is trying to say. The verbal signals in coherent writing affect readers in the same way that road signs affect drivers: Both guide them on their way and eliminate mistakes. Your ideas in written form are an unmapped territory to the reader unless you structure your thoughts carefully and provide aids to understanding along the way.

Exercise C   Look for ways the writer achieves coherence in the following paragraphs. Refer to the *Guides to Writing Coherent Paragraphs* and

1. Underline the words and phrases that provide coherence.

2. Identify the specific technique the author uses for each word, phrase, or passage you underlined.

   a. The *shinkansen* or "bullet train" speeds across the rural areas of Japan giving a quick view of cluster after cluster of farmhouses surrounded by rice paddies. This particular pattern did not develop purely by chance, but as a consequence of the technology peculiar to the growing of rice, the staple of the Japanese diet. The growing of rice requires the construction and maintenance of an irrigation system, something that takes many hands to build. More importantly, the planting and the harvesting of rice can only be done efficiently with the cooperation of twenty or more people. The "bottom line" is that a single family working alone cannot produce enough rice to survive, but a dozen families working together can produce a surplus. Thus the Japanese have had to develop the capacity to work together in harmony, no matter what the forces of disagreement or social disintegration, in order to survive.[1]

b. Persons beginning a business career will be more apt to find appropriate work if they follow a three-part study plan. First, job-seekers must follow the ancient maxim, "know thyself." They should carefully inventory their skills, experiences, and personal preferences. With that list in hand, the second step is to study the world of work. What kind of work provides the best match between work requirements and preferences and skills? Only when they have thus narrowed the possibilities should applicants start the third step—investigating individual firms. Being knowledgeable about a company's policies and prospects is a great advantage during the final phase of job seeking—interviews for specific positions. Studying themselves, the job market, and individual firms will help job-seekers become successful applicants.

Review   Unity and coherence help you keep the reader's interest after you capture it with an interesting topic sentence. Unity demands that every sentence of the paragraph relate to the topic. Thus, the reader will not be distracted from the subject. Coherence is a writer's term for logic and order. A coherent paragraph follows a plan of development and uses special techniques to carry the reader easily from one fact or detail to the next. Successful writers use both techniques in writing paragraphs.

Expanded   Before writing a first draft, write answers to these questions.
Writing
Checklist   1. Who is the audience for this message?

2. What is the purpose of the message?

3. What is the subject of the topic sentence?

4. What is my generalization about the topic?

5. What order shall I use for the message?

6. What words can I use in the topic sentence to capture the reader's interest?

7. What are the facts or details needed to explain or support the topic sentence?

8. What writing plan will achieve coherence?

9. Should the concluding sentence be a restatement or summary sentence?

10. What format is appropriate for this message?

[1]William G. Ouchi, *Theory Z: How American Business Can Meet the Japanese Challenge* (Reading, Massachusetts: Addison-Wesley Publishing Company, 1981), p. 64.

Cases   1. Describe a bulletin board located in the hall of your classroom building (or a particular bulletin board your instructor selects).

2. You are a sales trainee for R & G Electronics, a medium-sized firm that makes a wide range of electronic gauges used by a variety of businesses to monitor automatic functions. You have completed the first phase of training and now work alone, but under very close supervision. For instance, you use a regular call report form, but your training supervisor, Carl Stob, wants more information about each day's work.

a. Use the information on the following *Daily Sales Call Report* and the *Mental Notes for Case 2* to write your daily memo to Stob. Use chronological order to achieve coherence.

b. Use the same information to write a memo to Stob using order of importance to achieve coherence.

c. Write a memo to your instructor indicating which memo you feel is more appropriate for the situation.

Mental Notes for Case 2 (in Order of Calls)

1. Tom explained that they are negotiating with a new client. If they land the contract, they will need some specialized controls. Our #1875 is very close to filling the bill. I said we could surely adapt it for the new testing program on a special order basis. Am I right? What is the procedure for this kind of special order? What about costs?

2. Bill looked very tired and harried. I actually got the order from his secretary.

3. Sales are way down. They are reducing inventory. No pick up expected until fourth quarter.

4. Took Ed to a really nice new Chinese restaurant about a block from the plant. He seemed interested in our product line though they are now serviced mostly by Ace Electric. He didn't sound too happy with their service. If I can convince him about our service, they could be a big new customer as their lines are all automatically monitored.

5. Business is good, and they are modernizing a couple of lines, for which they will need new monitors. They have new trainees and need 10 additional manuals for using our B73 gauge.

6. Could be an important customer. I researched the city looking for companies which might be ready to change manufacturing processes and figured they must be ready. I was right. Had a really good session with Al Stine showing him all the kinds of things we could help him do automatically. He was so excited about some of the possibilities that he got a spot purchase order to experiment with some models. I'll keep in touch and have

DAILY SALES CALL REPORT

SALESPERSON Gordon Knight   DAY OF WEEK Wed.   TERRITORY St. Louis   MONTH Feb.   ROUTE _____   DAY 23   19 84   SHEET 1 of 1

	ACCOUNT NAME AND ADDRESS	PERSON'S NAME AND TITLE	REMARKS	NEXT CALL DATE	NEXT CALL TIME	CALL CODE	AMOUNT OF SALE
1.	M-X Testing Labs 224 N. 14th	Thomas Doakes Asst. Purch. Agt.	Nelson out of town. New client may need special controls.	3/22	am	R	—
2.	Hinton Mfg. 1800 W. Jefferson	Bill Tonne PA	regular order	3/28	9am	R	5895 00/
3.	P+R Electric Warehouse 1422 May St.	A.G. Lilly Mgr.	order reduced cutting inventory	June		R	1500 00/
4.	Bain Manufacturing 701 W. Harrison	Ed Bain (Lunch) Pres	Serviced by Porter Electronics. Not happy with them.	Lunch next time I'm in town.		F	—
5.	LB Bottles 184 Tyler	Marion Feller Adm. Asst.	needs manuals for B73 gauge	3/22		R	15,000 00/
6.	Jones Tube 3348 S. Maple	Al Stine Production Supervisor	Bought 8 meters to experiment with. May be big customer.	3/28	open	F	8940 00/
7.	Midtown Gas 1880 S. Portland	Leo Vantini PA	Phoned to cancel. No problems. Will mail small order.			X	—
8.	Midwest Manufacturing P.O. Box 18	Vern Strachlaken Product Engineer	New line to open. Our engineers might be useful.			S	18,900 00/
9.							
10.							
				TOTAL CALLS			
				TOTAL SALES			$

INSTRUCTIONS TO SALESPEOPLE: Mail this report daily. Retain a copy for your file. Use additional sheets as necessary. When writing a supplemental letter or name refer to it in the "Remarks" column. Write a separate letter about each customer or prospect. Code each call as follows: F—for first call on prospect or new account; M—if call was made and person missed; R—Regular call on established account; S—for special call on established account; X—if call planned but not made.

TOPS FORM 1203

LITHO·IN·U·S·A

Reprinted with permission.

a definite appointment to follow up in a month. I might need to take an engineer with me then.

7. Stayed so long at Jones Tube that I just cancelled this one because Midwest was such an important appointment that I didn't want to be late.

8. They are in the blueprint stages of opening a whole new product line. Apparently it will be 100% automated, and they already have some of our line so we have a good chance at the new line. Can we get an engineer down here next month to work with Vern to be sure we can meet their specifications?

3. After reading the report you wrote (Case 2), Carl Stob sends the following rapid letter about the situation at Midwest Manufacturing.

TO *Gordon Knight*
P O Box 88
East St. Louis, IL

SUBJECT *Midwest Mfg.*

MESSAGE

DATE *2/27/84*

Verlan Stokes from Engineering can be in St. Louis March 10, 11, or 12. Make arrangements for him to meet appropriate personnel. Overnight OK if needed.

SIGNED *Carl*

REPLY

DATE

SIGNED

TOPS FORM 3801 LITHO IN U.S.A. **RECIPIENT : REPLY ON PINK COPY — RETAIN WHITE COPY**
SENDER .. RETAIN THIS COPY

Reprinted with permission.

Use the information that follows to compose an answer to Stob's rapid letter.

You talked with the purchasing agent, Walter Van Buren, three times before you found out why he was so reluctant to arrange a meeting of your engineer with people in his plant who are working on the new product line; namely, all the competition also wants to send engineers to "help." Midwest doesn't want to spend that kind of time or give out that much information. They will prepare specifications and take bids in early May. We will be on the mailing list.

EXPANDED WRITING CHECKLIST

Before writing a first draft, answer these questions.

1. Who is the audience for this message?

2. What is the purpose of the message?

3. What is the subject of the topic sentence?

4. What is my generalization about the topic?

5. What order shall I use for the message?

6. What words can I use in the topic sentence to capture the reader's interest?

7. What are the facts or details needed to explain or support the topic sentence?

8. What writing plan will achieve coherence?

9. Should the concluding sentence be a restatement or summary sentence?

10. What format is appropriate for this message?

EXPANDED WRITING CHECKLIST

Before writing a first draft, answer these questions.

1. Who is the audience for this message?

2. What is the purpose of the message?

3. What is the subject of the topic sentence?

4. What is my generalization about the topic?

5. What order shall I use for the message?

6. What words can I use in the topic sentence to capture the reader's interest?

7. What are the facts or details needed to explain or support the topic sentence?

8. What writing plan will achieve coherence?

9. Should the concluding sentence be a restatement or summary sentence?

10. What format is appropriate for this message?

EXPANDED WRITING CHECKLIST

Before writing a first draft, answer these questions.

1. Who is the audience for this message?

2. What is the purpose of the message?

3. What is the subject of the topic sentence?

4. What is my generalization about the topic?

5. What order shall I use for the message?

6. What words can I use in the topic sentence to capture the reader's interest?

7. What are the facts or details needed to explain or support the topic sentence?

8. What writing plan will achieve coherence?

9. Should the concluding sentence be a restatement or summary sentence?

10. What format is appropriate for this message?

EXPANDED WRITING CHECKLIST

Before writing a first draft, answer these questions.

1. Who is the audience for this message?

2. What is the purpose of the message?

3. What is the subject of the topic sentence?

4. What is my generalization about the topic?

5. What order shall I use for the message?

6. What words can I use in the topic sentence to capture the reader's interest?

7. What are the facts or details needed to explain or support the topic sentence?

8. What writing plan will achieve coherence?

9. Should the concluding sentence be a restatement or summary sentence?

10. What format is appropriate for this message?

Chapter 7

Describing
a Process

To the Student:
    As you read chapter 7 and complete the exercises and cases, you will be asked to
       . . . define process description
       . . . understand the need for writing process descriptions
       . . . break complex actions into smaller steps
       . . . sequence the steps into a process
       . . . use parallel structure to write instructions
       . . . write process descriptions.

When the reader needs to know how to do something, the writer describes a process. A process is a series of actions which a person takes to do a job such as developing a roll of film or to operate a piece of equipment such as computer terminal. Such process descriptions may be general or specific.

WHAT IS A GENERAL PROCESS DESCRIPTION?

The general description gives the reader a picture of the total process or system. A supervisor in charge of several employees, all of whom are doing separate tasks to produce a finished product, or a consumer engaged in shopping for a product might both read general process descriptions.

Why Are General Process Descriptions Useful?

General process descriptions help people understand entire operations either of jobs or products. They enable people to get an overview of how something fits into a system. A person, for example, who is a dedicated amateur photographer wants to learn to develop her own film. She goes to a photo supply store and asks about it. Here is what she is told.

"To develop film, the photographer needs access to a darkroom, a canister to hold the undeveloped film, developing fluid and purified water, a cup to measure the liquids, a watch to time the process, other chemicals, and a drying rack. He or she also has to know the film speed, the room temperature, the temperature of the developing fluid and water, the freshness of the developing fluid, and the developing time recommended by the chemical manufacturer.

"To develop black and white film, agitate a roll of exposed film in a chemical bath to make negatives, wash the strip of developed film, fix the negatives in another chemical, clean the fixed film and, finally, dry the strip of negatives."

This description, which outlines the five steps in developing film, is true of any kind of black and white film. However, a photographer could not use this general description to develop a roll of film because it gives only an overview of the process.

Employment descriptions are another kind of general description. They are used by any organization which hires people for work. Employment descriptions range from 25-word write-ups that you can find in the help wanted section of any newspaper to long position descriptions of four pages or more which organizations use not only as guides for hiring but also for evaluating employees on the job.

How Do You Write a General Process Description?

Before you can write a general description of any job or product, you must know about all its components. For example, if you work for an architectural firm and are preparing a presentation for the city planning commission, you want to show that your building will meet standards and code requirements. One requirement in the zone where the firm proposed to erect a warehouse has to do with "maintaining the esthetic beauty of the area." Your firm's plan calls for a 40-foot-long screen planting of Tsuga canadensis and Cornus florida. This planting will grow naturally to the height of the building and require little care. Planning commission members are not apt to be botanists, so you tailor your general description to their interests.

> A screening hedge of evergreen and flowering trees at the west end of the building will contribute to the beauty of the area.

In the same architectural office, another person must prepare a general description of this planting for a nursery. He or she might write

> We will require sufficient 3-year-old Cornus florida and Tsuga canadensis to fill a planting strip 10' wide and 40' long located on the west side of the warehouse at 2325 Acorn Road.

The writer for the planning commission presentation had to discover that Tsuga canadensis is an evergreen and Cornus florida is a flowering tree to write a general process description for the commission. The writer for the nursery had to look at site plans to determine the size of the planting, but neither writer had to be a botanist or be able to plant a tree. Both writers had to spend time thinking about the needs of the audience:

(1) Who will read the message?

(2) What will the reader do with the information?

The planning commission will be satisfied that the architect is planning to meet esthetic standards. The nursery can draw a planting diagram and complete the job.

If, on the other hand, the architectural firm does not know what trees will be best at the site, it might prepare a general description of its needs and send the description to several nurseries who would then inspect the site, make a plan, and bid for the job. Such a general description might read

> Prepare a plan and estimate costs to plant three-year-old flowering shrubs which will mature at about 20' and three-year-old evergreens which may be trimmed to 6' to fill the 10' by 40' space on the west side of the warehouse at 2325 Acorn Road.

If the architects send that description to several nurseries, they hope to receive several different plans from which they can choose one on the basis of price or of esthetic appeal.

When you must write a general process description, begin by investigating the job or process. You may find that reading specific descriptions or studying drawings and photographs will help you understand the job or process. You may need to talk to people who do the job or use the product. You may need to look in a dictionary to understand some technical terminology. You may read some articles in trade or professional journals. You do not have to become an expert, but you must have a broad understanding of the subject about which you must write.

When you have some understanding of the subject, investigate the audience for the message. Does the reader need general information?

> This submersible pump operates on a 115-volt power supply and provides water for a normal one-family home.

Or does the reader need technical information?

> The $\frac{1}{2}$ HP motor in this submersible pump will provide 10.8 gallons per minute from the 60-foot-deep well at 40 lbs. of pressure using 115 V.

Should the reader take action?

> Marco pumps will send information about durable submersible pumps for farm irrigation needs if you write to
> P. O. Box 24
> Galesburg, IL 61634

Once you understand a product or job and know your reader's needs, you are ready to write a general process description. You begin this description, as you would any other paragraph, with a topic sentence. In the topic sentence, name the product or job you are describing, state its function, and give other information which helps the reader understand the description. If asked to describe his job duties, the news producer of a radio station might write this topic sentence.

> As news producer of radio station WMUK-FM, I prepare, produce, and present materials covering news, sports, and public affairs for broadcast.

In the body of the paragraph, the news producer details the duties he performs to "prepare, produce, and present" material for broadcast. The resulting paragraph is a general process description of his job.

> As news producer for radio station WMUK-FM, I prepare, produce, and present materials covering news, sports, and pub-

lic affairs for broadcast. First, to prepare material for broadcast, I collect and research background material, attend newsworthy events, interview follow-up "leads," and write and edit copy for presentation. Second, as producer, my primary duties include developing ideas and formats for shows, choosing guests and topics for discussion, and scheduling programs. Because WMUK-FM is a university radio station, I also select and train student interns and guide them in developing, gathering, and writing news stories. My final duties as producer are reading and answering mail from listeners and other interested persons such as lobbyists and politicians and maintaining and updating a file of background and news story lead information from many sources. Third, as presenter, I host "on-the-air" shows.

As you can see from the use of first-person pronouns *I* and *my* in the previous paragraph, the news producer wrote from a first-person or personal viewpoint. If he wanted to write from the third-person or objective viewpoint, he could replace the first-person pronouns with the the noun *news producer* and third-person pronouns *he* or *she, his* or *her.* Changing the viewpoint from first to third person would make the description of duties more useful to the organization, in this case a university. The university could use the description written from the third-person viewpoint as part of its personnel records or in a job advertisement. If this paragraph were prepared for a formal, organizational purpose, the news producer might also list his duties rather than write them in paragraph form. Here is how his paragraph rewritten in the third person would look.

The news producer for radio station WMUK-FM prepares, produces, and presents materials covering news, sports, and public affairs for broadcast. Specific duties are

1. Preparing materials for broadcast which includes
   a. collecting and researching background material
   b. attending newsworthy events
   c. interviewing follow-up "leads"
   d. writing and editing copy for presentation.
2. Producing materials for broadcast which includes
   a. developing ideas and formats for shows
   b. choosing guests and topics for discussion
   c. scheduling programs
   d. selecting and training student interns
   e. guiding interns in developing, gathering, and writing news stories

  f. reading and answering mail from listeners and other interested persons such as lobbyists and politicians

  g. maintaining and updating a file of background and news story lead information from many sources.

 3. Presenting materials which includes hosting "on-the-air" shows.

What Is the Relationship Between General and Specific Process Descriptions?

Sometimes a general process description is just a first step. Other people must build on your work. A department store floor manager might write the following general job description:

> Salespeople will perform the following tasks: serve customers, wrap merchandise, record sales, stock shelves from inventory, and clean display cases.

Then a clerk in the employment office could use this general process description to write a classified advertisement for sales help. In the personnel department, an interviewer could prepare a checklist for interviews based on the information:

> Is the applicant able to
>
>   move about the department
>
>   wrap merchandise
>
>   stock shelves
>
>   clean display cases?
>
> Can the applicant read labels?
>
> Can the applicant learn to operate the register?
>
> Will the applicant deal pleasantly with the public?

The same general process description can go to the training department where someone with special knowledge can start preparing a training manual with five major divisions:

> How to Give Effective Customer Service
>
> How to Wrap Merchandise
>
> How to Record Sales
>
>   Cash Sales
>
>   Credit Sales
>
>   Lay Away Sales

How to Stock Shelves from Inventory

    Inventory Records

    Shelving Procedures

How to Clean Display Cases

The applicant checklist and training manuals are both forms of specific process descriptions. Specialists will write the specific process descriptions, but if the floor manager had not given a complete general process description, all the specialists' work would be incomplete or incorrect. The manager had to examine the job carefully, take notes, and then formulate the simple sentence which covered ALL the duties.

Similarly, the person who inquired about developing film got a general description of the process used. The general description helps her to decide whether she has the time, interest, and money to learn the specific steps of the developing process and to invest in the necessary supplies and equipment. If she decides to develop her own film, she needs a list of specific instructions like the one that follows. Notice that while the general description you read earlier is true of any kind of film, the specific description is tailored to the particular kind of film the photographer is using.

DEVELOPING FILM
WITH COMPATIBLE KOROID CHEMICALS

Developing film is an intermediate process the photographer must complete to convert exposed film to prints. Following these directions in a darkroom which is 68°F will produce high-quality negatives from any 20-exposure roll of 400 ASA black and white film.

Assembling Materials

Before starting the developing process, be sure to have the following materials:

1. One 20-exposure roll of exposed ASA 400 black and white film

2. One Fahrenheit thermometer which registers temperatures to 75°

3. One individual film canister complete with film reel and stem

4. One 16-ounce graduate and one container for used fluid

5. Fourteen ounces of KO-211 developer stock

6. Timer

7. Sixteen ounces of Konso 7 fixer solution

8. Ko-flo

9. Two film clips

10. One double squeegee

Preparing Developing Fluid

1. Use a thermometer to measure tap water temperature and mix hot and cold water to assure that the running water is 68° F.

2. Run 14 ounces of 68° F water into a graduate.

3. Leave the water running to use later.

4. Add 2 ounces of KO-211 developer stock to the water in the graduate.

5. Pour the mixed solution into the developing canister.

Loading the Canister

1. Take the roll of film and the canister filled with developing fluid to the darkroom.

2. Set a warning light or lock the darkroom door.

3. Set the timer for 7½ minutes.

4. Turn off all the lights in the darkroom.

5. Remove the spool of film from its cassette and thread it onto the film reel.

6. Activate the timer.

7. Insert the reel into the developing canister and lock the lid on tightly.

8. Turn on the room lights.

9. Insert the stem into the film reel and agitate the reel by turning the stem continuously for 5 seconds every 30 seconds.

Stopping the Developing Process

1. Go to the sink just before the buzzer sounds.

2. Remove the stem from the film reel when the buzzer sounds.

3. Pour the developing fluid down the sink without removing the top of the canister.

4. Fill the canister with 68° F water from the tap.

5. Pour this rinse water down the drain.

6. Refill the canister with water.

7. Pour the second rinse water down the drain.

Fixing Negatives

1. Pour 16 ounces of Konso 7 fixer into the graduate.

2. Pour the fixer into the closed canister.

3. Set the timer for 10 minutes and activate it.

4. Insert the stem into the film reel and agitate the reel gently by turning the stem continuously for 5 seconds every minute.

5. Pour the Konso 7 fluid into a container labeled "used Konso 7" when you hear the buzzer.

Washing Film

1. Remove the lid from the canister.

2. Set the open canister under the water tap and rinse the film in 68° F running water for 6 minutes. (Set and activate the timer for 6 minutes.)

Applying Wetting Agent

1. Remove the canister from the flowing water, leaving it full of water.

2. Add 2 drops of Ko-flo to the water in the canister.

3. Leave the canister open.

4. Insert the stem in the film reel.

5. Agitate the reel gently for 5 seconds.

6. Turn off water tap.

Drying Film

1. Remove the film from the canister.

2. Attach a film clip to the tab at one end of the film strip. IMPORTANT: Clean the double squeegee before Step 3 to avoid scratching the film.

3. Hold the film by the clip and use a double squeegee to strip the water from the strip of negatives.

4. Attach another clip to the other end of the strip of film.

5. Hang the film to dry in a dust-free cabinet.

WHAT IS A SPECIFIC PROCESS DESCRIPTION?

The specific description isolates one part of the total process or system so that the reader who needs to perform a particular job or use a particular product may do so from a set of step-by-step written instructions. A specific description tells how to do something. It applies only to specific or particular items, as opposed to all items, because each kind of film, food processor, or clothing store differs in some way from every other similar kind. Thus, each specific description fills a specific need. In the rest of this chapter, you will learn how to write specific process descriptions.

Why Are Specific Process Descriptions Useful?

Specific process descriptions enable people who lack knowledge of how to do a particular task or use a particular product to learn to do so. Companies use process descriptions to train employees. After a general orientation session, many companies assign a newly hired worker to an experienced worker for on-the-job training. The new worker watches the experienced worker and listens to step-by-step instructions about how to carry out a task. Some companies also give new employees a list of specific instructions to follow. Similarly, most products come with operating instructions. Some even require the buyer to assemble part of the product. People's performance on the job and their satisfaction with products they buy depend in part at least on the depth of their understanding which, in turn, depends on the quality of written process descriptions.

How Do You Write a Specific Process Description?

The Audience
Accurate audience analysis is as important in writing a specific process description as in any other kind of writing. The best course for the writer to take is to assume that the reader is completely unfamiliar with the process to be performed. A person with some knowledge will not mind reading a complete set of instructions because every job or product differs at least slightly and the user must be aware of the differences. On the other hand, a person with little or no knowledge of a process needs absolutely clear and complete instructions. Almost all of us have experienced the frustration of working from incomplete or confusing instructions. Thus, the writer of specific process descriptions must never take the reader's knowledge for granted. Indeed, as a writer, your most difficult problem is not allowing personal knowledge to cause you to overlook putting down on paper the steps you do automatically.

The Writer
Besides keeping the reader in mind, you, the writer, have other serious obligations in writing specific process descriptions. First, you always describe a particular job or product. If you are giving instructions on developing black and white film, for example, you must specify the kind of film. Instructions for developing ASA 400 black and white film do not work for developing ASA 200 black and white film because each requires a different developing time.

Second, you must have access to whatever you are describing. Trying to describe a process from memory will almost surely produce instructions that lack important steps. To insure completeness, you may take some precautions. For example, if you are writing a set of instructions on how to access a mainframe computer from a terminal, you can sit at the terminal and take notes on each step. Or you can make notes and check them for completeness by using the notes to perform the process, adding to them as necessary to complete the process description. A final test of your instructions is to give them to a person unfamiliar with the process. If this person can perform the process from your instructions, you know the instructions are complete.

Third, you must be able to name each part of the item being described. The reader will have difficulty following instructions with vague references to the "oblong thing," the "button at the left of the gizmo," the "part near the top of the machine." For example, if the second step in accessing the computer from a terminal were "Depress the control key at the bottom of the keyboard" instead of "Depress the control key (marked *CTRL*)," the reader would have several possible keys to choose from. Picking the wrong key would not produce the desired result and would keep the reader from completing the process. As you will see, one way writers get around this problem of naming parts is to use pictorial aids.

Fourth, you must separate each step in the process and describe one action at a time. For example, if you are describing the process of activating a Decwriter 2 computer terminal, you might begin with the following steps:

1. Turn the terminal on by flipping the on/off switch at the upper left corner of the keyboard to the ON position.

2. Depress the control key (marked *CTRL*).

3. Hold the control key down.

4. Strike the letter *C*.

5. Release the control key.

Because each step describes a single action, the process is easy to follow even for a person who has never used a computer terminal. By the same token, the writer must avoid lumping steps together and giving double-barreled instructions such as those in Step 2 of the following example.

1. Turn the terminal on by flipping the on/off switch at the upper left corner of the keyboard to the ON position.

2. Type Control-C by depressing the control key (marked *CTRL*) and, while depressing the control key, striking the letter *C*.

Fifth, you must give the steps in an order that allows a person to complete the process most efficiently. A person who uses a computer terminal frequently may forget to write the first step in the instructions although he or she would never personally forget to turn the terminal on. Instructions out of the normal order look like this.

1. Depress the control key (marked *CTRL*) after turning on the terminal.

2. Strike the letter *C* with the control key down.

The effect of instructions given out of order is to confuse the beginner and waste the reader's time.

Exercise A   1. This writer omitted some obvious directions. Insert the missing step or steps.

TO CLEAN YOUR FREEZER

1. Unplug the electric power cord.

2. Remove and clean the baskets, removable shelves, and parts.

3. Wash the inside with a baking soda solution (two tablespoons of baking soda mixed in a quart of warm water). Strong or concentrated detergents can damage plastic parts, and the odor may get into food packages. Remove stubborn stains with mild soap and water.

4. Rinse the inside with clear water.

5. Wipe dry.

6. Wash the door gasket carefully with baking soda solution.

7. Replace food in the freezer.

2. This writer gives all the information necessary to start an engine, but the result is confusing. Can you reorganize these directions so the reader can follow step-by-step directions efficiently?

TO START THE ENGINE

1. Depress the accelerator pedal about half way and hold it without pumping unless the engine is cold when you should depress the accelerator pedal to the floor and raise it slowly two or three times. Or if the engine is flooded, depress the pedal slowly to the floor and hold it there.

2. Crank the engine by turning the ignition key to the START position. If the engine is flooded, hold the key in START position for as long as 10 seconds before starting over with step 1.

3. Release the ignition key and the accelerator pedal as soon as the engine starts. However, if the engine is flooded, let the accelerator pedal up gradually.

4. If the engine starts but fails to run, repeat steps 1, 2, and 3.

5. If the engine is cold, let it idle for about 30 seconds after starting and then tap the accelerator pedal lightly to reduce engine
speed.

SPECIAL NOTES ABOUT STARTING

***Don't pump the accelerator except as needed in item 1 above.

***To prevent engine damage, wait three or four seconds be-
tween each attempt to start the engine.

The Structure of the Specific Process Description

A process description has three main parts: the general statement about the
job or product, a list of tools or materials needed to complete the process,
and the description of the series of actions the reader takes to perform the
job or to use the product. The first step in writing a specific process description is identifying the topic of the message and explaining its purpose. The
method used to develop the general statement differs, depending on
whether you are writing about a job or a product.

General Statement about a Job

The general statement about a job has three parts: (1) it names the job, (2)
qualifies it (see chapter 5), and (3) specifies its purpose.

A busperson at McBurger Restaurants prepares tables for new
customers.

is a general statement about a job. "Busperson" names the job. "At
McBurger Restaurants" qualifies or distinguishes this job from busperson
jobs at any other restaurant. "Prepares tables for new customers" describes
the purpose of the job. Another way to make the same general statement is

Busing tables at McBurger's Restaurants prepares them for new
customers.

This statement is similar to one you read earlier:

Developing film is an intermediate process the photographer
must complete to convert exposed film to prints.

This statement names the job and specifies its purpose. The qualification
comes in the next sentence:

Following these directions in a darkroom which is 68°F will produce high-quality negatives from any 20-exposure roll of 400 ASA black and white film.

General Statement about a Product

A possible beginning for a process description on using a computer terminal is

A Decwriter computer terminal is a machine used to access a mainframe computer.

The general statement about a product has three parts: (1) it names the item to be discussed ("A Decwriter computer terminal"), (2) it tells what the product is ("a machine"), and (3) it describes what the product does ("accesses a mainframe computer").

The second step in writing a specific process description about a product is to give a physical description of the product. To help the reader picture a computer terminal, you may use a statement like

The Decwriter computer terminal is similar to the ordinary typewriter.

This statement compares an unfamiliar item with a familiar one. A second method to describe a product is to give characteristics such as size, weight, and material such as this description:

An individual sheet of this laser-cut fanfold form measures 8½" by 11" and consists of 20-lb. white sulphite paper.

A third method is to identify the parts of a product and to give a brief description of what it does:

The number pad on the keyboard of a minicomputer consists of 10 Arabic numeral keys, a decimal point key, and an enter key. This section of the keyboard resembles a 10-key calculator keyboard and enables the operator to enter figures rapidly and accurately using the 10-key touch method.

A fourth method of describing a product is to provide an illustration of the product.

Figure 7.1 Decwriter 2 Computer Terminal. Reprinted with permission.

This illustration may be a simple line drawing or a photograph. On the illustration, you enumerate the parts of the product that you will refer to when giving instructions. To make your illustration fully understandable to the reader:

1. Number the illustration: Figure 1, Figure 2, etc. (see Figure 7.1).

2. Give the illustration a title: Figure 7.1 Decwriter 2 Computer Terminal.

3. Place the illustration number and title below the illustration.

4. Point out parts you want the reader to refer to in the description

a. by labeling the parts with words if you can keep the number of words to a minimum (see Figure 7.2) or

b. by numbering or lettering the parts if you have so many parts that their names would clutter the illustration (see Figure 7.3).

5. List the numbered or lettered parts separately (see Figure 7.3).

6. Place the illustration as close as you can to the physical description.

pusher

cover with feed tube

work bowl

motor base

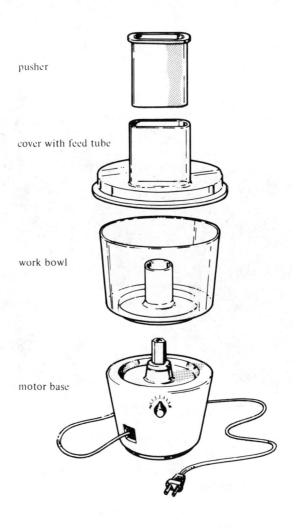

Figure 7.2 Food Processor.

PARTS LIST

		No. Rec'd.
1.	Firebox	1
2.	Door Handle	1
3.	Door Assembly (see below)	1
4.	Damper	1
5.	Damper Cotter Pin	3
6.	Damper Rod	1
7.	Fireplace Opening Cover Panel	1
8.	1"x3" Fiberglass Insulation	9ft.
9.	Hand Knob	2
10.	Sliding Lock Cover Plate	2
11.	½"x2"x10" Fiberglass Insulation	2
12.	Locking Clamp	2
13.	¼"x½" Bolt	2
14.	¼" Hex Nut	2
15.	3/8"x2" Bolt	2
16.	Locking Clamp Angle	2
17.	5/16" Flat Washer	4
18.	5/16"Hex Nut	4
19.	5/16"x½" Bolt	16
20.	Leg	1
21.	Leveler Screw	2
22.	Draft Slide	1
23.	Draft Slide Bracket	2
24.	Door Gasket	1
25.	Door Handle Thrust Washer	1
26.	Thrust Washer Set Screw	1
27.	Heat Deflector (not shown)	1

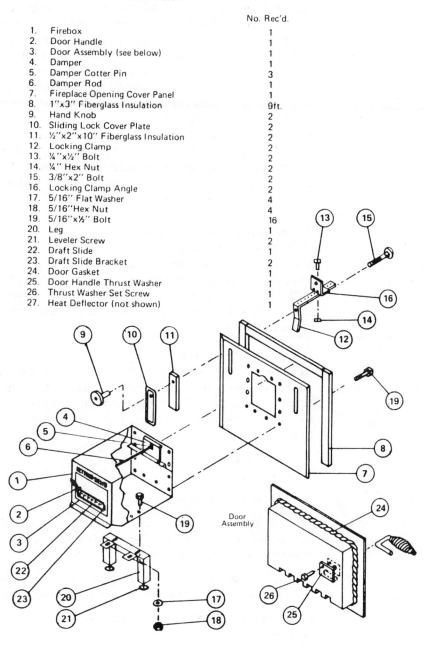

Door Assembly

Figure 7.3 Parts List. Reprinted with permission of Hayes-Te Equipment Corporation.

Listing Materials

Before beginning a task, readers need to know more than a general statement about any process. To work efficiently, they also need a list of the
tools or materials they need to complete the process. If you have ever scanned
a recipe, you have noticed that it begins with a list of ingredients. Cooks
check the list against their supplies to make sure that they have everything
they need before getting halfway through the cooking process and having to
stop to go out to buy the missing item. They then assemble all the ingredients as well as the utensils they will need before beginning to cook so that
everything will be at hand and the process can go forward without unnecessary delays to find missing items. Whether you give instructions for baking
a cake, painting a wall, developing film, or assembling a home computer
kit, the same rule applies. Readers need a list of tools or materials they will
use to complete the process.

Giving Step-by-Step Instructions

This section of the message, which is the same for a job or product description, lists the actions that the reader must take to complete the process. To
write this section of your paper, check your notes to make sure that your instructions are complete and ordered properly from first to last. Then,
itemize the steps in the process. Itemizing means listing and numbering the
steps consecutively.

Using Parallel Structure

To make your lists of instructions easy to follow, you must keep them parallel. Parallelism means that the items in the list follow the same grammatical
structure or pattern. The most prevalent structure used in lists is a command. It follows a verb-object pattern. For example, look at these instructions:

> Turn the terminal on.
>
> Depress the control key.
>
> Hold the control key down.

"Turn," "Depress," and "Hold" are all verbs; "terminal" and "control key"
are nouns that act as objects. Another familiar pattern is formed with present participles (-*ing* forms of verbs):

> The chief duties of the receptionist are *greeting* customers,
> *answering* the telephone, and *making* appointments.

Other patterns repeat nouns, verbs, infinitives, and various kinds of
phrases.

Exercise B Rewrite the following instructions so that each employs a parallel writing structure. You may vary the pattern from exercise to exercise, but in any one exercise you must use a single structure.

BANKCARD PURCHASES

1. If you are an early day-shift worker or work after midnight, check the date on the imprinter to be sure it is correct.
2. Check the amount of sale on the imprinter. It should be zero.
3. Set the amount of your sale on the imprinter.
4. Place the bankcard on the imprinter, face up.
5. To place the charge slip on the imprinter, fit it into the guides, face up.
6. Move the imprinter handle from left to right and back to the original position.
7. Remove the charge card and the charge slip.
8. Reset the register windows to zero on the imprinter.
9. Using the number on the charge slip, check the Hot Card list.
   a. If the number is on the list, refer to instruction Book C and call the manager.
   b. If the number is not on the list, proceed with the transaction.
10. Underline the account number.
11. Circle the date.
12. Print your initials under the date.
13. You only have to write "merchandise" in the description column.
14. But you do have to record the bankcard number in the cash register for validation.
15. Write in the total amount of the sale.
16. Be sure to compare the card signature with charge slip signature.
17. Staple the register receipt to the customer copy (yellow).
18. Give the yellow copy and the charge card to the customer.
19. Place the store copy under the cash drawer in the register.

TO RESET THE TIME ON AN AMB DIGITAL CLOCK

1. You will first want to know the correct time.
2. Looking at the controls on the top of the clock, find the one labeled *Time.*
3. Depress the *Time* button and hold it down.
4. Depress the button labeled *Fast* until the time is ½ hour before the present time.
5. While still depressing the *Time* button, stop depressing the *Fast* button.
6. Find the *Slow* button and depress it until you reach the present correct time.
7. Release all buttons.
8. If you pass the correct time, you must repeat all steps.

POSITION OF SERVING PERSON

A serving person has duties that involve

1. setting tables
2. greeting customers
3. taking orders
4. serving meals
5. billing customers

and after the restaurant closes, the serving person must stay to

1. clear late tables
2. total checks
3. collect, record, and distribute tips.

Cases   1. Write specific directions for walking from your classroom to some other place in the building; or, write specific directions for getting from your classroom building to some other campus building.

2. Revise the instructions you wrote in Case 1 to make them useful to a blind person.

3. Write a general process description of your duties in a job you have held.

4. Write a specific process description of the activities necessary to complete an assignment in this class.

5. To improve the efficiency of its operation, Packard Telephone Company, which serves part of northern Maine, has decided to upgrade its equipment. The company has decided to replace its customers' old telephones with newer models. To make a call with the old telephone, the cus-

tomer picked up the receiver, listened to be sure the line was free, cranked the handle at the side of the phone, and gave the operator the number. The new phones are direct dial. Because few of Packard's customers have ever used a direct dial phone, they need instructions.

Assignment: Write a specific description of the process of dialing a local number on the new telephone.

Assignment: Write a specific description of the process of direct dialing a long distance number

   a. collect

   b. billed to a third-party telephone.

Hint: Your writing task will be easier if you provide an illustration.

6. You have seen members of a restaurant staff going from table to table during the slow time after lunch and before the dinner rush to replenish condiments. Write both a general and specific process description of this job for a restaurant which requires the following items on each table.

1 full salt shaker

1 full pepper mill

1 full sugar bowl (individual sugar packets)

1 full bottle of each of the following condiments:

   ketchup

   steak sauce

   mustard

You will need to include a purpose statement and a list of materials as well as step-by-step directions for the specific process description.

Chapter 8

Writing Longer Messages

To the Student:

As you read chapter 8 and complete the exercises and cases, you will be asked to

. . . outline a longer message

. . . sequence ideas for effectiveness

. . . state your purpose and message plan in an introductory paragraph

. . . link paragraphs

. . . use side headings

. . . write a concluding paragraph.

Some of the writing you will do on the job will require a message of more than one paragraph. Although the length of the message may increase, you will still use the writing techniques you have learned already. For example, you will have to select the proper format for your message. You will also have to choose between direct and indirect orders depending on message content and audience. Finally, you will have to decide on the most efficient method of organizing individual paragraphs.

A longer message requires a few more aids to the reader than does a single-paragraph message. For example, you will have an introductory and concluding paragraph. You will also have to develop a method for linking paragraphs within the body of the message.

HOW DO YOU PLAN A LONGER MESSAGE?

When writing a longer message, you will benefit from spending more time in the planning phase than was probably necessary with one-paragraph messages. Planning time is well spent because it will actually save you writing time. Two important steps in planning are identifying the subject of your writing and outlining the ideas you will use to support the subject.

Identify the Subject

You studied identifying the subject in chapter 2. In that chapter, you learned that by answering the questions *why, what, when, where,* and *who* and combining the answers you were able to write a single descriptive sentence which identifies the subject. Once you have identified the subject, you can prepare an outline.

Prepare a Preliminary Outline

An efficient method you may use to plan your message is to prepare a topic outline. A topic outline uses words or phrases to indicate the main ideas you are trying to convey. When placed in a logical pattern, these words and phrases allow you to see your ideas as a whole and to decide whether you need to shift them around to develop a more effective organizational pattern for your message. You can use either a Roman numeral or a decimal form for outlining your ideas.

Here is an example of the process an office manager might go through in outlining a message. Sharon LaRocque has received the following memo.

INTER-OFFICE MEMORANDUM

DATE July 11, 198-

TO _____ Sharon LaRocque, Office Manager

FROM _____ A. P. Watts, Purchasing Agent *apw*

SUBJECT___ Recommendation for Office Copier Replacement

Let me know what copier you recommend to replace
the old Phillips in your office. Also please
note the reasons for your choice.

LaRocque decides to recommend the Model 6. Her reasons—size, price, production capabilities, and service record—form the major divisions of a topic outline.

REASONS FOR CHOOSING MODEL 6 COPIER

I. Size

II. Price

III. Production capabilities

IV. Service record

Sequence the Paragraphs

In outlining her reasons for choosing the Model 6 copier, she puts down her main reasons as they occur to her. That order may not be the most effective one for getting the response she wants from her audience, however. Before a writer adopts any plan of organization, he or she must consider the audience's needs. What does the reader want or need to know first, second, third, and fourth? When LaRocque considers her audience, the purchasing agent, again, she asks herself, "What is he most interested in?"

The answer is clearly *cost*. Since the price of the Model 6 is competitive with that of other leading copiers, she decides to mention *price* first in her report. She looks over her other ideas and decides *service record* should go second because of its relationship to *price*. After all, if the copier breaks down all the time, it probably is not a very good choice despite the price. She has *production capabilities* and *size* left. Which is more important? Probably *production capabilities* is more important because getting the work out rapidly saves money by freeing the machine operator for other jobs. Thus, *size* goes last. Although *size* is important to her in her crowded office, it is the least important consideration for A. P. Watts. After she has filled in the supporting details, her revised outline looks like this in the Roman numeral outline form.

REASONS FOR CHOOSING MODEL 6 COPIER

I. Cost

    A. Price

        1. Installation

        2. Warranty

    B. Operating costs

        1. Paper

        2. Toner

        3. Electricity

II. Service

    A. In-house

    B. Outside

        1. Fast

        2. Efficient

III. Production

    A. Copies per minute

    B. Exposure control

    C. Digital counter

IV. Size

    A. Copier

    B. Supply cabinet

As you review this outline, keep two points in mind. First, outlines are divisions of an idea. When you divide anything, you have to make at least two parts out of what was formerly a whole. Thus, each item that is divided has at least two parts under it. For example, the first main idea, *I*, is divided into two parts, labeled *A* and *B*; *B* is divided into three parts, labeled *1, 2,* and *3*. Although an item may stand alone such as *II. A. In-house*, it cannot logically be divided into only one part. Therefore, you cannot have *II. A. 1.* without having *II. A. 2.* as well.

Possible	*Not Possible*
II.	II.
A.	A.
1.	1.
2.	B.
B.	

Second, this outline is a topic outline. It uses words and short phrases rather than complete sentences to convey key ideas.

When you prepare your own outlines, remember these format rules.

1. Indentation shows the relative importance of items in the outline.

2. Each item lines up vertically with every other item in the same class.

3. Each item is parallel in grammatical structure to other items in its class.

4. The first word of each item begins with a capital letter.

The Roman numeral outline is probably the most commonly used outlining format. The decimal outline, however, is growing in use, especially in business and government, because it allows for even greater expansion than the Roman numeral outline, and it is easier to type on automatic machines. Once you have a grasp of the Roman numeral outline, translating it to decimal form is simple because only the designations of the divisions change. The content in the outline remains the same. Compare the two systems below:

Roman Numeral Outline	*Decimal Outline*
I.	1.
A.	1.1
B.	1.2
1.	1.2.1
2.	1.2.2
C.	1.3
II.	2.
A.	2.1
1.	2.1.1
a.	2.1.1.1
b.	2.1.1.2
2.	2.1.2
B.	2.2

When you have completed the outline form, you can see the interrelationship of ideas flowing from the purpose statement through the topic sentence and support sentences. You also know the order to follow in the message plan of the introductory paragraph.

Exercise A   Rewrite Sharon LaRocque's Roman numeral outline in decimal outline format.

HOW DO YOU WRITE THE MESSAGE?

After identifying the subject and outlining the ideas, you are ready to begin writing your message. It will consist of an introductory paragraph, several central paragraphs, and a conclusion. The introductory paragraph includes all the material your audience needs to have a clear idea of your purpose for writing and of the plan you will follow in explaining your ideas. The central paragraphs develop and support the idea expressed in the purpose statement. The concluding paragraph sums up what you have said in the paper.

Compose the Introductory Paragraph

The introductory paragraph has two purposes: to inform the reader of the main idea you are trying to convey and to give the reader an overview of your supporting ideas. The introductory paragraph, the first paragraph of any message, is extremely important because it serves as a map for the rest of the paper.

Purpose Statement
The purpose statement, often called a thesis statement, is usually expressed in one sentence. It should be both concise and precise so that the reader understands the nature of the message easily. Further, the purpose statement has the same features, a specific subject and a general statement about the subject, as the topic sentence of a single paragraph. However, the purpose statement summarizes the ideas of several paragraphs, while the topic sentence relates only to one idea expressed in a single paragraph. When you have written a sentence to identify the subject of your message, you have much of the information you need for the purpose statement.

The purpose statement, then, states the main idea of the message in the introductory paragraph. A typical purpose statement may convey information:

The Model 6 copier is a great improvement on other photocopy machines.

It may state a position:

The Model 6 copier will improve office output.

It may also give a decision:

The Model 6 copier is a cost-effective choice for our office.

When you were planning topic sentences, you learned that the way you phrased the sentence determined the content of the paragraph. In the same way, a purpose statement governs the content of a longer message. In later chapters, you will learn how to decide which purpose statement you need to use in a particular situation.

Message Plan

The second part of the introductory paragraph, the message plan or summary of supporting ideas, gives the reader an overview of the entire message.

What Goes into the Plan?

To find ideas for the message plan, look at the major divisions of the outline form. If your purpose statement is

> The Model 6 copier is a great improvement over other photocopy machines.

you may have supported that idea by explaining two features of the machine, speed and flexibility, which will form major sections of the outline. If you took these words and combined them with the purpose statement, you would have a sentence like

> The Model 6 copier is a great improvement over other photocopy machines because of its speed and flexibility.

How Do You Write the Plan?

First, as you have already seen, the ideas in the message plan may be part of the purpose statement. The sentence

> The Model 6 copier is a great improvement over other photocopy machines because of its speed and flexibility.

uses a subordinate clause introduced by *because of* to join the message plan with the purpose statement. Another way to give this information in one sentence might be to write a sentence like

> The speed and flexibility of the Model 6 make it superior to other photocopy machines.

You can probably think of other ways to combine purpose statements and message plans in one sentence in your own writing.

Second, the message plan may be in a sentence separate from the purpose statement:

> The Model 6 will improve office output. It will reduce ledger- and legal-size paper, chain feed originals, and collate copies.

A simple way to decide whether to separate the message plan from the purpose statement is to make a word count to test readability. If the combined purpose statement and message plan number about 20 words, they are readable as a single sentence. If together they much exceed 20 words, they have a high degree of reading difficulty and should be divided into two sentences.

After you have written the message plan in the introductory paragraph, remember that the central paragraphs must follow the same order you used in the message plan. For example, if you use the message plan statement

It will reduce ledger- and legal-size paper, chain feed originals, and collate copies.

your central paragraphs will first deal with reducing, second with chain feeding, and third with collating.

Link Paragraphs Together

The introductory paragraph usually requires more thinking than writing, but once you have completed the introductory paragraph you have an effective plan for the rest of your paper. Writing the central paragraphs of the body of the paper is just like all the writing you have been doing up to now. You must remember that each central paragraph has its own topic sentence and supporting sentences. An important added feature to longer messages, however, is to link supporting paragraphs to each other and to the introductory paragraph. Some of the same methods you used to achieve coherence by linking sentences together in a single paragraph will also work well in longer messages. Remember, however, that in one-paragraph messages, you were linking sentences together. In longer messages, you are linking paragraphs together. Thus, some of the guides to coherent writing from chapter 6 need to be extended for use in the longer message.

Guides to Coherence in Longer Messages

1. Repeat key words of the purpose statement in the topic sentence.

Purpose statement: Word processing machines improve office efficiency by saving time and cutting costs.

Topic sentence: Production time is a major factor in improving efficiency.

Topic sentence: Cost is the other important office efficiency factor.

2. Repeat sentence structures in topic sentences.

Purpose statement: Word processing machines improve office efficiency by saving time and cutting costs.

Topic sentence: Saving time improves office efficiency.

Topic sentence: Cutting costs improves office efficiency.

3. Use transitions to lead the reader from one paragraph to another.

    A. Number ideas: *first, second, third*, and so forth.

    B. Signal additions of similar material with words like *another, also, in addition*, and *furthermore.*

    C. Signal contrasts with words like *although, however, by contrast, in contrast to*, and *on the other hand.*

    D. Sum up ideas with *thus, therefore, as a result*, and *finally.*

You will find that the best ways to use the transitional words in item 3 is in combination with the repeated sentence structures in item 2. For example:

Purpose statement:	Word processing machines improve office efficiency by saving time and cutting costs.
Topic sentence:	First, saving time is an important efficiency factor.
Topic sentence:	Second, cutting costs is also vital to efficiency.

or

Topic sentence:	Efficiency ratings climb when time requirements shrink.
Topic sentence:	Efficiency ratings can climb further not only when time requirements shrink but also when costs shrink.

4. Use side headings to link paragraphs together. When you get to chapter 14, which discusses formal reports, you will study degrees of headings. For informal messages, you should learn to use side headings. Side headings serve much the same purpose as the transitional devices you have just studied. They allow the reader to move from one part of your message to another without getting lost.

What Are Side Headings?
Side headings are markers for the main ideas of the message. If you have used a topic outline to organize your message, side headings are the topics — words or phrases — that follow the Roman numerals in the Roman numeral outline or the whole numbers in the decimal outline.

What Is the Value of Side Headings?
Side headings are valuable first because they stand out from the rest of the message. In business writing, your readers are often interested in only a part of your message. Headings help them locate a particular part they are interested in. When they read the whole report but want to refer only to a particular section of it, they can easily find the section because you have marked it clearly with a side heading. Second, when you use side headings, you can omit long transitional phrases.

What Is the Format for Side Headings?

Side headings appear at the left margin of your message. To insure that headings stand out from the rest of the message, follow these suggestions.

1. Leave an extra space above and below headings.
2. Capitalize the first letter of each important word in the heading.
3. Underline the heading.

How Are Side Headings Written?

All side headings follow the same grammatical structure. In other words, you follow the rules for parallel structure you learned in chapter 7. Since side headings are words and phrases rather than sentences, you have to repeat the idea of the heading in the first sentence of the paragraph. In a paper about photocopiers, for example, if you are writing a section about cost, the side heading and topic sentence might look like this:

Cost

The cost of the Model 6 copier is competitive with that of other leading machines.

Where Are Side Headings Placed?

The first side heading follows the introductory paragraph. It comes before the first main idea in the body of the paper. Each time you begin a new idea and, thus, a new section of your message, you place a heading before the new section. Sometimes a section is one paragraph long; sometimes it is a few paragraphs in length. For example, in a paper about a photocopy machine, you might need two paragraphs to describe the machine's functions. One heading could cover both paragraphs because they discuss the same main idea, the machine's functions.

Conclude the Message

Like the opening section, the concluding paragraph is also dependent on the purpose of your message and the audience for your message. In the chapters that follow, you will learn to tailor the final paragraph to the content of the message. But, in general, all concluding paragraphs or sections do one or more of the following things:

1. Summarize the highlights of your message by reminding the reader of the most important points you made.

2. Draw a logical conclusion by showing the reader the results which stem from the facts you presented.

3. Facilitate decisionmaking by asking for or suggesting an action that could be taken as a result of the information you provided.

Whatever your purpose in the conclusion, remember that everything in this section must refer to something you have already written. The reader wants you to wrap up all your ideas in a neat package that is easy to remember or to act on. You can help the reader by sticking strictly to the subjects you have already written about.

Sample Message

In the sample message which follows, you see that Sharon LaRocque combined two strategies to conclude the memo. She briefly summarized the basis for her recommendation, but the last short paragraph facilitates decisionmaking by requesting a specific action.

```
                          MEMO

        TO:  A. P. Watts, Purchasing Agent

      FROM:  Sharon LaRocque, Office Manager 𝒮𝒥.

   SUBJECT:  Replacing Our Phillips Copier with a Model 6

      DATE:  July 13, 198-
```

The Model 6 copier is a cost-effective replacement for our
Phillips machine. The Model 6 is inexpensive to buy and
operate, has a good service record, meets our output needs,
and will fit conveniently into present office space.

Costs

The initial cost of the Model 6 is $2107.50, which includes
installation and 90 days' free service. We can then purchase
a service contract for $30 a month or $300 a year. The contract
may be renewed for one year at the same price even if new contracts are at higher rates.

Operating the Model 6 will also be inexpensive. The machine
uses plain paper (or our letterhead) so paper costs will be
only $.006 per copy. Powdered toner costs $30.25 for about
5,000 copies or $.006 a copy. Operating cost, then, is $.012
per copy. Further, the Model 6 uses a cold copy process and
requires less electricity than machines which rely on heat in
the copy process. It may be switched off after each use, thus
reducing heat and noise as well as electricity consumption.

Service

The Model 6 will require regular service. However, it has one
feature which should help to avoid some service calls. The machine opens easily to provide full access to the entire paper
track. This feature means our own operators can easily solve
paper feed problems.

When other problems arise, local repair service is available.
The company maintains a technical staff of six and guarantees
owners of service contracts that a service representative will
reach the premises within two hours of a call for service.

I called three local firms who own Model 6 copiers to ask about
their experience with service. All three indicated that service
was fast and efficient. One of the companies, ACE, relies
entirely on small copiers rather than on a central copy center.
Mr. James, therefore, has records of many copiers. His records
show that the average Model 6 requires some service after 8,000

copies. Other copiers in the same price range require service
after producing only 6,500 copies.

Production

The Model 6 is entirely adequate for the low-volume production
in this office. It produces 10 copies per minute on either
8 1/2" x 11" or 8 1/2" x 14" paper. A visible exposure control
lets us adjust the machine to make copies from pen, pencil, or
typed originals.

An operator can make a test copy to set exposure and then use the
digital counter to produce from 1 to 99 copies automatically.
The copy control resets to 0 after each run so the next operator
will not inadvertently make too many copies.

One special feature of copy control will increase operating efficiency. Long copy runs can be interrupted for single copies.
After the interruption, the machine's microprocessor automatically
completes the initial run without resetting or manual counting.

Size

The Model 6 is only 20" by 14" by 12". It will fit on the small
cabinet which now stands next to the larger Phillips machine.
We will store supplies for the copier inside the cabinet and
move the smaller unit to the files area which will be convenient
for all users.

If you agree that on the basis of cost, service, production, and
size the Model 6 is an efficient machine for this office, I will
place the order and plan to have the machine in service by
August 1.

147

Exercise B   1. Read the response to A.P. Watts' memo. Then answer these questions.

      a. What format did the writer choose?

      b. Why is this format appropriate for the message?

      c. Give quotations from the message which answer each of the following questions:

        1. What is the subject of the message?

        2. Why is the message needed?

        3. Where will the information in the message be used?

        4. When will the information be used?

      d. What words in the message plan are represented by each of these side headings?

        1. Costs

        2. Service

        3. Production

        4. Size

      e. The writer tried and rejected the following subject lines for this message. Why are these lines inadequate?

        1. New Copier

        2. Model 6 Copier

        3. A Good Copier

        4. The Copier that is Needed in our Office

    2. Review the Guides to Coherence in Longer Messages. Then mark the message wherever you find effective use of coherence techniques.

        Example: "The initial cost of the Model 6 . ." #1

Review   In this chapter, you have learned to organize material for longer messages. To write longer messages, you learned first the need to plan both through sequencing main ideas and outlining the message. After developing a feasible plan, you were able to (1) introduce your purpose for writing and give an overview of your message in an introductory paragraph; (2) follow your plan through the central paragraphs of your message; (3) link your ideas together to produce a readable message; and (4) conclude your message appropriately.

WRITING CHECKLIST FOR LONGER MESSAGES

1. Why does this message need to be written?

2. What will the message accomplish?

3. Who will read the message?

4. What order is appropriate for the message?

5. What major topics should I discuss in the message?

6. What is the most effective order for these topics?

7. What supporting information do I need for each topic?

8. What purpose statement will direct the reader's attention to the subject of the message?

9. What message plan will highlight the topics in the message?

10. Should the final paragraph be a summary, a conclusion, or a request for action?

11. What format is appropriate for this message?

Use the back of this sheet to complete a message outline.

WRITING CHECKLIST FOR LONGER MESSAGES

1. Why does this message need to be written?

2. What will the message accomplish?

3. Who will read the message?

4. What order is appropriate for the message?

5. What major topics should I discuss in the message?

6. What is the most effective order for these topics?

7. What supporting information do I need for each topic?

8. What purpose statement will direct the reader's attention to the subject of the message?

9. What message plan will highlight the topics in the message?

10. Should the final paragraph be a summary, a conclusion, or a request for action?

11. What format is appropriate for this message?

Use the back of this sheet to complete a message outline.

WRITING CHECKLIST FOR LONGER MESSAGES

1. Why does this message need to be written?

2. What will the message accomplish?

3. Who will read the message?

4. What order is appropriate for the message?

5. What major topics should I discuss in the message?

6. What is the most effective order for these topics?

7. What supporting information do I need for each topic?

8. What purpose statement will direct the reader's attention to the subject of the message?

9. What message plan will highlight the topics in the message?

10. Should the final paragraph be a summary, a conclusion, or a request for action?

11. What format is appropriate for this message?

Use the back of this sheet to complete a message outline.

WRITING CHECKLIST FOR LONGER MESSAGES

1. Why does this message need to be written?

2. What will the message accomplish?

3. Who will read the message?

4. What order is appropriate for the message?

5. What major topics should I discuss in the message?

6. What is the most effective order for these topics?

7. What supporting information do I need for each topic?

8. What purpose statement will direct the reader's attention to the subject of the message?

9. What message plan will highlight the topics in the message?

10. Should the final paragraph be a summary, a conclusion, or a request for action?

11. What format is appropriate for this message?

Use the back of this sheet to complete a message outline.

WRITING CHECKLIST FOR LONGER MESSAGES

1. Why does this message need to be written?

2. What will the message accomplish?

3. Who will read the message?

4. What order is appropriate for the message?

5. What major topics should I discuss in the message?

6. What is the most effective order for these topics?

7. What supporting information do I need for each topic?

8. What purpose statement will direct the reader's attention to the subject of the message?

9. What message plan will highlight the topics in the message?

10. Should the final paragraph be a summary, a conclusion, or a request for action?

11. What format is appropriate for this message?

Use the back of this sheet to complete a message outline.

Cases   1. Write the copy for a brochure for the Chamber of Commerce in your city. The Chamber wants to attract new industry, so your copy should stress such city assets as the labor force, transportation, industrial parks, tax structures, and quality of life. If you live in a large transportation center, you will want to stress transportation. If, however, you live in a smaller city or village that has no railroads or bus service, you will find other reasons to attract industry.

2. In many business positions, you will be assigned to work on long-term projects. Your supervisor may remember to say, "Keep me informed," or he or she may simply assume you will report your progress. The project may require regular reports (especially true for government-funded projects) or may be planned in several separate steps, and you will naturally plan to report at the end of each step.

If the project is ahead of schedule, you will want to report your success. More often, projects meet unexpected delays. Some employees make the mistake of trying to hide bad news. It will all come out someday, so smart workers always send progress reports to explain delays and failures as well as successes.

In this case, Moira MacDonald is in charge of a market research project to interview customers at a local shopping mall to discover their buying patterns. The mall's management will use the information to help mall tenants plan merchandising strategies and successful promotions to draw customers to the mall during slow shopping periods.

MacDonald set up this work schedule on January 5, leaving one week's leeway between the end of her work and the contract deadline date when the report is due in the client's office.

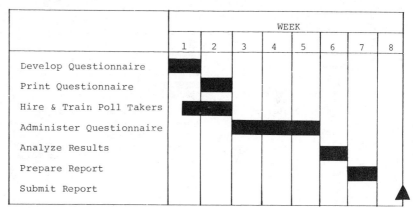

She completed the questionnaire in three days and submitted it to the statistical department for correction and coding. They raised some pertinent questions about the sampling techniques she employed, so she had to spend extra time revising the questionnaire. She sent this progress report to the division manager when the questionnaire cleared the statistical department.

MEMO

TO: M. L. Hernandez, Division Manager

FROM: Moira MacDonald *MᵐM*

SUBJECT: Modern Mall Customer Survey--Status Report

DATE: January 14, 198-

The Modern Mall survey is slightly behind schedule because of
statistical and printing problems. However, as the original
plan allowed one week's leeway, the final report should be
ready on March 2.

Statistical Delay

I sent the proposed questionnaire to the statistical department
on January 8. They suggested that I revise the eligibility questions and print six forms to capture full-year data during our
short, intensive survey period.

The revisions strengthened the questionnaire so it will provide
better information to the Modern Mall staff.

Printing Delay

The printer expected this copy on January 12. Of course, when I
told him the copy would be late, he scheduled another job. Our
survey will probably be available on January 23 or 26.

Revised Schedule

As the survey requires three full weeks for validity, I have revised
my work schedule.

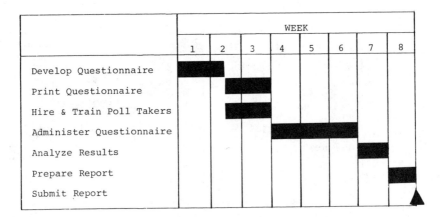

	WEEK							
	1	2	3	4	5	6	7	8
Develop Questionnaire	████							
Print Questionnaire		████						
Hire & Train Poll Takers		████						
Administer Questionnaire				████	████	████		
Analyze Results							████	
Prepare Report								████
Submit Report								▲

Now the date is February 4, and MacDonald is in trouble through no fault of her own. She hired six polling people. They completed nearly 300 good interviews before the heavy snow started on January 30. The mall shut down completely for the weekend. More snow arrived on Monday and Tuesday. The weather service predicts additional snow for the coming weekend. MacDonald and three of her assistants were at the mall on February 2 and 3, but they saw only 12 customers in the deserted and half-closed mall. The study will not be statistically valid unless the interviewers work through three full seven-day weeks of interviews.

MacDonald wants the division manager to renegotiate the contract, giving her two weeks to analyze results and to prepare the report — AFTER she has a total of 21 more or less normal shopping days for interviews.

Write the progress report for MacDonald. You will not need to complete a new work schedule, as the schedule she is seeking is dependent on the weather, not the calendar.

3. Write a narrative record of your employment history which you can use as background or supplementary material at a job interview. Remember, the application blank usually asks for a chronological outline of your employment history; don't simply repeat that outline. Instead, re-examine each job you have held to sort out particular knowledge you gained or good work habits you developed. Organize your message to impress a potential employer; do not bore him or her with lists of names, dates, and job titles.

If you are a young person with a very short employment history, you may also include chores, odd jobs, and baby sitting. Any regular duties that you performed built some good habits, and you learned something about "working for a living."

3a. *Alternate assignment.* If you are a person who so far has spent more time and energy looking for work than working, write a narrative history of your job searches. Again, avoid just making a list of disappointments. Analyze the disappointments and try to find a pattern so you can avoid meeting the same problems again.

4. Your employer is the public relations or information service department of your college or university. The Alumni Association has asked your department to prepare a historical brochure it can enclose with the news of reunion plans during the spring graduation week. It plans a three-fold brochure with two small pictures. One picture is of the first building on campus and the other picture is of ground breaking for the newest building. You are to write at least 250 words and not more than 300 words about the history of the institution. If you wish, you may write the last paragraph of the copy about future plans for the institution.

Chapter 9

Defining
an Abstraction

To the Student:

    As you read chapter 9 and complete the exercises and cases, you will be asked to

        . . . list criteria to define an abstract term

        . . . write a definition of an abstract term

        . . . draw up a checklist to gather information

        . . . write a report to describe your findings.

In chapter 7, you described a process: how to do something. In writing this description, you had the advantage of being able to give your readers a visual representation, an illustration, in addition to a word picture. Whether you were describing how to bake a cake or to set the timing on an automobile, your readers already knew how the process should come out. Your job was to make sure the readers could follow all the steps you described to them.

WHAT ARE ABSTRACT AND CONCRETE TERMS?

In chapter 9, you will be working with abstract terms rather than concrete things, as you did in chapter 7. Because these terms are abstract, you will not be able to illustrate them or label their parts. Usually you will not be able to measure them with a scale, or tape, or any standard measuring device you could use to measure a concrete thing. In many cases, you will not even be able to learn about abstractions through your senses. You cannot see, hear, taste, touch, or smell them. Yet your job as a writer is to make these abstract terms as clear to readers as the concrete things in chapter 7 were. To make abstractions clear, you will use the process of defining, which is telling what something is in precise terms upon which all your readers can agree. You will be able to make such definitions even of abstract terms.

Exercise A   Place a *C* before concrete items and an *A* before abstract items in the following list.

1. clean	11. neatness
2. tensile strength	12. water
3. acceleration	13. value
4. speed	14. bargain
5. car	15. time
6. oil	16. distance
7. efficiency	17. money
8. floor space	18. courtesy
9. height	19. cost
10. accountability	20. weight

WHY DO YOU DEFINE AN ABSTRACT TERM?

In the preceding exercise, you probably correctly said that *clean* is one of the abstract words. Because it is abstract, it exists first in a person's mind. Thus, your idea of clean may be very different from your neighbor's idea of clean. Before you and your audience can apply the term *clean* to any object, you must analyze the term to make sure you all have the same understanding of it.

Undefined Terms Cause Confusion

If your supervisor walks into your work area and says, "You'd better clean it up around here," you and your co-workers may all interpret his words differently. Some of you may think he is talking about your language, some about your behavior, your clothes, or your work surface. Even if all of you decide he is talking about your work surface, what action do you take? Do you remove all your tools or papers from the work surface and put them in storage places? Do you dust the work surface? Do you scrub it with a strong disinfectant?

Defined Terms Make Action Clear

Although you know "in general" that clean refers to work surface, you need specific information to fulfill your supervisor's request. This specific information may show a picture or model of the perfect work bench with every tool in place; it may include a list of actions to take: "After completing each die cutting, use the power vac to remove all metal shavings from bench or floor."

If you have been sweeping metal shavings from your work bench to the floor and leaving the shavings on the floor, you know you must use the vacuum to remove shavings from the floor.

If written carefully, each item in your list of specific responsibilities about cleanliness in the work area is part of the total definition of clean in one particular application.

HOW DO YOU DEFINE ABSTRACT TERMS?

You cannot transfer a definition of an abstraction, such as the one you just read, from one situation to another. *Clean* in a tool and die plant is not the same as *clean* in a doctor's office or in a hospital operating room. In fact, a definition of *clean* can change as one person's duties change in a day. You want your doctor to wash his or her hands before giving you a routine office examination, but when the same doctor prepares to remove your appendix, you expect his or her hands to meet operating-room standards for cleanliness. Hot water and antiseptic soap will clean the doctor's hands adequately in the office, but hospitals require several minutes of vigorous scrubbing with special soap and brushes in sterile surroundings. Even these precautions only produce hands clean enough to be covered by sterile gloves.

Write Criteria

You have already studied two requirements for writing definitions: (1) a term to be defined and (2) a situation in which the term exists. Once you have determined both of these, you have one further requirement. You must figure out the criteria you need to make your definition.

Criteria are tests you apply to the term or object you are defining. For example, all boxing fans are familiar with the term "a clean break." How does the referee decide whether two boxers in a clinch in the middle of the ring "break clean"? He applies three tests to their behavior:

1. Did the boxers step back when told to?

2. Did they step back at the same time?

3. Did they refrain from punching while stepping back?

But when a doctor examines the X-ray of a broken bone, he or she applies only one test to determine if the mishap may be defined as a "clean break": Does the X-ray confirm that the bone did not splinter at the point of the break?

When you understand a situation, you can write criteria for a definition that applies to it. Take a few minutes to jot down some criteria that will help you define the word *clean* in the phrase "a clean plate."

You should have refused to write any criteria. You needed to know the situation in which your criteria will operate. "A clean plate" may refer to a dinner plate or to a dental appliance for holding false teeth. A whole sentence will help you understand the problem thoroughly: "Each meal must be served on a clean plate," or "If you don't finish your vegetables and leave a clean plate, you can't have dessert." The criteria for a clean plate before a meal are different from the criteria for a clean plate after a meal. Now that you see two problems, list two criteria for each of them.

A Clean Plate *Before Dinner*	*A Clean Plate* *After Dinner*

Read over your criteria. Are you satisfied that a stranger could use them exactly as you meant them to be used? Or did you use one abstract term to try to define another abstract term? Did you write something like "no dirt on the plate" as one criterion for a clean plate after dinner? What "dirt" did you mean—garden soil, a greasy film, or actual food particles from the last meal? To insure that others would rate the plate as you would, you need a complete list which might contain all the following criteria:

1. No visible food particles clinging to either the service side or the underside of the plate

2. No chips or cracks harboring bacteria

3. No grease to stain paper towel rubbed over the plate.

How did you define the "after dinner" clean? If you thought of your own dishes after a meal, you did not write

> There is no food left on the plate.

Did you perhaps read the problem sentence again and adjust your definition of *clean* to the circumstances:

> No single identifiable piece of vegetable should be left on the plate.

Or perhaps you have a more lenient view of a child's duty to *clean* the plate and wrote:

> No more than one teaspoonful of each food served should remain on the plate.

Writing criteria requires the same precision of thinking and language that you used in chapter 7 to describe a process. You must use words that your reader cannot misinterpret and that are appropriate to the situation. The "clean plate" which prevails in most households would not meet the needs of a biologist who needs a "clean plate" on which to test a culture.

Test Criteria

Each time you face a new definition problem, you must complete the same steps to solve it:

1. Read or study the complete situation several times so that you understand exactly what you must do to help the reader.

2. Make some preliminary notes about factors that you will definitely have to take into account.

3. Observe the place or situation (or go to a library) to learn every detail you can about the place, situation, or action you must define.

4. Write tentative criteria that cover everything you saw or read.

5. Try out your tentative criteria in the particular situation.

6. Make revisions and try again. (You sometimes repeat this step several times in a complex situation.)

7. Apply your final list to the situation.

8. Write your findings in a clear report which describes what you discovered and summarizes the findings.

Exercise B Use concrete language to set standards appropriate for each of the following situations.

1. Set criteria for *accuracy* for
   a. a beginning typing student after eight weeks of lessons
   b. a newspaper compositor with five years' experience at the machine and at the job
   c. a typesetter for a special edition of a book which will sell at retail for at least $100 a copy

2. Define *safe driving speed* on a four-lane highway
   a. at 3 p.m. on a sunny spring day
   b. at 10 p.m. in a driving rain storm (winds are 60 miles an hour and the rain is 1" an hour)
   c. at 6 a.m. the morning after an ice storm

3. What are evidences of *high mathematical ability* or *high verbal ability* in each of these school situations?
   a. third grade
   b. ninth grade
   c. first year in college

4. Define a *prudent savings program* for
   a. a 10-year-old child who earns a small allowance for completing household chores
   b. a 16-year-old student with a part-time job (15 hours a week)
   c. a young, single adult with three years' work experience who just received a significant promotion and a 20 percent increase in salary

After completing these exercises, you are ready to use your abilities to define an abstract concept in a real-life case. Here is an example of using criteria to define an abstract term as the basis of an informational report which summarizes your work.

Sample Case 1 The building supervisor receives complaints from several workers in the buildings. They say that the drinking fountains are so messy they don't want to use them. The supervisor wants to give janitors some guidelines to follow to insure that the drinking fountains are clean.

The supervisor first inspects the fountains in the complex and finds the workers are right: Most of the drinking fountains are "messy." She writes notes about some of the "mess":

1. Some fountains have wads of chewing gum and/or cigarette butts in the basin.

2. Many fountains have water spots and mineral deposits.

3. Some basins have rust stains or other stains on the surface.

4. The outsides of fountains have fingermarks and many other un-identified marks and stains.

Before the supervisor can effectively write directions for the janitorial staff, she must first define "a clean fountain." Here is her definition.

A FOUNTAIN IS CLEAN WHEN

1. The basin contains no
    a. cigarette butts, chewing gum, or other debris
    b. water spots, mineral deposits, or other stains
2. The fixtures are free of
    a. water spots and mineral deposits
    b. grease and fingerprints
    c. rust stains
3. The exterior is free of
    a. water spots and mineral deposits
    b. grease and fingermarks

This definition of a "clean fountain" provides information that the supervisor uses to write instructions for janitors:

1. Remove foreign matter from the basins.
2. Scrub spigots, drains, and the on-off fixtures with a soft brush and nonabrasive cleanser.
3. Wipe out the basin with nonabrasive cleanser.
4. Use a grease-cutting cleanser to sponge the exterior to remove grease and fingermarks.

A week later the building supervisor gives you the criteria and list of janitors' instructions and sends you to the third floor of your building to check the drinking fountains because they have received the most complaints. You read the definition of "a clean fountain" and the list of instructions, and you prepare a simple checklist to help you assess the condition of the drinking fountains.

Figures 9.1, 9.2, and 9.3 show the results of your inspection.

Inspector's Name *Wilbur Johnson*   Time of Inspection *10:30 a.m.*

Inspection Site *North Bldg, 3rd Floor* Date of Inspection *11/5/8-*
                    Fountain 1

<u>Item</u>

Assessment

Yes   No

Basin contains
    cigarette butts   ____   ✔
    chewing gum   ____   ✔
    other debris   ____   ✔
    water spots   ____   ✔
    mineral deposits   ____   ✔
    rust stains   ____   ✔
    other stains   ____   ✔

Fixtures show
    water spots   ____   ✔
    mineral deposits   ____   ✔
    rust stains   ____   ✔
    fingermarks   ____   ✔

Exterior shows
    water spots   ____   ✔
    mineral deposits   ____   ✔
    grease   ____   ✔
    fingermarks   ____   ✔

Comments:

Figure 9.1 Completed Checklist for Fountain 1.

Inspector's Name _Wilbur Johnson_____ Time of Inspection ___10:35 a.m.___

Inspection Site _North Bldg., 3rd Floor_ Date of Inspection ___11/5/8-___

Fountain 2

Item	Assessment	
	Yes	No
Basin contains		
cigarette butts	_____	✓
chewing gum	_____	✓
other debris	_____	✓
water spots	_____	✓
mineral deposits	_____	✓
rust stains	_____	✓
other stains	_____	✓
Fixtures show		
water spots	_____	✓
mineral deposits	_____	✓
rust stains	_____	✓
fingermarks	_____	✓
Exterior shows		
water spots	_____	✓
mineral deposits	_____	✓
grease	_____	✓
fingermarks	_____	✓

Comments:

Figure 9.2 Completed Checklist for Fountain 2.

Inspector's Name *Wilbur Johnson*   Time of Inspection *10:40 a.m.*

Inspection Site *North Bldg., 3rd Floor* Date of Inspection *11/5/8-*

              Fountain 3

Item	Assessment	
	Yes	No
Basin contains		
cigarette butts		✓
chewing gum		✓
other debris		✓
water spots		✓
mineral deposits		✓
rust stains		✓
other stains		✓
Fixtures show		
water spots	✓	
mineral deposits	✓	
rust stains	✓	
fingermarks		✓
Exterior shows		
water spots		✓
mineral deposits		✓
grease		✓
fingermarks		✓

Comments:

Figure 9.3 Completed Checklist for Fountain 3.

Now are you ready to begin your report.

Step 1. Analyze the information you have gathered. The checklists show that the janitors have done a fairly good job. Fountain 1 and 2 got straight "no" ratings. Fountain 3 got "yesses" in three of the four categories. It had water spots and mineral deposits on the fixture.

Step 2. Put the information together in a direct report in memo form. Remember that in direct order, your most important finding goes in the first paragraph. Your supporting evidence goes in the following paragraphs where you explain your findings. Your report looks like Figure 9.4.

```
                              MEMO

         TO:  Gale Elliot, Building Supervisor

       FROM:  Wilbur Johnson, Inspector ₩

    SUBJECT:  Cleanliness of Drinking Fountains in North Building,
              Third Floor

       DATE:  November 5, 198-
```

As you see on the attached checklists, Fountains 1 and 2 are
clean. The janitors have followed your instructions carefully
and have done a thorough job.

Fountain 3 does not meet the high standards of the other two
fountains. Although the basin and exterior are clean, the
janitors have forgotten to scrub the fixtures with nonabrasive
cleanser. Water spots as well as mineral deposits coat the fixtures of Fountain 3.

Att.

Figure 9.4 Memo Report to Gale Elliot.

Exercise C Read the checklist that appears below. Analyze the information the checklist gives you. Put the information together in direct order memo format, following the model memo.

Inspector's Name *K. C. Collins*   Time of Inspection *2:30 p.m.*

Inspection Site *Lobby, North Bldg.* Date of Inspection *11/7/8-*

Item	Assessment	
	Yes	No
Basin contains		
cigarette butts	✔	
chewing gum	✔	
other debris		✔
water spots		✔
mineral deposits		✔
rust stains		✔
other stains		✔
Fixtures show		
water spots		✔
mineral deposits		✔
rust stains		✔
fingermarks		✔
Exterior shows		
water spots		✔
mineral deposits		✔
grease	✔	
fingermarks	✔	

Comments:

Sample Case 2

You work in the maintenance department of a small college. Your supervisor tells you that next summer the department must systematically go through every classroom making furniture repairs. The first step is to prepare checklists which the regular janitorial staff can use to make a comprehensive list of the furniture that must be repaired. When you have reports from the staff in each building, you will be able to place orders for replacement parts and schedule time and personnel in the shop for making repairs. Your superior asks you to "take care of the paper work."

You begin by visiting several classrooms to examine the furniture carefully and to make the following notes:

STUDENT CHAIRS: They are one-arm desk chairs constructed of plastic and metal. Some backs are missing; a few are cracked. Writing arms are loose on some desks. A few desk arms are missing entirely, and some seem twisted so they actually slant toward the floor. Feet missing from some chair legs cause the chairs to wobble. A few chair seats are cracked, missing, or broken in two parts. Screws have worked loose or are missing in the assembly where legs are attached to chair seats.

TABLES: On some tables the screws that hold the legs to the table top have worked loose, leaving the table top only partially secured to the leg assembly. A few table legs are dented and actually bent. Some metal feet are missing from table legs causing the table to rest unevenly on the floor.

SIDE CHAIRS: The chairs are made of metal with padded leatherette seats and a matching back pad. On a few chairs the seat cover has been torn, exposing the padding. The matching chair backs also are torn on some chairs. At least one chair has no leatherette on the back at all. Some metal feet have fallen off chair legs.

Back at your desk, you write the specific criteria which will tell you when a piece of furniture needs repair:

Student Chairs A student chair needs repair when an inspector finds one or more of these defects:

1. A chair back is loose, missing, or broken

2. A writing arm is loose, missing, or broken

3. A writing arm slants toward the floor

4. One or more chair legs lack metal feet

5. One or more scews are loose or missing in the leg/chair seat assembly

6. A chair seat is cracked, broken, or missing

Tables A table needs repair when an inspector finds one or more of these defects:

1. One or more screws are loose or missing in the leg/table top assembly

2. One or more table legs lack metal feet

3. One or more table legs are bent

Side Chairs A side chair needs repair when an inspector finds one or more of these defects:

1. Leatherette cover on chair back is torn or missing

2. Leatherette cover on chair seat is torn

3. One or more chair legs lack metal feet

Using these criteria, you prepared checklists for the staff to use in identifying furniture that must be repaired. You were careful to make up the forms to isolate each kind of repair so you could use the reports to order replacement parts and to estimate the time needed to make the repairs.

The maintenance staff used a separate form to check the furniture in each classroom and sent the data to you. You added the numbers from each form and compiled the total figures on one form. These data are shown in Figure 9.5.

Building *(Total - all buildings)*   Inspector *Janitorial Staff*

Room _____   Date *4/1/8-*

Furniture displaying one or more of the defects listed below should be marked for repair. Whenever you mark furniture for repair, indicate all the repairs each piece requires.

Number of tables inspected	57
Number of tables needing repair	8
Repairs required	
Table leg bent	1
Table leg lacking metal foot	12
Screws loose in table top/leg assembly	2
Screws missing in table top/leg assembly	15
Number of side chairs inspected	160
Number of side chairs needing repair	81
Repairs required	
Chair leg lacking metal foot	104
Seat cover torn	58
Leatherette back torn	6
Leatherette back missing	2
Number of student chairs inspected	764
Number of student chairs needing repair	243
Repairs required	
Chair back loose	131
Chair back missing	84
Chair back cracked	2
Writing arm loose	125
Writing arm missing	14
Writing arm broken	22
Writing arm slants toward floor	28
Chair leg lacking metal foot	301
Screws loose in chair seat/leg assembly	197
Screws missing in chair seat/leg assembly	590
Chair seat missing	2
Chair seat cracked	11
Chair seat broken	7

Comments:

Figure 9.5 Composite Furniture Checklist.

Using the information from Figure 9.5, you write a memorandum to your superior describing the repairs needed and suggesting the number of replacement parts you will need to make the repairs. The memo is shown as Figure 9.6.

```
                                MEMO

          TO:  Hazel Sturgis, Director, Physical Plant

        FROM:  Arthur Ermisch, Maintenance Supervisor  AE

     SUBJECT:  Classroom Furniture Repair

        DATE:  April 2, 198-

     After inspecting all classroom furniture, the janitorial staff
     found that 8 tables, 81 side chairs, and 243 student chairs need
     repairs to be ready for use next term.

     Tables

     The janitors found two main problems with tables:  metal feet
     missing from table legs and loose or missing screws in the
     table top/leg assembly.  To get the tables in good condition,
     the maintenance crew will have to replace 12 missing metal
     feet, tighten loose screws, and replace 15 missing screws.
     They will also have to straighten one bent table leg.

     Side Chairs

     Eighty-one side chairs need repairs.  We'll have to replace 104
     metal feet, 58 seat covers, and 8 leatherette backs.

     Student Chairs

     Student chairs need extensive repairs.  Two hundred forty-three
     of them have defective backs, arms, feet, seat/leg assemblies,
     and seats.

     1.  Chair backs:          131 need tightening
                                86 need to be replaced

     2.  Writing arms:         125 need tightening
                                36 need to be replaced
                                28 need to be bent back to level
                                   position

     3.  Metal feet:           310 replacements are needed

     4.  Seat/leg assembly:    197 need tightening
                               590 have missing screws

     5.  Chair seats:           20 replacements are needed
```

Figure 9.6 Memo Report to Hazel Sturgis.

Review   In this chapter, you have learned the distinction between abstract and concrete terms, the relationship of an abstract term to the situation in which it operates, and a method of gathering information. More important, you can now use information to determine criteria you need to write definitions. These definitions allow you to develop checklists useful for evaluating abstract terms. Most important, when you have completed all of these steps, you can be sure that the report you write will contain valid information which is useful to your reader.

Cases   1. Re-read the sample case and report on classroom furniture to prepare yourself to write a report on damaged furniture in your classroom.

   a. List all the furniture you see in your classroom.

   b. Examine the furniture and make notes on any signs of damage you observe.

   c. Write a definition of "damaged classroom furniture."

   d. Write criteria for every separate category of furniture. For example, "A desk is damaged when. . . ."

   e. Construct a checklist you can use as an inspection form.

   f. Re-examine the furniture and make an accurate count on your inspection form of each evidence of damage you note.

   g. Tally your findings.

   h. Write a memo to your instructor describing your findings.

   2. Your writing task is to determine the quality of a convenience store you are familiar with. Some factors you may wish to investigate are parking lot layout, building layout, organization of merchandise, and customer service.

PART 1. PARKING LOT LAYOUT

Step 1. Collect your ideas about convenience store parking lots. When you think of convenience store parking lots you have driven into, you may come up with some questions like these.

—What was the condition of the lot surface?

—Were enough stalls available for all the customers who entered the lot?

—Did gas pumps, trash barrels, or other obstacles block access to stalls?

—Did gas customers parked at pumps block access to stalls?

—Were the lines separating the stalls clearly marked?

—Were customers able to leave the lot and get back on the street without delay?

Step 2. Go to a convenience store and observe the parking lot. Remove items that do not apply and add items that do apply to the list you have made in Step 1.

Step 3. Define "adequate parking lot."

Step 4. Construct an inspection form to rate a convenience store parking lot.

PART 2. BUILDING LAYOUT

Step 1. After you have parked your car, you are ready to enter the store to evaluate its layout.

— What kind of entrance does the store have? double doors? a single door?

— Do any obstacles block the door?

— Do leaving customers block the path of entering customers?

— Where is the checkout counter in relation to the entrance?

— Do customers at the checkout counter block the entrance?

— Does the cashier have a clear view of all parts of the store from the checkout counter?

— Can the cashier check areas out of the line of sight by looking in mirrors mounted on the walls?

— Do cases or display racks block aisles?

— Can two customers pass each other in the aisles?

Step 2. Observe the layout of a convenience store. Remove items that do not apply and add items that do apply to the list you made in Step 1.

Step 3. Define "adequate building layout."

Step 4. Construct an inspection form to rate the layout of a convenience store.

PART 3. ORGANIZATION OF MERCHANDISE

Step 1. Look carefully at the merchandise in the store.

— Are like items grouped with like items?

— Are all the snack foods together in one place?

— Are all the paper products together?

— Do you notice any items obviously out of place as you walk down the aisles?

— Is all the merchandise visible?

—Do crates, cases, or display racks in the aisles keep you from reaching items on shelves?

—Is the checkout counter cluttered with items like gum, candy, lighters, or magazines?

—Are small items like candy and batteries jumbled together on a shelf?

Step 2. After inspecting the merchandise in a convenience store, eliminate items that do not apply and add more important items to the list you made in Step 1.

Step 3. Define "adequate organization of merchandise."

Step 4. Construct an inspection form to rate the organization of merchandise in the store.

PART 4. CUSTOMER SERVICE

Step 1. Make notes on how store personnel serve customers.

—Do personnel greet customers?

—Can they help customers find merchandise?

—Does the cashier check customers out as soon as they have selected their merchandise?

—Does the store accept checks or credit cards in payment for merchandise?

—Do customers get refunds on unsatisfactory merchandise?

—Do employees wear uniforms?

Step 2. Correct your list after you have visited the convenience store.

Step 3. Define "adequate customer service."

Step 4. Construct an inspection form to rate the customer service provided at the convenience store you have inspected.

PART 5. WRITING ASSIGNMENT

When you have completed your fieldwork, observation of the convenience store, you can prepare to report your findings.

1. Using the inspection forms you have constructed, rate a convenience store.

2. Tally the findings on your inspection forms.

3. Write a memo report to your instructor, describing your findings.

3. You are the inspector for a group of retail outlets. (You may choose an outlet you are already familiar with such as a gas station, clothing store, fast-food restaurant, or similar facility.) Competition for customers is so fierce that you must not only provide quality goods and services, you must also make certain that your outlet is attractive to your customers.

1. Name the outlet you will inspect.

2. List the areas in the outlet that customers use.

3. Write tentative criteria for attractiveness in each area you listed.

4. Visit an outlet of the kind you have chosen and revise your criteria.

5. Define attractiveness in relation to the facility you have chosen.

6. Draw up a checklist to cover the items in your definition.

7. Rate the outlet you have selected for attractiveness to customers.

8. Write a report of your findings.

Chapter 10

Sorting Things or Ideas

To the Student:
　　As you read chapter 10 and complete the exercises and cases, you will
be asked to
　　. . . define classification
　　. . . understand the importance of
classification
　　. . . follow logical steps to classify
a subject
　　. . . write a message that relies on
classification as a method of organization.

In the distant past, a person was capable of knowing everything that had been thought or said. Now a person would have difficulty knowing everything about even a single field. With rapid advances in science and technology, we are experiencing an information explosion. How can we cope with new information that is produced every day as well as with information that has accumulated over time? Classification is one technique that allows us to handle large amounts of information.

WHY IS CLASSIFICATION IMPORTANT?

Classification lies at the heart of most human enterprises, of computer and accounting systems, of all branches of science, and even of the selective service system which rates or classifies adult males according to their suitability to serve in the armed forces. Every time you fill out an income tax form, a census form, or a questionnaire, you classify yourself as fitting into any number of different groups. When you complete forms, however, you are participating in only the second step of the process. The first step is the more important and demanding of the thinker, writer, or manager.

Business pays premium salaries to people who can set up classes and minimum salaries to people who fill them in. For instance, an accountant or comptroller decides on an account name for every possible transaction in a company. Each account has a number and a definition. Then the company hires clerks to enter transactions in the correct accounts.

In much the same way, computer programmers earn large salaries by spending weeks or months investigating all kinds of information that a group of users needs. Then they spend more time following the trails of information and classifying it for use in different parts of a business or technical operation. Finally, they write a program that captures all the information and divides it into specific regular reports for different users in the same company. Because dividing information is the difficult part of the classification process, programmers spend a great deal of time "de-bugging" a program that sends odd bits of information into the wrong report. When the program runs smoothly, various clerks (or even punched paper tapes) can place information in the program without worrying about sorting it. The computer will classify information according to divisions made by the programmer.

People who work with computers talk about GIGO, an acronym for "garbage in, garbage out." If the initial step of setting up classes is incorrect, no amount of changing the way items are placed on line will produce a good report. On the other hand, a well thought out system of classification takes what would otherwise be a random collection of facts and ideas and puts them in a form that allows people to learn from them and use them profitably.

WHAT IS CLASSIFICATION?

Classification is a basic system of thought used to sort large amounts of information into useful form. It is really a two-step process: (1) setting up the classes and (2) placing items into them. Trouble occurs when a writer tries to do both processes at once or to do Step 2 before Step 1.

WHAT ARE THE STEPS IN CLASSIFICATION?

To classify information, you follow four steps. First, select a subject suitable for classification. Second, limit the subject. Third, divide it into major classes useful to the audience. Fourth, subdivide the major classes. When you apply each of these steps, you will be able to take a body of information and transform it into useful form.

Select a Subject for Classification

The first step in any classification is to find a subject capable of being classified. To be capable of being classified, a thing or an idea must be plural in fact or in nature. A single item can be separated into its constituent parts, but it cannot be classified. For example, we can classify transportation as public or private or as air, water, or land transportation, but we cannot classify the luxury ship, Queen Elizabeth II. We can only divide the Queen Elizabeth into its constituent parts.

Of course, in selecting a subject for classification, as for any form of writing, you as writer must either have knowledge of or be capable of gathering data about a subject. For example, if you have lived all your life in an urban area, you probably do not know much about farm equipment and would have to do considerable research to classify such equipment. By the same token, if you are from a small town or rural area, you would have little first-hand knowledge of urban transportation systems and would have to rely upon research if you selected such a subject. However, both farm equipment and urban transportation systems are possible subjects because they are knowable. A subject like the social customs of Australopithecus is impossible to write about because no information on the subject exists.

Exercise A   1. Some of the subjects in the following list can be classified; some cannot. Write *Yes* in front of each subject that can be classified and *No* in front of each subject that cannot be classified. Be prepared to explain why certain subjects cannot be classified.

industry   candlepower
skilled trades   electricity

pollution	ounces
light	land
heat	landlords

2. Read the following classified lists. Supply an accurate classification title for each list.

A	B
debits	eagles
credits	owls
assets	robins
income	sparrows
interest earned	wrens

C	D
eagles	herons
condors	kingfishers
owls	pelicans
hawks	egrets
falcons	flamingos

Limit the Subject for Classification

As you have learned already, you must limit the subject of any message, a rule that certainly applies to subjects for classification. A subject like "transportation" implies that the writer is preparing a history of transportation because it is not limited by time or place. By contrast, a subject like "public transportation in Los Angeles in 1980" is workable because it describes only one kind of transportation system and covers only one place at a particular time. Your method of limiting the subject is not arbitrary, however; it depends on your purpose in writing.

Exercise B
1. Limit each of these broad subjects to bring it to manageable size. For each subject, indicate the reason for your particular limitation. Follow the example shown for hospital work.

Subject	Limited Subject	Purpose
Hospital work	Employment opportunities for nurses in hospitals	To provide occupational information to students in a school of nursing
Skilled trades		

College courses

Art

Medication

Research &
   Development

2. Cross out the item or items that do not belong in each of the following classified lists:

Office Furniture	Uses for Wood
tables	fire
desks	paper
chairs	buildings
file cabinets	stage scenery
adding machines	furniture
telephones	pencils

Federal Income Tax
Deductions

state & local taxes
charities
medical expenses
robberies
moving expenses

Classify the Subject

Once you have limited the subject, you are ready to classify it. Many subjects can be classified in several different ways. For example, you can classify bicycles by model, maker, country of manufacture, market share, price, or features, depending on your purpose in writing. An American bicycle maker investigating foreign competitors might be most interested in foreign models, makers, countries of manufacture, or market share. A racing magazine might look at particular features like weight. A consumer magazine might require an exhaustive classification of all bicycles available to potential consumers who want to make a comparison of models to buy.

After deciding on a system of classification, you must make sure that your classes have the same value. For example, if you decide to describe foreign competitors, you might classify bicycles by country of manufacture. If you further limit the topic to chief foreign competitors, a possible classification might be *England, France, Italy*, and *Japan* because each item is a unit equal to the others. By contrast, the classification *England, Europe*, and *Japan* is incorrect because *England* fits into the class *Europe*. Thus, the writer could put English bicycles in either of two classes, *England* or *Europe*. The two classes overlap, an error in logic. To be correct, each item of information should fit only in a single class.

Here is another example of an overlapping classification. A writer wants to classify a group of bicycles of the same price according to their features. She selects *size, weight, safety, handling, pedaling*, and *braking*. Which class overlaps into the others? If you picked *safety*, you are correct. *Safety* depends in part on the other five features but also on the bicyclist's knowledge of traffic rules, concentration, and riding skill among other variables.

Exercise C   1. Use the limited subjects you developed in Exercise A in this chapter and develop comparable classes for each subject. For example, Employment Opportunities for Nurses in Hospitals might be classified as Special Duty, General Duty, and Management Duty, or as Day Shift, Night Shift, Swing Shift, and Part Time, or as Out-patient, Emergency, Recovery, Orthopedic, Obstetric, and Surgical.

2. If you find overlapping classes in any of the following lists, point them out and explain why they overlap other classes in the list.

Traits of Character	*Carpet Features*
honesty	density
loyalty	color
charity	warp threads
kindness	woof threads
personality	pile height

Travel

intercity
intracity
transcontinental
intercontinental
space

Subdivide the Classification

Once you have determined the major classes into which you will divide a subject, you are ready to subdivide each class. Why is further classification necessary? The chief reason for subclassification is to organize a great deal of information so that it is understandable to the reader. Let us see how a writer confronted with a classification problem goes about the task.

Sample Case   Stan Ryder works in the marketing division of Fleetwing, an American bicycle manufacturer. His supervisor, Lewis Van Fleet, the vice president for marketing, asks him to report on foreign competitors. Ryder finds they have captured almost 20 percent of the U.S. market. In other words, nearly 20 percent or one of every five bicycles sold in the United States is made in a foreign country. Since less than one percentage point represents millions of dollars in sales in some industries, market share is an extremely important figure. Ryder gathers figures on market share and price of each foreign model and determines that Fleetwing's greatest competition comes from France, England, and Japan. Fleetwing's laboratory tests bicycles made in these countries and sends the results to Ryder who puts them together with the information he has collected in a series of notes.

NOTES ON 3-SPEED FOREIGN BICYCLES

Plassy Classic. Ferrand et Cie. France. $236. 31 lbs. Mx frame. 22 in. Pedaling 1. Handling 1. Braking 3. S ½.

Ferrand III. Ferrand et Cie. France. $230. 30 lbs. C frame. 22 in. Pedaling 1. Handling 1. Braking 3. S 1.

Challenger 2681. Rally Bicycles, Ltd. England. $170. 33 lbs. C frame. 21 in. Pedaling 2. Handling 1. Braking 4. S 2 ½.

Challenger 2682. Rally Bicycles, Ltd. England. $175. 33 lbs. O frame. 21 in. Pedaling 2. Handling 1. Braking 3. S 2.

Rally Roadster. Rally Bicycles, Ltd. England. $140. 35 lbs. C frame. 23 in. Pedaling 2. Handling 2. Braking 2. S 3.

Tokyo City Bike. Yahama. Japan. $215. 34 lbs. C frame. 21 in. Pedaling 2. Handling 2. Braking 3. S ½.

Rival Roadster. Yahama. Japan. $165. 35 lbs. O frame. 20 in. Pedaling 3. Handling 2. Braking 4. S 1 ½.

Alpha L47. Zaibatsu, Inc. Japan. $135. 37 lbs. C frame. 22 in. Pedaling 3. Handling 4. Braking 3. S 1 ¾.

Alpha L96. Zaibatsu, Inc. Japan. $138. 37 ½ lbs. O frame. 21 in. Pedaling 3. Handling 4. Braking 3. S 1 ½.

Ryder's notes list the model of bicycle, maker, country of manufacture, price including shipping, weight, type of frame (C = closed; O = open; Mx = mixed), size in inches, pedaling, handling, and braking capabilities (1 = excellent; 2 = very good; 3 = good; 4 = fair; 5 = poor), and percentage of market share of three-speed foreign bicycles sold in the United States.

After reading through his notes, Ryder decides country of manufacture will be his major class. He subdivides each class by brand of bicycle and each brand by its features. Then he prepares a preliminary outline.

3-SPEED BICYCLES IN COMPETITION
WITH FLEETWING MODELS

I.   French bicycles
    A. Plassy Classic
      1. Handling
      2. Pedaling
      3. Braking
    B. Ferrand III
      1. Handling
      2. Pedaling
      3. Braking

II.   English bicycles
    A. Challenger 2681
      1. Handling
      2. Pedaling
      3. Braking
    B. Challenger 2682
      1. Handling
      2. Pedaling
      3. Braking
    C. Rally Roadster
      1. Handling
      2. Pedaling
      3. Braking

III. Japanese bicycles
    A. Tokyo City Bike
      1. Handling
      2. Pedaling
      3. Braking
    B. Rival Roadster
      1. Handling
      2. Pedaling
      3. Braking

      C. Alpha L47
        1. Handling
        2. Pedaling
        3. Braking
      D. Alpha L96
        1. Handling
        2. Pedaling
        3. Braking

Ryder has written a technically correct outline: None of his classes overlap, and each is subdivided in exactly the same way. Yet do you see where he has gone wrong? Remember, his original assignment was to report on foreign competitors in the U.S. bicycle market. Has Ryder given his supervisor much idea of which company or which model of bicycle is Fleetwing's strongest competitor? If you look at the information he has at his disposal, you realize that while he has classified bicycles, he has not supplied the information his supervisor really wants. He has used the wrong information. If he were to write a report based on the preliminary outline, he would be describing a good deal about the features of each bicycle but very little about them as competition. Although features are useful for a comparison with Fleetwing's bicycles, they are less important to an understanding of competition than market share.

Ryder learned an important lesson which you should consider also. At the beginning of any writing task, the writer usually has more information than he or she needs. Classification helps to sort this information, but it is useless unless it meets a specific need. What is the right information? It is that information which the audience asks for. The object of this writing assignment as of any other is to focus on the purpose for writing before wasting time doing the wrong assignment.

Fortunately for Ryder, he realizes his mistake and prepares a new outline based on market share of each maker.

3-SPEED BICYCLES IN COMPETITION
WITH FLEETWING MODELS

I.   Market Share of Rally Models
      A. Rally Roadster
        1. Price
        2. Features
          a. Frame
          b. Pedaling
          c. Handling
          d. Braking

B. Challenger 2681
  1. Price
  2. Features

    a. Frame
    b. Pedaling
    c. Handling
    d. Braking

C. Challenger 2682
  1. Price
  2. Features

    a. Frame
    b. Pedaling
    c. Handling
    d. Braking

II.   Market Share of Zaibatsu Models

A. Alpha L47
  1. Price
  2. Features
    a. Frame
    b. Pedaling
    c. Handling
    d. Braking

B. Alpha L96
  1. Price
  2. Features

    a. Frame
    b. Pedaling
    c. Handling
    d. Braking

III.   Market Share of Yahama Models

A. Rival Roadster
  1. Price
  2. Features

    a. Frame
    b. Pedaling

        c. Handling
        d. Braking
    B. Tokyo City Bike
      1. Price
      2. Features
        a. Frame
        b. Pedaling
        c. Handling
        d. Braking

IV.   Market Share of Ferrand Models
    A. Ferrand III
      1. Price
      2. Features
        a. Frame
        b. Pedaling
        c. Handling
        d. Braking
    B. Plassy Classic
      1. Price
      2. Features
        a. Frame
        b. Pedaling
        c. Handling
        d. Braking

Ryder feels much more satisfied with his second outline because it answers the questions his supervisor had about competition with Fleetwing's bicycles. Now he has to write his report. He has all the information he needs. He wants to make sure he puts it in the most readable format. He comes up with two options. Read each option carefully.

OPTION 1

MEMORANDUM

TO: Lewis Van Fleet, Vice President
      Marketing Division

FROM: Stan Ryder, Assistant Manager

SUBJECT: Foreign Competitors in the U.S. Market

DATE: May 11, 198-

Foreign makers control 18.75 percent of the U.S. market for three-speed bicycles. Of this total, nine different models have a 14.25 percent share. (Several other models compete for the remaining 4.5 percent.) I have listed each model by maker in descending percentage of market share and have given the prices and features of each model.

Rally Bicycles

Three bicycles made by Rally, the Challenger 2681, Challenger 2682, and Rally Roadster, have the biggest market share at 7.5 percent. The Challenger 2681 sells for $170. It is a closed-frame model which our test lab rates as very good in pedaling, excellent in handling, and fair in braking. The second Rally model, the Challenger 2682, sells for $175. An open-frame model, it rates as very good in pedaling, excellent in handling, and good in braking. The third Rally model, the Rally Roadster, sells for $140. It is a closed-frame model which rates a very good in pedaling, handling, and braking.

Zaibatsu Models

Zaibatsu controls 3.25 percent of the market. Zaibatsu manufactures the Alpha L47 and Alpha L96. The Alpha L47, a closed-frame model, sells for $135 and rates as good in pedaling, fair in handling, and good in braking. The Alpha L96, an open-frame model, sells for $138. It rates as good in pedaling, fair in handling, and good in braking.

Yahama Models

Yahama controls 2 percent of the market. Yahama makes the Rival Roadster, an open-frame model, which sells for $165 and the Tokyo City Bike, a closed-frame model, which sells for $215. The Rival Roadster received a good rating

for pedaling, very good for handling, and fair for braking.
The Tokyo City Bike had very good ratings for pedaling and
handling and a good for braking.

Ferrand Models

Two bicycles made by Ferrand, the Model III and Plassy
Classic, share 1.5 percent of the market. The Ferrand III
at $230 is a closed-frame model which received excellent
ratings in pedaling and handling and a good in braking.
The Plassy Classic at $236 is a mixed-frame model which
also received excellent ratings in pedaling and handling
and a good in braking.

OPTION 2

MEMORANDUM

TO: Lewis Van Fleet, Vice President
        Marketing Division

FROM: Stan Ryder, Assistant Manager *SR*

SUBJECT: Foreign Competitors in the U.S. Market

DATE: May 11, 198-

Foreign manufacturers control 18.75 percent of the U.S. market for
three-speed bicycles. Of this total, nine different models have a
14.25 percent market share.

As you can see from the chart below, Rally leads with 7.5 percent
of the market, followed by Zaibatsu with 3.25 percent, Yahama with
2 percent, and Ferrand et Cie. with 1.5 percent. The chart also indicates some other facts about each bicycle such as market share/model,
price, frame style, and pedaling, handling, and braking capabilities.

MARKET SHARE OF FOREIGN MANUFACTURERS OF THREE-SPEED BICYCLES

	% of Market Share (Total)	% of Market Share (by model)	Price (incl Shipping)	Frame*	Pedaling+	Handling+	Braking+
Rally Bicycles, Ltd.	7 1/2						
Challenger 2681		2 1/2	$170	C	2	1	4
Challenger 2682		2	$175	O	2	1	3
Rally Roadster		3	$140	C	2	2	2
Zaibatsu, Inc.	3 1/4						
Alpha L47		1 3/4	$135	C	3	4	3
Alpha L96		1 1/2	$138	O	3	4	3
Yahama	2						
Rival Roadster		1 1/2	$165	O	3	2	4
Tokyo City Bike		1/2	$215	C	2	2	3
Ferrand et Cie.	1 1/2						
Ferrand III		1	$230	C	1	1	3
Plassy Classic		1/2	$236	Mx	1	1	3

*C=closed; O=open; Mx=mixed
+Pedaling, handling, and braking were rated as
   1=excellent; 2=very good; 3=good; 4=fair; 5=poor

Consider Ryder's audience, Lewis Van Fleet. Which memo do you think Stan Ryder sent to Van Fleet? You are right if you chose Option 2. Ryder reasoned that Option 2 says everything Option 1 says but is much more concise. Van Fleet is a high-ranking, busy executive. Option 1 would take him more time to read, and the figures would be harder to retrieve from the sentence format than from the tabular form in Option 2. (Notice, however, that Ryder put his main conclusions and introduced his table in sentence form in his memo.)

Data dictated Ryder's choice of Option 2, a choice you, too, will be able to make when you complete the next chapter on Summarizing Data.

Review   In this chapter, you learned how to classify, an important technique for sorting large amounts of information, a task that confronts professional people every day. You learned that classification is more than an exercise in logic. It is a tool that writers rely on to structure the content of their messages in a readable form.

Cases   1. Butler-Taggert, one of the big five machine tool manufacturers, started operations in Pocatawba 73 years ago when Fred Butler and Jack Taggert, two enterprising bicycle repairmen, began making their own tools in a shed behind Butler's father's house. Since its humble beginnings, the company has expanded and diversified. Five years ago, it added a nuclear components division. For the last 50 years, Butler-Taggert (B-T) has been one of the chief employers in Pocatawba.

To celebrate the company's Diamond Jubilee, Frederick Butler Taggert III, the company president, has asked you, as head of the public relations department, to prepare a community-wide celebration. Taggert tells you that he wants you to use the Jubilee to raise the visibility of the company in the community by once again involving it in community affairs as it was involved in the time of his father.

Taggert also wants to enhance the company's reputation and to raise company morale through the Jubilee. B-T still attracts more applicants than it needs for jobs in its plant because of its high salary scale and liberal benefits plan. But the best graduates in communications, accounting, marketing, and engineering from the Pocatawba campus of the state university look for jobs in Chicago, Detroit, and other metropolitan areas. The community as a whole takes B-T for granted, Taggert feels, and is only aware of the company when management-labor relations get publicity or when environmentalists inspect the furnaces.

Taggert's main goal, however, is to provide lasting benefits to the community during the Jubilee year. He has remained a loyal son of Pocatawba. He and his children are graduates of the local schools. In fact, he serves on the boards of both the state university and of Pocatawba General Hospital. In her younger years, his daughter Joan was active in the Pocatawba Civic Theatre. His late wife was president of the Pocatawba Art Guild.

Although he has not yet discussed finances with you, Taggert has mentioned that he will expend both corporate and personal funds on a good program.

Write a report detailing areas where Butler-Taggert can make a contribution to the community. Family interests are a good starting point. You want to involve as many sectors of the Pocatawba community as possible.

2. Explain how your college or university uses the principle of classification to divide itself into manageable units.

3. Your supervisor at the small newspaper for which you work calls you into his office one Wednesday morning. He is looking at the classified section of the paper. "Our classifieds aren't classified," he says. "Just look at these help wanted ads. They're scattered over the page. What kind of system do you people use?"

Somewhat taken aback, you try to respond: "We just take the descriptions the advertisers give us and put them in alphabetical order."

"Obviously," he answers, "and the mess on Sunday is four times as bad as this because we have four times as many ads. Take these ads and come up with some sensible classification system that our readers can get some use out of."

HELP WANTED

ACCOUNTING — dept. in progressive downtown law firm has excellent full time opportunity for person possessing good accounting background and typing skills. Pleasant surroundings, good pay & benefits.

ALCOHOLISM COUNSELOR — To work variable shifts in a residential treatment center. Master's Degree in Human Services or equivalent experience required.

Assembler Programmer — COLORADO - Requires 2 yrs. DEC RT II MACRO or NCR 270 or Burroughs Assembler. To $24,000.

ASSISTANT SERVICE MANAGER

Trainee position requiring mechanical aptitude & excel. communication skills. A 4 yr. degree is mandatory. $20,000. Fee pd. Call or send resume.

Asst. Tax Mgr. — Requires Federal, State & Local Corp. Tax experience for large mfg. To $32,000.

BOOKKEEPER — company is seeking an exper., ambitious person. Must be flexible in responsibilities with excel. personality. Mag card & data entry exper. very helpful. Salary to $12,000 plus full benefits.

BUILDINGS & GROUNDS — Maintenance Worker II/Electrician ($14,264-$17,084). Change light fixtures, ballast; hook up computers to mechanical equipment; work on equipment controls; install, construct, repair, and maintain all electrical equipment. Utilizes blueprints and may oversee a helper when assigned to specific projects. May be required to perform routine maintenance jobs, as assigned. Journeyman's sta-

tus or equivalent in electrical area. Must have own vehicle and pass security check. Ability to follow orders and get along with others.

CHIEF ENGR. — BSME. Exper. in management, product liabilities, testing, stress analysis. Elec. exper. a plus. Fee pd. $25-$35,000. Affirmative Action Employer.

CLEANING POSITION — Part time. Looking for hard working, well groomed, self motivated man or woman for an in-home cleaning service. Applicants must be at least 18 & have own transportation. Earnings will average $5 to $10 per hour depending on production. Hours to suit your schedule.

COMPANION — Lady to live in & help around the house, some personal care required, must be able to drive, room & board offered, salary negotiable.

Controller — Growing mfg. needs person with degree and solid accounting, cost and planning skills. To $30,000.

COUNSELOR — Must possess degree in social work counseling or related field and at least 1 year of related work experience. Downtown office.

CRAWLER PICKERS & WORM DIGGERS — needed. Work for yourself. Bring bucket & pitchfork. Sportsman's Bait.

CRISIS SOCIAL WORKER — Full time to counsel children, adolescents and their families. Counsel youngsters in pre and after care from psychiatric hospital. M.S.W. and experience required. Salary $14,000-$16,000.

CYTOTECH

Laboratory Service, Inc., located in Grand Rapids, has

full-time & part-time positions available for Registry Eligible or Registered Cytotechs. Our technical staff includes 2 full-time Pathologists. Starting salaries are commensurate with experience, & our fringe benefit program includes: yearly bonus, profit sharing, & paid insurance.

DAIRY FARM OPENING — help wanted milking cows in parlor. Must like cows.

DENTAL ASSISTANT — No experience necessary.

DENTAL SEC'Y/RECEPTIONIST — Experienced only.

DENTAL TECHNICIAN — Crown & bridge finisher, experienced or will train, starting salary $5 hr., insurance.

DESIGN DRAFTING — Mechanical parts and hydraulic valves. 2-5 years experience required. Growing company with advancement potential.

DRAFTER

Part time Draftsperson for ten to thirty hours per week in Mechanical Engineering Department. Must have several years of drafting experience, preferably with material handling equipment.

ELEC. ENGR. — Projects. Machine, automation, robots. Programmable controls, relay logic, electro-mechanical. Fee pd., to $34,000.

ENGINEER — Rapidly growing packaging machinery company is looking for an engineer with a mechanical & electronic background with design experience. This is a challenging growth oriented position.

EXEC. SECY — to Exec. Dir. Good comm. skills, type 60 wpm, dictaphone, min. of board & staff meetings, supv. other clerical, switchboard.

Reprinted with permission of the *Kalamazoo Gazette*, Kalamazoo, MI.

FARM HELP — with some experience, also part time.

HOUSEKEEPER — needed, live-in. Must love children & farm life. Own furn. apt. Must swim. Three Rivers area. More for room, board & a family than pay.

INDUSTRIAL
Illustrator-Drafter

Opening exists for an Industrial Illustrator/Drafter in the Transportation Division of a Grand Rapids based manufacturing firm.

Position will work directly with Product Designer and be responsible for the formulation of a Product Parts List and perspective view drawings during product processing. Additional duties will include the setting up, maintenance and updating of a master parts catalog file. Flexibility to perform mechanical drafting duties, experience with tolerances and the ability to determine how piece parts relate to the whole assembly are definite pluses.

The ideal candidate should possess a minimum of two (2) years industrial illustrating experience and an Associates degree from an industrial arts college which could include mechanical drafting background.

We offer an excellent starting salary plus a complete Company paid benefits program.

Internal Audit — Degree and corporate operation and compliance audit experience required. Light travel.

JANITOR WANTED — full-time. Apply in person at Schwarz's.

JR. IND. ENGINEER

Immediate opening for individual with 1-2 years of time standards experience along with educational background in industrial engr./mgmt. Mechanical background and familiarization with data processing systems desirable.

LEGAL SECRETARY — part-time. Excel. skills, must be exper.

LIVE-IN — Immediate position in Allegan area for mature and responsible individual to care for elderly lady. Light housekeeping and cooking. Experience required. Nurses Aide training a plus.

LIVE-IN HOUSEKEEPER — care for 2 boys, cooking, laundry, housekeeping. Rm. & board plus salary, refs.

LPN TEAM LEADER — to work 5 evenings (3-11) in two-week pay period, three shifts one week, two the next.

MAINTENANCE MAN WANTED — Millwright exper., no other need apply. Also cable crane operator.

MANAGER — for mobile home park. Reply to Box 77, Gazette, 1 S. Burd.

MANAGER — Looking for aggressive person to manage private club. Management experience with good background in food. Send resume to Box 80, Gazette, 1 S. Burd.

MANAGER INDUSTRIAL ENGINEERING — $35-$40,000. Fee paid. Responsible for all I.E. functions. Contact Paul Peters, Executive Employment, 75 W. Mich. Ave.

MEDICAL RECEPTIONIST — Experienced. Needed part time, perhaps full time, rural office. Duties include scheduling patients, typing & filing and using the peg board system. Salary based on experience.

MEDICAL SOCIAL WORKER

Challenging opportunity to work in a progressive, hospital setting. Responsibilities will include casework and counseling with patients and families in our Oncology, Pediatrics, and Open Heart Programs. Crisis intervention skills a necessity. This position offers an excellent opportunity for professional growth along with competitive salary and benefits. An M.S.W. required. Previous medical experience desired.

MEDICAL TECHNICIAN — to work in medical specialty office. Previous patient contact desirable. Will assist with EKG's, blood pressures and diagnostic testing. Also will be involved in computerized data analysis.

MENTAL HEALTH CASE MANAGER — $18,470 to $24,682. Provides assessment, planning, coordination of multiple services and advocacy for developmentally disabled individuals and their families in health, residential, vocational, legal, financial and educational areas. MA/MS in a human service area with at least 1 year of experience in developmental disabilities or related field. Knowledge of community resources, valid drivers license and availability of a car to transport clients is required.

MENTAL HEALTH WORKER — (30 hrs/wk) BA/BS degree in Occupational or Rehabilitation Therapy and experience working with previously hospitalized adults and children. Responsibilities include assistance providing community placement and client services management as well as day treatment services to adults and children. Excellent salary and fringe benefits. AA/EOE.

MICROBIOLOGY LAB TECH — Degree plus exper $18-20,000.

MKTING. MGR. — Bus. products, establish/measure mkting. mix, track record. $35,000.

NEEDED FOR TEEN BOY — Supervision in my home or yours. Afternoons, 3-11:30.

NIGHT AUDITOR — Experienced. For 100 room house. Full night audit. Must have prior exp.

NIGHT SHIFT — residential program for developmentally disabled adults. Duties: supervision of night time needs, cleaning, laundry, record keeping, $3.50/hr. plus benefits.

NURSES

We offer you a challenging opportunity to work with developmentally disabled. Good salary, benefits, & orientation. Full time or part time openings on 2nd & 3rd shifts.

OCCUPATIONAL THERAPIST, REG. — Full time 80 bed private care psychiatric facility. Min. 1 yr. experience in general or adolescent psychiatry preferred. Excellent salary & benefits.

OFFICE STAFF POSITION

Permanent full time, Monday through Friday, 9-6. Previous office experience required. Duties will involve working with all phases of an office operation including payroll, accounts payable, keypunching, switchboard, etc. Call for interview.

PAYROLL CLERK — Also know accts receivable & payable. Freight bill exper. a plus. $11-$12,000.

PLASTICS ENGR. — Process trouble shooting/tooling, injection molding. $28,000

POWER CO. — is interested in qualified persons to fill the position of draftsperson at its Nuclear Plant. Candidates must have 2-3 yrs. general drafting experience to be considered for this position.

PRODUCTION MANAGER — $35-$38,000, fee pd. Exper. in a heavy machining environment.

PROGRAMMER ANALYST — $25-$30,000. Fee paid. Writing business application program in PL/I, COBOL, MIMS using VM/CMS.

PROJECT ENGR. — Design solid state circuitry to mech. equip. To $33K.

QUALITY CONTROL MANAGER — $25-$30,000. Fee

paid. Metal working related to machining or wire drawing. Contact Paul Peters, Executive Employment, 75 W. Michigan. Open Sat. 9-12.

RETAIL MANAGER — Ladies' ready-to-wear. Rapidly expanding chain in Southwest. Employer ''turned on'' by experience. $12,000, fee pd.

RESPIRATORY THERAPIST

With our expanded role for the therapist and active involvement of a medical and associate medical director our Cardio-Neuro and Pulmonary Department remains a vital component in our commitment to be forerunners in the health care field.
We are currently seeking registered or registry eligible and certified or certified eligible therapists who have a strong desire to fulfill their potential in their professional specialty.
This is a full time position with flexible scheduling. We offer an excellent wage and salary program and an attractive benefit package.

RN'S

Two full-time RN positions are available in Oaklawn Hospital's OR and Recovery Room. Applicant must have OR and Recovery experience with Orthopedic and Out-Patient experience desirable. Some float to Medical/Surgical floor. Wage range of $8.80 to $10.07 and full benefit package are available.

SECRETARY — CPA firm seeking experienced secretary with demonstrated ability to relate with clients and professional personnel. Must have excellent typing skills and pride in workmanship. Salary open.

Systems Analyst — Excellent opportunity. Must have 3 yrs. COBOL and analyst experience in mfg. systems. Midwest. To $26,000.

SYSTEMS PROGRAMMER — 2-5 years experience with VTAM, CICS, SOLC, & MVS. Will be working with AMDAHL 470/V6 connected to over 300 CRTs & 29 minicomputers. (Series/1) Fee paid. $28-$31,000.

TELEPHONE OPERATOR

To operate cordless switchboard & perform general typing & clerical duties, 3 to 6 months, telephone experience preferred. Must type 60 wpm or better, must have pleasant phone personality. Only qualified applicants need apply. Salary commensurate with ability & experience, fringe package. Apply in person or phone for appt.

TOOL ENGINEER — $25-$35,000. Fee paid. Familiar with machines and cutting tools.

TRAINER — Part time, to work with developmentally disabled adults in community settings. Trainers teach variety of independent living skills. Experience and/or education in human services required.

TYPIST — Experienced in word processing or typesetting for operating a compugraphic edit writer. Part time. Pleasant working conditions.

WANTED — person with much enthusiasm & a positive attitude to run a small grain elevator & feed store. Must have agricultural background & be willing to work.

WANTED — Working manager for a 300-400 sow operation. Total confinement. Farrow to finish. Must be production oriented. This job includes good pay for a good days work, incentive bonus based on production, Blue Cross/Blue Shield Ins., meat & house furn.

4. Reclassify Mr. Ryder's nine foreign bicycles showing which are the "best buys." (You will need to use the techniques you learned in chapter 9 to define an abstraction.)

Chapter 11

Summarizing
Data

To the Student:

As you read chapter 11 and complete the exercises and cases, you will be asked to

. . . select appropriate graphic aids for a message

. . . plan appropriate graphic aids

. . . construct tables, line graphs, bar graphs, and circle graphs

. . . incorporate graphic aids into a message.

In chapter 10, you learned to classify information and, in the example, you saw how Stan Ryder could have saved writing time as well as make his message clearer by organizing facts into a table. In this chapter, you will learn more about tables and other graphic aids which will help you make messages clear to readers.

WHAT ARE GRAPHIC AIDS?

A graphic aid is a visual representation of data. It can help make a message clear. It can often make the written message shorter, but it can rarely stand alone as a complete message. For instance, study the following table.

HEIGHTS OF STUDENTS IN ROOM 212
1983

Height	Number of Students
Under 3' 4"	0
3' 4" - 3' 6"	10
3' 6¼" - 3' 8"	9
3' 8¼" - 3' 10"	8
3' 10¼" - 4'	3
Over 4'	2

You have information, but you have no message. The writer actually wrote this memo.

```
                              MEMO

          TO:  Purchasing Agent

        FROM:  Beryl Lego   BL

     SUBJECT:  New Furniture for Room 212

        DATE:  January 18, 1983

As you can see from the chart below, our fourth grade students
vary in height.  I recommend buying

            20 chairs for students between 3' 4" - 3' 8"
            10 chairs for students between 3' 8¼" - 4'
             5 chairs for taller elementary students

              HEIGHTS OF STUDENTS IN ROOM 212
                          1983
```

Height	Number of Students
Under 3' 4"	0
3' 4" - 3' 6"	10
3' 6¼" - 3' 8"	9
3' 8¼" - 3' 10"	8
3' 10¼" - 4'	3
Over 4'	2

Now the reader has a recommendation as well as the evidence on which the recommendation is based.

Some kinds of information are better suited to graphic display than others. You will want to consider a visual enhancement for your message when you must

1. provide detailed statistical information

2. explain trends or relationships

3. describe what something looks like or where something is.

These visual or graphic aids are usually considered in two large categories: tables and figures.

WHAT ARE TABLES?

Tables are rows and columns of data. Tables may be as short as two lines and two columns, or they may be large folded pages containing hundreds of lines and columns. They may be simple open tables (no lines or underlines as in Table 11.1), or they may use horizontal lines (as in Table 11.2), or they may need both horizontal and vertical lines (as in Table 11.3). They may contain only figures, words and figures, or only words.

Table 11.1

**REPRESENTATIVE COMMON STOCKS
AND THEIR TICKER SYMBOLS**

Company	Ticker Symbol	Stock Exchange
Allis-Chalmers	AH	NY
Computone Systems, Inc.	CTON	OTC
Lilly (Eli)	LLY	NY
New Process	NOZ	AM
SCM Corporation	SCM	NY

Table 11.2

JULY PRODUCTION: PLANT X

Department	Units Ordered	Units Completed
A	612,380	612,380.5
B	909,447	910,420
C	1,148,092	1,148,092.75
D	1,119,662	1,114,981
E	2,464,000	2,465,781.125
Total Units	6,253,581	6,251,655.375

Table 11.3
HOUSEHOLD TYPE, BY INCOME LEVEL AND MEDIAN INCOME: 1979

Item	All Households	Family Households				Nonfamily Households			
		Total	Married Couple	Male Hhldr., Wife Absent	Female Hhldr., Husband Absent	Total	Single-Person Household		Multiple Person Household
							Total	Male Hhldr.	Female Hhldr.	

Item	All Households	Total	Married Couple	Male Hhldr., Wife Absent	Female Hhldr., Husband Absent	Total	Total	Male Hhldr.	Female Hhldr.	Multiple Person Household
Number, all races (1,000).....	79,108	58,426	48,180	1,706	8,540	20,682	17,816	6,793	11,022	2,867
Under $5,000..............	10,411	3,945	1,870	146	1,929	6,467	6,295	1,562	4,732	172
$5,000-$9,999............	13,006	7,788	5,323	247	2,218	5,218	4,810	1,594	3,217	108
$10,000-$14,999.........	12,574	9,084	6,958	314	1,812	3,489	2,988	1,297	1,692	501
$15,000-$19,999.........	11,099	8,740	7,444	267	1,030	2,360	1,828	1,008	819	531
$20,000-$24,999.........	9,783	8,428	7,496	222	710	1,355	940	635	305	416
$25,000-$34,999.........	12,380	11,309	10,441	270	598	1,071	610	434	177	462
$35,000-$49,999.........	6,577	6,076	5,745	156	175	501	224	175	51	277
$50,000 and over........	3,276	3,055	2,904	84	68	219	118	89	30	101

Source: U.S. Bureau of the Census

When Should You Use a Table?

When you have groups of exact data which the reader may need to study, you should use a table. Tables save both writing and reading time. They save time for writers because writers do not have to repeat the same words in succeeding sentences. They save time for readers because the facts are displayed in a central position for easy reference.

In real life, Stan Ryder (Sample case, chapter 10) might have started to write the first long memo, but by the second paragraph he would have realized that he was repeating the same words in every sentence. So he would have stopped writing and started to construct a table for his report.

How Do You Construct a Table?

As you studied sample Tables 11.1-11.3, you saw that they share certain characteristics. All are horizontally centered on the page, and all contain at least four separate parts: a table number, a descriptive title, short column headings, and a body of data.

Table Number

If you use more than one table in your message, give each one a number. In formal papers, writers usually use Roman numerals (I, II, III) to identify tables. If the message is written in several chapters, modern writers usually number tables consecutively in each chapter. In chapter 1, the table numbers would be 1.1, 1.2, etc. In chapter 2, the table numbers would be 2.1, 2.2, etc.

Title

The title for a table must identify the subject so that readers will understand what the numbers in the body mean. The title must be long enough to be accurate but not so long as to confuse the reader. PRODUCTION does not tell the reader enough. PRODUCTION FOR 6 DEPARTMENTS IN PLANT X FOR THE MONTH OF JULY tells too much. JULY PRODUCTION: PLANT X tells the full story. Many titles are simply typed using capital letters. Otherwise, capitalize all important words in the title.

Column Headings

Column headings are another part of the identification process. Each column of data should have a title which shows the reader what the data in that column represents. Most column headings are just one word (or often, one year or one month). Because the title often appears over a rather narrow column, writers try to write column headings in the fewest possible words. Column headings should be centered over the columns they identify. They are often underlined, and the first letters of important words are capitalized.

Body

The body contains the facts. The left hand column is called the stub column. Each line in the stub identifies the data that appear across that line. Short tables are usually single spaced. Longer tables may be double spaced to separate information for easy reading.

Information in the body should be organized in some logical order. By date is one common way of organizing. Another common organizing method is alphabetic. The method chosen should help the reader find important information quickly.

Look carefully at the vertical alignment in the sample tables. The information in the stub column is aligned at the left margin of the table; all the stub lines begin "flush left." The data columns, however, are aligned "flush right" in each column or are aligned so that all the decimal points remain in a straight line when the table contains numerical data. When the data columns contain words rather than numbers, the words are aligned "flush left" in each column.

Some writers prefer to leave equal spacing between all columns, including the stub column. Others leave extra space after the stub column and then use equal spacing between all the data columns. Writers should select a spacing method that looks attractive and that helps readers find information readily.

In addition to these standard parts of a table, you may need to add footnotes and source information. Table 11.4 shows both footnotes and source information.

Table 11.4
ALL GOVERNMENTS – REVENUE, EXPENDITURE, AND DEBT: 1950-1980

Item and Year	All Governments (bil. dol.)	Federal[1]		State and Local (bil. dol.)			Annual Percent Change[2]		Per Capita[3] (dollars)		
		Total (bil. dol.)	Percent of Total	Total	State	Local	Federal	State and Local	Total	Federal	State and Local
Revenue:											
1950	67	44	65.3	23	11	12	–3.3	7.3	440	287	153
1955	106	72	67.6	34	17	18	12.9	9.3	644	435	209
1960	153	100	65.2	53	26	27	6.8	7.8	851	554	296
1965	203	126	62.1	77	39	38	4.8	8.5	1,045	649	396
1970	334	206	61.6	128	69	60	3.0	13.3	1,642	1,011	631
1972	383	223	58.3	159	84	75	4.5	11.5	1,839	1,073	766
1973	432	254	58.8	178	97	81	12.7	12.6	2,059	1,211	850
1974	484	288	59.5	196	108	88	13.6	9.9	2,289	1,367	927
1975	519	302	58.2	217	119	98	5.0	10.7	2,436	1,418	1,018
1976	571	324	56.6	248	139	109	7.0	14.2	2,661	1,507	1,154
1977	658	383	58.1	275	156	120	18.1	11.1	3,039	1,766	1,272
1978	732	430	58.7	302	172	130	12.3	9.4	3,356	1,971	1,385
1979	829	500	60.3	330	190	140	16.3	9.3	3,768	2,270	1,498
1980	932	564	60.5	369	213	156	12.8	11.8	4,116	2,489	1,627

Year											
1950	70	42	60.3	28	11	17	11.1	15.5	464	280	184
1955	111	70	63.5	40	14	26	10.8	7.4	670	426	244
1960	151	90	59.7	61	22	39	5.2	8.8	841	502	339
1965	206	119	57.9	87	31	55	5.7	7.4	1,061	614	447
1970	333	185	55.5	148	56	92	4.5	12.1	1,638	910	728
1972	399	209	52.3	190	72	118	6.2	12.7	1,917	1,002	915
1973	437	231	53.0	205	78	127	9.4	8.7	2,081	1,103	978
1974	478	253	52.8	226	86	139	9.2	10.1	2,263	1,195	1,069
1975	560	292	52.1	268	107	161	15.5	18.8	2,628	1,370	1,259
1976	625	322	51.5	303	123	180	10.3	14.6	2,912	1,500	1,417
1977	682	359	52.8	323	129	194	11.5	6.6	3,154	1,661	1,494
1978	745	400	53.7	345	137	209	11.5	7.5	3,418	1,835	1,584
1979	832	452	54.3	380	149	232	13.0	10.2	3,782	2,054	1,728
1980	959	526	54.8	432	173	259	16.4	13.7	4,232	2,324	1,909
Debt outstanding:[4]											
1950	281	257	91.4	24	5	19	.6	12.4	1,856	1,697	159
1955	319	274	86.1	44	11	33	1.3	12.9	1,928	1,660	268
1960	356	286	80.4	70	19	51	.9	9.7	1,979	1,591	389
1965	417	317	76.1	100	27	72	2.1	7.4	2,150	1,637	513
1970	514	371	72.1	144	42	102	4.8	7.5	2,351	1,825	706
1972	602	427	71.5	175	54	120	8.5	9.9	2,938	2,100	838
1973	657	468	71.3	188	59	129	7.1	7.4	3,130	2,232	898
1974	693	486	70.2	207	65	141	3.8	9.6	3,278	2,300	977
1975	764	544	71.1	220	72	148	11.9	6.4	3,591	2,553	1,038
1976	872	631	72.4	241	85	156	16.0	9.4	4,061	2,941	1,121
1977	969	709	73.2	260	90	169	12.3	8.0	4,477	3,278	1,200
1978	1,061	780	73.5	280	103	178	10.0	8.9	4,865	3,759	1,286
1979	1,138	834	73.3	304	112	192	6.9	8.4	5,170	3,788	1,382
1980	1,250	914	73.1	336	122	214	9.6	10.5	5,518	4,037	1,481

[1] Data adjusted to system for reporting State and local data and therefore differ from figures in section 9 tables. shown; for 1950, change from 1948. For explanation, see Guide to Tabular Presentation. Minus sign (−) denotes decrease. estimated population as of July 1; 1970 and 1980 based on resident population enumerated as of Apr. 1. Includes Armed Forces abroad through 1955; thereafter, resident population. Excludes intergovernmental amounts. [4] As of end of fiscal year. [2] Represents average for period of intervals [3] All years except 1970 and 1980 based on

Source: U.S. Bureau of Census, *Census of Governments: 1977*, vol. 4, No. 5, *Compendium of Government Finances*, and vol. 6, No. 4, *Historical Statistics on Government Finances and Employment*; and *Governmental Finances*, series GF No. 5, annual.

The writer used footnotes to keep the headings short. Without footnotes, each column heading would have to explain assumptions and details of little interest to the casual reader. The information in this table came from an outside source: the United States Bureau of the Census. Because census information is compiled in many volumes, this writer had to search through four volumes to gather all the information which was summarized in one table. The writer acknowledges all four sources at the end of the table. If the writer develops the information or it comes from internal company sources the reader would recognize, no source line is needed.

Typing Tables

Most writers like to have tables typed by a professional or at least a proficient typist. Good typists who have little statistical typing experience can learn to type tables by re-reading directions in a typewriting text book. Average typists who have to type tables only infrequently often ask a friend to type the tables on separate sheets of paper. Then they use rubber cement (regular glue wrinkles the paper) to paste tables in place in their finished manuscripts. The final step in this cut-and-paste method is to make a photocopy of the finished product so the reader will not see the paste-on.

If you must produce the table alone, experiment on separate sheets of paper until the table is readable and the headings are correctly centered. Then employ the cut-and-paste method to insert the table at the proper place in your message.

Exercise A

1. You used the J & H Company's time records to compile statistics about the number of absences on each day of the week during the past year. Set up a table that will display the information clearly. Do not use figures; just plan for titles and spacing. The table is the first of three you plan to use in your report to the personnel manager.

2. Use the information that follows to create a short table.

According to U.S. Census figures, the city of Portage has grown nearly ninefold in only 40 years. In 1940, the village population was 4,250; 10 years later the population had nearly doubled to 7,946. The next decade produced the greatest expansion as population reached 20,181. Such explosive growth could not last, and the 1970 census counted only 33,590 people living in the city. The rate of growth has continued to slow as the 1980 population is only 37,650.

3. Use the information in the following table to write a short paragraph similar to the paragraph in Exercise A, problem 2.

PROPERTY TAX EXPENDITURES
FOR THE CITY OF TALLAHASSEE
1983

Item	Percent of Tax Dollar
Public schools	63
City government	18
County government	11
Intermediate school district	4
Community college	3
Collection fee	1

4. Use the following information to create a table that shows the percent of overhead charged to each department in Liston's Department Store in February. Liston charges each department a percent of total store overhead based on the floor space of each department. The total overhead for February was $300,000 for the month.

Department	Square Feet
Men's Wear	1,000
Ladies' Wear	1,300
Furniture	2,600
Cosmetics	900
Customer Services	750
Notions	500
Shoes	500
Total floor space	7,550

WHAT ARE FIGURES?

Figures may be charts, graphs, maps, pictures, or other visual aids—anything except a table. The most commonly used figures in business writing are the line graph, the bar graph, and the circle graph. These graphs usually do not present specific data, but they can give readers a general picture much faster than a table can.

When Should You Use a Line Graph?

The line graph is one of the best ways to show a trend occurring over a period of time. As you can see in Figure 11.1, time is laid out on the horizontal axis. The amount of change is shown on the vertical axis, with the starting point beginning at the vertical axis. This method of assigning values lets readers' eyes move normally from left to right to get an instant picture of the direction of the trend.

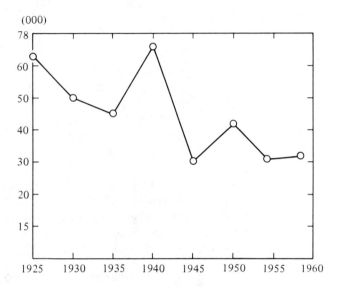

Figure 11.1 U.S. Silver Production (1925-1960) (thousands of fine ounces). *Source: Department of Commerce.*

Sometimes you may want to use a simple line graph to compare two or more trends as shown in Figure 11.2.

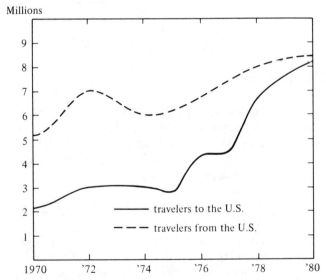

Figure 11.2 Travel to and from the U.S. (1970-1980). *Source: Department of the Treasury.*

You can easily compare two or even three items in one figure, but be careful not to draw so many trend lines as in Figure 11.3 that you leave the reader confused.

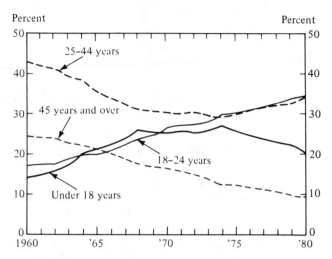

Figure 11.3 Persons arrested — Percent by Age (1960-1980). *Source: U.S. Bureau of the Census.*

What Are the Parts of a Line Graph?

A graph is only as useful as its labels. You can see in the sample figures that each figure has a general title and each axis of the graph has a label. In addition, some graphs also add identification near a trend line (see Figure 11.3), and Figure 11.2 contains a special inset (legend) to identify the different lines.

General Identification
If you use more than one figure in a message, each one has a number. The numbers are consecutive. If you use both tables and figures, the tables are numbered consecutively beginning with Table 1, and the figures also are numbered consecutively beginning with Figure 1.

In addition to the number identification, each figure must have a short descriptive title. Unlike table titles, figure numbers and titles usually appear below the actual graph. Placing the title and number below the figure helps to separate the general identification from the trend line and axis labels.

Axis Labels
Each axis in a line graph has a general label. However, if the axis is years, most writers do not bother to write the word "year." Then each major grid

on the axis has a specific label showing the time, number, or amount represented by that particular grid mark. You can see in Figure 11.1 that the writer avoids writing very large numbers by labeling the vertical axis "in thousands." Then the actual grid label could be 70 rather than the harder to read, 70,000.

How Do You Construct a Line Graph?

Most modern computers have special graphics programs which will print perfectly proportioned graphs if you provide accurate labels and appropriate numbers. If you do not have access to such a computer program, you need graph paper to produce an accurate and attractive line graph. Most writers use graph paper for a rough draft and then trace the figure so that readers will not be distracted by individual grid lines. Therefore, you should prepare all your figures before you begin to type your message so you will know how much space to save for tracing figures onto the final typed message.

When you first begin to draw graphs, you will probably have to experiment to determine the most attractive spacing. One general rule is to select spacing so that you have room to write all the labels horizontally. If your readers have to turn their heads to read vertical writing, they may lose track of the pictorial message you are trying to convey.

Once you have selected appropriate horizontal spacing, use the same number of graph spaces in each vertical grid. Look at the three examples below. They all use the same figures, but they give the reader different images of the speed and velocity of change.

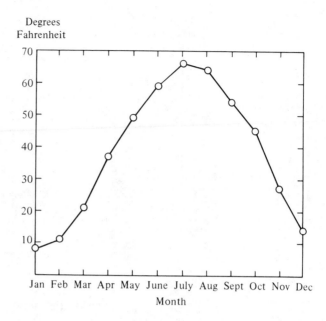

Figure 11.4 Average Mean Temperature in Duluth, Minnesota. *Source: Department of Commerce.*

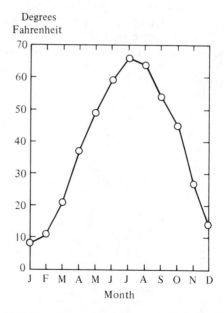

Figure 11.5 Average Mean Temperature in Duluth, Minnesota. (Shows incorrect vertical spacing.) *Source: Department of Commerce.*

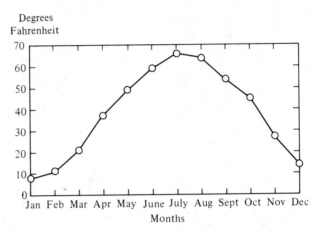

Figure 11.6 Average Mean Temperature in Duluth, Minnesota (shows incorrect horizontal spacing). *Source: Department of Commerce.*

Figure 11.4 uses square grids and presents a true picture. Figure 11.5 uses extra spaces on the vertical axis, and the trend looks faster and larger than it actually is. Figure 11.6 uses extra spaces on the horizontal axis, and this error gives the reader a visual impression that the changes are slower and smaller than they actually are.

Similarly, each square must represent an equal amount of time or an equal number or quantity. Study Figures 11.7 and 11.8 to see what happens to the visual image if the grids represent different quantities.

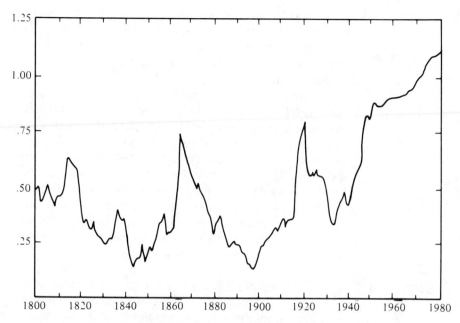

Figure 11.7 U.S. Wholesale Price Index (1800-1980) (converted to 1967 dollar = 100).

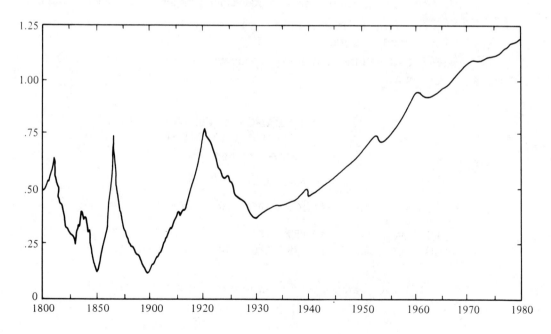

Figure 11.8 U.S. Wholesale Price Index (1800-1980) (converted to 1967 dollar = 100).

If you must show trends over a 100-year period, you have two choices—a long fold-out graph or grids that represent 5 or 10 years each. You cannot make one grid equal to 5 years and another equal to 10 years. The same is true for the vertical axis; each square must stand for an equal number or amount.

Professional graphic artists and typists can determine exact placement for axis labels and general identification by measuring and counting. Less experienced people who want to produce high quality graphic representations can use the "cut-and-paste" method. Draw lines on the figure at each place where you will need typed titles and labels. Then type the material on a clean sheet of paper. Cut the typed words and letters out and use rubber cement or transparent tape to hold them in place. When you trace the line graph into its correct place in your message, you can make a light pencil dot at each place where you must type a title or label. Then you can put your page in the typewriter and adjust the paper to begin typing at each dot. After typing, you can easily erase the light dots.

Exercise B

1. Lay out and provide appropriate titles and labels for a line graph which will show the reader the number of accidents at a dangerous traffic intersection in your city during each month of the past year. You do not need actual figures; just plan for the possibility that no accidents might occur in a month and as many as 50 accidents might occur in another month.

2. Use the information in Exercise A, problem 2, to construct and label a simple line graph.

3. Use the information in the following table to construct and label a line graph.

OCCUPANCY RATES IN PERCENT
PINE VIEW MOTEL
SARASOTA, FLORIDA

Year	Ja	Fe	Ma	Ap	Ma	Ju	Ju	Au	Se	Oc	No	De
1982	96	96	94	89	81	78	76	72	73	79	84	92
1983	95	96	92	88	80	74	72	68	72	81	87	88

4. Write a paragraph using the information in Figure 11.9 below.

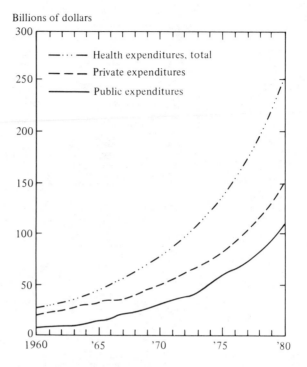

Billions of dollars

Figure 11.9 National Health Expenditures (1960-1980). *Source: Statistical Abstract of the United States.*

When Should You Use a Bar Graph?

A second common graph is the vertical or horizontal bar graph. This figure is used to highlight comparisons rather than trends. It may show a situation at one time or at a series of separate times, but it does not have the intermediate information that a line graph presents. A bar graph may be drawn either horizontally, as in Figure 11.10, or vertically, as in Figure 11.11.

Department

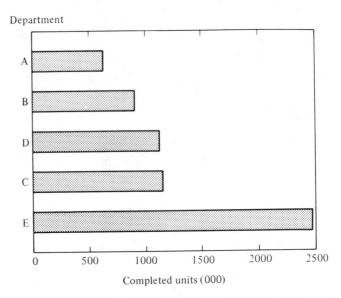

Completed units (000)

Figure 11.10 July Production in Plant X (thousands of completed units).

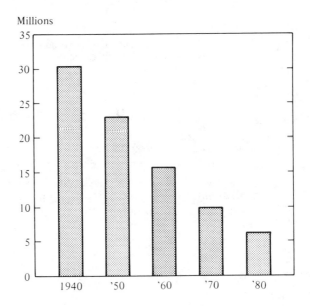

Figure 11.11 U.S. Farm Population (1940-1980). *Source: U.S. Bureau of the Census.*

Figure 11.10 graphically represents data that happened in a single period of time—in July. For best visual effect, bar graphs showing a comparison of figures for a single time period should be represented horizontally. Other data that should be represented horizontally are data about length or distance as in Figure 11.12.

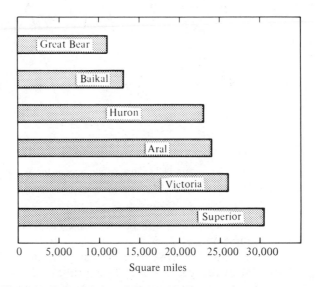

Figure 11.12 Great Lakes of the World. *Source: National Geographic Atlas of the World.*

On the other hand, Figure 11.11 shows data at several different times. In this case, the vertical bar is used so the time scale can be written on the horizontal axis as in a line graph. If the graph were used to compare height instead of length, the bars should also be arranged vertically to leave a mental picture of height in the reader's mind.

What Are the Parts of a Bar Graph?

Like the line graph, the bar graph uses two axes, each of which is labeled. Unlike the line graph, the vertical bar graph axis usually starts at zero. However, if the numbers are large, the graph usually shows a break line between zero and the first significant grid identification as in Figure 11.13.

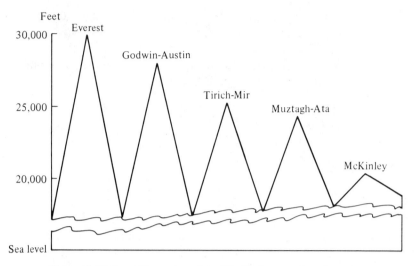

Figure 11.13 Great Mountains of the World. *Source: Encyclopaedia Britannica World Atlas.*

Of course, the graph has a figure number, a short descriptive title, and a source line.

Figure 11.14 shows how the bar graph can be used to compare several sets of related data at different times. The bars must be different colors or at least must show contrasting hatch marks. Notice that the color or hatch pattern must also be identified in a special corner of the figure called the legend.

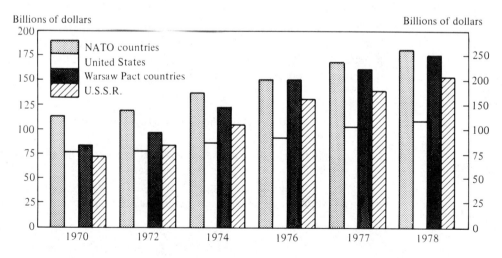

Figure 11.14 Worldwide Military Expenditures (1970-1978). *Source: U.S. Bureau of the Census.*

One special feature of the bar graph is that zero can be in a center position to show both gains and losses as in Figure 11.15.

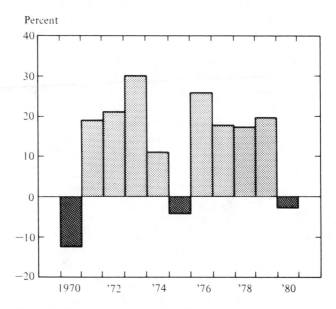

Figure 11.15 Corporate Profits after Taxes—Annual Percent Change. *Source: U.S. Department of Commerce.*

The bar graph can also display several kinds of information in each bar as in Figure 11.16.

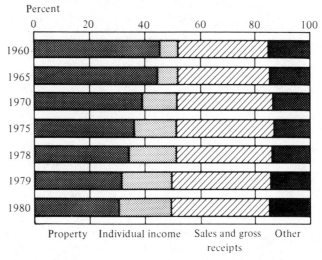

Figure 11.16 State and Local Government Taxes—Percent Distribution, by Type (1960-1980). *Source: U.S. Bureau of the Census.*

This figure shows an overall change in state and local government tax structure in the two decades since 1960. Readers can see the percentage of each kind of tax as well as the trend away from property taxes and toward income taxes.

How Do You Construct a Bar Graph?

Modern computers will construct and print bar graphs if you input accurate information. Many computers will even print the graph in more than one color to show contrast. However, if you must prepare the graph by hand, use graph paper and a ruler for accuracy and attractiveness.

You will need the same identifications on a bar graph that you needed for a line graph: a consecutive figure number, a general title, axis labels, and individual grid point labels. And, as on line graphs, you must plan the space on the graph to allow room for axis and grid labels. Most often, the figure number and general title appear below the finished graph. Bar graphs are somewhat easier to read if the bars are not the same width as the blank spaces between bars (see Figure 11.10). If the bar graph compares two or more items, the comparison bars are juxtaposed without space between them as in Figure 11.14. Comparison bars must be different. You may use different colors or different shading patterns to distinguish them. A small key should identify the bars as in Figure 11.14. Plan to assemble the graph in a logical order — most to least, least to most, or by time or distance.

The first step in producing a bar graph is to draw and identify the two axes. Remember to plan horizontal bars for time and distance. Next, consider the largest number that must be represented on the graph. Obviously, this bar sets an effective size limit for a bar graph. Most graphic designers plan bar graphs to the next largest 0. That is, if your largest number is $962, plan the largest grid for $1,000 instead of stopping at $962. Planning to the nearest 0 makes accurate proportional layout easy. Each grid mark equals a multiple of 10 instead of an odd fraction. For instance,

$$1000/20 \text{ grids} = 50 \text{ units per grid}$$

but

$$962/20 \text{ grids} = 48.1 \text{ units per grid.}$$

Obviously, working with 50 and 100 is easier than counting by 48.1 to 96.2, etc. Further, you will identify grids with large whole numbers which readers can remember easily.

On your rough draft graph paper, you may want to lightly mark the value of each grid to make drawing easier. After you have drawn all the bars, erase the interim markings and type in the large guide numbers your reader should remember. On bar graphs, you usually only need to type in grid marks in three or four places. If you need more detailed information, you probably should be using a table. In a bar graph, you want to show accurate but approximate relationships. If you add too many details, your readers may become confused.

Exercise C

1. Lay out and label the major grids for a bar graph which will show the relative heights of five popular urban shade trees. The tallest tree will grow to a mature height of 180 feet; the shortest tree will be 75 feet tall when mature.

2. Use the information in Figure 11.1 to create a bar graph that will emphasize the position at ten-year intervals.

3. Use the information in Figure 11.17 to write a paragraph explaining the same facts.

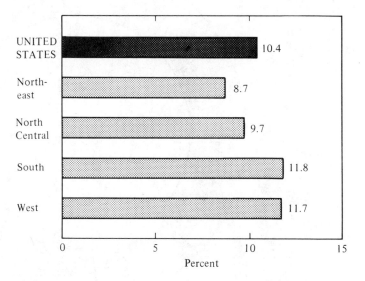

Figure 11.17 Personal Income by Region (1970-1980): Annual Percent Change. *Source: U.S. Bureau of the Census.*

4. Use the following information to create a simple bar graph.

Every continent has its great rivers. In North America, the Mississippi-Missouri system flows 3,785 miles to the Gulf of Mexico. In Latin America, the mighty Amazon stretches nearly 4,000 miles from headwaters to the Atlantic Ocean. The Great Blue Nile begins deep within Africa and winds its way 4,145 miles to the Mediterranean Sea. China's Yangtze River flows 3,400 miles to the sea. Across the border, the Volga drains westward through 2,290 miles of Russian countryside. The historic Rhine River of central Europe (only 820 miles) seems puny by comparison.

5. Use the information in Figure 11.2 to create a comparative bar graph.

When Should You Use a Circle Graph?

Business writers often use one other graph form—the circle graph or "pie chart." This graphic form shows the parts of a single whole as in Figures 11.18 and 11.19.

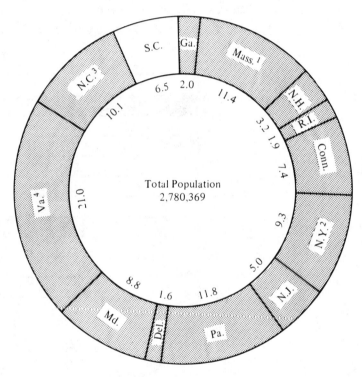

[1] Includes Maine
[2] Includes Vermont
[3] Includes Tennessee
[4] Includes Kentucky

Figure 11.18 Percent Population of the American Colonies: 1780.

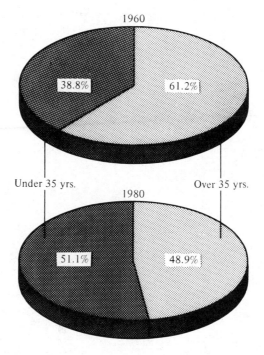

Figure 11.19 Labor Force — Age Composition. *Source: U.S. Bureau of the Census.*

What Are the Parts of a Circle Graph?

Circle graphs may have general titles and figure identification above or below the graph. If the message contains other figures, the title and number are usually placed below the graph for continuity's sake. Because a circle graph or pie chart is only used to show parts of a whole, the value of each "slice of the pie" is almost always stated as a percentage. Occasionally, a pie chart is used to show allocation of money; the values are in monetary terms as in Figure 11.20.

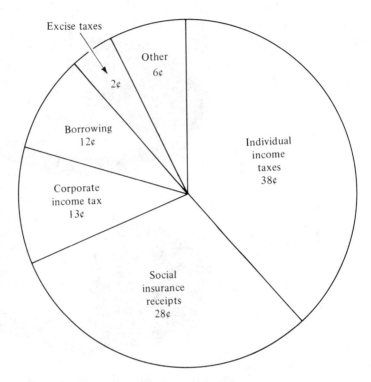

Figure 11.20 How the Federal Government Raised Revenues: 1980.

How Do You Construct a Circle Graph?

Although great variation is possible, the clearest circle graphs usually follow these rules.

1. The largest slice begins at "12 o'clock" on the circle.

2. The slices are arranged in descending order of size.

3. The "other" or "miscellaneous" category is last in the circle, even if it is larger than some other segments as in Figure 11.20.

Again, some modern computers will construct a circle graph. However, if you must prepare your own pie charts, you need two tools—a compass and protractor (Figure 11.21).

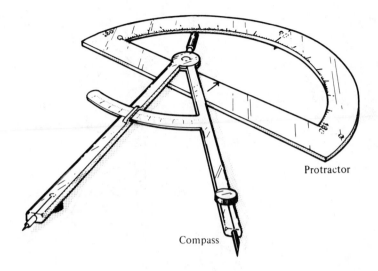

Protractor

Compass

Figure 11.21 Compass and Protractor.

You can manage without a compass, but you must have a protractor for accuracy. If you do not have a compass to draw the basic circle, go through the kitchen cupboards to find a cup, glass, or cookie cutter that seems to be an appropriate size for the visual image you wish to convey.

These graphs are not as easy to produce as line and bar graphs. You have to work with percentages and convert them to degrees of a circle to divide the circle into segments that accurately represent the data you wish to present.

Use plain paper (not graph paper) and begin by drawing a circle of any size you find easy to work with. You can enlarge the circle or shrink it after you draw the radii to divide the circle. Place the compass somewhere near the center of a sheet of paper and draw the basic circle (Figure 11.22).

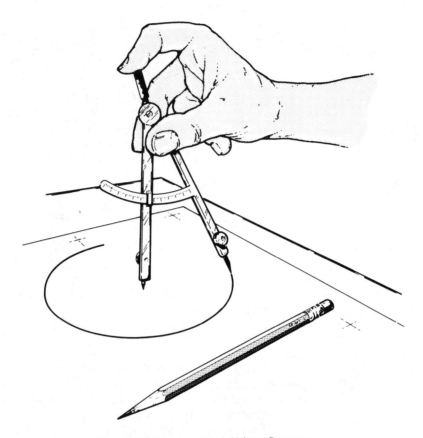

Figure 11.22 Drawing a Circle Using a Compass.

Here is an example of constructing a circle graph from tabular data.

Table 11.5
U.S. LAND HELD BY FEDERAL
DEPARTMENTS IN 1979

Department	Millions of Acres
Interior	649
Agriculture	188
Defense	30
Other	4

First, add the figures. The federal departments hold 871 million acres of land. Acres of land do not translate directly into parts of a circle. The circle is a whole (100 percent), so you must determine what percent of that 100 percent each department holds:

$$649/871 \quad = \quad 74.5\%$$
$$188/871 \quad = \quad 21.8\%$$
$$30/871 \quad = \quad 3.44\%$$
$$4/871 \quad = \quad .459\% \text{ (nearly 1/2 of 1 percent)}$$

Double check by adding the percentages. In this case, the figures add to 100.199 percent, so the percentages are probably close enough to make an accurate graph.

A circle of any size always contains 360 degrees (the "grids" of a circle graph). You must now use these percentages to determine how many degrees of the circle each percent represents.

$$.745 \times 360 = 268 \quad \text{degrees}$$
$$.218 \times 360 = \quad 78.5 \quad \text{degrees}$$
$$.034 \times 360 = \quad 12.24 \text{ degrees}$$
$$.0045 \times 360 = \quad 1.65 \text{ degrees}$$

Once again, double check by adding the degrees to see if they total to approximately 360. In this case, the total is 360.39 degrees. As you work only with whole numbers, this slightly large total will not distort the visual message.

Now draw the "12 o'clock" radius. (A radius is a line reaching from the edge of a circle to its center.) Figure 11.23 shows the circle with the first radius.

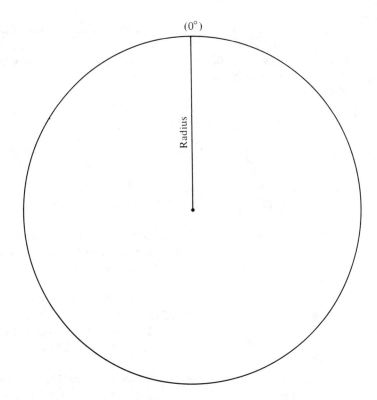

Figure 11.23 The "12 o'clock" Radius in a Circle Graph.

The point where the radius touches the circumference is the "0" point on your circle. You need a "slice of the pie" that is 268 degrees clockwise farther around the circle from this "0" point. To measure 268 degrees, you need the protractor. This handy half circle measures only 180 degrees at a time. You know you will need the whole 180 degrees plus 88 more degrees (268 − 180 = 88). So put the arrow of the protractor at the center point of the circle and align the straight edge of the protractor with the radius you drew (see Figure 11.24). Mark the bottom of the circle with a tiny mark to show half the circle (180 degrees) as in Figure 11.24.

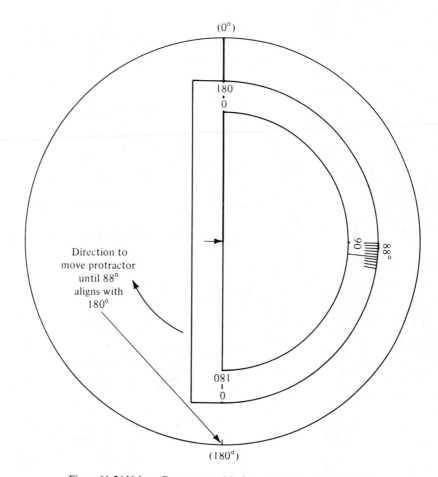

Figure 11.24 Using a Protractor to Mark 180° on a Circle Graph.

Now keep the arrow on the center point of the circle and swing the protractor in a clockwise direction until you see 88 degrees line up with the mark you made to indicate half the circle (180 + 88 = 268). Draw a radius line from the center of the circle to the left hand "0" mark as in Figure 11.25.

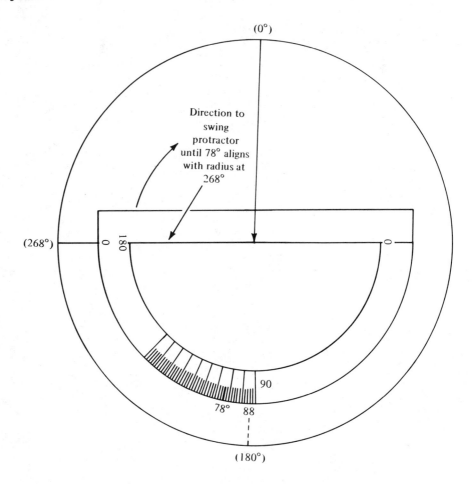

Figure 11.25 Using a Protractor to Mark 268° on a Circle Graph.

You have now marked a large section of the pie to indicate the land held by the Department of the Interior. Keep the arrow at the center of the circle and again swing the protractor in a clockwise direction until you align 78 degrees with the radius you just drew. Again, draw a radius from the center to the edge of the circle as in Figure 11.26.

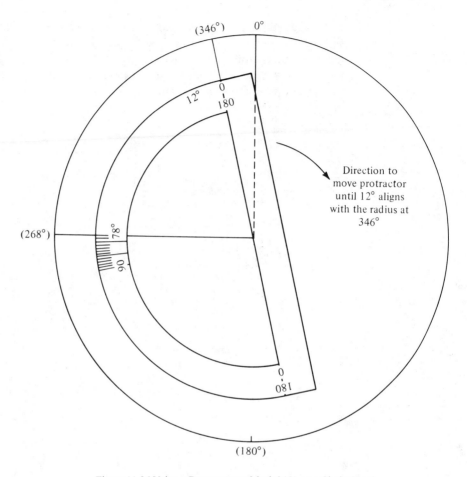

Figure 11.26 Using a Protractor to Mark 346° on a Circle Graph.

Now you have accounted for 649 million acres held by the Department of the Interior (268 degrees) and 188 million acres held by the Department of Agriculture (78 degrees). You have used up 346 degrees of the circle (96%). If you check the percentage calculations you did, you see that 74.5% and 21.8% equal 96.3%, so your radius lines are projecting a true visual image. Repeat the process one more time to account for land held by the Department of Defense (30 million acres or 12 degrees). Keep the arrow at the center of the circle; swing the protractor in a clockwise direction until 12 degrees aligns with the line you just drew. Draw another radius along the straight edge of the protractor. The tiny space left is land held by "other" federal departments.

Now you can label the graph. As the table from which you worked showed millions of acres, that is the unit you should use to identify segments of the graph. You converted to percentages for your own convenience, but you do not want to show percentages to your reader. Your finished graph should resemble Figure 11.27.

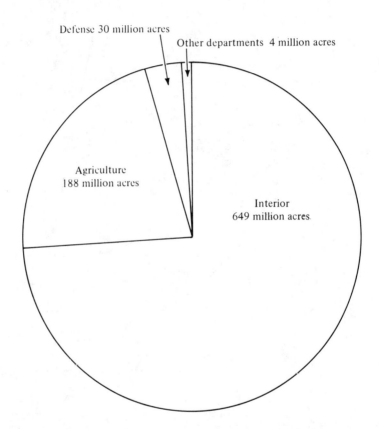

Figure 11.27 Federal Departments Owning U.S. Land in 1979.

If you need a smaller circle, simply draw it inside the rough draft circle. The proportions of the pie will remain the same. The graph can be enlarged by drawing a larger circle and extending the radii to meet the new circumference.

Exercise D   1. Complete the calculations you need to convert the figures in Exercise A, problem 4, into a circle graph which has this title.

FLOOR SPACE ASSIGNMENTS
IN LISTON'S DEPARTMENT STORE
(In percent)

2. Use the information in Exercise A, problem 4, to represent as a circle graph the dollar amount of overhead charged to each department. Do the calculations; do not draw the graph.

3. What title should you write to identify the circle graph you planned in Exercise D, problem 2?

4. Use the information that follows to construct and label a circle graph.

> In 1979, federal government departments and agencies owned 871 million acres of American real estate. This federally held land is used for four main purposes: forest and wildlife habitat, 573 million acres; leased grazing land, 163 million acres; national parks and monuments, 69 million acres; military bases and test sites, 18 million acres. Various other uses such as government buildings, rights of way, experimental farms, and reserved lands occupy another 48 million acres.

5. Write a paragraph using the information in Figure 11.19.

WHERE DO YOU PLACE VISUAL AIDS IN MESSAGES?

You remember that a table or figure cannot convey a complete message. The writer must introduce each table or figure and tell the reader what to expect in the visual aid. Compare the following excerpts from a report about gasoline sales.

Excerpt A. "The gas war won't be short lived. As cars become more fuel efficient, retail distributors will have to fight harder to keep market share in a diminishing market. Indeed, many retailers have already closed their doors."

Excerpt B. "The gas war won't be short lived. The shrinking market has already forced 79,500 dealers out of business.

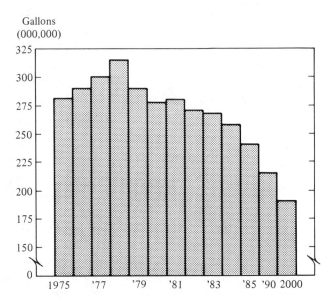

Figure 11.28 Daily U.S. Gasoline Sales (millions of gallons). *Sources: 1975-81, Department of Energy; 1982-2000, forecasts by Standard Oil of California.*

More will probably follow as competition increases to keep a share of the diminishing market."

Excerpt C. "The gas war won't be short lived. In the past ten years, the number of gas stations has declined from 226,000 to 146,500. As Figure 11.29 shows, these surviving retail distributors must plan to fight harder to keep market share as customers consume less gasoline in more fuel-efficient cars.

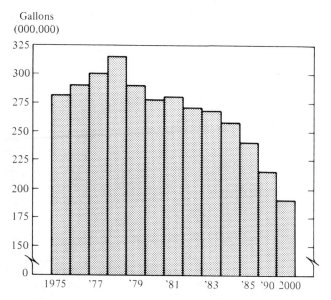

Figure 11.29 Daily U.S. Gasoline Sales (millions of gallons). *Sources: 1975-81, Department of Energy; 1982-2000, forecasts by Standard Oil of California.*

The sharp decline predicted in the next two years will force even more stations to close."

Excerpt A paints a general picture, unsupported by any fact. The reader has no idea of the magnitude of the problem and no mental picture to carry to the writer's next idea.

Excerpt B puts a table into the report, but the writer does not tell the reader what to see in the table. The reader must stop to figure out the reason for the table and thus loses the writer's train of thought.

In Excerpt C, the writer introduces the table so readers can understand the size of the problem and almost predict the first sentence which follows the figure. This writer makes good use of a simple bar graph.

In general, the writer prepares a reader for a table or graph by mentioning the number of the figure and indicating the most important information readers can expect to see in the visual representation. The table or graph should be placed in the manuscript immediately after that "highlight" introduction. If the writer wants to call attention to less important points in the visual aid, other comments can follow the visual as in the following example.

The center of population is that point at which an imaginary, flat, weightless and rigid map of the United States would balance if weights of identical value were placed on it so that each weight represented the location of one person on the date of the census. The stars in Figure 11.30 below show the long march to the west, starting 23 miles east of Baltimore, Maryland, in 1790 and crossing the Mississippi River to Jefferson County, Missouri, in 1980.

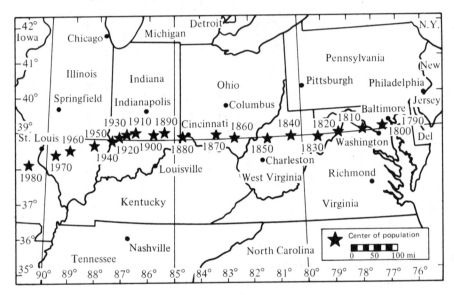

Figure 11.30 U.S. Centers of Population: 1790-1980. *Source: Statistical Abstract of the United States.*

The figure also shows that only since World War II has the center of population moved toward the south. The north-south center was virtually the same in 1950 as it was in 1850, but the balance has moved slowly southward since 1950.

A few formal reports require large, complex tables and figures. These are usually placed in an appendix at the end of the report so they do not interrupt the reader's concentration on the flow of ideas in the report. Often the writer will incorporate a short version of the large table or figure in the body of the report for emphasis.

Exercise E

1. Write the introductory sentence or sentences that might precede the table in Exercise B, problem 3.

2. Write the sentences that might precede and follow the line graph in Figure 11.31.

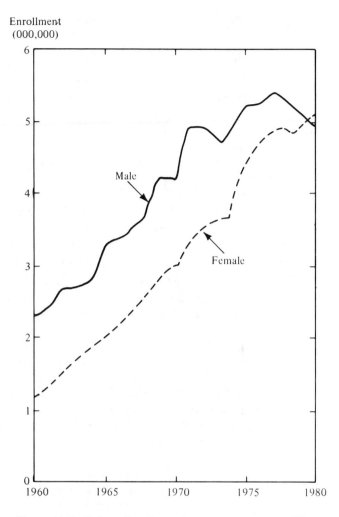

Figure 11.31 College Enrollment by Sex (1960-1980) (millions). *Source: U.S. Bureau of the Census.*

Review   In studying chapter 11, you have learned to create tables and graphs to help readers remember highlights of your messages. You use tables to display precise data which the reader may want to study. Sometimes you use tables to arrange words in a special order so readers can compare features. You use line graphs to show trends continuing through time. You use bar graphs to show data at separate times, and you use circle graphs to show parts of a whole.

Each table or figure has a separate, consecutive number and a descriptive title. Each column in a table must have a subtitle, and each axis in a graph must be identified. In a circle graph, each "slice of the pie" is labeled.

Tables and figures appear in text immediately after they are introduced. The writer explains what highlights will appear in the table or figure, inserts the table or figure, then continues the discussion.

Cases   1. You work in the publications department of a large pension fund. The date is July 15, 1982. The Board of Trustees has just completed a major report explaining current investments to its 630,000 members. The writing staff has polished the report and turned it over to you. Your job is to add tables and figures that will summarize important information in the report. Some figures you must illustrate are in the body of the report. Other figures appear in summary form at the end of the report. Be sure to write titles for the figures or tables you design and indicate where they belong in the report.

ANNUITY INVESTMENTS

The hallmark of our times is uncertainty. Will the volatile economic conditions of the last few years prevail for years to come, or will inflation and interest rates come down and stabilize at lower levels? Will long-term interest rates remain higher than short-term rates as they have for all but a few of the last 50 years? Or will the interest rate inversion of the past few years—with short-term higher than long—return again? Or none of the above? No one knows, of course, but both short- and long-term rates have been at historic highs in recent years. And since 1979 your annuity fund has been building an investment portfolio that captures for participants not only the high long-term fixed interest rates currently available, but also some of the responsiveness to inflation normally associated only with short-term investing. This we do, as discussed below, by incorporating in long-term loans various features that can provide extra returns if we have higher-than-expected inflation while the investments are outstanding.

Virtually all mortgage commitments made since 1980 have included inflation-adapted features that provide an opportunity for extra returns over and above the interest rate set at the time the loan is committed. The extras come either from sharing in future gross rent increases or resetting the mortgage interest rate. The most frequently used feature is the one that shares in future gross rent increases. Examples of such loan commitments include:

An agreement to lend $7 million for a three-building research/office complex in California's Silicon Valley. This loan carried a fixed interest rate of 13.8% and will pay us 35% of gross rental income above a preset level. Since leases have already been signed that provide rental income in excess of the preset level, our effective yield will rise to 14.4% on this loan in its very first year.

In the center of St. Louis, a four-story enclosed shopping center mall will be financed with a $38 million mortgage loan. Pedestrian bridges and skyways will link the mall to two adjacent department stores, an office building, and a parking garage. The loan has a fixed interest rate of 13.25% and provides that we will receive 25% of the mall's gross rents above a predetermined level.

Near the newly expanded international airport in Tampa, Florida, two industrial buildings will be constructed, financed by our $2 million mortgage loan. This loan carries a 14.125% fixed interest rate and a 25% participation in future gross rent increases. The space can be used as a showroom, distribution center, or light manufacturing facility.

The other type of inflation-adapted feature in our mortgage loan commitments is one that will increase the loan's interest rate automatically and, in addition, give us an option to increase the rate still further. For example, during 1982, we agreed to make a $13 million, 20-year mortgage loan to build a research facility in New York State's Hudson Valley. The interest rate on this loan, set initially at 14.5%, will rise automatically by one-half percentage point every five years. And each time the rate goes up, we have the option to increase the rate for the balance of the loan period by as much as an additional two percentage points. If we exercise that option, the borrower can elect to repay the loan instead of accepting the higher rate.

We also have been active in the purchase of prime-location office buildings during the past few years. These real estate investments provide a dependable flow of rental income; and, to help future rents keep pace with inflation, tenant leases in our buildings are being negotiated for shorter time periods than in the past.

Figure I, below, shows our progress in making mortgage and real estate investment commitments with inflation-adapted features. Also illustrated below, in Figure II, are our recent loan commitments to business and industry, which contain other types of inflation-adapted features.

For more than a decade, our program of direct loans to business and industry has included loans with equity participation features. Some of these direct loans are negotiated so that in return for making a long-term loan at a fixed interest rate, we acquire stock of the corporate borrower. Today this is usually done through a "leveraged buy-out," an arrangement in which a management/investor group forms a new corporation that borrows money to buy an existing business. The new owner/managers generally apply some of the loan to revitalize or expand their business, and if the move is as successful as expected, we can share in that success through realizing capital gains on our stockholdings in the firm, over and above the interest payments on the loan.

We also seek equity participation through other types of direct loans. One such loan to an oil and gas drilling company to purchase three offshore drilling platforms for $6 million at 15.5% interest includes our right to buy 185,000 shares of the company's common stock at any time prior to 1990 at a preset price. From this type of loan, realized capital gains over the last three years have been about $60 million, substantially increasing our total yield above the interest payments on these loans.

Some direct loans have rate reset provisions, with the initial interest rate set at a specified percentage above the current rate for long-term U.S. Treasury bonds. Then, at predetermined intervals, such as six months, a year, or two years, the rate is adjusted to prevailing long-term interest rates, again at the specified premium above Treasury bond rates. We have committed ourselves to make $585 million of these variable rate loans since 1980—such as a $25 million, 20-year loan to a northwestern gas pipeline company, with an initial interest rate of 16.9%, adjustable every year.

In addition to loans with equity participation or adjustable interest rate features, we also invest in fixed-rate-only loans with maturities that range from just a few years to 20 or more.

ANNUITY SUMMARY
The increasing earnings from our investments over the years have benefited participants through the dividends declared year by year by the Board, raising the interest rates credited to annuity owners' accumulations during the pay-in years and raising lifetime income payments during the pay-out years.

MARKET INVESTMENTS
The common stock component of the pension plan takes a long-term approach to investing the funds participants allocate to it. We do not seek spectacular returns at the risk of substan-

tial loss; we don't bet on market timing, and we don't specialize
in any particular segment or segments of the market. Instead, we
hold stocks widely across many industries and companies
throughout the U.S. and, to some extent, in other countries. Our
objective is to seek total returns (market value changes plus dividends) that are about the same from year to year as those of the
stock market in general, and somewhat better over the long
term.

Our holdings both at home and abroad are more widely
diversified than any single index, but for benchmark purposes,
the "S&P Equivalent" is of general interest as a surrogate for the
market in comparing performance. As shown in Figure III, from
our founding in 1952 until 1973, our average annual net rate of
total return was 11.1%, compared to 10.7% for the S&P Equivalent. Then in the mid-1970s, like most managed equity funds,
we underperformed the market: minus 4.3% compared to minus
0.8% for the S&P Equivalent. Early in 1976, we began to phase
in a new stock selection system based on newly available computer technology and developing financial theory; the new system became fully operational on April 1, 1977. For the five-plus
years since then (through June 30, 1982), we have done somewhat better than the market, averaging 7.8% per year compared
to the market's 7.4% per year. Measuring the entire period from
our beginning, our average annual net rate of total investment
return, still feeling the drag of the 1973-75 period, was 8.2%
compared to the 8.4% for the S&P Equivalent.

Over the years our portfolio has included shares of multi-
national firms that are traded on U.S. stock exchanges — corporations that sell goods and services to the world at large. And
since 1973, we have held shares of Japanese firms traded on Japanese stock exchanges. Beginning in 1979, we began expanding
our international investing, toward an objective of having 10%
of our assets invested in shares traded on major foreign stock exchanges around the world. Historical studies have shown that
since the early 1950s a broadly diversified representation of international stocks would have produced a cumulative return better than that of the U.S. market. Also, the ups and downs of foreign stock markets generally have occurred at different times
than those of the U.S. market. While similar results may or may
not prevail in the future, we expect our foreign stock holdings to
help reduce swings in the market value of our portfolio as a
whole, and in the process, to increase long-term total returns.
The table below shows the percentage of our holdings purchased

through foreign stock exchanges, which amounted to $587 million as of the end of June, 1982.

In July, 1981, we began adjusting our U.S. stockholdings so that a major portion of the portfolio will track the results of the entire U.S. stock market with as little active management as possible. Most of the stocks in this portion of the portfolio, representing about 80% of our U.S. stocks as of mid-1981, will be invested in stocks in Standard & Poor's 500-stock average, held in proportion to their weights in this well known indicator. The rest will be a representative sampling of stocks which comprise the rest of the U.S. stock market. The balance of our domestic stocks, now some $1.5 billion, will continue to be actively managed, with stock selection based primarily upon analysis of the relationship between a company's long-term earnings prospects and the current market price of its stock. Figure IV shows the percentage distribution of our portfolio as of June 30, 1982.

MARKET INVESTMENT SUMMARY

Our year-by-year investment results, like those of other widely diversified equity funds, largely reflect the returns on common stocks in general. But over the long run, the combination of some foreign stock holdings, most of the domestic stocks tied closely to overall U.S. stock market experience, and the rest actively managed, is expected to further our objective of achieving long-term total returns somewhat better than the market.

Stock Portfolio as of June 30, 1982

International investments, $587,000,000
Actively managed stocks, $1,509,428,500
Non-S&P stock holdings, $335,428,500
S&P weighted holdings, $5,953,857,000

International Investments as of June 30, 1982

Country	Amount Invested
Australia	$ 31,698,000
Belgium	8,218,000
Canada	42,851,000
France	18,784,000
Hong Kong	19,371,000
Japan	225,995,000
Mexico	1,175,000

Netherlands	17,024,000
Singapore/Malaysia	15,262,000
Spain	9,979,000
Sweden	9,393,000
Switzerland	27,589,000
United Kingdom	116,814,000
West Germany	42,852,000

Mortgage and Real Estate Commitments, 1980-June 30, 1982

*Fixed-Rate-Only
Mortgages*

1979, $444,420,000
1980, $ 78,100,000
1981, $ 9,009,000
1982, $ 5,285,000

*Fixed-Rate Mortgages
with Contingent
Interest Features*

1979, $238,670,000
1980, $484,220,000
1981, $810,810,000
1982, $940,730,000

*Mortgages with Rate
Reset Features*

1979, $ 0
1980, $ 46,860,000
1981, $ 70,070,000
1982, $ 5,285,000

*Income Producing
Real Estate*

1979, $139,910,000
1980, $171,820,000
1981, $120,120,000
1982, $105,700,000

Loan Commitments, 1980-June 30, 1982

*Fixed-Rate Loans
with Maturities More
than 10 Years*

1979, $924,560,000
1980, $818,400,000
1981, $532,180,000
1982, $217,140,000

*Fixed-Rate Loans
with Maturities 10 Years
and Shorter*

1979, $ 20,320,000
1980, $ 40,920,000
1981, $259,600,000
1982, $151,340,000

*Fixed-Rate Loans
with Equity
Participation Features*

1979, $ 71,120,000
1980, $163,680,000
1981, $142,780,000
1982, $ 72,380,000

*Direct Loans
with Variable-Rate
Features*

1979, $ 0
1980, $ 0
1981, $363,440,000
1982, $217,140,000

2. Your superior is preparing a proposal in which he wants to include a little company history. He will need a table for the written message, but he wants to use graphs in his oral presentation. You are to prepare the table and graphs from the following raw data. Be sure to provide an appropriate title.

Number of Employees: In 1950, 15 professional and 98 nonprofessional; 1955, 22 professional and 138 nonprofessional; 1960, 31 professional and 153 nonprofessional; 1965, 54 professional and 542 nonprofessional; 1970, 75 professional and 865 nonprofessional; 1975, 102 professional and 1,054 nonprofessional; 1980, 135 professional and 1,254 nonprofessional.

Gross Sales: In 1950, $935,000; in 1955, $2,987,654; in 1960, $3,639,024; in 1965, $7,693,997; in 1970, $9,386,233; in 1975, $14,638,693; in 1980, $19,648,396.

Net Profits: In 1950, $13,287; in 1955, $68,398; in 1960, $201,583; in 1965, $648,307; in 1970, $963,106; in 1975, $1,157,398; in 1980, $2,648,099.

3. The editor for your firm's annual report calls you over to read the message from the company president which is, traditionally, the first section of the report. "This report is really pretty interesting, but a lot of people will get turned off by these first two paragraphs full of numbers. Why don't you put this information into a couple of nice tables? We can run the tables on a page facing the president's message. After you get the tables, I'll rough out a layout and go upstairs to see if we can just condense the first two paragraphs into a one-liner, 'As the tables on the facing page show, the company's overall financial picture was strengthened in the past year.' That will get us out of the numbers business and into the interesting part. See what you can come up with."

Here are the "two paragraphs full of numbers" that you must put into a chart.

"Despite serious pressures from both recession and inflation, your company enjoyed record high revenues in this past year—$1,414,414,000 as compared to $1,258,018,000 in the previous year. Our total dividends ($30,827,000) were up 15% from $26,788,000, and dividends per share of common stock were up 10% from $1.45 to $1.60. This new record was possible in spite of the fact that net income fell from $72,086,000 to $69,535,000 while net income per share of common stock fell from $4.13 to only $3.78.

"At year's end we can report that total company assets stood at $1,214,722,000, a healthy 11% increase from $1,095,538,000 last year. Working capital is up $15,655,000 to $190,630,000. Of course, new long-term debt accounted for much of that increase as it rose from $99,880,000 to $113,587,000. However, the stockholders' equity also showed a large gain moving as it did from $438,955,000 to $503,459,000.

The number of stockholders has risen only slightly from 19,379 to 20,014."

4. Most data is accumulated in table form. Writers study the information, draw conclusions, and then prepare a message. Because they know readers are more apt to retain mental images of pictures than to retain details from tables, writers use graphs rather than tables to emphasize the conclusions they draw from research.

The tables in this case are reprinted from a special pamphlet issued by the Department of Commerce to celebrate America's Bicentennial. [*U.S. Bureau of the Census, Bicentennial Statistics.* Reprinted from *Pocket Data Book, USA, 1976.* Washington, D.C., 1976.] They show some of the great changes that have occurred in the United States since its founding. Study the tables, draw some conclusions about working in the United States, and write a short report that you highlight with figures constructed from the data in the tables. Be sure to classify and synthesize your information to avoid writing a report that is merely a paragraph by paragraph rehash of statistics.

Table 598
LABOR FORCE

In millions. Prior to 1947, persons 14 years old and over; thereafter, 16 and over. Data prior to 1947 not entirely comparable with later years.

Year	Labor force, total	Civilian labor force	Employed Total	Employed Agricul- tural	Year	Labor force, total	Civilian labor force	Employed Total	Employed Agricul- tural
1900.....	28.5	28.4	27.0	11.1	1947.....	60.9	59.4	57.0	7.9
1910.....	36.9	36.7	34.6	11.3	1950.....	63.9	62.2	58.9	7.2
1920.....	41.7	41.3	39.2	10.4	1960.....	72.1	69.6	65.8	5.5
1930.....	48.8	48.5	44.2	10.3	1970.....	85.9	82.7	78.6	3.5
1940.....	56.2	55.6	47.5	9.5	1975.....	94.8	92.6	84.8	3.4

Table 599
WOMEN IN THE CIVILIAN LABOR FORCE

In millions, except percent. Persons 15 years old and over, 1890-1930; 14 and over, 1940-1960; and 16 and over, thereafter. Data prior to 1940 not entirely comparable with later years.

Year	Total	Per- cent[1]	Single	Mar- ried	Year	Total	Per- cent[1]	Single	Mar- ried
1890.....	3.7	18.9	2.5	.5	1947.....	16.3	29.8	6.2	7.5
1900.....	5.0	20.6	3.3	.8	1950.....	17.8	31.4	5.6	9.3
1910.....	7.6	25.4	4.6	1.9	1960.....	22.5	34.8	5.4	13.5
1920.....	8.3	23.7	[2]6.4	1.9	1965.....	26.0	36.7	5.9	16.2
1930.....	10.6	24.8	5.7	3.1	1970.....	31.2	42.6	7.0	19.8
1940.....	13.8	27.4	6.7	5.0	1975.....	36.5	45.9	8.5	22.7

[1] Percent of female population.   [2] Includes widowed and divorced.

Table 600
NONAGRICULTURAL EMPLOYMENT, BY INDUSTRY GROUP

Percent distribution

Year	Total (mil)	Manu- factur- ing	Whole- sale, retail	Services	Govern- ment	Trans- port., public util.	Contract construc- tion
1900.........	15.2	36.0	16.5	11.5	7.2	15.0	7.6
1910.........	21.7	36.1	16.5	11.1	7.5	15.5	6.2
1920.........	27.4	39.0	16.3	8.6	9.5	14.6	3.1
1930.........	29.4	32.5	19.7	11.5	10.7	12.5	4.7
1940.........	32.4	33.9	20.8	11.4	13.0	9.4	4.0
1950.........	45.2	33.7	20.8	11.9	13.3	8.9	5.2
1960.........	54.2	31.0	21.0	13.7	15.4	7.4	5.3
1970.........	70.9	27.2	21.2	16.4	17.7	6.4	5.0
1975.........	77.0	23.8	22.0	18.2	19.2	5.8	4.5

Table 602

PERCENT DISTRIBUTION BY OCCUPATION OF WORKERS

Covers employed and unemployed in civilian labor force by job last held.

Occupation	1900	1920	1930	1940	1950	1960	1970	1975
White-collar workers	17.6	24.9	29.4	31.1	36.6	42.3	47.5	47.9
Professional, technical	4.3	5.4	6.8	7.5	7.3	11.0	13.8	14.2
Managers, administrators	5.8	6.6	7.4	7.3	10.4	10.3	10.2	9.9
Clerical	3.0	8.0	8.9	9.6	12.6	14.7	17.4	17.5
Sales	4.5	4.9	6.3	6.7	6.3	6.3	6.1	6.3
Blue-collar workers . . . . , . .	35.8	40.2	39.6	39.8	40.2	37.7	36.0	34.2
Craftsmen, foremen	10.5	13.0	12.8	12.0	13.0	13.0	12.8	12.9
Operatives	12.8	15.6	15.8	18.4	20.8	18.8	18.2	16.0
Laborers	12.5	11.6	11.0	9.4	6.4	5.9	5.0	5.3
Service workers	9.0	7.8	9.8	11.8	11.2	12.3	12.5	13.8
Farm workers	37.6	27.0	21.2	17.4	12.1	7.7	3.9	3.3

Table 603

AVERAGE ANNUAL WAGES AND SALARIES – SELECTED INDUSTRIES

In dollars. Per full-time employee. Data prior to 1950 not entirely comparable with later years.

Item	1900	1920	1930	1940	1950	1960	1974
Mining	479	1,684	1,424	1,388	3,467	5,724	12,935
Contract construction	593	1,710	1,526	1,330	3,380	5,756	12,206
Maufacturing	487	1,532	1,488	1,432	3,331	5,548	10,834
Transportation	505	1,645	1,610	1,756	3,641	5,836	12,616
Wholesale, retail trade....	508	1,270	1,569	1,382	3,042	4,478	8,749
Services...............	340	912	1,066	953	2,212	3,684	8,141
Government	584	1,245	1,553	1,344	3,014	4,646	10,632

Table 604

AVERAGE EARNINGS AND HOURS OF PRODUCTION (MFG.) WORKERS

Year	Hourly Earnings	Weekly Earnings	Weekly Hours	Year	Hourly Earnings	Weekly Earnings	Weekly Hours
1909....	$.19	$10	51.0	1945....	$1.02	$44	43.5
1914....	.22	11	49.4	1950....	1.44	58	40.5
1920....	.55	26	47.4	1955....	1.86	76	40.7
1925....	.54	24	44.5	1960....	2.26	90	39.7
1930....	.55	23	42.1	1965....	2.61	108	41.2
1935....	.54	20	36.6	1970....	3.36	134	39.8
1940....	.66	25	38.1	1975....	4.81	190	39.4

Table 605

MANUFACTURING – AVERAGE DAILY WAGES

Occupation	1860	1865	1870	1876	1880
Skilled occupations	$1.62	$2.50	$2.61	$2.24	$2.26
Blacksmiths..........	1.64	2.61	2.68	2.32	2.31
Carpenters..........	1.65	2.68	2.64	2.12	2.15
Engineers...........	1.61	2.33	2.47	2.17	2.17
Machinists..........	1.61	2.56	2.67	2.34	2.45
Painters............	1.62	2.31	2.67	2.20	2.21
Laborers	1.03	1.48	1.52	1.33	1.32

Table 584
Resident Population, by States

Covers some States as territories or before statehood.

Population[1] (1,000)

State	1790	1820	1840	1860	1880	1900	1920	1940
U.S.[1]	3.9	9.6	17.1	31.4	50.2	76.0	105.7	131.7
Ala	x	128	591	964	1,263	1,829	2,348	2,833
Alaska	x	x	x	x	33	64	55	73
Ariz	x	x	x	x	40	123	334	499
Ark	x	14	98	435	803	1,312	1,752	1,949
Calif	x	x	x	380	865	1,485	3,427	6,907
Colo	x	x	x	34	194	540	940	1,123
Conn	238	275	310	460	623	908	1,381	1,709
Del	59	73	78	112	147	185	223	267
D.C.	x	23	34	75	178	279	438	663
Fla	x	x	54	140	269	529	968	1,897
Ga	83	341	691	1,057	1,542	2,216	2,896	3,124
Hawaii	x	x	x	x	x	154	256	423
Idaho	x	x	x	x	33	162	432	525
Ill	x	55	476	1,712	3,078	4,822	6,485	7,897
Ind	x	147	686	1,350	1,978	2,516	2,930	3,428
Iowa	x	x	43	675	1,625	2,232	2,404	2,538
Kans	x	x	x	107	996	1,470	1,769	1,801
Ky	74	564	780	1,156	1,649	2,147	2,417	2,846
La	x	153	352	708	940	1,382	1,799	2,364
Maine	97	298	502	628	649	694	768	847
Md	320	407	470	687	935	1,188	1,450	1,821
Mass	379	523	738	1,231	1,783	2,805	3,852	4,317
Mich	x	9	212	749	1,637	2,421	3,668	5,256
Minn	x	x	x	172	781	1,751	2,387	2,792
Miss	x	75	376	791	1,132	1,551	1,791	2,184
Mo	x	67	384	1,182	2,168	3,107	3,404	3,785
Mont	x	x	x	x	39	243	549	559
Nebr	x	x	x	29	452	1,066	1,296	1,316
Nev	x	x	x	7	62	42	77	110
N.H.	142	244	285	326	347	412	443	492
N.J.	184	278	373	672	1,131	1,884	3,156	4,160
N. Mex	x	x	x	²94	120	195	360	532
N.Y	340	1,373	2,429	3,881	5,083	7,269	10,385	13,479
N.C.	394	639	753	993	1,400	1,894	2,559	3,572
N. Dak	x	x	x	5	37	319	647	642
Ohio	x	581	1,519	2,340	3,198	4,158	5,759	6,908
Okla	x	x	x	x	x	790	2,028	2,336
Oreg	x	x	x	52	175	414	783	1,090
Pa	434	1,049	1,724	2,906	4,283	6,302	8,720	9,900
R.I.	69	83	109	175	277	429	604	713
S.C.	249	503	594	704	996	1,340	1,684	1,900
S. Dak	x	x	x	x	98	402	637	643
Tenn	36	423	829	1,110	1,542	2,021	2,338	2,916
Tex	x	x	x	604	1,592	3,049	4,663	6,415
Utah	x	x	x	40	144	277	449	550
Vt	85	236	292	315	332	344	352	359
Va	692	938	1,025	1,220	1,513	1,854	2,309	2,678
Wash	x	x	x	³12	75	518	1,357	1,736
W. Va	56	137	225	377	618	959	1,464	1,902
Wis	x	x	31	776	1,315	2,069	2,632	3,138
Wyo	x	x	x	x	21	93	194	251

na Not available.   x Not applicable.   [1]U.S. figures in millions, State figures in thousands.

Table 584
Resident Population, by States

Population[1] (1,000)			Population per square mile of land							
1960	1970	1975	1790	1840	1880	1920	1960	1970	1975	State
179.3	203.2	213.1	4.5	9.5	16.9	35.0	49.6	56.2	60.3	U.S.
3,267	3,444	3,614	x	11.5	24.6	45.8	64.2	67.9	71.3	Ala.
226	300	352	x	x	na	.1	.4	.5	.6	Alaska
1,302	1,771	2,224	x	x	.4	2.9	11.5	15.6	19.6	Ariz.
1,786	1,923	2,116	x	1.9	15.3	33.4	34.2	37.0	40.7	Ark.
15,717	19,953	21,185	x	x	5.5	22.0	100.4	127.6	135.5	Calif.
1,754	2,207	2,534	x	x	1.9	9.1	16.9	21.3	24.4	Colo.
2,535	3,032	3,095	49.4	64.3	129.2	286.4	520.6	623.6	636.6	Conn.
446	548	579	30.1	39.7	74.6	113.5	225.2	276.5	292.1	Del.
764	757	716	x	486	3,063	7,293	12,524	12,402	11,738	D.C.
4,952	6,789	8,357	x	1.0	4.9	17.7	91.5	125.5	154.5	Fla.
3,943	4,590	4,926	.6	11.8	26.3	49.3	67.8	79.0	84.8	Ga.
633	769	865	x	x	x	39.9	98.5	119.6	134.6	Hawaii
667	713	820	x	x	.4	5.2	8.1	8.6	9.9	Idaho
10,081	11,114	11,145	x	8.5	55.0	115.7	180.4	199.4	199.9	Ill.
4,662	5,194	5,311	x	19.1	55.1	81.3	128.8	143.9	147.1	Ind.
2,758	2,824	2,870	x	.2	29.2	43.2	49.2	50.5	51.3	Iowa
2,179	2,247	2,267	x	x	12.2	21.6	26.6	27.5	27.7	Kans.
3,038	3,219	3,396	1.8	19.4	41.0	60.2	76.2	81.2	85.6	Ky.
3,257	3,641	3,791	x	7.8	20.7	39.6	72.2	81.0	84.4	La.
969	992	1,059	3.2	16.8	21.7	25.7	31.3	32.1	34.2	Maine
3,101	3,922	4,098	32.0	47.3	94.0	145.8	313.5	396.6	414.3	Md.
5,149	5,689	5,828	47.1	91.7	221.8	479.2	657.3	727.0	744.7	Mass.
7,823	8,875	9,157	x	3.7	28.5	63.8	137.7	156.2	161.2	Mich.
3,414	3,805	3,926	x	x	9.7	29.5	43.1	48.0	49.5	Minn.
2,178	2,217	2,346	x	8.1	24.4	38.6	46.0	46.9	49.6	Miss.
4,320	4,677	4,763	x	5.6	31.6	49.5	62.6	67.8	69.0	Mo.
675	694	748	x	x	.3	3.8	4.6	4.8	5.1	Mont.
1,411	1,483	1,546	x	x	5.9	16.9	18.4	19.4	20.2	Nebr.
285	489	592	x	x	.6	.7	2.6	4.4	5.4	Nev.
607	738	818	15.7	31.5	38.4	49.1	67.2	81.7	90.6	N.H.
6,067	7,168	7,316	24.5	49.7	150.5	420.0	805.5	953.1	972.7	N.J.
951	1,016	1,147	x	x	1.0	2.9	7.8	8.4	9.4	N. Mex.
16,782	18,237	18,120	7.1	51.0	106.7	217.9	350.6	381.3	378.8	N.Y.
4,556	5,082	5,451	8.1	15.5	28.7	52.5	93.2	104.1	111.7	N.C.
632	618	635	x	x	.9	9.2	9.1	8.9	9.2	N. Dak.
9,706	10,652	10,759	x	37.3	78.5	141.4	236.6	260.0	262.6	Ohio
2,328	2,559	2,712	x	x	x	29.2	33.8	37.2	39.4	Okla.
1,769	2,091	2,288	x	x	1.8	8.2	18.4	21.7	23.8	Oreg.
11,319	11,794	11,827	9.7	38.5	95.5	194.5	251.4	262.3	263.0	Pa.
859	947	927	64.5	102.0	259.2	566.4	819.3	902.5	883.7	R.I.
2,383	2,591	2,818	8.2	19.5	32.6	55.2	78.7	85.7	93.2	S.C.
681	666	683	x	x	na	8.3	9.0	8.8	9.0	S. Dak.
3,567	3,924	4,188	.8	19.9	37.0	56.1	86.2	94.9	101.3	Tenn.
9,580	11,197	12,237	x	x	6.1	17.8	36.4	42.7	46.7	Tex.
891	1,059	1,206	x	x	1.8	5.5	10.8	12.9	14.7	Utah
390	444	471	9.4	32.0	36.4	38.6	42.0	47.9	50.8	Vt.
3,967	4,648	4,967	11.6	19.3	37.6	57.4	99.6	116.9	124.9	Va.
2,853	3,409	3,544	x	x	1.1	20.3	42.8	51.2	53.2	Wash.
1,860	1,744	1,803	na	na	25.7	60.9	77.2	72.5	74.9	W. Va.
3,952	4,418	4,607	x	.4	23.8	47.6	72.6	81.1	84.6	Wis.
330	332	374	x	x	.2	2.0	3.4	3.4	3.8	Wyo.

[2]Includes part of Arizona Territory.   [3]Includes Idaho and parts of Montana and Wyoming.

5. Here are a few more tables from the same Bicentennial booklet. You may want to use some information from the tables shown in Case 4 to help you to draw conclusions about prices and income in the United States. Write a short report explaining your conclusions and emphasizing your main points with graphic representations.

Table 609
CONSUMER AND WHOLESALE PRICE INDEXES

						Consumer			
							Food		
Year	Con-sumer	Year	Con-sumer	Whole-sale	Year	All items	at home	Hous-ing	Whole-sale
1800.....	51	1860.....	27	na	1915....	30	29	na	36
1805.....	45	1865.....	46	na	1920....	60	62	na	80
1810.....	47	1870.....	38	na	1925....	53	48	na	53
1815.....	55	1875.....	33	na	1930....	50	46	na	45
1820.....	42	1880.....	29	na	1935....	41	37	49	41
1825.....	34	1885.....	27	na	1940....	42	35	52	41
1830.....	32	1890.....	27	29	1945....	54	51	59	55
1835.....	31	1895.....	25	25	1950....	72	75	73	82
1840.....	30	1900.....	25	29	1955....	80	84	82	88
1845.....	28	1905.....	27	31	1960....	89	90	90	95
1850.....	25	1910.....	28	36	1965....	95	96	95	97
1855.....	28				1970....	116	114	119	110
					1975....	161	176	167	175

1967 = 100   na   Not available.

Table 610
WHOLESALE PRICES OF SELECTED COMMODITIES

In dollars. Figures in parentheses reflect changing market locations of commodities priced and possible changing uniformity in commodity composition.

Year	Wheat flour[1]	Sugar (lb.)	Cotton, raw (lb.)	Wool (lb.)	Coal, anthracite (ton)	Copper (lb.)
1800	10.03	.13	.24	na	na	.53
1810	9.65	.13	.16	na	na	.43
1820	4.71	.12	.17	.75	na	.29
1830	4.99	.07	.10	.39	9.05	.22
1840	5.30	.06	.09	.39	4.91	.25
1850	5.55	.07	.12	(.83)	3.64	.23
1860	5.19	(.10)	.11	1.03	3.40	(.23)
1870	(9.28)	.14	.24	.90	4.39	.21
1880	8.90	.10	.12	1.03	4.53	.22
1890	(4.65)	(.06)	(.11)	(.72)	(3.35)	.16
1900	3.35	.05	.10	.66	3.92	.17
1910	4.69	.05	.15	.69	4.81	.13
1920	11.58	.13	.34	1.60	9.50	.18
1930	4.87	.05	.14	.76	12.72	.13
1940	4.31	.04	.10	.97	9.55	.12
1950	(5.43)	.08	.36	1.98	12.58	.22
1960	4.99	.09	.31	1.16	13.95	.33
1970	5.57	.11	.25	1.03	16.57	na
1975	9.37	.31	.45	1.49	44.86	.64

na Not available.   [1]Prior to 1950, 196-lb. barrel; thereafter, 100 lb.

Table 611
RETAIL PRICES OF SELECTED FOODS

Year	Flour (5 lb.)	Bread (lb.)	Sugar (lb.)	Round Steak (lb.)	Pork chops (lb.)	Butter (lb.)	Eggs (doz.)	Milk Delivered (½ gal.)	Potatoes (10 lb.)
1890	.15	na	.07	.12	.11	.26	.21	.14	.16
1900	.13	na	.06	.13	.12	.26	.21	.14	.14
1910	.18	na	.06	.17	.19	.36	.34	.17	.17
1920	.41	.12	.19	.40	.42	.70	.68	.33	.63
1930	.23	.09	.06	.43	.36	.46	.45	.28	.36
1933	.20	.07	.05	.26	.20	.28	.29	.21	.23
1940	.22	.08	.05	.36	.28	.36	.33	.26	.24
1946	.35	.10	.08	.52	.49	.71	.59	.35	.47
1950	.49	.14	.10	.94	.75	.73	.60	.41	.46
1955	.54	.18	.10	.90	.79	.71	.61	.46	.56
1960	.55	.20	.12	1.06	.86	.75	.57	.52	.72
1965	.58	.21	.12	1.08	.97	.75	.53	.53	.94
1970	.59	.24	.13	1.30	1.16	.87	.61	.66	.90
1975	1.00	.36	.37	1.89	1.86	1.03	.77	[1].75	1.34

In dollars.   na Not available.   [1]1973 price.

Table 614
NATIONAL INCOME MEASURES

Year	NI	PI	DPI	Year	NI	PI	DPI
1897-1901 avg	15	14	14	1935	56	60	58
1902-06 avg	21	20	20	1940	80	78	75
1907-11 avg	27	27	26	1945	181	170	149
1912-16 avg	35	34	33	1950	236	226	206
1917-21 avg	67	63	61	1955	328	309	273
1925	78	75	73	1960	412	400	349
1929	85	85	82	1965	566	537	472
1930	74	76	74	1970	798	801	686
1933	40	47	45	1975	1,208	1,246	1,077

In billions of dollars. NI = National income, PI = Personal income, DPI = Disposable personal income.

Chapter 12

Comparing Things, People, Situations, and Ideas

To the Student:

As you read chapter 12 and complete the exercises and cases, you will be asked to

. . . state the problem to be solved

. . . develop criteria to help solve it

. . . use the criteria to analyze information

. . . outline your solution clearly

. . . write the results of your analysis in an appropriate format.

Like other methods of inquiry you have studied, comparison is a way of organizing information for a useful purpose. Because it is basic to our thought processes, we engage in it naturally many times a day. When we wonder "Should I wear the brown suit or the blue suit," "Should I stop at the bank before or after work," "Who should I discuss the new plan with first, Barbara or Jerry," we are comparing the merits of things, people, situations, and ideas. Thoughts like these pass through our minds almost unconsciously, just as we make decisions about them without submitting them to prolonged analysis. We decide to wear the blue suit because it's closer to the front of the closet. We cash the check before going to work because, as we approach the bank, we notice a free drive-in window. We talk to Jerry first because we happen to meet him on the way in to work. These informal comparisons result in equally informal decisions. In this chapter, you will study comparison as a formal way of organizing information to help make decisions.

WHAT IS COMPARISON?

Comparison is a statement of likenesses or differences between things, people, situations, and ideas. To make the distinction between likenesses and differences clear, we generally say that comparison is a statement of likeness while contrast is a statement of difference.

Traditionally, comparisons and contrasts have been limited to choices between two items like the comparisons you read in the first paragraph. Yet in any real situation, the decision may be among three or four items. For example, if you are buying a new television set, you may limit your choice initially to sets with black matrix picture tubes. That initial decision leaves you with sets from at least three different manufacturers to compare before deciding which to buy. Thus, while some comparisons are between two items, all comparisons are not necessarily limited to two.

Why Make Comparisons?

You make comparisons to assess the relative merits of two or more items so that you can make a decision about them. For example, you may want to find out which utility might be the best investment, what tape recorder is the best buy, or whether working for a small company is more advantageous than working for a large one. Because decisions like these are important, they deserve point-by-point analysis. Only through this kind of systematic analysis can one reach a wise decision.

What May Be Compared?

To make valid comparisons, you must have at least two items in the same class. Your first task, then, is to make sure items for comparison are in the same class. No one would compare Saks Fifth Avenue and Johnny's Gas Station because their only similarity is that they are both retail outlets. Most people would recognize immediately that they are not in the same class. Items to be compared must share traits or characteristics beyond superficial similarities.

Can you compare Reggie Jackson, right fielder of the California Angels, and Dave Gantz, right fielder of the Loganport Vultures, a Little League baseball team? They seem to have many characteristics in common. Both play right field; both use the same kinds of skills to hit, run, and field. A paragraph comparing them might look like this.

> Last season, Dave Gantz played better than Reggie Jackson. Gantz was more productive offensively than Jackson. For example, his batting average was higher than Jackson's. Gantz hit .451 while Jackson hit .299. Gantz stole 35 bases; Jackson stole 12. Gantz was never caught stealing. Jackson was thrown out three times. Gantz also played better defensively. Gantz's record shows he played right field flawlessly. No errors were recorded against him last season. By contrast, Jackson made five fielding errors. Thus, statistics for last season show that Dave Gantz outplayed Reggie Jackson both offensively and defensively.

Although the writer has used the same criteria to judge each player, does this paragraph convince you that Dave Gantz is a better baseball player than Reggie Jackson? Why not? This paragraph reduces comparison to the absurd. By choosing only information that supports Gantz's case and leaving out all the information that supports Jackson's case, the writer "proves" Gantz is superior to Jackson. Leaving out pertinent information biases writing. Such writing hides rather than reveals information.

HOW DO YOU WRITE COMPARISONS?

Preparing a message that uses comparison as the chief technique for organizing information includes several steps both in pre-writing and in writing. You are already familiar with some of these steps. Others will be new to you.

Define the Subject

Your first step is defining the subject by answering why, what, where, when, and who about the subject. In writing comparisons, you will have two or more subjects because you will be comparing two or more items. Completion of this step will help you focus on your purpose for writing.

Select Criteria

Criteria, as you learned in chapter 9, are tests you apply to an item you are defining. You also call criteria standards or bases for judgment. They are factors outside the items you are comparing which give you common ground upon which to make a comparison.

To be useful, criteria must be the same for all the items you are comparing. For example, if three people applied for a position as senior auditor, and the first were judged on his relationship to the president of the company, the second on his physical characteristics, and the third on his work experience, the comparison would be unfair because different criteria were applied to each of them. The criteria must be the same for each job candidate for a true comparison to take place.

Exercise A List several criteria upon which you might base your judgment on the following topics.

1. Choice of a used car

2. Choice of an apartment

3. Choice of an employer with whom you would like to interview

4. Choice of employees who have earned pay raises

Criteria must also relate directly to the solution of the problem you are working on. For example, physical characteristics would not be a useful criterion by which to compare job candidates for the senior auditor position because whether the candidates are short or tall, handsome or ugly, fat or skinny has no bearing on their ability to do the work. On the other hand, physical characteristics would be a useful criterion for modeling or acting jobs. As you can see, criteria change for each different problem you are working on.

The order in which you organize criteria also changes according to the problem. For instance, a student living on a small income might rank price as the first, or most important, criterion for choosing a used car. A person buying a used car as a second vehicle for getting back and forth to work might rank gas mileage as the most important criterion.

Exercise B   Rank criteria you have selected in Exercise A from most to least important according to the situations that follow.

1. a. Your part-time job is to deliver papers on a rural route in your own car.

   b. You just won $100,000 in the state lottery.

2. a. You do not own a car and the city has no bus service.

   b. You must take in a room-mate to make ends meet financially.

3. a. You've been out of work for a year.

4. a. The boss's son works in your department.

b. You have severe asthma.

b. The new system is for merit, not seniority.

Analyze Information

To be useful as a method of inquiry, comparison requires the writer to give facts as well as to interpret them. Giving facts without interpretation does only half the work because it leaves interpretation up to the reader. By the same token, giving an interpretation without the facts, for example, saying, "A is superior to B" or "C is more efficient than D" without saying why, is not sufficient either. Without the facts, the reader cannot judge how the writer arrived at the interpretation or whether the interpretation is correct. After defining the subject and selecting criteria, your next step is to gather facts relevant to making a decision, as you will see Dave Benedict do in his analysis of sites in the sample case. Then you can outline and write your message.

Outline the Message

You can outline the body of the message based on comparison in two different ways. You can begin with the first criterion and examine each choice on that basis, proceeding through the list of criteria. Or you can begin with the first choice and examine it in relation to all the criteria, proceeding through the list of choices. Your outline will follow either Form A or Form B.

Form A	*Form B*
I. Introductory paragraph	I. Introductory paragraph
II. Body	II. Body
A. Criterion 1	A. Choice 1
1. Choice 1	1. Criterion 1
2. Choice 2	2. Criterion 2
3. Choice 3	3. Criterion 3
B. Criterion 2	B. Choice 2
1. Choice 1	1. Criterion 1
2. Choice 2	2. Criterion 2
3. Choice 3	3. Criterion 3
(and so forth)	(and so forth)
III. Conclusion	III. Conclusion

Write the Purpose Statement

The purpose statement of your message must indicate more than that you are making a choice. It must state clearly what your choice is. The following guidelines will help you make your choice clear in the purpose statement.

1. *Name the items you are comparing.* If you have two candidates for a job, name both candidates: Kerry Wilvert and Fran McCall. If you are comparing products, such as calculators, name them: PH-57, Duosonic, DataCalc.

2. *Indicate your choice by the order in which you name items.* If you select Kerry Wilvert instead of Fran McCall, put Wilvert's name first. If your purpose statement is a complex sentence, put your choice in the main clause and subordinate other items: "Although PH-57 and Duosonic are capable of numerous functions, the DataCalc performs more of the functions we need."

3. *State your preference clearly in the predicate.* "Kerry Wilvert rather than Fran McCall is Trendex's choice for the senior auditor position." "The DataCalc calculator performs more functions at a lower cost than do the PH-57 and the Duosonic."

Sample Case

Dave Benedict is site inspector on the locations staff of Finn and Sons, a company that franchises Flying Finn outlets, an automotive service specializing in one-stop fast oil change and lubrication.

Dave's job is a traveling one. He visits cities large enough to support one or more stations that offer such service and evaluates possible sites that may later be franchised. He looks for closed full-service gas stations which may be purchased and remodeled to meet the special requirements of the new service business. He automatically refuses to consider sites that are not located on main city roads or sites that cannot be modified for "drive-through" service. He also does not consider stations that need extensive remodeling or repair. Because the new business requires pits rather than hoists in the service bays, Benedict can only consider property that is for sale rather than for lease.

These many restrictions often mean that a city of 100,000 will have only three or four possible sites. Benedict fills out a site evaluation form for each possible site and writes a memo report to Frank Finn, Jr., the marketing manager, explaining his findings. This week he is visiting Plainfield, Wisconsin. Here is the raw material from which he must write his weekly report.

Area map showing possible sites in Plainfield, Wisconsin

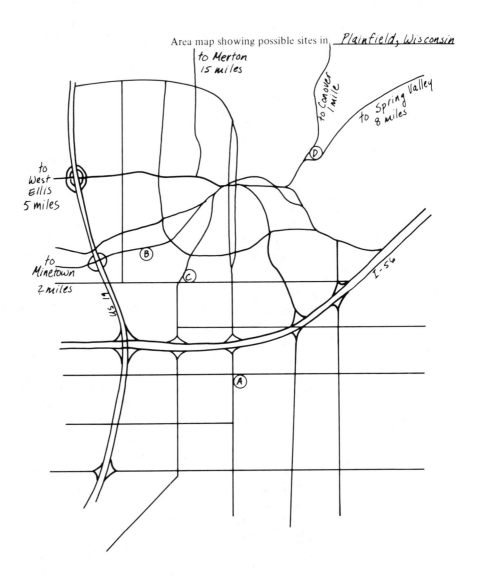

to Merton
15 miles

to Conover
1 mile

to Spring Valley
8 miles

D

to
West
Ellis
5 miles

to
Minetown
2 miles

B

C

A

US 19

I-56

SITE EVALUATION FORM

Site Designation: ___A___

Address: ___6004 S. Evergreen_____

___Plainfield, Wisc._____

Cost: ___Asking $57,500. (for sale) (5 yrs.)___   Taxes: ___$2700._____

Visibility from road: Good __✓__ Fair _____ Poor _____

On-site parking: Room for __15__ cars

Size: Office area: _____8' X 14'_____

No. of car bays: ___3___

Other:

2 cement platforms for gas pump must be removed

Speed limit at site: __35__ miles per hour (Evergreen)
              25 m.p.h. (Walnut)

Traffic volume:

Comments:

Evergreen is a 5-lane major north-south route for local traffic from 3 southern suburbs to city center. Walnut is one of 3 through streets from western residential area to eastern industrial area. Traffic light at intersection. Station access from both streets. Evergreen volume high all day. 60% of Walnut volume in rush hours.

Nearby businesses:

Comments:

Evergreen is a commercial strip. Nearest self-service gas is ½ mile north or 1½ miles south. Nearest full-service station is 1 mile south on west side of Evergreen & 2 miles on East side. No gas on walnut.

Area Analysis (1/2 mile radius):

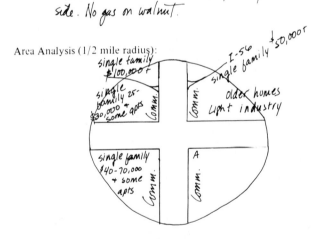

Comments:

Except for the strip which goes north 2miles and south 2miles, the west of Evergreen is single-unit housing with a few small apt. complexes. On the east, the housing is a mix of inexpensive plat and older houses, then light industry.

SITE EVALUATION FORM

Site Designation: ___B___

Address: ___4508 West Brookings___

___Plainfield, Wisc.___

Cost: ___$50,000.___   Taxes: ___$2300___

Visibility from road: Good ____ Fair _✓_ Poor ____

On-site parking: Room for __10__ cars

Size: Office area: ____7' x 15'____

No. of car bays: ___2___

Other:

Small outside storage shed

Speed limit at site: __40__ miles per hour

Traffic volume: ↑N

_____

_16,900_ ⟶

_____

⟵ _15,700_

                              ⓑ

Comments:

Brookings is the business route for I-56 and US-19. A 5-lane road. It also leads west to a suburb just 3 miles after US-19. Commuters from the west and south use the road to reach city center and the state university.

Nearby businesses:

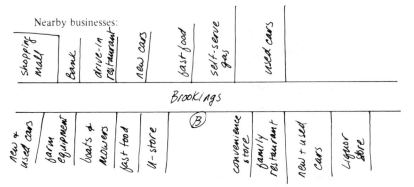

Comments:

The area pays only county, not city taxes. Highway businesses fairly well patronized.

Area Analysis (1/2 mile radius):

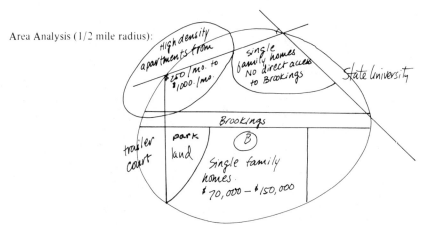

Comments:

Area to the NW is multiple dwelling for nearly 2 square miles. State university enrolls 20,000 students. Many patronize businesses on Brookings or use the road to reach US 19

SITE EVALUATION FORM

Site Designation: _____C_____

Address: ___910 S. Arlington Ave._____

___Plainfield, Wisc._____

Cost: ___$42,000._____ Taxes: ___$3000._____

Visibility from road: Good __✓__ Fair _____ Poor _____

On-site parking: Room for __6__ cars

Size:

Office area: ___8' x 8'_____

No. of car bays: __1__

Other:

Speed limit at site: __25__ miles per hour

Traffic volume:

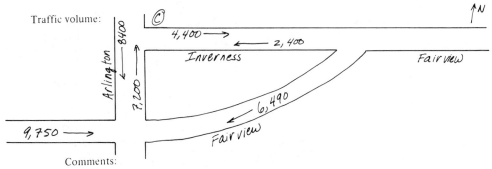

Comments:

    Site is accessible from both Inverness and Arlington. Traffic Light at Fairview and Arlington. No left turn southbound on Arlington to Fairview; traffic must turn left at Inverness. Inverness dead ends at Arlington. Fairview is one of 4 east-west thorofares on the south side of the city. 70% of Arlington traffic is in rush hours. (7-9am, 3:30-5pm)

Nearby businesses:

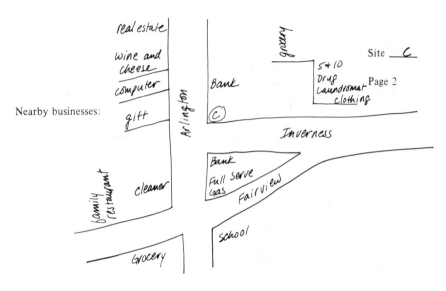

Site ___C___

Page 2

Comments: Corner business center patronized heavily by local residents

Area Analysis (1/2 mile radius):

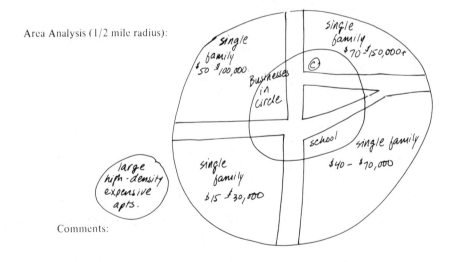

Comments:

276

SITE EVALUATION FORM

Site Designation: _____D_____

Address: _____3801 Maryhill Rd._____

_____Plainfield, Wisc._____

Cost: _____$32,000._____ Taxes: _____$1580._____

Visibility from road: Good _____ Fair _✓_ Poor _✓_ (good south and west but obscured by bridge northbound)

On-site parking: Room for _15_ cars

Size:

    Office area: _____12' X 15'_____

    No. of car bays: _____3_____

    Other: _Unusually deep lot_

Speed limit at site: _25_ miles per hour

Traffic volume:

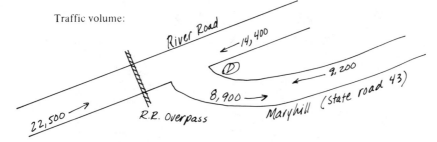

Comments:

    80% of River Road volume is commuter; 70% of Maryhill is commuter. Access to site from both streets.

Nearby businesses:

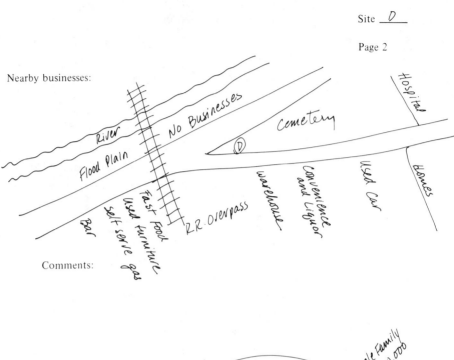

River

Flood Plain

No Businesses

Cemetery

Hospital

Used Car

homes

warehouse

Convenience and Liquor

R.R. Overpass

Fast Food

Used furniture

self serve gas

Bar

Comments:

Area Analysis (1/2 mile radius):

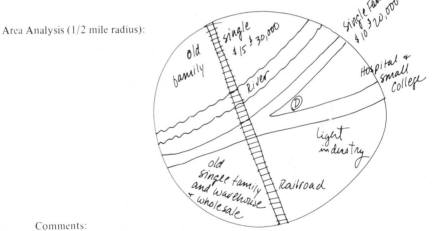

old family

single $15 $30,000

River

single Family $10 $20,000

Hospital & small College

light industry

old single family and warehouse + wholesale

Railroad

Comments:

Working class neighborhood. May become more industrial.

Dave Benedict's assignment is clear: to write a memo to Frank Finn, his supervisor, recommending one of the four sites he has visited in Plainfield. Before he can begin his memo, he must review the information he has gathered in relation to the company's criteria for site selection. The company looks for the following characteristics, in the order given, in its sites.

1. Availability of customers
2. Traffic pattern
3. Access to the site
4. Visibility of the site from the road
5. Space available at the site
6. Price of the site

Benedict uses these criteria to judge each site he has visited. Here are his notes.

NOTES ON SITE SELECTION

	Facts	*Interpretation*
1. Availability of Customers		
Site A	V. Good	In Plainfield's busiest commercial area near low-middle income, single-family housing, a few small apt. complexes.
Site B	V. Good	Busy commercial area. High density apts., middle-income, single-family housing, State U.
Site C	Good	Residential area with a few businesses. Range of single-family housing from low to high income.
Site D	Poor	Industrial area. Some old, low-income, single-family housing.
2. Traffic Pattern		
Site A	V. Good	26,300 daily volume on Evergreen; 14,448 on Walnut. Volume continuous on Evergreen, 60% at rush hours on Walnut. Speed limits: 35 mph on Evergreen, 25 on Walnut.

Site B	Good	32,600 daily on W. Brookings. Heavy commuter traffic to city center. Speed limit: 40 mph.
Site C	Good	6,800 on Inverness; 16,240 on Fairview; 15,600 on Arlington. 70% of Arlington traffic during rush hours. Speed limit: 25 mph.
Site D	V. Good	36,900 daily on River Rd.; 18,100 on Maryhill. 80% commuter on River Rd; 70% commuter on Maryhill. Speed limit: 25 mph.

3. Access to Site

Site A	V. Good	Traffic light at corner. Turn lane on Evergreen. 2-way traffic on intersecting streets. Accessible from dwellings and both streets.
Site B	Good	No traffic light. Turn lane. Good access from W. Brookings. Surrounding homes have poor access to W. Brookings.
Site C	Poor	No traffic light. No cross traffic. Traffic backs up on Arlington and Inverness, waiting to make turns.
Site D	Poor	No traffic light. Access to site from both streets. Poor access from area homes — cut off by river. 2-mile detour to reach site.

4. Visibility of Site from Road

Site A	Good	Site is on corner. View unobstructed from road.
Site B	Fair	Site in middle of strip. Signs from other businesses obstruct view.
Site C	Good	Site on corner; no obstructions.

Site D	Fair	Good visibility for south- and westbound traffic. View obscured by bridge for north- and eastbound traffic.

5. Space Availability

Site A	V. Good	Parking for 15 cars. 3 car bays. 8'x14' office.
Site B	Good	Parking for 10 cars. 2 car bays. 7'x15' office.
Site C	Poor	Parking for 6 cars. 1 bay. 8'x8' office.
Site D	V. Good	Parking for 15 cars. 3 bays. 12'x15' office. Deep lot.

6. Price of Site

Site A	Highest	Cost, $57,500 (on market for 5 years). Taxes, $2,700. (2 cement gas pump platforms must be removed.)
Site B	2nd high	Cost, $50,000. Taxes, $2,300.
Site C	3rd high	Cost, $42,000. Taxes, $3,000.
Site D	Lowest	Cost, $32,000. Taxes, $1,500.

Dave Benedict comes to several conclusions on the basis of his notes.

1. He will recommend Site A. It got the highest ratings possible in each criterion except price, the least important of Finn and Sons' criteria. Further, because the site has been on the market for five years, the asking price may come down if Finn makes a firm offer.

2. Site B is his second choice because it is inferior to A in several high-ranking criteria—traffic pattern, access, and visibility.

3. Sites C and D are unacceptable in nearly all of the criteria except price.

Benedict's next step is to outline his message. He decides to use direct order so that Finn will not have to read to the end of the memo to learn his recommendation and the reasoning behind it. He will also use a Form B outline to give Finn a clear picture of each site as a whole. Here is how his outline looks.

OUTLINE: SITE SELECTION

I. Introduction

   A. Recommendation of Site A

   B. Reasons for recommending Site A rather than Site B according to the criteria

II. Body

   A. Site A

      1. Availability of customers: very good
      2. Traffic pattern: very good
      3. Access to site: very good
      4. Visibility of site: good
      5. Space availability: very good
      6. Price: highest

   B. Site B

      1. Availability of customers: very good
      2. Traffic pattern: good
      3. Access to site: good
      4. Visibility of site: fair
      5. Space availability: good
      6. Price: second highest

   C. Site C

      1. Availability of customers: good
      2. Traffic pattern: good
      3. Access to site: poor
      4. Visibility of site: good
      5. Space availability: poor
      6. Price: third highest

   D. Site D

      1. Availability of customers: poor
      2. Traffic pattern: very good
      3. Access to site: poor
      4. Visibility of site: fair
      5. Space availability: very good
      6. Price: lowest

As you can see, Benedict outlined the body of the memo in descending order of importance from best site to worst. He places Site A first because that is his first choice, the site he will recommend. He talks about Site B second because it is his second choice and so forth through Sites C and D, his third and fourth choices. Having finished these preliminaries, he prepares the following memo to submit to his supervisor.

MEMO

To: Frank Finn, Jr., Marketing Manager

From: Dave Benedict, Site Inspector 🖉

Subject: Site Recommendation in Plainfield, Wisconsin

Date: October 13, 198-

I recommend purchasing the service station at 6004 South Evergreen (designated as Site A on the attached evaluation forms) for purchase. Of the four sites available in Plainfield, Site A best fits company criteria for establishing Flying Finn franchises. It received "very good" or "good" ratings in (1) availability of customers, (2) traffic pattern, (3) access, (4) visibility, and (5) space.

The other possible choice for a Flying Finn franchise was the service station at 4508 West Brookings (Site B). However, as you will see from the following description of each site, Site B got the same rating, "very good," as Site A in availability of customers but ranked lower in traffic pattern, access, visibility, and space.

Site A: 6004 South Evergreen

Site A rated a "very good" in availability to customers. It is in Plainfield's busiest commercial area, near low- and middle-income, single-family housing and a few small apartment complexes. The volume of traffic passing the site is high: 26,300 vehicles daily on Evergreen and 14,448 on Walnut. While 60 percent of the traffic on Walnut occurs during rush hours, the traffic is continuous on Evergreen throughout the day. Further, speed limits of 35 m.p.h. on Evergreen and 25 m.p.h. on Walnut, the traffic light at the intersection of Evergreen and Walnut, and the turn lane on Evergreen let drivers stop at Site A without danger.

Its position at the intersection makes the site visible and accessible to people living in the area as well as to commuters. Because Site A has 15 parking spaces, customers can leave their cars to be serviced while they shop at nearby retail outlets. The three bays also offer the possibility of future expansion, and the 8-foot by 14-foot office provides enough space for the service counter and waiting room.

The asking price for this site is $57,500. Because it
has been on the market for five years, the owners may lower
the price if a firm offer were tendered. City taxes are
$2,700 a year. Additionally, two cement platforms which
formerly held gas pumps need to be removed.

Site B: 4508 West Brookings

In a busy commercial area, Site B also has very good
customer availability. High density apartments, middle-
income, single-family housing, and the state university
surround the site. Traffic volume along Brookings is heavy
(32,600 daily); however, much of it is commuter traffic
traveling at the speed limit of 40 m.p.h. Commuters are
less likely to stop going to and from work than are residents or shoppers.

Although Site B is far from traffic lights at the
intersection, Brookings does have a turn lane; access from
Brookings itself is also good. However, because Site B is
in the middle of the commercial strip, surrounding homes
and apartments have little direct access to it. The site
has only fair visibility from the road because signs of
other businesses obstruct the view. It is large enough for
our purposes with parking for 10 cars, 2 car bays, and a
7-foot by 15-foot office. Site B costs $50,000. County
taxes are $2,300 a year.

Site C: 910 South Arlington Avenue

Site C, which got a "good" rating for customer availability, is in a small commercial complex in the middle of
a residential area of single-family dwellings. Homes in
this area range from low to high income. Traffic volume is
good (38,600 daily), traveling at 25 m.p.h. Seventy percent of the 15,600 cars using Arlington represents commuter
traffic, however.

Access to Site C is poor. Site C has no cross traffic
(Inverness deadends at Arlington). Motorists may not turn
left from Arlington onto Inverness, and the traffic light
is at the next corner. Traffic backs up on Arlington and
Inverness during rush hours, causing jams which make access
to the site difficult.

Although visibility is good, Site C is too small for
our purposes. It parks six cars and has only one bay. The
office is 8 feet by 8 feet. Site C costs $42,000 plus
$3,000 in yearly taxes.

Site D: 3801 Maryhill Road

Availability of customers at Site D is poor. This
site is in an industrial area near some old, low-income,
single-family housing. Daily traffic volume is high;
36,900 vehicles pass along River Road and 18,100 along
Maryhill. However, this traffic, traveling at 25 m.p.h.,
is 80 percent commuter on River Road and 70 percent
commuter on Maryhill. Although Site D is accessible from
both River Road and Maryhill, I rated access as poor
because the corner has no traffic light and because area
homes are cut off from the site by a river. Residents
living across the river would need to make a two-mile
detour to reach 3801 Maryhill. Visibility is good from the
north and west but poor from the south because a bridge
obscures the site from the south.

Site D ranks well in the least important criteria,
space availability and price. It can park 15 cars, has 3
bays, a 12-foot by 15-foot office, and a deep lot. It
costs $32,000. Taxes are $1,580 a year.

Conclusion

Although Site A costs more than the other three sites
I visited, it offers the best return on investment. This
site has the biggest volume of casual traffic--customers on
errands who will use our services, rather than commuters
bound on getting to and from home without stopping. For
these reasons as well as others I've already mentioned,
Site A is the best location for a Flying Finn franchise.

Attachments: Outline map of Plainfield, Wisconsin
              Evaluation Forms for Site A
                                    Site B
                                    Site C
                                    Site D

Review   In this chapter, you studied comparison as a method of inquiry which will aid you in making decisions about items in the same class. This method enables you to state which of two or more items you would choose, develop criteria to help you make your choice, outline your solution, and write a message that conveys your decision clearly through statement and interpretation of facts.

Cases   1. Your employer is Kay's Potato Chips, a locally owned, small, specialty manufacturer. Since its founding in 1919, the company has expanded from selling in one city to delivering in three states. Gross sales for the last five years are shown in the table below.

Year	Gross Sales
Current	$15,487,632
19– –	15,846,139
19– –	16,001,648
19– –	16,011,437
19– –	16,021,761

Although Kay's has increased prices each year to adjust for inflation, total sales (in both units and dollars) are decreasing. Apparently, some previously loyal customers are deserting the local brand.

Informal investigation shows that Kay's products get good "eye-level" shelf space at most retail outlets. Its prices are the same or slightly lower than national brand prices; and two years ago, Kay's introduced a "No Salt Added" line at regular prices. A pilot taste test showed that Kay's chips are fresh and crisp. Furthermore, no Kay's chip had the slight taste of rancid grease which sometimes can be detected in chips shipped farther to market from the national warehouse centers that larger companies must use as an interim distribution step.

Kay's maintains a fleet of trucks and vans for distribution. The trucks all carry the brand name, logo, and slogan to help advertise the brand on streets and highways. The company spends about $75,000 each summer to sponsor baseball broadcasts on eight key radio stations. This advertising is to keep the company name before the public during the picnic season.

Three times a year, the company takes space in 30 newspapers in the tri-state distribution area to advertise Kay's chips and to offer a "cents-off" coupon for purchases. The ads cost about $4,000 each time, and expenses in redeeming the coupons average $8,000 for each coupon offering. (Only about 10 percent of coupons printed are redeemed at retail outlets.)

Additionally, the company offers all major retail outlets the opportunity to advertise a special price on Kay's chips four times a year. Kay's discounts the wholesale price by 10 or 15 percent during the special promotion week but pays none of the direct advertising costs. (The discount is 10 percent if the chips are listed by name and 15 percent if a picture of the package appears in the ad.) This form of price discounting, charged to the advertising budget, cost the company $30,000 last year.

The company officers agree that these traditional advertising methods are neither holding customers nor attracting new ones. For the next fiscal year, they are willing to double the advertising budget and ask you to plan an effective campaign.

You will want to build your campaign around a single theme to take advantage of the repetition factor in advertising. You will also want to direct your campaign toward a specific audience which regularly buys potato chips. And you will need a schedule to reach your target audience frequently during the year. Re-read the facts in this case to determine your budget for the advertising year. Then prepare a proposal for an advertising campaign which you will submit directly to the company president, Irving Kaye.

Use the following data to make decisions about the kinds and numbers of promotional activities you want to include in your campaign.

MEDIA COSTS

Newspaper space—$14 a column inch

For this price, the newspaper lays out the ad, provides artwork, and prints the ad in one edition. A column inch is one inch deep in one column of the paper. A typical coupon is 2" deep and 2 columns wide, or 4 column inches.

Radio—$10 a minute (7 p.m.-7 a.m.)

17 a minute (6 a.m.-10 a.m. and 3 p.m.-7 p.m.)

25 a minute (10 a.m.-3 p.m.)

Thirty-second ads are billed at 80 percent of the one-minute price.

Television—$400 for 30 seconds during prime time

200 for 30 seconds during evening news

100 for 30 seconds during afternoon

70 for 30 seconds during a.m. news

Local TV stations will produce a 30-second spot of colored slides and voice for as little as $150. Advertising agencies will write and tape a quality 30-second spot for about $3,000.

Billboards

Producing copy for billboards costs about $200 per board. Boards are rented for a small geographic area on one-month contracts in a mixture of illuminated and nonilluminated boards. In each geographic area, boards are arranged by "showing" of 25, 50, 75, and 100. A "25 showing" guarantees that the message will reach 25 percent of the potential audience in the area. A "25 showing" consists of 9 billboards and costs $1,700 a month plus production costs. A "100 showing" consists of 32 boards and costs $6,250 for one month. Costs between the extremes are proportionate.

Handbills

Handbills may be distributed under windshield wipers in parking lots, on street corners, or door to door. Cost of production varies according to the size of the handbill and choice of color and paper. An average price for 100,000 bills is $500. For street corner and parking lot handouts, the distribution cost is $4 an hour. Targeted door-to-door distribution costs three cents a delivered bill. (Targeted delivery means the buyer selects areas of a city to receive handbills according to marketing surveys which show approximate income and family size in each area.)

Mass Mailing

The cost of a letter delivered to "resident" or "occupant" is fifteen cents in quantities of 100,000 or more.

Magazines

Regional magazines have very low circulation. Advertising in national magazines costs too much to waste the money on readers outside the local marketing area.

POPULATION FIGURES

The rural tri-state area has a population of nearly four million people. They live in 1,342,780 separate households.

MEDIA OUTLETS

Outlet	Number
Daily newspapers with 10,000 circulation	30
with 25,000 circulation	3
with 50,000 circulation	1
TV stations with 100,000 viewers	25
Radio stations with 500,000 listeners	2
with 100,000 listeners	20
with 50,000 listeners	40
Billboard showing areas	50

2. You are retail sales manager for Sherman-Gilliam, Inc., a manufacturer of paint and wallpaper. The company is mounting a national advertising campaign built on free public demonstrations of do-it-yourself home decorating techniques.

The demonstrators are all former professional decorators. They are skilled in their craft but unskilled at public speaking. During the four-week training course, regional training directors have to turn these trainees into competent company representatives who can sell the product through their demonstrations. You hope that the trainees' knowledge will make up for any lack of rhetorical skills they may have. The training directors, instead, will concentrate on the program summarized below:

Week One: Create Confidence. The trainees will speak before the group for one minute. They will receive praise for their effort, irrespective of its quality as a speech, to build their confidence. The length of time each trainee speaks will increase gradually.

Week Two: Develop Enthusiasm. Enthusiasm here means sincere effort to communicate decorating skills to audiences who know little or nothing about home decorating.

Week Three: Act Naturally. Trainees will be instructed to use their normal accents to get their messages to the audience. Plain talk is the goal. Grammar will not be corrected. Trainees will be corrected, however, for making their talks unnecessarily technical and for adopting unnatural "high brow" accents.

Week Four: Plan the Talk. Training directors will help trainees outline their talks and move logically from topic to topic without losing the audience. Directors will not write speeches for the trainees but will, instead, encourage them to deliver the talks in their own styles.

Your supervisor, Marta Smodzy, Promotions Manager, expects you to complete your selection of regional training directors shortly. In fact, you have selected four of the five training directors already. However, you have left the position of training director for the midwest region for last, thinking it would be easiest to fill because the midwest is your home region. You have already invited two candidates for an interview for the position. You are having a difficult time choosing the third candidate to be interviewed. The pressure of time has forced you to narrow your choice to two applicants. You review the resumes from Charles Johnson and Phillip Woods again. Report your choice for the third person to be interviewed to your superior. Support your choice with facts and remember to interpret the facts.

Charles Johnson
1728 West Maple
Angola, IN 46703

Phone: (219) 198-3030

EDUCATION

Institution	Major	Degree
Chicago State University Chicago, IL	Communications	M.A. (1959)
DePaul University Chicago, IL	English	B.A. (1950)

EXPERIENCE

Teaching

Institution and Classes	Dates
Tri-State University, Angola, IN Creative Writing, Advanced Composition, Speech	1973–
Indiana University, Gary, IN Composition, Film Criticism, Persuasion	1965-72
Wilson Comm. College, Chicago, IL Composition, Reading and Study Skills	1960-64
DuSable H. S., Chicago, IL English and Driver Education	1955-60

Other Employment
    Staff Sgt. in U.S. Army
    Salesman for Chi-town Appliance, Chicago, IL
	1951-52
	1948-50

PROFESSIONAL ACCOMPLISHMENTS

Publications

"Selling Yourself," *Sales Management Journal*, 15, No. 1 (1973), 26-30.
"Film as Criticism," *Journal of American Film*, 10, No. 4 (1963), 43-51.
"Teaching Reading in the Community College," *Chicago City College Review*, 3, No. 2 (1963), 7-8.

Presentations

"Overcoming Stage Fright," Midwest Regional Speech Conference, Springfield, IL, 1981.
"The Old Soft Sell," MLA Workshop, Chicago, IL, 1971.

Consulting

Writing Seminars for over 25 companies (1978–)
    Representative companies: Mark Equipment
                            Gayles & Hill

Sales Seminars for over 50 companies (1975–)
    Representative companies: Miller Bakeries
                            Auto Dealers Assn.

PHILLIP WOODS
Phone: (216) 190-0204

3713 Navoo Trail
Aurora, OH 44202

EXPERIENCE

Teaching

Institution and Classes	Dates
Cleveland State University Advanced Business Writing, Salesmanship	1976 –
Champaign Community College Business Writing, Report Writing	1973-76

University of Illinois
    Teaching assistant for Basic Communication
    Technical Writing
	1965-70

Nonteaching

U.S. Army	1971-73
Clerk, Greentree Lumber Co.	1962-65
Asst. Mgr., Big Burger Restaurant	1961-62

EDUCATION

Institution	Major	Degree
University of Illinois Champaign, IL	English	Ph.D. (1976)
University of Illinois Champaign, IL	English	M.A. (1973)
Ohio State University Columbus, OH	English	B.A. (1965)

PROFESSIONAL ACCOMPLISHMENTS

Publications

Writing for Business (New York: Random House, 1978). 242-page text.

"Writing Sales Letters: 6 Easy Steps," *Journal of Communications*, 63, No. 1 (1975), 101-132.

"How to Prepare Letters of Application that Sell," *Business Communication Bulletin*, 14, No. 2 (1974), 38-39.

Presentations

"What Business Wants from College Graduates," Conference on Communication, Cincinnati, 1981.

"Career Preparation for Business Majors," Midwest Conference on Business Communication, Minneapolis, 1979.

"No Product Sells Itself," National Association of Advertising Managers, Cleveland, 1982.

3. You work for a public relations firm. One of the firm's clients is a consortium of 45 small colleges (enrollments of 500 or fewer). Some colleges are directly affiliated with a religious denomination. Others are non-denominational but do emphasize or at least provide classes in Bible study and religion. Still others are secular, but they find that over 80 percent of their students have strong religious convictions and attend church services regularly.

Your firm has a good four-page article about the special advantages of attending a small college instead of a large one. The plan is to submit the article for publication to one of two religious magazines that publish a college issue each October. When the article is accepted, you will alert all members of the consortium, let them see a copy of the article, and invite them to prepare an ad for that issue. The advertisement can then relate directly to points made in the article.

As the article will be ready for submission nine months ahead of press deadline and as it is tailored for a special college issue, your firm anticipates no difficulty in placing it. Your firm will make up a reader reply card to bind into the magazine. Readers can use this card to request information from any or all of the colleges in the consortium.

However, the article can only be run once and in only one magazine. You have been asked to study the demographic information from each magazine and to recommend the magazine for this public relations program. When you have made your decision, report to the Media Placement Manager, Monica Haines.

MAGAZINE A

Circulation Information:
  Guaranteed circulation, 50,000
  Average readership per copy, 2.8 persons
  Total readership, 112,000 per issue
Readership Information:
  100% paid subscriptions ($13.50 for members, and $16.50
    for leaders). Of these, only 1% are gifts
  94% of readers report they read each issue
  48% of readers are young people (Average age, 16.5 years)
  52% of readers are adult youth group leaders
  54% of readers are female
  46% of readers are male
  86% of leaders advise members about college attendance
  93% of leaders recommend particular colleges
Advertising Rates for a One-time B/W Insertion:
  Bind-in reply card for $1,450 ($32.22 per college)
  Full page, $1,950
  2/3 page,   1715

1/2 page,   920
1/3 page,   730
1/6 page,   540
1/12 page,   155

MAGAZINE B

Circulation Information:

Guaranteed circulation, 40,000

Average readership per issue, 2.1 persons

Total readership per issue, 84,000

Readership Information:

Average age of readers, 47

Average family income of readers, $21,411

21% of subscribers have children who will enter college within two years

59.5% of readers are pastors or are on pastoral staff

    92.9% of these recommend colleges to young people

    74.7% of these have written to colleges for information

    61% of these desire to receive college catalogs

71.5% report they spend at least an hour reading each issue.

Sex of readers

    70.9% male

    29.1% female

Education of readers

    44% have post-graduate degrees

    78% have graduated from college

Advertising Rates for a One-time B/W Insertion:

Bind-in reply card for $1,965 ($43.66 per college)

Full page, $2,200

2/3 page,   1,760

1/2 page,   1,364

1/3 page,   924

1/6 page,   550

Chapter 13

Showing Cause and Effect

To the Student:

As you read chapter 13 and complete the exercises and cases, you will be asked to

. . . define "cause"

. . . distinguish between real and apparent causes

. . . define "effect"

. . . perceive the relationship of causes and effects

. . . use your knowledge of cause and effect to help you solve problems.

Nearly every day, we hear the question Why? Everyone asks this question, from small children just learning to talk to our supervisors at work. And each time it comes up, the questioner is delving into the cause-effect relationship. For children, asking why is a means of gathering information about the environment in which they live. For business people, these questions are the first step in the problem-solving process. Why is absenteeism high? Why is productivity low? Why did our competitor have greater profits than we did last year? They gather information on these topics and similar ones for a purpose such as effecting a change or bettering the business. In this chapter, you will study the cause-effect relationship as a means of gathering information, and you will learn some techniques to apply to solving business problems.

WHAT ARE CAUSES?

Causes are the reasons why something happened. As students, you are probably used to answering cause and effect questions because they are favorite examination questions. Why did the Roman Empire fall? What were the causes of the Civil War? State the reasons for the Depression. If you have done well on test questions like these, you have probably observed two important rules of cause and effect. (1) You have looked for answers beyond a single cause. For example, to say the stock market crash caused the Depression is an incorrect answer because several factors or causes contributed to that event. (2) You have also distinguished between causes and coincidental events. For example, to say that Herbert Hoover caused the Depression is likewise incorrect. Because of the economic factors in effect in 1932, the Depression would have occurred no matter who was president. Thus, Hoover's presidency and the Depression were coincidences in that they occurred at the same time, but his presidency did not cause the Depression.

Many events have multiple causes that must be distinguished from coincidental but often simultaneous occurrences. Here is how the chairman of a major oil company accounted for the loss of income his company suffered: "a surplus of crude supplies that led to a reduction in petroleum product prices around the world, higher than normal industry crude oil and product inventories and, in particular, a marked reduction in the consumption of oil."[1]

---

[1] Clifton C. Garvin, Jr., "Chairman's Remarks to Shareholders," Exxon's 100th Annual Shareholders' Meeting, *Exxon News*, June, 1982, p. 2.

WHAT ARE EFFECTS?

Effects are the results of causes. When actions are taken or decisions are made, something happens. These happenings are effects. Effects may be good or bad. When a new factory opens in a small town, for example, the effects are good. Local people are employed and taxes that the factory pays help the town's economy. These effects in turn produce other effects and themselves become causes. Because people are employed, they have money. They spend some of their money at other local businesses which also improve. They also use some of their money for local and state taxes which help to pay for better schools, better roads, and a number of other services which improve the quality of life. When the opposite happens, a business closes, the reverse takes place. Employees lose their jobs, and the business stops paying taxes. Because of loss of income, the unemployed spend less at area businesses. They not only contribute less in taxes, but apply for funds in the form of unemployment insurance and other benefits to which they are entitled. Since the tax base has shrunk, states and municipalities have less to spend. Roads go unrepaired, schools cut programs, and the town offers fewer services. Compression rather than expansion occurs along the whole chain of effects.

Exercise A   List possible causes and effects for the following situations:

A. Your school has announced a 10 percent increase in tuition, effective next semester.

	Causes	*Effects*
1.		
2.		
3.		
4.		
5.		

B. The electricity in your house has just failed.

Causes	*Effects*
1.	
2.	
3.	
4.	
5.	

HOW DO YOU USE CAUSE AND EFFECT?

Once you understand the nature of cause and effect, you can see how they are useful in analyzing and solving problems. You will follow a four-step process in preparing a message using cause and effect: (1) isolate the problem, (2) gather information, (3) analyze information, and (4) analyze the audience.

Isolate the Problem

In examining a problem, you will sometimes know the causes and have to find effects. Sometimes you will know effects and have to search for causes. Your first task as a writer is to analyze the problem and decide which you have and which you must find.

Gather Information

When you know whether you are dealing with a cause or an effect, your second task is gathering information. Depending on the problem, you can gather facts through observation or experimentation or through such techniques as library research, interviews, and questionnaires. When gathering information, two possible difficulties face the writer: too much information or too little information. The first leads to faulty or unreliable conclusions or, in some cases, to no conclusion. The second often delays action. Sometimes the desire to gather more information is only a means of putting off tackling a problem. The real danger is putting off making a decision beyond the point when it could have done some good. In most practical pursuits, time and money keep the writer/researcher from finding out everything about a particular situation. Your work supervisor and your writing instructor both have deadlines. You must be as thorough as possible in solving problems within the framework they give.

Analyze and Synthesize

The information you have gathered is called raw data at this point because it is in the form of notes, tapes, or stacks of questionnaires. In this state, it is fairly useless to anybody but you. If you have used a questionnaire, your first step is to tally the answers to each question. Then, unless you have exactly 100 responses to every question, you will need to convert these totals to percentages. Percentages provide equivalent data which you can analyze, refine, and put into useful form. If you know exactly the problem you are working on, you can eliminate all the facts that are unrelated to solving it. Then you can begin to synthesize the remaining facts. A preliminary step in synthesis is to classify: put together all similar facts under general topics related to the causes or effects you are trying to establish. When you have classified your facts, you can organize them in relation to the audience's needs.

Analyze the Audience

The person to whom you are reporting may want only an analysis of causes and effects or an analysis with recommendations on what action to take based on your findings. The wish for a recommendation is usually specified. If it is not, don't make one. Making recommendations when not asked to do so is likely to seem pushy to the person who reads them. When you are asked to give recommendations, don't forget to include your analysis. Your reader will want to know on what you based the recommendations. Make sure also that your recommendations derive directly from your findings. For example, you might have been asked to determine why production was low in Plant 7. You discovered a bottleneck at the end of line 1. Your recommendation must be "to study ways to eliminate the bottleneck" rather than "fire the workers." Further study may show that the machinery needs to be retooled or that workers need special training. Or it may show that this particular group of employees does not work well together and should at least be moved if not fired. The point is that "finding a bottleneck" is only the first step to solution, not the last. Finally, make reasonable recommendations. Some writers get carried away and recommend actions that are so radical that they are beyond the decisionmaker's authority to carry out.

When you write, be sure to choose tactful wording in your recommendations. Avoid sounding bossy or know-it-all because such an attitude will lessen your own influence.

Sample Case

Here is a cause-effect problem that confronted Rollin Hogaboom, a small businessman. Rollin Hogaboom opened his first Sun Bright laundromat in 1975 at a location near his home. It prospered, and in 1978, he opened a second one near two mobile home parks at the edge of town. In 1981, he opened a third laundromat in the new shopping center south of town.

Each facility has 10 triple load washers, 20 double load washers, 10 single load washers, 20 driers, 2 extractors, a sink with hand-operated wringer, as well as the usual vending machines for supplies, snacks, and change. Each center is open from 8 a.m. to 8 p.m. on weekdays and Saturdays and noon to 6 p.m. on Sundays. He employs three full-time managers who, in turn, hire nine part-time workers. During working hours, the employees stock the supply and change machines, do limited recordkeeping, and keep the facility clean. Only one employee is on duty at any particular time. Full-time employees work a regular 8 a.m.-4 p.m. schedule, Monday through Friday. Part-time employees work weekends and after 4 p.m.

Hogaboom has followed a strict schedule for replacing machinery. He has also learned over the years to make most machine repairs. He prides himself on visiting each center on a regular twice-a-week schedule Monday through Friday to make repairs and discuss operations with the attendant on duty.

He chose his locations well, and all three operations have been successful. In the last six months, however, his second center (near the mobile home parks) has not been as profitable as in the past. Nor is it as busy as the other two facilities. Hogaboom toured the area but could not discover any new competition. He has also discussed the situation with the manager, Sandra Slavinsky, but she has no suggestions that would account for the recent sizable drop in business.

Hogaboom has isolated the problem. He knows he is dealing with an effect, the loss of business at his second center. He knows he must find the causes. He sits down one day to try to figure out why business has fallen off. He makes a list of possible causes:

1. Maybe everybody at the mobile home parks has bought a washer and drier.

2. Maybe the population at the mobile home parks is aging and no longer has loads of diapers to wash in Sun Bright machines.

3. Maybe all the people who used to live at the mobile home parks have bought their own homes somewhere else in town, and a new group, unaware of Sun Bright's existence, has moved in.

Hogaboom thinks he is on the right track at last, but what should he do now? He figures reason 3 is his best possibility. After all, if nobody knows Sun Bright exists, they can't very well wash clothes there. He remembers seeing a competitor's ad in the newspaper. It offered free detergent for every load of wash. Maybe he could do the same. He might also get some coin-operated, personal-sized TVs like the kind he saw at the Snow Queen center on Rose Street.

Really enthusiastic now, Hogaboom shows his list to his wife and tells her what he plans to do. She points out the causes on his list have no basis in fact. He may be right; he may be wrong about why he's losing business. Since he's losing money already, can he really afford to put ads in the paper, give away free detergent, and buy TV sets that will probably break down all the time anyway? Maybe he should just cut his losses and close the ailing laundromat.

Hogaboom rejects the idea of closing the laundromat but concedes his wife has a point about putting more money into the facility without knowing whether it will do any good. His information gathering has not been scientific, to say the least. He needs more information, but he doesn't know how to get it. He can't very well track down the customers who aren't coming to Sun Bright anymore to ask them why not.

Finally, Hogaboom takes his problem to the association of small businesses to which he belongs. They put him in contact with the Retired Executives Council, a free consulting service of retired business executives who help people like him. Hogaboom gets an appointment to talk with Sal Rotunda about his problem. Somewhat warily, he shows Rotunda his list of possible reasons for the decline in business. Rotunda notes them down and promises to get in touch with Hogaboom within two weeks.

Gathering Information

Rotunda's first task is to find out what answers to Hogaboom's questions will reveal about causes for decline in the second laundromat's business. He calls the managers of the two mobile home parks. Their answers are pretty much the same.

1. The residents are not allowed to use automatic washers because both mobile home parks are on septic systems too small to accommodate them.

2. The age mix has remained about the same. Most residents are young married couples just starting families.

3. No major population shift has occurred recently.

Rotunda investigates two more possibilities. First, he finds that neither mobile home park has opened a laundry facility on its grounds. Second, he checks prices at competing laundromats and finds that Hogaboom's prices are comparable.

With this information in hand, Rotunda realizes that the causes for the decline in business are probably inside the laundromat rather than outside in the community. Now he can focus his search for information. To see whether the second laundromat differs from the other two in any significant way, Rotunda develops a questionnaire which is administered to 200 patrons at each of the three locations (30 each weekday and Saturday and 20 on Sunday) to pinpoint the reasons why the second laundromat has become less profitable.

Here are the results of the investigation. The three columns of figures represent the users of Hogaboom's first laundromat (near his home), the second laundromat (near the mobile home parks), and the third laundromat (in the shopping center).

QUESTIONNAIRE AND ANSWERS

1. How many times a week do you use this or any other laundromat?

	Laundry No.		
	1	2	3
Less than once a week	40	20	34
Once a week	82	44	72
Twice a week	32	56	62
Three times a week	36	62	26
More than three times a week	8	18	6

2. What day(s) of the week do you prefer to use this or any other laundromat?

Monday	50	55	50
Tuesday	42	38	33
Wednesday	32	55	51
Thursday	55	50	75
Friday	50	65	40
Saturday	52	97	63
Sunday	26	70	35

3. What time of day do you prefer to use this or any other laundry facility?

8 — 12 am	100	56	90
12 — 4 pm	72	30	67
4 — 8 pm	24	58	38
Other	4	56	6

4. Last week, what day(s) of the week did you use this laundromat?

None	6	15	10
Monday	45	40	40
Tuesday	41	30	32
Wednesday	15	40	54
Thursday	43	45	68
Friday	42	55	44
Saturday	51	55	60
Sunday	20	30	40

5. Last week, what day(s) of the week did you use a laundromat other than this one?

None	170	130	181
Monday	5	15	10
Tuesday	1	8	4
Wednesday	17	12	1
Thursday	12	8	2
Friday	8	10	2
Saturday	1	38	3
Sunday	6	36	2

6. Last week, what time(s) did you use this laundromat?

8 — 12 am	110	67	80
12 — 4 pm	61	50	72
4 — 8 pm	17	33	35

7. Last week, what time(s) did you use a laundromat other than this one?

6 — 8 am	2	20	6
8 — 12 am	26	5	8
12 — 4 pm	12	8	9
4 — 8 pm	4	28	4
8 — 10 pm	6	45	9

8. Do you have to wait for the machines you want to use at this laundry facility?

Single load washer

yes	10	5	12
no	180	180	170
sometimes	10	15	18

Double load washer

yes	22	15	10
no	147	153	150
sometimes	31	32	40

Triple load washer

yes	16	10	16
no	156	170	148
sometimes	28	20	36

Extractor

yes	39	32	22
no	121	120	124
sometimes	40	48	54

Drier

yes	12	10	6
no	150	149	132
sometimes	38	41	62

Sink and wringer

yes	0	0	0
no	199	200	200
sometimes	1	0	0

9. When you use this laundromat, do you find the laundry supplies you need in the vending machine?

Always	60	30	24
Usually	55	64	89
Sometimes	20	54	11
Rarely	5	12	3
N/A	60	40	73

10. When you use this laundromat, do you find the change you need in the coin and bill changing machine?

Always	3	1	8
Usually	145	110	154
Sometimes	20	56	30
Rarely	7	23	5
N/A	25	10	3

11. Do you consider the machines in this facility are in

Good condition	170	172	168
Fair condition	28	25	23
Poor condition	2	3	9

12. Do you consider the machines in this facility are

Modern	160	165	155
A little old	34	30	35
Quite old	6	5	10

13. Do you consider the machines in this facility are

Very clean	84	16	75
Clean	112	152	123
Somewhat dirty	2	27	1
Dirty	0	5	1

14. Are the lavatory and sorting tables in this facility

Very clean	120	60	107
Clean	45	50	77
Somewhat dirty	30	60	16
Dirty	5	30	0

15. Are the floors, walls, etc., in this facility

Very clean	120	50	173
Clean	50	60	78
Somewhat dirty	30	70	7
Dirty	0	20	2

16. Have you needed help from the attendant at this facility?

yes	180	191	178
no	20	9	22

17. Could the attendant solve your problem?

Yes	170	130	160
No	30	70	40

18. Was the attendant pleasant while giving you assistance?

Yes	190	60	180
No	10	140	20

Analyzing Information

Having compiled all the answers he received from laundromat customers, Rotunda analyzes the answers to find out what each one means in relation to the problem he is trying to solve. Here are his notes on responses to each question.

NOTES

Question No.	Facts and Interpretation
1.	The second laundromat gets heavy repeat customers each week. Sixty-eight percent of its customers use it 2-3+ times a week compared to 38% and 47% for the first and third laundromats.
2.	Monday is still the preferred wash day for many people. Interest slacks off on Tuesday-Wednesday and picks up again at the end of the week. Preference totals (232 customers) for second laundromat from Friday-Sunday far outstrip those for the first (128 customers) and third (139 customers).
3.	Most people in Groups 1 and 3 prefer doing their laundry between 8 a.m. and 4 p.m. Group 2 prefers later hours (4-8 p.m. and "other"). (Possible problem: second laundromat's hours don't fill customers' needs?)
4.	The second group had the highest nonuse total (15) for the previous week (as opposed to 6 and 10 for the other groups). In Groups 1 and 3, 90% actually used the laundromat on the day noted as preferred in Question 2. In Group 2, 232 people stated Friday-Sunday as preferences, but only 140 actually used the laundromat those days. (Why the discrepancy?)
5.	Customer loyalty is 85% for Group 1 and 90% for Group 3, but only 65% for Group 2. Total use figures show that while 50 people in Group 1 and 24 people in Group 3 actually used another laundromat, 137 people from Group 2 went elsewhere. Notably, 74 people who like to wash on Saturday and Sunday did so—at a competing laundromat. (Possible answer to Question 4?)
6.	Only 60% in Group 2 used the facilities at the time of day listed as a preference in Question 3.

Question No.	Facts and Interpretation
7.	Sixty-five customers in Group 2 used a competitor's laundromat at either 6-8 a.m. or 8-10 p.m. when Hogaboom's laundromats are closed. Figures of outside use by other groups are negligible. (Possible answer to Question 3?)
8.	OK. Most people have access to the machines they want to use.
9.	OK for Groups 1 and 3 in finding the laundry supplies they need. Note bulge in "Sometimes" and "Rarely" categories for Group 2. (Possible problem keeping the supply machine stocked?)
10.	Same as Question 9. 13.5% and 17.5% in Groups 1 and 3 report trouble getting change; 39.5% of Group 2 have trouble. (Problem with keeping change machine working?)
11.	OK. Most customers satisfied machines are in working order.
12.	OK. Most customers think equipment is up to date.
13.	Groups 1 and 3 satisfied with cleanliness of machines. Group 2 reports "Somewhat dirty" (23.5%) and "Dirty" (2.5%). (Problem: upkeep of machines at second laundromat?)
14.	Dissatisfaction with lavatory/folding table cleanliness: Group 1 − 17.5%; Group 2 − 45%; Group 3 − 8%. (Problem: upkeep of personal use items at second laundromat?)
15.	Dissatisfaction with general conditions of laundromats: Group 1 − 15%; Group 2 − 45%; Group 3 − 4.5%. (Problem: general upkeep at second laundromat?)
16.	Almost all customers need attendant's assistance at some time.
17.	Customers in Groups 1 and 3 received help in solving their problems 85% and 80% of the time. Group 2 customers received help 65% of the time. (Problem: lack of help from attendant at second laundromat?)
18.	Attendants at first and third laundromats pleasant 95% and 90% of the time but only 30% of the time at second laundromat. (Problem: attendant often unpleasant at second laundromat?)

Synthesizing Information

After analyzing the results of the questionnaire, Rotunda is ready to synthesize the information he has gathered. His first step is to eliminate facts that don't help him solve the problem. Thus answers to Questions 8, 11, 12, and 16 may be eliminated. Because the answers are the same at all three laundromats, they don't give him any specific insight on the problem at the troubled facility.

Rotunda reviews the facts and ideas he has left. Several points concerning the second laundromat stand out. He lists these points separately.

POINTS TO CONSIDER

1. Customers preferred using facilities Friday-Sunday at 4-8 p.m. and at "other" times.

2. Many customers didn't actually use the laundromat on the preferred days. No loss of customers on Friday. Saturday, 55 came to second laundromat, and 38 went somewhere else. 70 said they preferred to wash on Sunday. 30 did, but 36 went somewhere else.

3. 74 customers went to competing laundromats Friday-Sunday.

4. Only 60% of the customers use the laundromat at preferred times of day. 56 people preferred other hours. Last week 20 washed between 6 and 8 a.m.; 45 washed after 8 p.m. 58 people prefer to wash between 4 and 8 p.m.; 33 did, but 28 didn't. 28 went somewhere else.

5. 65% report problems with supply machine.

6. 94.5% report problems with the change machine.

7. 23.5% say the machines are "Somewhat dirty"; 2.5% say they are "Dirty."

8. 45% dissatisfied with cleanliness of lavatory/folding tables.

9. 45% dissatisfied with general cleanliness of facility.

10. 35% say attendant doesn't help them solve their problems.

11. 70% say attendant was not pleasant in giving them assistance.

Now that Rotunda has picked out the points that he thinks bear directly on the second laundromat's decline in business, he is ready to classify them under some general headings. Because he has structured the questionnaire carefully, the headings seem readily apparent. Hours is one major category heading, Upkeep is a second, and Attendant is a third. "Too easy," he says to himself. A closer look shows the categories Upkeep and Attendant overlap. Since upkeep is a responsibility of the attendant, it is really a subcategory under Attendant rather than a category equal to it. His reclassification looks like this:

I. Hours
II. Attendant
  A. Upkeep
  B. Customer service

One further bit of information keeps nagging him: Item 4 in *Points to Consider*. If 58 people expressed a preference for the hours from 4 to 8 p.m., but only 33 actually used the laundromat at that time, the problem isn't hours. The laundromat is open, but 25 people are going to a competing facility. This fact points to a problem with the attendant about which the answers to the questionnaire reveal nothing more. He makes a note to mention the fact in his report to Hogaboom.

Analyzing the Audience

As far as Rotunda is concerned, the hard tasks — gathering, analyzing, and synthesizing information — are finished. Now thoroughly familiar with the facts, he doesn't anticipate any difficulty getting them down on paper in a way that will satisfy his client, Rollin Hogaboom. But Rotunda is responsible for more than simply transmitting facts. He also has to make some recommendations to Hogaboom — some suggestions about what Hogaboom can do to stop the decline in business. Recommendations are always the touchy part, Rotunda thinks, especially when they come from an unpaid consultant. People value what they pay for, and the more they pay, the higher the value. Rotunda reminds himself that Hogaboom was sent to him because Hogaboom could not solve his own problem and could not afford to hire anyone else. If the explanations are clear and the recommendations reasonable, they should help him halt the losses at his laundromat.

Here is the report that Rotunda sends to Hogaboom.

August 1, 198-

Mr. Rollin Hogaboom
Sun Bright Laundromat
126 Flowerfield Rd.
Pittsburg, KS 66762

Dear Mr. Hogaboom:

The decline in business at the laundromat near the mobile home parks stems from customer dissatisfaction with hours and attendants. In the following report, I've outlined the methods used to gather information, the results, and conclusions and recommendations for actions you may consider taking to return the laundromat to profitability.

Method

Information came from three sources: (1) phone calls to the managers of the two mobile home parks near the laundromat; (2) my own investigation of competing laundromats; and (3) a questionnaire distributed to customers at all three of your facilities. Two hundred customers (30 each weekday and 20 on Sunday) were polled at each laundomat for the purpose of comparing information from the profitable laundromats to that gathered at the unprofitable one. The differences in customers' answers helped to reveal the causes for the decline at the second laundromat, as you can see point by point on the enclosed copy of the questionnaire with answers.

Results

The decline in business stems from factors within the laundromat itself rather than from changes outside the facility. The mobile home parks' managers report no major changes. The age mix of residents and their occupancy rate have remained the same. Because of drainage systems at both parks, residents may not use automatic washers in their homes. For that reason among others, the parks' management has not installed laundry facilities on the premises. Parks' residents are still using public laundry facilities, either yours or a competitor's. Further, a comparison of your prices with the competitions' showed no

significant differences. Thus, factors outside the laundromat may be eliminated from consideration as possible
causes for the decline in business.

The answers to the questionnaire show two areas of concern:
(1) with hours and (2) with service.

Hours. Twenty-eight percent of the customers indicated
they preferred to do their laundry at times when the second
laundromat is closed. During the week of the survey, 32.5
percent of the customers had done at least one load of
laundry at a competitor's laundromat between 8 am. and 8
pm. Ten percent (20 customers) did laundry between 6 am.
and 8 am, and 22.5 percent (45 customers) did laundry
between 8 and 10 pm.

Many customers appear to be avoiding the second laundromat
during hours when it is open. Of the people surveyed, 38
percent preferred to use the facility on Saturday and Sunday. While 28.8 percent actually used it at their preferred time, 27.7 percent patronized a competing laundromat. Furthermore, while 29 percent of the customers indicated a preference for using the facility between 4 and 8
pm, only 16.5 percent actually used your facility during
that time period. Another 14 percent used a competitor's
facility between 4 and 8 pm.

Attendants. Two other areas of customer dissatisfaction
concern the attendants' responsibilities for upkeep of the
facility and service to the customers. At the second
laundromat, for example, 94.5 percent of the customers reported difficulties getting change, 23.5 percent and 2.5
percent reported the machines were "somewhat dirty" and
"dirty," and 45 percent reported dissatisfaction with items
like lavatories and folding tables as well as with general
conditions.

Many customers also expressed concern about the service
they received from attendants at the second laundromat.
For example, 35 percent claimed the attendant failed to
help them solve problems, and 70 percent felt the attendant
was not pleasant in giving assistance.

Conclusions and Recommendations

1. The hours that the second laundromat is open do not
    suit the customers' needs. To remedy this problem,
    you might consider changing or extending business hours
    at this laundromat, especially on weekends.

Mr. Rollin Hogaboom
Page 3
August 1, 198-

2. The attendants do not appear to be fulfilling their
    duties. Customers complain about upkeep and service.
    They are avoiding the facility after 4 pm and on
    weekends, which seems to indicate that the part-time
    attendants rather than your full-time employee are at
    fault. You will have to verify this conclusion from
    personal observation. Perhaps the easiest way is to
    change your own work schedule, staggering the days
    and times of your visits so that you arrive at times
    other than when your full-time employee is working.

I have discussed your possible personnel problem with Linda
Ganis, a former head of personnel at GVC Industries and a
member of the Council. She is available to advise you
further in the personnel area. Should you wish any other
explanation about this report, please call me at 232-0343.
I will be happy to discuss it with you.

Sincerely,

S. Rotunda

Sal Rotunda

SR/dz

Enc.

QUESTIONNAIRE AND ANSWERS

1. How many times a week do you use this or any other laundromat?

Laundry No.

	1	2	3
Less than once a week	40	20	34
Once a week	82	44	72
Twice a week	32	56	62
Three times a week	36	62	26
More than three times a week	8	18	6

2. What day(s) of the week do you prefer to use this or any other laundromat?

	1	2	3
Monday	50	55	60
Tuesday	42	38	33
Wednesday	32	55	51
Thursday	55	50	75
Friday	50	65	40
Saturday	52	97	63
Sunday	26	70	35

3. What time of day do you prefer to use this or any other laundry facility?

	1	2	3
8 — 12 am	100	56	90
12 — 4 pm	72	30	67
4 — 8 pm	24	58	38
Other	4	56	6

4. Last week, what day(s) of the week did you use this laundromat?

	1	2	3
None	6	15	10
Monday	45	40	40
Tuesday	41	30	32
Wednesday	15	40	54
Thursday	43	45	68
Friday	42	55	44
Saturday	51	55	60
Sunday	20	30	40

5. Last week, what day(s) of the week did you use a laundromat other than this one?

None	170	130	181
Monday	5	15	10
Tuesday	1	8	4
Wednesday	17	12	1
Thursday	12	8	2
Friday	8	10	2
Saturday	1	38	3
Sunday	6	36	2

6. Last week, what time(s) did you use this laundromat?

8 – 12 am	110	67	80
12 – 4 pm	61	50	72
4 – 8 pm	17	33	35

7. Last week, what time(s) did you use a laundromat other than this one?

6 – 8 am	2	20	6
8 – 12 am	26	5	8
12 – 4 pm	12	8	9
4 – 8 pm	4	28	4
8 – 10 pm	6	45	9

8. Do you have to wait for the machines you want to use at this laundry facility?

Single load washer

yes	10	5	12
no	180	180	170
sometimes	10	15	18

Double load washer

yes	22	15	10
no	147	153	150
sometimes	31	32	40

Triple load washer

yes	16	10	16
no	156	170	148
sometimes	28	20	36

Extractor			
yes	39	32	22
no	121	120	124
sometimes	40	48	54
Drier			
yes	12	10	6
no	150	149	132
sometimes	38	41	62
Sink and wringer			
yes	0	0	0
no	199	200	200
sometimes	1	0	0

9. When you use this laundromat, do you find the laundry supplies you need in the vending machine?

Always	60	30	24
Usually	55	64	89
Sometimes	20	54	11
Rarely	5	12	3
N/A	60	40	73

10. When you use this laundromat, do you find the change you need in the coin and bill changing machine?

Always	3	1	8
Usually	145	110	154
Sometimes	20	56	30
Rarely	7	23	5
N/A	25	10	3

11. Do you consider the machines in this facility are in

Good condition	170	172	168
Fair condition	28	25	23
Poor condition	2	3	9

12. Do you consider the machines in this facility are

Modern	160	165	155
A little old	34	30	35
Quite old	6	5	10

13. Do you consider the machines in this facility are

Very clean	84	16	75
Clean	112	152	123
Somewhat dirty	2	27	1
Dirty	0	5	1

14. Are the lavatory and sorting tables in this facility

Very clean	120	60	107
Clean	45	50	77
Somewhat dirty	30	60	16
Dirty	5	30	0

15. Are the floors, walls, etc., in this facility

Very clean	120	50	173
Clean	50	60	78
Somewhat dirty	30	70	7
Dirty	0	20	2

16. Have you needed help from the attendant at this facility?

yes	180	191	178
no	20	9	22

17. Could the attendant solve your problem?

Yes	170	130	160
No	30	70	40

18. Was the attendant pleasant while giving you assistance?

Yes	190	60	180
No	10	140	20

Review   This chapter shows that cause and effect can be put to work to solve a problem. As you read through the sample case, you noticed that the laundromat owner, Rollin Hogaboom, knew immediately that he was dealing with an effect, a loss of business. He did not know its causes and found out that making up "causes" with no basis in fact was not helpful. Only through a structured process of gathering, analyzing, and synthesizing information was the consultant able to help Hogaboom understand the nature of the problem and to develop some ideas for solving it.

Cases   1. Some state legislatures in northern industrial states are considering laws that would require an industry that plans to leave the state to file what amounts to an "environmental impact" statement explaining the local effects of the plant closing. Assume such a law is in effect in your state. Select a major employer in your city and consider the effects on your city if the business were to move to another state and close this operation.

2. If you live in a large city, Case 1 would be difficult to do with accuracy, but you could consider the effects to expect if financial difficulties caused your college to close at the end of this academic year. Be careful to make this report a general assessment; don't write about how the closing would affect you personally.

3. You are on the staff of the customer relations department at Jarndyce and Company, an exclusive department store. The head of the department, Phyllis Dern, has received three complaints about poor employee-customer relations on the telephone. She asks you to get the details of each incident and report them to her. At the same time, you are to suggest methods for correcting the problem. Here is what you discovered.

Incident 1: Joan Taggert, chairperson of the Christmas committee for a large local charity, had phoned to discuss the charity's annual toy order. "The secretary who answered the phone was unbelievably rude. Before I could say more than 'I'd like to speak to Mr. Edwards in the Toy Department,' she yelled 'Hang on' and left the phone. When she returned, she barked, 'Whadadya want?' I gave her my name and again asked for Mr. Edwards. She left the phone without a word.

"When she returned to the phone again, she was a changed person. She politely said, 'Mr. Edwards will be glad to speak with you.' Of course, by that time, it was just too late. I didn't feel like talking to him. I said I would call again. So far, I just haven't got around to it."

Incident 2: Mrs. Johnstone phoned to complain about a billing error. She had to explain her problem to the operator who connected her to the billing department. The clerk who answered the phone listened to the complaint and then said, "The man who handles that kind of problem is on his coffee break right now. You'll have to try again when he's around."

Mrs. Johnstone was so irritated that she exploded, "Just cancel my account. I never want to do business with you again." To that the clerk responded with a line from the training manual, "I will relay the message. Thank you for shopping at Jarndyce."

Incident 3: Warren Grovenor went to customer service to pick up a dozen expensive gifts that he had left to be wrapped. He turned in his claim check, and the clerk left to gather the packages. The phone rang, and the clerk returned to answer it. Apparently, the caller was another customer with a problem. After waiting five minutes, Mr. Grovenor headed for the executive offices and Phyllis Dern. He told her the incident and added, "My time is as valuable as anyone's. If you want to be paid for those gifts, YOU get them to the banquet hall of the Tilton Hotel by noon today." Then he left the store.

4. In the competition for business, the bank that employs you has undertaken to survey both its current customers and customers who have closed accounts in the past year. The short survey form looks the same, but two forms have actually been used. "Dear Customer" surveys were sent to current customers. "Dear Friend" forms were mailed to former customers. Read the information on the two forms that follow this case; study the list of comments that accompanies the forms. Then draw such conclusions as you can from the results and write a memo to Gerald Painter, Vice President for Personnel, to suggest steps the bank might take to keep its present accounts and create an image that will attract new accounts.

Dear Customer:

　　Please help us become a better bank by giving us the benefit of your comments and suggestions. Be assured that your comments will be taken seriously.

1. Please tell us why you closed one of your accounts with us.

   _230_ Moving to _____　　　　_180_ Location not convenient

   _____ Hours not convenient　　　　　　_67_ Service not satisfactory

   _289_ Service charges　　　　　　　　　_2_ Turned down on a loan

   _562_ Interest rates　　　　　　　　　_____ Other_____

2. Please rate our employees' ability to service your banking needs.

	EXCELLENT	GOOD	AVG.	FAIR	POOR
Lobby Tellers	1 _268_	2 _419_	3 _504_	4 _40_	5 _12_
Drive-In Tellers	1 _28_	2 _391_	3 _450_	4 _312_	5 _80_
Branch Managers	1 _74_	2 _101_	3 _34_	4 _14_	5 _4_
Receptionist at Branch/ New Accounts	1	2 _301_	3 _607_	4	5
Other FNB Personnel	1 _12_	2 _56_	3 _720_	4 _27_	5 _5_

3. Account # _____-_____-__. Branch _____
   　　　　　　　　　　　　　　　　　　　　FNB OFFICE USED MOST OFTEN

4. Comments:_____

   _____

   Signature (if you wish) _____ Phone _____

   Thanks very much for letting us know how you feel about First National.

   　　Number mailed: 4310　　　_Number returned: 1289_

   TEAR OFF AT PERFORATION, ENCLOSE COMPLETED FORM IN ENVELOPE BELOW, SEAL AND MAIL. POSTAGE IS PAID BY US!

Dear Friend:

Please help us become a better bank by giving us the benefit of your comments and suggestions. Be assured that your comments will be taken seriously.

1. Please tell us why you no longer have this account with us.

_102_ Moving to _____   _12_ Location not convenient

_2_ Hours not convenient   _8_ Service not satisfactory

_22_ Service charges   _37_ Turned down on a loan

_____ Interest rates   _____ Other _____

2. Please rate our employees' ability to service your banking needs.

	EXCELLENT	GOOD	AVG.	FAIR	POOR
Lobby Tellers	1 5	2 130	3 27	4 41	5
Drive-In Tellers	1	2	3 31	4 98	5 40
Branch Managers	1 3	2	3	4	5 10
Receptionist at Branch/ New Accounts	1	2	3	4	5
Other FNB Personnel	1	2	3 168	4	5 30

3. Account # _____-_____-__ . Branch _____
                                        FNB OFFICE USED MOST OFTEN

4. Comments: _____

_____

Signature (if you wish) _____ Phone _____

Thanks very much for letting us know how you feel about First National.

Number mailed : 600   Number returned: 200

TEAR OFF AT PERFORATION, ENCLOSE COMPLETED FORM IN ENVELOPE BELOW, SEAL AND MAIL. POSTAGE IS PAID BY US!

SIGNIFICANT COMMENTS

Compliments

Large number of branches (346)
Check cashing card (245)
Evening banking (199)
Variety of services at one place (178)
Help with real estate problems (123)
Autotellers (122)
Christmas calendar (99)

Complaints

Slow service at drive-in windows (435)
Long lines at drive-in windows (344)
Computer is down too often (301)
Autotellers broken (214)
Tellers don't respect the fact that they are
        dealing with MY money (178)
Need early morning banking (100)
Want a branch in Oakmont (82)
Time to straighten out account errors is
        too long (81)

Chapter 14

Writing
Formal Reports

To the Student:

As you read chapter 14 and complete a research project, you will be asked to

. . . distinguish between primary and secondary research

. . . know the parts of reports based on primary research

. . . use the format of reports based on primary research

. . . know how to prepare a bibliography

. . . know how to take and organize notes

. . . use the format of reports based on secondary research.

In earlier chapters of this book, you used memos and letters to convey written messages. In this chapter, you will study the formal report. If you have produced term papers or library research papers for your college classes, you have already written one kind of formal report. Formal reports based on secondary research share many of the characteristics of term papers or library research papers. Formal reports based on primary research, however, will probably be new to some of you. Both kinds of reports are useful in business and other professional settings, and this chapter will give you the opportunity to study both of them. The first part of the chapter covers primary research; the second part covers secondary research.

Whether primary or secondary, research is the basis of reports because research is the means by which writers gather information for reports. Some reports are based solely on primary research, some only on secondary research, and some on a combination of primary and secondary research. Your subject and purpose for writing dictate the kind of research you need to do to gather data.

REPORTS BASED ON PRIMARY RESEARCH

Primary research is based on first-hand information. This kind of information is usually generated to solve a particular problem. Because the information is new, it does not exist in published form. First-hand information comes from various sources. Observation, polls, questionnaires, interviews, market surveys, product tests, and various kinds of laboratory tests all produce first-hand information.

Sometimes the report writer is responsible for doing the research that produces the data for a report. In large organizations, the writer often directs other people in gathering information by requesting information from other departments or commissioning studies. The writer is in charge of production of the report but, because of the scope of the report or because of technical expertise required, may not personally engage in research. In chapter 10 on classification, you saw an example of research done by someone other than the author. In that example of primary research, Fleetwing's laboratory tested the bicycles. Stan Ryder, the report writer, used the information as the basis of his report. By contrast, in chapter 13 on cause and effect, Sal Rotunda does his own research, using a questionnaire to gather information on the decline in business at the Sun Bright laundromat. Neither of these writers used formal report structure to deliver his message, however. Two variables often dictate the choice of formal report format: (1) the importance to the organization of the information being reported on and (2) the importance of the audience for whom the report is being written.

The structure of the formal report has never been standardized in the way that parts of the letter have been. Structure depends partly on the size of the report, on the audience, and even in some cases on the organization that the writer works for. Many organizations have developed their own report formats to meet their own specific needs. Reports based on primary research, however, have many of the same parts although these parts may be named and organized differently from report to report and even from organization to organization. Reports typically include prefatory parts (title page, letter of transmittal, and abstract) and the body of the report (introduction, method, results, conclusions, recommendations). They often end with one or more appendices.

Prefatory Parts of the Report

Title Page

This page includes the title of the report, identification of the person the report was prepared for, identification of the writer, and the date on which the report was submitted.

Well written titles are often neglected parts of reports. A good title informs readers of the report's contents and enhances their desire to read the report. The following guidelines should help you to write informative titles.

Guidelines for Titles

1. Give complete information about the contents of your report in the title. To insure completeness, answer the 5 Ws: why, what, where, when, who.

Why:	To inform Rollin Hogaboom
What:	To find causes for a decline in profit
When:	Current
Where:	Sun Bright Laundromat #2
Who:	—

2. Make titles concise by

   (a) excluding needless words such as "A Study of," "A Report on," or "An Investigation of" and

   (b) avoiding use of complete sentences.

3. Use either Example A or Example B as models in preparing the title page of your report.

Causes for Declining Profits
at Sun Bright Laundromat's Second Facility

Prepared for

Rollin Hogaboom
Sun Bright Laundromat
126 Flowerfield Road
Pittsburg, KS 66762

Prepared by

Sal Rotunda
Retired Executives Council
2500 Russell Drive (Suite B)
Pittsburg, KS 66762

August 1, 198-

Example A. Cover Page for a Professional Report.

Selecting the Correct Word Processing Equipment

Prepared for

Dr. T. R. Rennals
Associate Professor
Department of Business Information Systems
Western Michigan University
Kalamazoo, MI 49008

Prepared by

Kelly Wolf
BIS 142-BC

December 4, 198-

Example B. Cover Page for a College Paper.

Letter of Transmittal

Following the title page is the letter of transmittal by which the writer officially turns the report over to the reader. This letter may be one of two kinds.

1. It may simply note that the assigned work has been completed and sent to the reader (see Example C).

2. It may contain a synopsis of the major results and conclusions of the report (see Example D).

The kind of letter of transmittal you choose depends on whether your report contains a separate abstract. If you include an abstract, the first kind of letter of transmittal is appropriate. If your report omits an abstract, use the second kind of letter of transmittal. Abstracts and synopses have the same purpose: to summarize the report's contents.

The letter in Example C is very brief because the writer will include a separate abstract with the report and does not want to repeat the information from the abstract in the letter. Thus, Example C contains only the most important information contained in the report. In the letter in Example D, the synopsis goes into more detail. Notice that the synopsis follows the same order as the report.

RETIRED EXECUTIVES COUNCIL
2500 Russell Drive (Suite B)
Pittsburg, KS 66762

August 1, 198-

Mr. Rollin Hogaboom
Sun Bright Laundromat
126 Flowerfield Road
Pittsburg, KS 66762

Dear Mr. Hogaboom:

Here are my findings on the decline in business at Sun
Bright Laundromat's second facility about which you asked
me to report on July 17.

My research indicates that the causes for the decline at
your second facility are customer dissatisfaction with the
laundromat's hours and with its attendants. To remedy
these problems, you should consider extending the laundromat's hours and more closely monitoring your employees'
performance.

Researching this report has been an interesting challenge.
Should you wish any further explanation, please call me at
232-0343, and I will be happy to discuss the report with
you. My colleague on the Retired Executives Council, Linda
Ganis, is also available to discuss your personnel problems
with you.

Sincerely,

S. Rotunda

Sal Rotunda

SR/dz

Example C. Cover Letter without Synopsis.

RETIRED EXECUTIVES COUNCIL
2500 Russell Drive (Suite B)
Pittsburg, KS 66762

August 1, 198-

Mr. Rollin Hogaboom
Sun Bright Laundromat
126 Flowerfield Road
Pittsburg, KS 66762

Dear Mr. Hogaboom:

Here are my findings on the decline in business at Sun
Bright Laundromat's second facility about which you asked
me to report on July 17.

My research indicates that the causes for the decline in
business at your second facility are customer dissatisfaction with the laundromat's hours and with its attendants.
Telephone interviews with managers of two mobile home parks
near your facility, a visit to a competing laundromat and,
most important, a questionnaire distributed to 200 customers at each of your three facilities helped me to reach
these conclusions. Specifically, 28 percent of the customers at the second facility prefer to do their laundry at
times when the laundromat is closed. Furthermore, many
customers patronize a competitor's laundromat, even during
hours when your facility is open. These customers expressed dissatisfaction with the upkeep of the laundromat
and with the service they received from the attendant.

To remedy these problems, you might consider changing or
extending the laundromat's hours. You might also make spot
checks at the laundromat during evening hours and on weekends rather than regularly scheduled visits during the day,
Monday through Friday.

Researching this report has been an interesting challenge.
Should you with any further explanation, please call me at
232-0343, and I will be happy to discuss the report with
you. My colleague on the Retired Executives Council, Linda
Ganis, is also available to discuss your personnel problems
with you.

Sincerely,

S. Rotunda
Sal Rotunda

SR/dz

Example D. Cover Letter with Synopsis.

Abstract

An abstract of Rotunda's report would be almost identical to the synopsis that appears in paragraphs two and three of Example D. (Remember: the terms *abstract* and *synopsis* as well as *precis, summary*, and *epitome* are often used interchangeably.) However, the synopsis included in the letter of transmittal is informal, a fact signaled by the use of personal pronouns. By contrast, the abstract as a separate piece of writing is formal. It should not contain personal pronouns. Some other guidelines that apply to abstracts follow.

Guidelines for Abstracts

1. Condense the report to about one-tenth its original size. Thus, a ten-page report produces a one-page abstract.

2. Cover each section of the report in the order that the section appears in the report.

3. Proportion parts of the abstract in relation to the length of each section in the report. That is, give the longest part of the report the most coverage in the abstract; the second longest part the second most coverage, and so forth.

4. Report only the major results, conclusions, and recommendations of the report.

If the report has been carefully structured, the abstract is easy to write; it becomes almost a matter of reproducing the main points of each section of the report.

Previously, abstracts were used only for extremely formal, usually lengthy, reports. Letters of transmittal with synopses served for less formal, shorter reports. Now, use of computers to store data has made the abstract a necessity in many organizations because the abstract has become an important part of computerized indexing systems.

The next example shows Rotunda's synopsis written as a separate part of the report.

                                                                    iv
                              Abstract

An examination of factors outside the laundromat and a
survey of customers to ascertain conditions inside the
laundromat show that causes for the decline in business are
customer dissatisfaction with hours and attendants in Sun
Bright Laundromat's second facility. Telephone interviews
with managers of two mobile home parks near the second facility, a visit to a competing laundromat, and a questionnaire distributed to 200 customers at each of Sun Bright's
three facilities reveal these conclusions. Specifically,
28 percent of the customers at the second facility prefer
to do their laundry at times when the laundromat is closed.
Many of these customers patronize a competitor's laundromat, even when the laundromat is open. These customers
also expressed dissatisfaction with the upkeep of the
laundromat and with the service received from attendants.
Changing or extending business hours and conducting spot
checks of the facility when part-time attendants are at
work might remedy these problems.

Example E. Abstract.

Contents

The contents page gives the page number of each major section of the report. Thus, the contents page is really an outline of the report which tells the reader on which page a major section of the report begins. Including a contents page is especially useful in reports of ten pages or more because it enables the reader to find a specific part of the report quickly and easily.

Contents

Example F. Contents.

The Body of the Report

The body of the report is the body of information that the writer is conveying to the reader by means of the report form. It is ordinarily made up of five sections: (1) introduction, (2) method, (3) results, (4) conclusions, and (5) recommendations. As you know from previous chapters, your audience may not ask for recommendations. In that case, you omit the recommendations section. You may also join conclusions and recommendations, especially if they are brief, in one section rather than write them as separate sections. Finally, a distinguishing feature of formal reports is a more elaborate system of headings than you have used so far.

Introduction

The introduction defines the problem to be solved, gives the purpose of the report, explains the scope of the research, and outlines the steps the writer will take in the rest of the report. When you read the introduction of Sal Rotunda's report to Rollin Hogaboom, you will see that Rotunda defines the problem as decline in business at the second laundromat. His purpose is to find the causes for the decline. The scope of the study includes factors outside the laundromat (as suggested by Hogaboom in chapter 13) and conditions inside the laundromat (ascertained through use of a customer survey).

Like any other message, the report may be written directly or indirectly. You noticed that Rotunda began his report with the conclusions he had reached as the result of his research. The reader, Rollin Hogaboom, was most interested in the conclusions because they directly answered his questions about the decline in business. The report may also begin with the recommendations if they are the reader's chief interest. Beginning with conclusions or recommendations has become increasingly common. As readers have less time to devote to reports, they want the important information first. They may read the rest of the report as time and interest dictate.

If your report mixes both primary and secondary research, the introduction may also contain references to the published work of other researchers engaged in the same kind of study. These references help fill in the background of the report, update readers on continuing research on a particular subject, and show the place your study has in an ongoing process. If you include secondary references in your introduction, remember that your task is to give only relevant and pertinent data—such as major facts, methods, results, and conclusions—rather than to give lengthy paraphrases of other studies.

Method

The method section of your report describes how you conducted your study. This description includes two parts, subjects and procedure.

Subjects are people, animals, or objects that the researcher gathers information about. In the subjects section of method, you answer three important questions.

(1) *How many subjects participated in the study?* The number of subjects may change from the beginning to the end of a research project. If the number does change, the writer must give both beginning and ending figures. For example, if the researcher sent out 200 questionnaires, of which 10 were completed and returned, the report would give both numbers to inform the reader of exactly how many responses the report was based on. To omit the number of returned questionnaires might be misleading. The reader would assume that a statement like "20 percent of the participants liked the fruit-flavored cereal" meant that 40 people liked the cereal because 20 percent of 200 is 40. In actuality, only two people stated a preference for the fruit-flavored cereal because 20 percent of the 10 people who answered the questionnaire is two.

(2) *Who were the subjects?* The answer to this question distinguishes the subjects of a study from everyone or everything else. For example, all the subjects in Rotunda's study were laundromat users. In some studies, the researcher identifies other characteristics such as age, sex, or economic or social status, depending on the purpose of the report. Animals may be identified by such characteristics as genus, species, age, and sex. Objects, such as the bicycles in Ryder's study, may be identified by brand or model number, or any other characteristic that distinguishes them from objects in the same class.

(3) *How were the subjects selected?* Some subjects are selected randomly. They are the first 20 people who walk in the door when the researcher is asking for volunteers to fill out a questionnaire. They may also be selected because they belong to a particular group, such as business communicators, chief executive officers of Fortune 500 companies, or high school teachers of consumer education courses, from whom the researcher wishes to gather information. People whose names appear on membership or mailing lists are often selected as subjects for research because the researcher can contact them easily. Objects are selected for much the same reason—because they form a group. Stan Ryder, as you will recall, selected only bicycles made by foreign companies controlling at least 1 percent of the U.S. market.

Procedure, the second part of the method section, details the specific steps the researcher uses to get information from the subjects. If a questionnaire is used to elicit information, the researcher notes whether he or she distributed the questionnaires personally, had other agents distribute them, or distributed them through the mail. Procedure also describes the way in which the researcher tallies the results of questionnaires or condenses and lists other information he or she has gathered.

Similarly, if interviews are used, the researcher mentions whether the interviews were conducted in person or by telephone. If information is the result of tests, the researcher mentions the kind of test, the test site, conditions, and materials. This section also sets forth any special instructions the researcher has given to the subjects.

Results

The results section reports the data the researcher has gathered. The first rule to remember is to report refined data. Up to this point, the researcher has concentrated on collecting raw data. After collecting the raw data, the researcher refines it by tabulation. Tabulation refers to any method such as tallying, condensing, or listing the researcher uses to put information into cohesive form. As you learned in chapter 11, one of the best ways to communicate large amounts of data clearly and concisely is in graphic form. The results section contains any graphs, charts, or tables you have prepared as well as an explanation of them.

The second rule is to report only facts resulting from the information-gathering process. Familiarity with the information tempts one to rush ahead at this point and to begin to interpret the facts. Such interpretations properly belong in the conclusions section.

A third rule is to report only the relevant facts. Most often, the research process produces much more information than the writer needs. Discriminating between information that helps to solve a problem and information that may be interesting in itself but has no direct bearing on the solution is one of the writer's greatest challenges. Making a correct choice about what to leave out strengthens the report. A word of caution is perhaps appropriate here: The writer must not leave out relevant information that runs counter to his or her expectations. In an informative report, the writer's goal is to report the truth as revealed by the facts, not to persuade the reader to accept a particular position by selecting only the facts that support that position.

The writing of the results section follows the same rules for organization as any other message you have already written. Once you have limited your information in relation to its relevance to solving the problem, you present it in what you judge to be the most efficient order. Refer to chapter 4 to refresh your memory on choices of organizational plan.

If you are writing a report that mixes primary and secondary research, you may also include comparisons of your results with those of the authors you mentioned in the introduction.

Conclusions

The conclusions section of your report is the proper place to analyze and interpret the factual material presented in the results section. First, conclusions must relate directly to the problem or question being studied. Second, they must derive from the facts the researcher has gathered. Third, they must inform the facts. That is, they must supply an overall meaning to the facts because arriving at logical conclusions is the reason for going through the research process and presenting the research in the form of a written report.

You may arrive at more than one conclusion as the result of research. When you have two or more conclusions to report, you can present them clearly by numbering and listing them. The order in which you give results dictates the order for presenting conclusions. Using the same order adds to the coherence of the report.

Recommendations

When you are asked to include recommendations, remember that careful audience analysis will serve you well. First, focus on the possible in your recommendations. Making recommendations not in the power of your reader to carry out is useless and better omitted. Second, avoid making suggestions not based on conclusions. Your recommendations should flow directly from conclusions. For this reason, the conclusions and recommendations sections are sometimes combined in one section. When each is short, it does not warrant its own separate section unless the reader expects or specifically requests writing each as a separate section.

End Parts of the Report

If the body of the report contains complete information, the writer simply stops with the last sentence in the conclusions or recommendations. However, if the report is a mixture of primary and secondary research, the writer must add a list of reference notes and a bibliography to give the sources of secondary information. If you have included secondary research, read the second part of this chapter for instruction on writing reference notes and bibliography.

Writers of formal reports based on primary research sometimes add one appendix or more to the report. An appendix is supplementary information. Appended information may go into more depth on a specific topic than is necessary in the body of the report, or an appendix may give information that helps fill in the background for the reader. Questionnaires (often with responses tallied); new computer programs used for the study; the text of a speech, interview, or unpublished report; or useful references not cited in the report itself are items appropriate to appendices.

SPECIAL CONSIDERATIONS

Headings

To this point, you have used side headings to identify various sections of messages. Side headings are sufficient for one- or two-page messages.

Longer messages like formal reports, however, require a greater degree of differentiation among headings to show the reader the interrelationship among parts of the body of the report. Thus, levels are assigned to headings. The placement of the heading in the text shows its level.

In most reports, three levels of headings are usually enough. Although reports begin with an introduction, *Introduction* is rarely written out as a heading because readers take for granted that the first thing they read after the title of the report is the introduction.

Guidelines for Headings

1. Center a first-level heading on a line by itself. First-level headings signal main sections of the report. First-level headings in this report structure are *Method, Results, Conclusions*, and *Recommendations*.

2. Place second-level headings on their own line at the left margin. Second-level headings signal divisions within the main sections of the report. For example, *Method*, the first main section, is divided into *Subjects* and *Procedure*. Thus, headings in this section would look like this:

Method

Subjects

Procedure

3. Indent third-level headings and place them at the beginning of the first line of the paragraph. Put periods after third-level headings to separate them from the paragraph. (Notice that third-level headings are the only ones that are punctuated.) Just as second-level headings are divisions of main sections of reports, third-level headings are divisions of subsections. Therefore, you will never have a third-level heading unless you have a second-level heading. Study the example that follows.

Method

Subjects
Procedure
    Site.
    Conditions.
    Materials.

4. Underline all headings to make them stand out from other written material.

5. Capitalize the main words of first- and second-level headings. Capitalize only the first word of third-level headings (except when you would capitalize a word normally).

Format Guidelines

1. Use single spacing on the title page.

2. Place the three title-page entries on the title page, beginning on line 16 with the title of the report. Information about the recipient begins at the middle of the page on lines 30-33. Information about the writer and the submission date starts on line 48.

3. Leave visible margins of 1 inch on each of the four sides of every sheet. (If you are putting your report in a binder, leave an actual margin of 1½ inches on the left side so that 1 inch of margin will be visible.)

4. Follow format instructions for the letter of transmittal as given on pages 327 to 329.

5. Organize the contents page in two columns beneath the centered title *Contents*. Give major sections of the report in the left column. Indent subheadings five spaces under each major heading. Give the page number on which the section begins in the right column under the column heading *Page*. The examples below show two ways to organize a contents page.

<u>**Contents**</u>

	Page
Abstract	iv
Preliminary Investigation	1
Method	1
Subjects	1
Procedure	2
Results	2

Or

<u>**Contents**</u>

	Page
Abstract	iv
I. Preliminary Investigation	1
II. Method	1
A. Subjects	2
B. Procedure	2
III. Results	2

6. Place the abstract on a separate page beneath the centered title <u>Abstract.</u>

7. Repeat the title of the report on the first page of the body of the report. Remember to center it.

8. See page 338 to format headings in the body of the report.

9. Begin typing or writing every page 1 inch from the top of the sheet.

10. Use double spacing for the rest of the report.

11. Place one appendix or more after all the other sections of the report, including reference and bibliography pages. Center the title <u>Appendix</u>. Two spaces beneath it, write the title of the appendix. Leave the rest of the sheet blank. Add whatever you wish to append in its original form rather than in rewritten form. For example, if you used a questionnaire in your research, include a copy of the actual questionnaire.

12. Use lower case Roman numerals for prefatory parts of the report. Convert Arabic numerals to Roman as shown below.

Roman numerals	i	ii	iii	iv	v	vi	vii	viii	ix	x
Arabic numerals	1	2	3	4	5	6	7	8	9	10

13. Count each page of the prefatory parts.

14. Write Roman numerals only on pages following the letter of transmittal. (Thus, the contents page is numbered iii.)

15. Use Arabic numerals for the body of the paper.

16. Count the first page of the body but don't put a number on it.

17. Place both Roman and Arabic numerals in the upper right corner of each sheet, four spaces from the top of the page and in line with the right margin stop.

SAMPLE FORMAL REPORT BASED ON PRIMARY RESEARCH

If Sal Rotunda had been reporting to an officer of a regional or national chain of franchised laundromats rather than to the owner of a chain of three laundromats, he would have submitted a formal report rather than a letter report. Rotunda's report is an example that shows you how the structure of his report changes from that which you studied in chapter 13 while the content remains the same. You can use Rotunda's report as a model. Together with the format guidelines, it will help you prepare the final copy of your own report for submission.

Causes for Declining Profits
at Sun Bright Laundromat's Second Facility

Prepared for

Rollin Hogaboom
Sun Bright Laundromat
126 Flowerfield Road
Pittsburg, KS 66762

Prepared by

Sal Rotunda
Retired Executives Council
2500 Russell Drive (Suite B)
Pittsburg, KS 66762

August 1, 198-

August 1, 198-

Mr. Rollin Hogaboom
Sun Bright Laundromat
126 Flowerfield Road
Pittsburg, KS 66762

Dear Mr. Hogaboom:

Here are my findings on the decline in business at Sun
Bright Laundromat's second facility about which you asked
me to report on July 17.

My research indicates that the causes for the decline at
your second facility are customer dissatisfaction with the
laundromat's hours and with its attendants. To remedy
these problems, you should consider extending the laundromat's hours and more closely monitoring your employees'
performance.

Researching this report has been an interesting challenge.
Should you wish any further explanation, please call me at
232-0343, and I will be happy to discuss the report with
you. My colleague on the Retired Executives Council, Linda
Ganis, is also available to discuss your personnel problems
with you.

Sincerely,

S. Rotunda

Sal Rotunda

SR/dz

Contents

Abstract   iv

An examination of factors outside the laundromat and a
survey of customers to ascertain conditions inside the
laundromat show that causes for the decline in business are
customer dissatisfaction with hours and attendants in Sun
Bright Laundromat's second facility. Telephone interviews
with managers of two mobile home parks near the second facility, a visit to a competing laundromat, and a questionnaire distributed to 200 customers at each of Sun Bright's
three facilities reveal these conclusions. Specifically,
28 percent of the customers at the second facility prefer
to do their laundry at times when the laundromat is closed.
Many of these customers patronize a competitor's laundromat, even when the laundromat is open. These customers
also expressed dissatisfaction with the upkeep of the
laundromat and with the service received from attendants.
Changing or extending business hours and conducting spot
checks of the facility when part-time attendants are at
work might remedy these problems.

Causes for Declining Profits at
Sun Bright Laundromat's Second Facility

An examination of factors outside the laundromat and a survey of customers to ascertain conditions inside the laundromat revealed that causes for the decline in business at Sun Bright Laundromat's second facility stem from causes within the laundromat itself. These causes are customer dissatisfaction with hours and attendants.

A preliminary investigation of possible outside causes for the decline in business at Sun Bright Laundromat's second facility proved negative. Telephone interviews with managers of two mobile home parks near the laundromat reveal no major changes in the age mix or occupancy rate of park residents. Further, because of drainage systems at both parks, residents may not use automatic washers in their homes. For the same reason, parks' management has not installed laundry facilities on the premises. Additionally, a comparison of Sun Bright's prices with those of competitors shows no significant differences. Thus, factors outside the laundromat may be eliminated from consideration as possible causes for the decline in business.

After eliminating outside factors, the next steps in the investigation were to survey customers at all three facilities, analyze the data revealed in the survey, and develop conclusions and recommendations from these data.

Method

Subjects

    Subjects were 600 customers, chosen randomly through-
out each day, at Sun Bright Laundromat's three facilities.
These customers who volunteered their time represented
three groups of 200 at each laundromat.

Procedure

    Three marketing interns from Eastern State University
distributed questionnaires for seven days to customers at
each of the facilities. The interns collected 30 responses
each weekday and 20 responses Sunday. They provided each
respondent with a copy of the questionnaire and a pencil
and asked the respondents to assess the laundromat.

    The interns returned to the Retired Executives Council
office and tallied the questionnaire results by hand. They
then transferred the results to a master copy of the questionnaire which is printed in the Appendix.

Results

    The answers to the questionnaire show two areas of
concern: (1) with hours and (2) with service.

Hours

    Twenty-eight percent of the customers indicated they
preferred to do laundry at times when the second laundromat
is closed. During the week of the survey, 32.5 percent of
the customers had done at least one load of laundry at a
competitor's laundromat between 8 am. and 8 pm. Ten percent (20 customers) did laundry between 6 and 8 am, and

22.5 percent (45 customers) did laundry between 8 and 10 pm.

Many customers appear to be avoiding the second laundromat during hours when it is open. Of these people, 38 percent preferred to use the facility on Saturday and Sunday. While 28.8 percent actually used it at their preferred time, 27.7 percent patronized a competing laundromat. Furthermore, while 29 percent of the customers indicated a preference for using the facility between 4 and 8 pm, only 16.5 percent actually used it during that time period. Another 14 percent used a competitor's facility between 4 and 8 pm.

Attendants

Two other areas of customer dissatisfaction concern the attendants' responsibilities for upkeep of the facility and service to the customers. At the second laundromat, for example, 94.5 percent of the customers reported difficulties getting change, 23.5 percent and 2.5 percent reported the machines were "somewhat dirty" and "dirty," and 45 percent reported dissatisfaction with items like lavatories and folding tables as well as with general conditions.

Many customers also expressed concern about the service they received from attendants at the second laundromat. For example, 35 percent claimed the attendant failed to help them solve problems, and 70 percent felt the attendant was not pleasant in giving assistance.

Conclusions and Recommendations

1. The hours that the second laundromat is open do not
    suit the customers' needs. A change or extension of
    business hours, especially on weekends, might remedy
    this problem.

2. The attendants do not appear to be fulfilling their
    duties. Customers complain about upkeep and service.
    They are avoiding the facility after 4 pm and on
    weekends, which seems to indicate that the part-time
    attendants rather than full-time employee are at fault.
    Spot checks of the second facility at times when
    part-time attendants are at work would verify this
    conclusion.

5

Appendix

Questionnaire with Results

QUESTIONNAIRE AND ANSWERS

1. How many times a week do you use this or any other laundromat?

<table>
<tr><th></th><th colspan="3">Laundry No.</th></tr>
<tr><th></th><th>1</th><th>2</th><th>3</th></tr>
<tr><td>Less than once a week</td><td>40</td><td>20</td><td>34</td></tr>
<tr><td>Once a week</td><td>82</td><td>44</td><td>72</td></tr>
<tr><td>Twice a week</td><td>32</td><td>56</td><td>62</td></tr>
<tr><td>Three times a week</td><td>36</td><td>62</td><td>26</td></tr>
<tr><td>More than three times a week</td><td>8</td><td>18</td><td>6</td></tr>
</table>

2. What day(s) of the week do you prefer to use this or any other laundromat?

<table>
<tr><td>Monday</td><td>50</td><td>55</td><td>60</td></tr>
<tr><td>Tuesday</td><td>42</td><td>38</td><td>33</td></tr>
<tr><td>Wednesday</td><td>32</td><td>55</td><td>51</td></tr>
<tr><td>Thursday</td><td>55</td><td>50</td><td>75</td></tr>
<tr><td>Friday</td><td>50</td><td>65</td><td>40</td></tr>
<tr><td>Saturday</td><td>52</td><td>97</td><td>63</td></tr>
<tr><td>Sunday</td><td>26</td><td>70</td><td>35</td></tr>
</table>

3. What time of day do you prefer to use this or any other laundry facility?

<table>
<tr><td>8 — 12 am</td><td>100</td><td>56</td><td>90</td></tr>
<tr><td>12 — 4 pm</td><td>72</td><td>30</td><td>67</td></tr>
<tr><td>4 — 8 pm</td><td>24</td><td>58</td><td>38</td></tr>
<tr><td>Other</td><td>4</td><td>56</td><td>6</td></tr>
</table>

4. Last week, what day(s) of the week did you use this laundromat?

<table>
<tr><td>None</td><td>6</td><td>15</td><td>10</td></tr>
<tr><td>Monday</td><td>45</td><td>40</td><td>40</td></tr>
<tr><td>Tuesday</td><td>41</td><td>30</td><td>32</td></tr>
<tr><td>Wednesday</td><td>15</td><td>40</td><td>54</td></tr>
<tr><td>Thursday</td><td>43</td><td>45</td><td>68</td></tr>
<tr><td>Friday</td><td>42</td><td>55</td><td>44</td></tr>
<tr><td>Saturday</td><td>51</td><td>55</td><td>60</td></tr>
<tr><td>Sunday</td><td>20</td><td>30</td><td>40</td></tr>
</table>

5. Last week, what day(s) of the week did you use a laundromat other than this one?

None	170	130	181
Monday	5	15	10
Tuesday	1	8	4
Wednesday	17	12	1
Thursday	12	8	2
Friday	8	10	2
Saturday	1	38	3
Sunday	6	36	2

6. Last week, what time(s) did you use this laundromat?

8 – 12 am	110	67	80
12 – 4 pm	61	50	72
4 – 8 pm	17	33	35

7. Last week, what time(s) did you use a laundromat other than this one?

6 – 8 am	2	20	6
8 – 12 am	26	5	8
12 – 4 pm	12	8	9
4 – 8 pm	4	28	4
8 – 10 pm	6	45	9

8. Do you have to wait for the machines you want to use at this laundry facility?

Single load washer

yes	10	5	12
no	180	180	170
sometimes	10	15	18

Double load washer

yes	22	15	10
no	147	153	150
sometimes	31	32	40

Triple load washer

yes	16	10	16
no	156	170	148
sometimes	28	20	36

Extractor			
yes	39	32	22
no	121	120	124
sometimes	40	48	54
Drier			
yes	12	10	6
no	150	149	132
sometimes	38	41	62
Sink and wringer			
yes	0	0	0
no	199	200	200
sometimes	1	0	0

9. When you use this laundromat, do you find the laundry supplies you need in the vending machine?

Always	60	30	24
Usually	55	64	89
Sometimes	20	54	11
Rarely	5	12	3
N/A	60	40	73

10. When you use this laundromat, do you find the change you need in the coin and bill changing machine?

Always	3	1	8
Usually	145	110	154
Sometimes	20	56	30
Rarely	7	23	5
N/A	25	10	3

11. Do you consider the machines in this facility are in

Good condition	170	172	168
Fair condition	28	25	23
Poor condition	2	3	9

12. Do you consider the machines in this facility are

Modern	160	165	155
A little old	34	30	35
Quite old	6	5	10

13. Do you consider the machines in this facility are

Very clean	84	16	75
Clean	112	152	123
Somewhat dirty	2	27	1
Dirty	0	5	1

14. Are the lavatory and sorting tables in this facility

Very clean	120	60	107
Clean	45	50	77
Somewhat dirty	30	60	16
Dirty	5	30	0

15. Are the floors, walls, etc., in this facility

Very clean	120	50	173
Clean	50	60	78
Somewhat dirty	30	70	7
Dirty	0	20	2

16. Have you needed help from the attendant at this facility?

yes	180	191	178
no	20	9	22

17. Could the attendant solve your problem?

Yes	170	130	160
No	30	70	40

18. Was the attendant pleasant while giving you assistance?

Yes	190	60	180
No	10	140	20

REPORTS BASED ON SECONDARY RESEARCH

Reports based on secondary research bring together other authors' published ideas in new wholes. Authors share their efforts with us through publication so that we do not have to replicate their work every time we are faced with a problem they have already solved or a question they have already answered. Your term papers or library research papers are examples of secondary research. Organizations also use secondary research to gather background material necessary to the decisionmaking process.

Organizing Your Time

Successful completion of a report based on secondary research depends a good deal on managing time well. Many people think that no other single factor determines the quality of the finished product more. Fortunately, doing this kind of report allows you to organize your time easily because fairly discrete steps make up the process. As in preparing any other kind of message, these steps divide into pre-writing and writing. You can make up a schedule to help you finish your report on time.

	Allotted Time	*Date*
I. Pre-writing		
A. Preparing a bibliography		
B. Taking notes		
C. Organizing notes		
II. Writing		
A. Preparing the first draft		
B Revising		
C. Producing the final copy		
D. Proofreading		
III. Due date		

A glance at the schedule seems to indicate that the writing steps should take more time than the pre-writing steps. However, many writers spend two-thirds of their time on the pre-writing phase and one-third on the actual writing. Completing the preliminaries, gathering sufficient information and organizing it carefully, allows you to concentrate only on writing and, thus, to use your writing time efficiently. If you have to spend some of your writing time in trips to the library to check a source or to take more notes, then "writing" becomes a burden.

Preparing a Bibliography

By definition, a bibliography is a list of sources of information published by other authors. Bibliographies may include unpublished materials such as theses, dissertations, and other reports and papers, however. Once you know what your topic is, you can begin preparing a bibliography. Before you go to the library to begin work, get some 3-inch by 5-inch index cards for recording your bibliographic references. Using index cards for your bibliography is helpful. As you add more references, you can re-alphabetize your cards easily to keep them in the correct order. At the library, you will find numerous resources to help you in the preparation of your bibliography.

Computer Searches

If your library is equipped for it, you can do bibliographic research electronically through on-line searches of computerized, commercial databases. Databases are computer-readable collections of records selected from databases using a computer terminal connected to a host terminal by telephone line or telecommunications network. Hundreds of databases covering all subject areas are now available.

An on-line search has many advantages over the traditional, manual search which relies on printed sources. The on-line search can retrieve bibliographic references representing two or more concepts or subject terms, thus allowing greater specificity. It can search for new or jargon words because the computer is instructed to search not only subject headings but also title and abstract words. Because of computer storage capabilities, on-line databases often index and record more publications than printed sources; thus, the on-line search can be more comprehensive. Since databases are updated more frequently than their printed equivalents, an on-line search can provide more recent references. Finally, an on-line search can cover a range of dates in one step, whereas a manual search is a volume-by-volume, year-by-year process.

Many libraries and information centers now offer computerized search services to their users. In some instances, the user is charged for the service, based on database royalty fees, telecommunications fees, and costs of records printed.

A few of the many available commercial databases are listed below. Your librarian or information specialist can describe the coverage and contents of the databases and tell you how an on-line search of them can assist you with your research.

Selected Databases

Database	Scope
ABI/Inform	Business, management, and industry
America: History and Life	American history
ERIC	Education
GPO Monthly Catalog	Government publications
Magazine Index	Popular magazines
Management Contents	Business
National Newspaper Index	*New York Times, Wall Street Journal, Christian Science Monitor*
Psycinfo	Psychology
P.A.I.S. (Public Affairs Information Service)	Social sciences

The Card Catalog

In preparing a bibliography manually, an important resource is the card catalog. The card catalog is a file cabinet of cards which contain information on the books your library owns. The card catalog lists books in at least three different ways: by author, by title, and by subject. This division corresponds to the three divisions of the card catalog itself. When you know the general topic of your report but don't know any specific book titles or authors on that topic, you can look in the subject section of the card catalog to see what books the library has. For example, a student preparing a bibliography on word processing found this card.

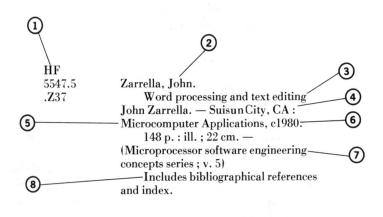

HF
5547.5
.Z37   Zarrella, John.
                  Word processing and text editing
            John Zarrella. — Suisun City, CA :
            Microcomputer Applications, c1980.
                  148 p. : ill. ; 22 cm. —
            (Microprocessor software engineering
            concepts series ; v. 5)
                        Includes bibliographical references
            and index.

        1. Word processing (Office practice)
I. Title

MiKW   24 MAY 82   6425285   EXWBaa 80-114189r80

Look carefully at the cards you find in the card catalog. Each card has information that enables you to locate a book as well as information necessary for your bibliography cards.

Familiarize yourself with the items on the catalog card.

1. Library call number
2. Author
3. Title
4. Place of publication
5. Publisher
6. Date of publication
7. Series
8. Contents

Many catalog cards briefly describe the book's contents. Scan this description for items relevant to your particular topic. Later, when you are ready to find the book in the library, you will be better informed on its particular use to you.

Indexes to Periodicals

Much information useful to the report writer appears in periodicals. Periodicals are publications such as scholarly and professional journals, magazines, and newspapers that are published at regular intervals: quarterly, monthly, weekly, or daily, for example. To find information published in periodicals, you can consult indexes to periodicals. These indexes generally list articles by both subject and author. Some indexes are for general use because they list articles from popular rather than specialized periodicals.

Indexes for General Use

1. *Readers' Guide to Periodical Literature* indexes over 100 well known magazines.
2. *New York Times Index* catalogs articles appearing in the *New York Times*. It covers agriculture, business, economics, history, military affairs, politics, religion, and science.
3. *Social Sciences and Humanities Index* lists articles of social and cultural interest.
4. *The Vertical File Service Catalog* concentrates on less widely circulated publications such as monographs and pamphlets.

Many indexes have a narrower scope because they list articles published in specialized periodicals. If you do not know the index for your particular area, consult your reference librarian or read through this partial list.

Indexes for Specialized Use

1. *Accountants' Index*
2. *Applied Science and Technology Index*
3. *Art Index*
4. *Biological Abstracts*
5. *Biological and Agricultural Index*
6. *Business Periodicals Index*
7. *Chemical Abstracts*
8. *CIJE* (Current Index to Journals in Education)
9. *Engineering Index*
10. *The Humanities Index*
11. *MLA* (Modern Language Association)
12. *P.A.I.S.* (Public Affairs Information Service)
13. *Psychological Abstracts*
14. *The Social Sciences Index*

Because of the large number of different articles they list, indexes shorten the form of entries to save space. The forms differ from index to index, but each index has a key to help you understand what each item in the entry means. Here is the January, 1982, entry on word processing from *Business Periodicals Index.*

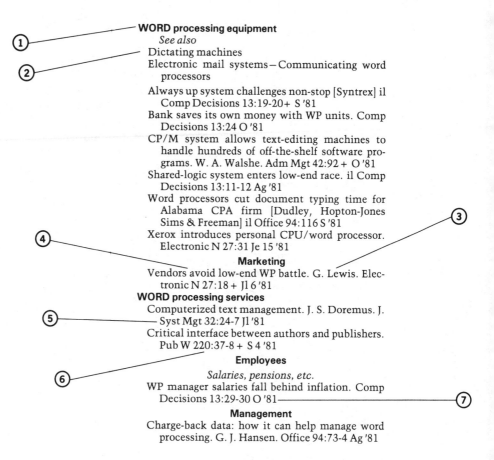

WORD processing equipment
    See also
    Dictating machines
    Electronic mail systems – Communicating word
       processors
    Always up system challenges non-stop [Syntrex] il
       Comp Decisions 13:19-20+ S '81
    Bank saves its own money with WP units. Comp
       Decisions 13:24 O '81
    CP/M system allows text-editing machines to
       handle hundreds of off-the-shelf software pro-
       grams. W. A. Walshe. Adm Mgt 42:92 + O '81
    Shared-logic system enters low-end race. il Comp
       Decisions 13:11-12 Ag '81
    Word processors cut document typing time for
       Alabama CPA firm [Dudley, Hopton-Jones
       Sims & Freeman] il Office 94:116 S '81
    Xerox introduces personal CPU/word processor.
       Electronic N 27:31 Je 15 '81
                Marketing
    Vendors avoid low-end WP battle. G. Lewis. Elec-
       tronic N 27:18 + Jl 6 '81
WORD processing services
    Computerized text management. J. S. Doremus. J.
       Syst Mgt 32:24-7 Jl '81
    Critical interface between authors and publishers.
       Pub W 220:37-8 + S 4 '81
                Employees
         Salaries, pensions, etc.
    WP manager salaries fall behind inflation. Comp
       Decisions 13:29-30 O '81
              Management
    Charge-back data: how it can help manage word
       processing. G. J. Hansen. Office 94:73-4 Ag '81

Business Periodicals Index, ©1982 by the H.W. Wilson Company.
Material reproduced by permission of the publisher.

Study the placement of contents in the entry.

1. Subject

2. Cross-reference to other subject sections which have information on word processing

3. Author

4. Title

5. Periodical, abbreviated

6. Volume number, followed by page numbers after the colon

7. Date of publication, abbreviated

Preparing Bibliography Cards

Once you have located your reference sources, you can begin making bibliography cards. Each card should contain two kinds of information: (1) library call numbers to lead you to different places in the library where books are stored; (2) bibliographic information on authors, titles, places of publication, publishers, and dates to use in the final bibliography of your report. Putting down complete bibliographic information, shown in items 2-6 on the sample card, in the order and form in which you will use it later in the bibliography of your report will save time in the final production stage of the report.

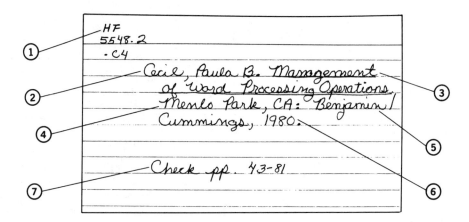

Study the sample bibliography card for a book.

1. Library call number
2. Author's name in inverted order, extended five spaces to the left of the rest of the entry
3. Book title, underlined
4. Place of publication
5. Name of publisher
6. Date of publication
7. Note on contents of particular interest

A bibliography card for a periodical article differs in some respects from a bibliography card for a book as the next example shows.

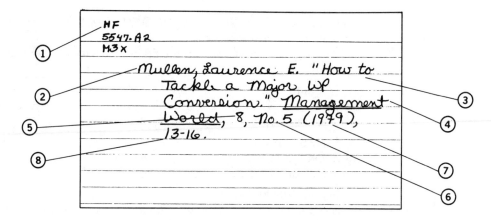

Study the sample bibliography card for an article.

1. Library call number, found by consulting your library's list of periodicals holdings

2. Author's name in inverted order, extended five spaces to the left of the rest of the entry

3. Article title, in quotation marks

4. Name of periodical, underlined

5. Volume number

6. Issue number

7. Date of publication

8. Total pages of article

As you study these bibliography cards and the sample entries that follow, pay particular attention to punctuation. Author, title, and publication information, the main parts of any entry, are separated by periods.

Sample Bibliographic Entries: Books

1. One author

Grossman, Lee. *Fat Paper: Diets for Trimming Paperwork.* New York: McGraw-Hill, 1976.

2. Author, more than one work

Cecil, Paula B. *Management of Word Processing Operations.* Menlo Park, CA: Benjamin/Cummings, 1980.

Cecil, Paula B. *Word Processing in the Modern Office.* Menlo Park, CA: Cummings, 1976.
(Arrange two or more entries by the same author in alphabetical order by book title.)

3. Two authors

Bergerud, Marly, and Jean Gonzalez. *Word Processing: Concepts and Careers.* New York: Wiley, 1978.

4. Three or more authors

Anderson, Ruth I., and others. *The Administrative Secretary: Resource.* New York: McGraw-Hill, Gregg Division, 1970.

5. Organizational author

British Computer Society. *Data Dictionary Systems Working Party Report.* Philadelphia: Heyden & Son, 1977.

6. Author and editor

Carter, Shirley G. *Word Processing & Other Automated Publication Systems.* Ed. Robert J. Zabielski. Washington, D.C.: Society for Technical Communication, 1981.

7. Editor, no author

House, William C., ed. *Data Base Management.* New York: Van Nostrand Reinhold, 1974.

8. Edition

Hanna, J. Marshall, and others. *Secretarial Procedures and Administration.* 6th ed. Cincinnati: South-Western, 1973.

9. Series

Zarrella, John. *Word Processing and Text Editing.* Microprocessor Software Engineering Concept Series. Suisun City, CA: Microcomputer Applications, 1980.

10. Volume

Seelye, E. *Design.* 3d ed. Vol. 1 of *Data Book for Civil Engineers.* 3 vols. New York: Wiley, 1960.

Sample Bibliographic Entries: Periodicals

1. Journals

Mullen, Laurence E. "How to Tackle a Major WP Conversion." *Management World*, 8, No. 5 (1979), 13-16.
(Inclusion of an issue number eliminates the need to give the month. Some journals do not have issue numbers but if they do, include the issue number.)

2. Journal, no author

"Cost Effectiveness of Word Processor Is Questioned." *International Management*, 36, No. 6 (1981), 3.

(If an article appears without an author's name, it is called an unsigned article. Put the title in the author position and alphabetize by the first word in the title unless it is *A, An,* or *The.*)

3. Magazine, no volume number

"PERT for Micros." *Industrial Management + Data Systems*, November, 1980, p. 46.

(When a magazine has no volume number, give the month and year [and day for weekly magazines] of publication. Use the abbreviations *p.* or *pp.* for *page* or *pages* because no volume number is present.)

4. Newspaper, daily

"IBM Word Processor Jolts the Industry." *Wall Street Journal*, March 24, 1981, p. 54, col. 1.

(Give the month and day of publication as well as the number of the column in which the article begins.)

Sample Bibliographic Entries: Other Forms

1. Interview

Wilhoit, Benjamin. Interview. Charlottesville, VA, Sept. 23, 1982.

2. Monograph

Erickson, Lawrence W. *Basic Components of Office Work — An Analysis of 300 Office Jobs.* Cincinnati: South-Western, 1971. (Monograph 123)

3. Pamphlet

U.S. Bureau of the Census. *Bicentennial Statistics.* Reprinted from *Pocket Data Book, USA 1976.* Washington, D.C.: Government Printing Office, 1976.

4. Annual report

Campbell Soup Company. *1981 Annual Report.* Camden, NJ, 1982.

After collecting your bibliography and alphabetizing your cards, you have what is called a working bibliography. You may add cards to it as your reading uncovers other sources of information. Integrate cards from additional sources alphabetically.

Taking Notes

As you gather your bibliography, you will notice that the books and articles fall into several loose categories. Kelly Wolf, a student writing on the general topic of word processing, found categories like costs, equipment, personnel, and management. Divisions in the indexes and notes on the cards in the card catalog suggested some of these categories. Others grew from scanning books and articles in her bibliography. To work efficiently, Kelly focused her research by following these steps: (1) reviewing collected material; (2) deciding on an area of interest within the general subject; (3) evaluating library resources to insure that sufficient information was available in her area of interest.

Having focused on word processing equipment, Kelly narrowed her topic in this way.

What:	to describe how to choose word processing equipment
Why:	to learn about the equipment selection process
Where:	U.S.
When:	current
Who:	companies

From these answers, she developed the following descriptive sentence: This report will describe how some U.S. companies choose word processing equipment.

Kelly next drew up a rough outline in the form of a list of questions to guide her in further research.

1. Does the size of the company affect choice?
2. Does the way a word processor works affect choice?
3. How does cost affect choice?
4. How much can companies save by their choice?
   Staff?
   Files?
5. Does the type of work affect choice?

This rough outline changed many times as the note-taking process revealed new and different ideas. It was nonetheless a valuable starting point because it directed Kelly in taking notes.

Preparing Note Cards

When you are gathering information from more than three or four sources, use cards rather than sheets of paper for your notes. The major advantage of cards is their flexibility. When you have finished taking notes, you can arrange and rearrange the cards so that they follow the order of your outline. Taking notes on sheets of paper makes rearrangement nearly impossible. Finding specific pieces of information on sheets of paper requires a time-consuming hunt-and-peek process.

Guidelines for Note Cards

1. Use 4-by-6 inch rather than 3-by-5 inch cards. (Four-by-six are preferable because they are distinguishable from 3-by-5 bibliography cards and provide more space for information.)
2. Limit information to one kind of item a card.
3. Note the source of the information on the card. (Some people copy the author's last name or the first few words of a title of unsigned articles from the bibliography card; others use a numerical system.)
4. Put the number of the page from which you took information on the note card.
5. Label the contents of each card to speed later organization.

Following these guidelines, you can begin using one of three forms (summary, paraphrase, or quotation) for taking notes.

Summary
Summary note cards condense large amounts of information, especially specific information. The advantage of summary note cards is time saved in not having to copy whole paragraphs of information. You can write summary note cards in sentence form or in phrases, as the following example shows.

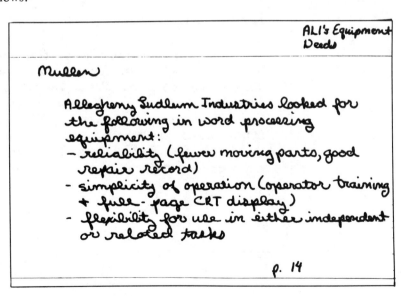

When you get to the writing stage of your report, you can refine the wording of facts on summary note cards to express them more smoothly. Even though you use your own words on summary note cards, remember to credit the author from whose book or article the ideas came.

Paraphrase

Paraphrasing is putting another author's ideas into your own words. Paraphrases differ from summaries in that summaries express a great deal of information in a few words while paraphrases use almost the same number of words as the original. Writers of reports based on secondary research paraphrase extensively. Through paraphrase, they can mold information written in different styles into a stylistically unified whole. Here is a short passage quoted directly from an article entitled "Work Measurement Justifies New WP System" by Sharon Hagelstrom, an employee of American Edwards Laboratories.

> A recent article quoted figures ranging from $7.50 to $12.00 to produce a page of text. The variables depend on whether overhead costs are included. Since my costs average less than $6.00 per page, this is ample justification for our existence, proving that I am providing my employer with a significant bargain for a vital supportive function.

A note card on which this information is paraphrased looks like this.

American Edwards: Savings

Hagelstrom

The average cost to yield a page of text is $7.50 to $12.00. American Edwards Laboratories has lowered the cost to $6.00 a page. The cost reduction insures continuance of the word processing center in an important support role while saving the company money.

p. 138

Quotation

Quotation note cards copy another author's words exactly. Quotations are enclosed in quotation marks. You are not permitted to change any words within quotation marks. However, you may omit words (or even whole sentences in long quotations) by using an ellipsis as long as you do not change an author's meaning. An ellipsis is three periods with a space before and after each period. Avoid using an ellipsis at the beginning of a quotation in your report by providing an introduction to the quotation, as the following example shows.

> J. R. "Reg" Little suggests that the primary factors to consider when establishing measurement standards are "quantity, quality, and time of production."

The advantage of quotations is in capturing the authority as well as the style and tone of the source. When paraphrasing is undesirable because of the clarity, economy, or individuality of an author's phrasing, you can use a quotation to good effect. But quote sparingly to avoid producing a report that is little more than a crazy quilt of quotations pasted together.

This paragraph quoted directly from an article entitled "What Is an Automated Office and How Does a Firm Make the Change?" describes the process of automating an office.

> According to Mr. Sinopoli, the office of tomorrow will require a system solution which merges office and data processing applications on the same data network. This, he says, will provide users with a single source of information, yet with access to a company's entire data base. Further, it will provide a foundation for true electronic document distribution, enabling users to file and distribute that filing. This will make information available to individual departments or persons, while providing access to a central data base for corporate level decisions. It also will allow users to network such time-consuming tasks as volume printing.[1]

If the report writer wanted to save this whole paragraph for future reference, he or she would copy it word for word onto a note card, enclosing it in quotation marks. If only one part of it were of interest, here is how the note card might look.

---

[1]"What Is an Automated Office and How Does a Firm Make the Change?" *The Office*, 91, No. 4 (1980), 48.

> *"What Is an Automated Office"*   document distribution
>
> [The merger of office and data processing applications] "will provide a foundation for true electronic document distribution, enabling users to file and distribute that filing. This will make information available to individual departments or persons, while providing access to a central data base for corporate level decisions."
>
> p. 48

Sample Reference Notes: Books

Notice that these reference notes are for the books and articles used in the sample bibliographic entries. Primary reference notes that give full information are followed by secondary notes used for each subsequent reference to the same author. Secondary notes are given only when they differ from the form of the secondary reference note in the first example.

1. One author
   Lee Grossman, *Fat Paper: Diets for Trimming Paperwork* (New York: McGraw-Hill, 1976), p. 43.
   Grossman, pp. 45-46.
   (Do not place a comma before the parenthesis in the first note. Use the abbreviation *p.* for *page* and *pp.* for *pages*. Write out page numbers fully: *pp. 45-46* rather than *pp. 45-6.*)

2. Author, more than one work
   Paula B. Cecil, *Management of Word Processing Operations* (Menlo Park, CA: Benjamin/Cummings, 1980), pp. 5-6.
   Cecil, *Management of Word Processing Operations*, p. 9.
   Paula B. Cecil, *Word Processing in the Modern Office* (Menlo Park, CA: Cummings, 1976), pp. 101-102.
   Cecil, *Word Processing in the Modern Office*, p. 111.
   (Give titles as well as the author's name when referring to different works by the same author or to two authors of the same name.)

3. Two authors

Marly Bergerud and Jean Gonzalez, *Word Processing: Concepts and Careers* (New York: Wiley, 1978), pp. 78-79.

Bergerud and Gonzalez, p. 89.

4. Three or more authors

Ruth I. Anderson and others, *The Administrative Secretary: Resource* (New York: McGraw-Hill, Gregg Division, 1970), p. 66.

Anderson and others, p. 67.

5. Organizational author

British Computer Society, *Data Dictionary Systems Working Party Report* (Philadelphia: Heyden & Son, 1977), p. 42.

British Computer Society, p. 48.

6. Author and editor

Shirley G. Carter, *Word Processing & Other Automated Publication Systems*, ed. Robert J. Zabielski (Washington, D.C.: Society for Technical Communication, 1981), pp. 202-203.

7. Editor, no author

William C. House, ed., *Data Base Management* (New York: Van Nostrand Reinhold), p. 98.

8. Edition

J. Marshall Hanna and others, *Secretarial Procedures and Administration*, 6th ed. (Cincinnati: South-Western, 1973), p. 36.

Hanna and others, pp. 40-41.

9. Series

John Zarrella, *Word Processing and Text Editing*, Microprocessor Software Engineering Concept Series (Suisun City, CA: Microcomputer Applications, 1980), p. 226.

10. Volume

E. Seelye, *Design*, 3d ed., Vol. 1 of *Data Book for Civil Engineers*, 3 vols. (New York: Wiley, 1960), p. 78.

Sample Reference Notes: Periodicals

1. Journals

Laurence E. Mullen, "How to Tackle a Major WP Conversion," *Management World*, 8, No. 5 (1979), 14.

Mullen, p. 15.

(Notice that the full reference note omits *p.* or *pp.*, the abbreviations for *page* and *pages*, because it has a volume number. By contrast, the shortened form uses the abbreviation for *page* because it has no volume number.)

2. Journal, no author

"Cost Effectiveness of Word Processors Is Questioned," *International Management*, 36, No. 6 (1981), 3.

"Cost Effectiveness," p. 3.

(Shorten titles of unsigned articles. Do not change the order of the words in the title, and give enough words to make the reference note understandable.)

3. Magazine, monthly

"PERT for Micros," *Industrial Management + Data Systems*, November, 1980, p. 46.

4. Newspaper, daily

"IBM Word Processor Jolts the Industry," *Wall Street Journal*, March 24, 1981, p. 54, col. 1.

"IBM Word Processor," p. 54, col. 1.

Sample Reference Notes: Other Forms

1. Interview

Benjamin Wilhoit, Interview, Charlottesville, VA, Sept. 23, 1982.

Wilhoit, Interview.

2. Monograph

Lawrence W. Erickson, *Basic Components of Office Work — An Analysis of 300 Office Jobs* (Monograph 123; Cincinnati: South-Western, 1971), p. 18.

3. Pamphlet

U.S. Bureau of the Census, *Bicentennial Statistics* (Rpt., *Pocket Data Book, USA 1976*; Washington, D.C.: Government Printing Office, 1976), p. 379.

4. Annual Report

Campbell Soup Company, *1981 Annual Report* (Camden, NJ, 1982), p. 6.

Campbell Soup Company, p. 7.

Organizing Notes

After you take notes on all areas indicated on your preliminary outline, sort the cards according to their contents into the broad categories of the outline. This step should reveal whether you have gathered enough information to write a final outline or whether you need to do more research. Kelly Wolf produced this outline from her notes.

Sample Topic Outline Selecting the Correct Word Processing Equipment

Purpose statement and message plan: In the United States, the selection of the correct word processing equipment varies with the needs of each business. Every company has different needs depending on the size of the business, the kind of business, and the savings goals of the business.

I.   Size of the business

   A. Small
   B. Medium
   C. Large

II. Kind of business

   A. Insurance
   B. Law
   C. Photographic products

III. Savings goals

   A. Michigan Consolidated Gas
   B. American Edwards Laboratories
   C. U.S. Army

This topic outline is sufficient for the short report that Kelly Wolf wrote. However, she could have written a sentence outline from the same material. If she had, here is how it would look. As you read this sentence outline, you can compare it with the report. You will notice that the sentences in the outline sometimes differ in structure and word choice though not in meaning from those in the report.

Sample Sentence Outline Selecting the Correct Word Processing Equipment

Purpose statement and message plan: In the United States, the selection of the correct word processing equipment varies with the needs of each business. Every company has different needs depending on the size of the business, the kind of business, and the savings goals of the business.

I.   The size of a business affects its choice of equipment.

   A.   Small businesses use stand-alone equipment.
   B.   Medium-sized businesses need computer systems distributed internally among offices.

      1.   Allegheny Ludlum Industries transformed its headquarters on the advice of a consulting firm.
      2.   Allegheny chose among a variety of machines.

         a. It looked for reliability and simplicity.
         b. It looked for continuing smooth function.
         c. It looked for full-page CRT display.
         d. It looked for flexibility.

      3.   Allegheny set up word processing "satellites" in key offices and stand-alones in its legal department.

    C. Large businesses require more sophisticated systems.

II. The kind of work a company does affects its selection of word processing equipment.

    A. Insurance companies have special needs.

      1. Before automating, claims writers wrote instructions by hand for typists.

      2. After automating, word processors produced individualized letters more quickly.

    B. Law firms have special needs.

      1. An OCR page scanner increased productivity.

      2. It helped to produce errorless copy.

    C. An international marketer has special needs.

      1. It must communicate between its European and U.S. headquarters.

      2. It joined word processing to telex.

III. Savings goals affect choice of word processing equipment.

    A. Michigan Consolidated Gas reduced printing costs by using word processors in its graphics department.

    B. American Edwards Laboratories lowered its cost per page by introducing a disk system.

    C. The U.S. Army reduced its staff by introducing word processing.

      1. Other government offices using word processors did not increase productivity.

      2. They need to systematize use of word processing equipment.

Writing the Report

At this point in the report writing process, you are in command of a well organized body of information. You can now concentrate on putting this information into readable form. Report writing is more than copying from note cards. You need to introduce information from secondary sources as well as to document the sources.

Introducing Information

The information you have gathered on note cards must form a smoothly flowing, coherent whole in the paper. One way to achieve coherence when you are using borrowed material is through careful introduction of quotations and paraphrases. You do not have to introduce summaries.

You must link each quotation and paraphrase to the material that comes before it. Common ways to introduce quotations and paraphrases are with phrases like the following:

— Jean Tomassi, Word Processing Supervisor at the firm, states . . . .

— In "Work Controls and Their Uses in Word Processing," Phyllis Smoot illustrates . . . .

— According to "Blending Word Processing and Telex," an article in *Modern Office Procedures*, ...

— Krois and Benson in "Word Processing and Personnel" discuss . . . .

Notice that each of these introductions includes the author's name and title, if available, or the title of a book or an article.

These introductions work equally well with paraphrases and with short and long quotations. Short quotations, fewer than four typed lines, are enclosed in quotation marks and are written continuously in the body of the report. Long quotations, four typed lines or more, are set off from the body of the report by indenting them five spaces. Because they are set off by indentation, you do not need quotation marks to identify them, as the following example shows.

Donna Taylor, the manager of word processing operations for a large corporation, offers this advice to companies switching to word processing systems:

> The biggest mistake people make when they are looking for word processing systems . . . is making no decisions at all. They look at every piece of equipment on the market, become confused, and forget it for a year. A better way . . . would be to select no more than five vendors, study the equipment carefully, narrow it down to two, and then evaluate on a feature-by-feature, benefit-by-benefit comparison to find the best equipment for their job.

Documenting Sources

Because the information you include in a report based on secondary research comes from other authors, you must give them credit for their work. Give credit by placing a number at the end of each summary, paraphrase, and quotation in your paper. Number borrowed material consecutively throughout your paper, beginning with the first item you borrow. Here is an example from Kelly Wolf's report.

According to J. R. "Reg" Little, a founder and first president of the International Word Processing Association: "There are over 50 word processing machines on the market, each with a variety of software packages, options, and features."[1]

Notice that the note number is outside the period and quotation marks, one-half space above the line. This number refers to the first reference note on the reference notes page:

[1]J. R. "Reg" Little, "Measured Typing Output: Does It Help or Hinder?" *The Office*, 91, No. 2 (1980), 31-32.

Crediting sources in this way lets readers know where you found your information. It also allows them to find a book or article in their own library if they are interested in reading more of what a particular author has written.

Preparing and Revising the First Draft

Kelly Wolf wrote the first draft of her report on word processing from her outline and note cards. Then she went through it carefully, making changes in word choice and sentence structure, correcting spelling and typing errors, and adding and deleting to improve the clarity of her report. Using her outline as a guide, Kelly also added headings to improve the readability of the final copy of her report.

Selecting the Correct Word Processing Equipment

According to J.R. "Reg" Little, a founder and first president of the International Word Processing Association: "There are over 50 word-processing machines on the market, each with a variety of software packages, options and features."[1] In the United States, the selection of the correct word processing equipment varies with the needs of each business. Every company has certain needs depending on the size of the business, the kind of business, and the savings goals of the business.

Size of the Business.

First, the size of the business is an important ~~a prominent~~ factor in choosing the best word processing equipment for a company. In their article on the office of the future, ~~According to~~ Steve Golen and M. Agnes Titkemeyer suggest that "a business should buy equipment that easily can be expanded with new programming features as they become available."[2]

Small Businesses

In everyday practice, small businesses usually need stand alone equipment which ~~either~~ produces only a hard copy or an exhibit on a screen.[3] Recently, Chase Manhattan's Corporate Banking Department, a small business in itself, wanted to take advantage of a small word processing system.[4] The department evaluated equipment from ten manufacturers. It looked for shared logic capability ~~was looked for~~, so that many operators would have access ~~admittance~~ to one data base. Through Wang Laboratories, it ~~they~~ found two OIS 140's and two System 5's.[5]

Medium-Sized Businesses

Next, medium-sized businesses usually need computer systems with ~~which have~~ terminal keyboards distributed ~~which are situated~~

among ~~the~~ offices, *for internal use* ~~to be used inside a business~~.   In 1977,

Allegheny Ludlum Industries (ALI) transformed headquarters

operations to a word processing structure.   The *company* ~~business~~

decided to try word processing because of the need for

greater productivity at less cost / *but* ~~The business~~ did not

know what equipment to select.   Meredith Associates, Inc.,

a consulting firm, assisted them. *6*

A variety of machines *was* ~~were~~ available, **S**ome ~~were~~ more

complicated than others. *First, ALI* ~~The company~~ wanted reliable,

simple machines. *Second, it* ~~They~~ looked for continuing smooth

function instead of individual features. *Third, it* ~~They~~ wanted units

which had full-page CRT displays because ~~the~~ CRT displays

supply a reference which ensures less strain on ~~the~~

employees and more efficiency. *Fourth, it* ~~They also~~ wanted

flexibility.   So, instead of a single word processing

center, ALI set up four word processing "satellites" in key

offices: personnel, accounting, financial planning and

analysis, and tax.   They also put three *independent* word processing

units in the legal department because of the "special

nature" of the work of this department. *7*

Large Businesses

Finally, large businesses usually need more

sophisticated systems which *they can use* ~~can be used~~ for exchanges

between branch offices in other areas and for

communication, by telephone connection, *between systems. 8* ~~from one complex to~~

~~another.~~ **X** Prudential needed a complicated system because

it *is* ~~was~~ so large. *Word processing* ~~The~~ equipment *gives* ~~grants~~ Prudential the

ability *to accomplish* ~~of accomplishing~~ various *kinds of jobs* ~~types of labor~~ with "finishing touches," such as letters typed error-free on expensive letterhead stationery, that are hard to get with conventional ~~other~~ equipment.[9]

Kind of Business

The second factor to consider in picking ~~the~~ word processing equipment for a company is the kind of work the company engages in. ~~type of business being run~~. Different types of businesses have diverse needs. Some companies fill their needs by purchasing word processing services from word processing service bureaus. Wordtronics Corp. has 120 such bureaus in operation.[10] Other companies have set up their own specialized word processing systems.

Insurance

Colonial Penn Insurance Company in Philadelphia is one example of a business with special needs because of the type of work it does ~~done~~. The company took 16 months to transform its typing pool ~~itself~~ into a word processing and central dictation/ transcription department. Before getting ~~the~~ word processing and dictating equipment ~~was put it~~, approximately 400 ~~250~~ claims department writers were writing instructions by hand, indicating the choice of stock paragraphs and ~~the~~ assorted contents for informative messages to the company's policyholders. Twenty-nine typists copied these drafts.[11]

The insurance company had ten Dictaphone System 293 multiple-cassette central dictation recorders, seven Thought Master desktop transcribers, four Display 2000 text processors, and a Master Mind word management computer system installed in the word processing center of the claims department. Within a few months, the company achieve**d** its goal, as an insurance company, of individualized letters completed quickly through ^*use of* ~~the~~ single-line display text processors. These processors ~~will~~ delete, add, rearrange, or assemble letters from stock paragraphs.[12]

Law Firm
~~Another~~ *A second* ^example of the needs of different types of businesses is Radison, Pfaelzer, Woodward, Quinn and Rassi, a law firm. The company has increased its productivity by introducing an OCR page reader to the company's word processing system.[13] Jean Tomassi, ^*Word Processing Supervisor at the firm,* states: ^"The suggestion that we consider suppl**e**menting word processing with ^an OCR scanning device prompted me to attend a seminar on OCR and visit other law offices that used scanners. We decided on the Alpha-Word because it was the most versatile."[14] The *firm uses* *an* OCR page reader ~~is used~~ for text editing and ~~test~~ revising. Because of the importance of quality needed on the final draft, the OCR page reader meets the requirements of the law firm.[15]

Photographic Products Marketer
A final illustration of ^*specialized* ~~specialization~~ needs be**c**ause of the type of business ~~being run~~ is Agfa-Gevaert, a**n** *international marketer* ^~~worldwide business~~ of photographic products. The company requires close communication between European headquarters and the United States headquarters in New Jersey. ~~The~~ *It* ~~company~~ ^has ~~the~~ *a* word processing/telex connection which is unique to ~~the~~ *its* word processing center~~ of Agfa-Gevaert.~~[16] *As a result, as reported in "Blending Word Processing and Telex,"* ^~~According to~~ an article in <u>Modern Office Procedures</u>: "One

telex ope~~R~~ator now sends more cables than two operators could send under the old system." [17] ~~The telex was created because of the special need of the Agfa-Gevaert company.~~

Savings Goals

A final factor to consider in deciding on the right word processing equipment is the savings goals of the business. Word processing can save a company money. ~~A company can save money through word processing.~~ ~~Steve~~ Golen and ~~M. Agnes~~ Titkemeyer suggest ~~feel~~ that "savings are possible by upgrading word processing equipment and adding inhouse photocopying and reprographics equipment to print brochures which were formerly sent to outside printers." [18]

Michigan Consolidated Gas

One example of a company's increasing income by saving money is Michigan Consolidated Gas Co. The company has reported saving ~~to have saved~~ approximately $150,000 above the price of equipment just in its graphics department, through preparation of ~~The company saved this money by making~~ documents with its ~~their~~ own word processing equipment. [19] ~~This is an excellent savings.~~

American Edwards Laboratories

Another illustration of a business' saving through word processing is American Edwards Laboratories. The company ~~business~~ changed from tape text processing to an NBI disk system. It ~~The company~~ increased productivity while saving time and money. The average cost to yield a page of text is $7.50 to $12.00. ~~the~~ American Edwards Laboratories has lowered the cost to less than $6.00 a ~~per~~ page of text. [20]

U.S. Army

A last example ~~sample~~ of savings is the United States Army. According to General Accounting Office (GAO) figures, the Army cut costs by reducing the number of workers through institution of a word processing system. By contrast, in

1977, the federal government spen~~d~~**t** $80,000,000 on word

processing. ~~and they~~ *The GAO* states that ~~their~~ productivity *of other government offices* has not

improved.[21]

As reported in The Economist, the GAO concludes that

three factors contribute to low productivity: "absence of

productivity standards, cost-eliminating criteria and

guidelines."[22] ~~It~~ *The GAO* recommends ~~that the General Services

Administration should remedy this by publishing~~ *publication of* a complete

word processing handbook. Such a handbook would ~~increase~~ *reduce costs by*

systematizing use of word processing equipment in government offices.[23]

~~the income of the United States government.~~[22]

Every business in the United States is *different* ~~unique~~.

Therefore, each business ha~~d~~**s** different needs, *depending on* ~~Three main~~

~~division of a company are~~ the size of the business, kind of

business, and savings goals of *the* ~~a~~ business. These factors

help *to determine the kind of* ~~in deciding on which~~ word processing equipment a

company should select~~, for its business~~. ~~According to~~ Donna

Taylor, the manager of word processing operations for a

large corporation~~,~~ *offers this advice to companies switching to word*
processing systems:

> The biggest mistake people make when they are looking
>
> for word processing systems . . . is making no
>
> decisions at all. They look at every *piece* ~~price~~ of
>
> equipment on the market, become confused, and forget
>
> it for a year. A better way . . . would be to select
>
> no more than five vendors, study the equipment
>
> carefully, narrow it down to two, and then evaluate
>
> on a feature-by-feature, benefit comparison to find
>
> the best equipment for their job.[24]

As you read through the first draft of Kelly Wolf's report, you probably noticed that she crossed out quite a few words and phrases. You also noticed she made other changes, using two common proofreader's symbols, the caret ($\wedge$) and the transposition sign (t/f). The caret indicates the exact point where something is to be inserted on a line. The inserted material is written in above the line. The transposition sign indicates that two letters (or words or phrases) should switch positions. After revising the first draft of her report, Kelly incorporated all the changes in the final copy of the report.

Selecting the Correct Word Processing Equipment

Prepared for

Dr. T. R. Rennals
Associate Professor
Department of Business Information Systems
Western Michigan University
Kalamazoo, MI 49008

Prepared by

Kelly Wolf
BIS 142-BC

December 4, 198-

Selecting the Correct Word Processing Equipment

According to J.R. "Reg" Little, a founder and first president of the International Word Processing Association: "There are over 50 word-processing machines on the market, each with a variety of software packages, options and features."[1] In the United States, the selection of the correct word processing equipment varies with the needs of each business. Every company has certain needs depending on the size of the business, the kind of business, and the savings goals of the business.

Size of the Business

First, the size of the business is an important factor in choosing the best word processing equipment for a company. In their article on the office of the future, Steve Golen and M. Agnes Titkemeyer suggest that "a business should buy equipment that easily can be expanded with new programming features as they become available."[2]

Small Businesses

In everyday practice, small businesses usually need stand-alone equipment which produces only a hard copy or an exhibit on a screen.[3] Recently, Chase Manhattan's Corporate Banking Department, a small business in itself, wanted to take advantage of a small word processing system.[4] The department evaluated equipment from ten manufacturers. It looked for shared logic capability so that many operators would have access to one data base. Through Wang Laboratories, it found two OIS 140's and two System 5's.[5]

Medium-Sized Businesses

Next, medium-sized businesses usually need computer systems with terminal keyboards distributed among offices for internal use. In 1977, Allegheny Ludlum Industries (ALI) transformed headquarters operations to a word processing structure. The company decided to try word processing because of the need for greater productivity at less cost but did not know what equipment to select. Meredith Associates, Inc., a consulting firm, assisted them.[6]

A variety of machines was available, some more complicated than others. First, ALI wanted reliable, simple machines. Second, it looked for continuing smooth function instead of individual features. Third, it wanted units which had full-page CRT displays because CRT displays supply a reference which ensures less strain on employees and more efficiency. Fourth, it wanted flexibility. So, instead of a single word processing center, ALI set up four word processing "satellites" in key offices: personnel, accounting, financial planning and analysis, and tax. They also put three independent word processing units in the legal department because of the "special nature" of the work of this department.[7]

Large Businesses

Finally, large businesses usually need more sophisticated systems which they can use for exchanges between branch offices in other areas and for communication, by telephone connection, between systems.[8] Prudential needed a complicated system because it is so large. Word processing equipment gives Prudential the ability to accomplish various types of jobs with "finishing touches," such as letters typed error-free on expensive letterhead stationery, that are hard to get with conventional equipment.[9]

Kind of Business

The second factor to consider in picking word processing equipment for a company is the kind of work the company engages in. Different types of businesses have diverse needs. Some companies fill their needs by purchasing word processing services from word processing service bureaus. Wordtronics Corp. has 120 such bureaus in operation.[10] Other companies have set up their own specialized word processing systems.

Insurance

Colonial Penn Insurance Company in Philadelphia is one example of a business with special needs because of the type of work it does. The company took 16 months to transform its typing pool into a word processing and central dictation/transcription department. Before getting word processing and dictating equipment, approximately 400 claims department writers were writing instructions by hand, indicating choice of stock paragraphs and assorted contents for informative messages to the company's policy-holders. Twenty-nine typists copied these drafts.[11]

The insurance company had ten Dictaphone System 293 multiple-cassette central dictation recorders, seven Thought Master desktop transcribers, four Display 2000 text processors, and a Master Mind word management computer system installed in the word processing center of the claims department. Within a few months, the company achieved its goal, as an insurance company, of individual-ized letters completed quickly through use of single-line display text processors. These processors delete, add, rearrange, or assemble letters from stock paragraphs.[12]

Law Firm

A second example of the needs of different types of businesses is Radison, Pfaelzer, Woodward, Quinn and Rassi, a law firm. The company has increased its productivity by introducing an OCR page reader to the company's word pro-cessing system.[13] Jean Tomassi, Word Processing Supervisor, states: "The suggestion that we consider supplementing word processing with an OCR scanning device prompted me to attend a seminar on OCR and visit other law offices that used scanners. We decided on the Alpha-Word because it was the most versatile."[14] The firm uses an OCR page reader for text editing and revising. Because of the importance of quality needed on the final draft, the OCR page reader meets the requirements of the law firm.[15]

Photographic Products Marketer

A final illustration of specialized needs because of type of business is Agfa-Gevaert, an international marketer of photographic products. The company requires close communication between European headquarters and the United States headquarters in New Jersey. It has a word processing/telex connection which is unique to its word processing center.[16] As a result, as reported in "Blending Word Processing and Telex," an article in Modern Office Procedures, "one telex operator now sends more cables than two operators could send under the old system."[17]

Savings Goals

A final factor to consider in deciding on the right word processing equipment is the savings goals of the business. Word processing can save a company money. Golen and Titkemeyer suggest that "savings are possible by upgrading word processing equipment and adding inhouse photocopying and reprographics equipment to print brochures which were formerly sent to outside printers."[18]

Michigan Consolidated Gas

One example of a company's increasing income by saving money is Michigan Consolidated Gas Co. The company has reported saving approximately $150,000 above the price of equipment just in its graphics department through preparation of documents with its own word processing equipment.[19]

American Edwards Laboratories

Another illustration of a business' saving through word processing is American Edwards Laboratories. The company changed from tape text processing to an NBI disk system. It increased productivity while saving time and money. The average cost to yield a page of text is $7.50 to $12.00. American Edwards Laboratories has lowered the cost to less than $6.00 a page of text.[20]

U.S. Army

A last example of savings is the United States Army. According to General Accounting Office (GAO) figures, the Army cut costs by reducing the number of workers through institution of a word processing system. By contrast, in 1977, the federal government spent $80,000,000 on word processing. The GAO states that productivity of other government offices has not improved.[21]

As reported in The Economist, the GAO concludes that three factors contribute to low productivity: "absence of productivity standards, cost-eliminating criteria and guidelines."[22] The GAO recommends publication of a complete word processing handbook. Such a handbook would reduce costs by systematizing use of word processing equipment in government offices.[23]

Every business in the United States is different. Therefore, each business has different needs, depending on the size of the business, kind of business, and savings goals of the business. These factors help to determine the kind of word processing equipment a company should select. Donna Taylor, the manager of word processing operations for

a large corporation, offers this advice to companies
switching to word processing systems.

The biggest mistake people make when they are looking
for word processing systems . . . is making no
decisions at all. They look at every piece of
equipment on the market, become confused, and forget
it for a year. A better way . . . would be to select
no more than five vendors, study the equipment
carefully, narrow it down to two, and then evaluate
on a feature-by-feature, benefit comparison to find
the best equipment for their job.[24]

Reference Notes

[1] J. R. "Reg" Little, "Measured Typing Output: Does It Help or Hinder?" The Office, 91, No. 2 (1980), 31-32.

[2] Steve Golen and M. Agnes Titkemeyer, "Word/Information Processing Implications for the Office of the Future," The Secretary, 41, No. 5 (1981), 7.

[3] Golen and Titkemeyer, p. 10.

[4] "Systems in Action," Administrative Management, 41, No. 9 (1980), 73.

[5] Golen and Titkemeyer, p. 10.

[6] Laurence E. Mullen, "How to Tackle a Major WP Conversion," Management World, 8, No. 5 (1979), 13.

[7] Mullen, pp. 14-15.

[8] Golen and Titkemeyer, p. 10.

[9] Ruby M. Price, "Prudential's Word Processing Center Saves $300,000 a Year," The Office, 91, No. 3 (1980), 138.

[10] "Integrated Word Processing Service Bureaus Organized," The Office, 92, No. 4 (1980), 270.

[11] "Central Dictation Wins Approval," Modern Office Procedures, 25, No. 7 (1980), 76.

[12] "Central Dictation," p. 76.

[13] Jean Tomassi, "Page Readers Uncork Bottleneck in Legal Firm's Word Processing," The Office, 91, No. 2 (1980), 95.

[14] Tomassi, p. 95.

[15] Tomassi, p. 95.

9

[16] "Blending Word Processing and Telex," Modern Office Procedures, 25, No. 10 (1980), 196.

[17] "Blending Word Processing," p. 196.

[18] Golen and Titkemeyer, p. 7.

[19] Golen and Titkemeyer, p. 7.

[20] Sharon Hagelstrom, "Work Measurement Justifies a New WP System," Modern Office Procedures, 25, No. 11 (1980), 138.

[21] "Words, Words, Words, Words, Words, Wo," The Economist, 271, No. 4 (1979), 95.

[22] "Words, Words," p. 95.

[23] "Words, Words," p. 95.

[24] Bette Primrose, "WP Perks by Primrose," Modern Office Procedures, 25, No. 9 (1980), 32.

Bibliography

"Blending Word Processing and Telex." Modern Office
Procedures, 25, No. 10 (1980), 196, 199.

"Central Dictation Wins Approval." Modern Office
Procedures, 25, No. 7 (1980), 76-77.

Golen, Steve, and M. Agnes Titkemeyer. "Word/Informa-
tion Processing Implications for the Office of the
Future." The Secretary, 41, No. 5 (1981), 7, 10-11.

Hagelstrom, Sharon. "Work Measurement Justifies a New WP
System." Modern Office Procedures, 25, No. 11
(1980), 138, 140.

"Integrated Word Procesing Service Bureaus Organized." The
Office, 92, No. 4 (1980), 270.

Little, J. R. "Reg." "Measured Typing Output: Does It
Help or Hinder?" The Office, 91, No. 2 (1980), 24,
26, 31-32.

Mullen, Laurence E. "How to Tackle a Major WP Conversion."
Management World, 8, No. 5 (1979), 13-16.

Price, Ruby M. "Prudential's Word Processing Center Saves
$300,000 a Year." The Office, 91, No. 3 (1980), 138,
140.

Primrose, Bette. "WP Perks by Primrose." Modern Office
Procedures, 25, No. 9 (1980), 28, 32.

"Systems in Action." Administrative Management, 41, No. 9
(1980), 73-74.

11

Tomassi, Jean. "Page Readers Uncork Bottleneck in Legal
     Firm's Word Processing." The Office, 91, No. 2
     (1980), 95-96.

"Words, Words, Words, Words, Words, Wo." The Economist,
     271, No. 2 (1979), 95.

Proofreading

Proofreading is the final step in producing a report. If you are typing your report, read each sheet before you take it out of the typewriter. If you find a simple spelling or typing error, you can easily return to it and correct it. If you find a more complex error, such as the omission of two or three sentences, you can stop and make whatever corrections are necessary before typing several more pages and only finding the omission when you are finished.

When you have finished the final copy of your report, check it against your last draft copy to insure that you have made all the changes you want to make. Ideally, you should have left enough time on your schedule to be able to put your report aside for a few days. When you pick it up again shortly before its due date, you should be able to concentrate on it better. Proofread it once more to remove any errors you may have overlooked previously. If you allow time to complete the steps in the proofreading process, your report should represent you well to your reader.

SUGGESTIONS FOR RESEARCH PROJECTS

Primary Research

1. Investigate the possibility of opening a business in your city. The following list of questions will start your thinking.

   a. Will the business be unique or in competition with similar businesses?

   b. If in competition, how will the business gain a market share (location, advertising, price, service)?

   c. What licensing requirements must the business meet?

   d. What are start-up costs such as rent, inventory, signs, advertising, and salaries?

   e. How can the start-up costs be financed?

   f. What taxes must be paid?

   g. What success can the owner expect in one year? in five years?

2. Complete a "market basket" survey in your area. Use the *Consumer Price Index* list of grocery staples or construct one that reflects your purchasing habits. Find the average price of each item in your shopping area. Compare it with the latest federal *CPI* figures.

3. Complete a comparison shopping report on one or several products to determine the prices available to consumers in your area. You may

want to compare prices of different brands of similar items in one store or you may compare prices in one store with prices for the same product in another store.

4. Write an informational report about some aspect of your present employment. Here are some ideas. Your job may make you think of other information that would be more interesting to casual readers.

a. Describe the duties and responsibilities of your position.

b. Describe or explain the business of the company for which you work.

c. Describe or explain pay scales, benefits, or special employee privileges at your place of employment.

d. Describe the product your company manufactures and explain how it is used and by whom it is used.

e. Describe the career tracks (ways to move up to more responsibility and higher salaries) available at your place of employment.

f. Explain training procedures at your place of employment.

g. Explain hiring procedures at your place of employment.

5. Interview at least five employed people age 25 or older. If you are secure in your own choice of career field, talk only with people in your field. If you are thinking about several different career possibilities, talk to people in each of your possible fields of interest.

Before you start your interviews, make a list of questions to be sure you ask each person for the same kind of information. Your instructor may ask to see the list of questions and your list of potential interviewees before you begin. Here is a list of questions to get your thinking started.

a. What is your job title?

b. What are your duties on this job?

c. How long have you held this position?

d. What position did you have before this one?

e. How did your previous position prepare you for this position?

f. What do you like best about this job? Why?

g. What do you like least about this job? Why?

h. What do you see as the next position in your career?

i. Why did you go into this field in the first place?

j. If you had to do it again, would you be in this field?

k. Why or why not?

NOTE: If you plan to interview a business person on business time, you should follow these steps:

    a. Phone first to explain your purpose. Be sure to indicate the amount of time you will need to complete the interview.

    b. Arrive promptly for the interview wearing clothing appropriate for the particular place of business.

    c. Leave at the end of your scheduled time unless the interviewee particularly urges you to stay.

    d. Write and mail a short letter thanking the person for the time he or she spent with you and for the information you received.

6. Account for the success of a particularly busy restaurant. You might like to complete the report as if you were a consultant. Someone who wants to open a restaurant has asked you to recommend some procedures that will insure "sure fire success."

7. Assess the food service at your college. Consider such factors as cost, hours of service, menu variety, menu quality, nutritional value, quantities served, convenience, cleanliness, and "atmosphere."

8. Prepare a report that new students at your college or university might use to decide whether to live on campus or independently off campus. Some factors to consider are cost (don't forget transportation costs if applicable), convenience, time spent on housekeeping, opportunities for developing friendships, studying, diet, and possible problems.

9. Prepare a guide to campus organizations at your college. Find the names of student organizations and classify them into interest groups such as sports oriented, career oriented, religious, hobby, social, etc. Then write a few lines about each organization. New students would probably like to know how often a group meets, where and when it meets, what costs are involved, and what activities are part of an organization's program. You may discover other factors of interest.

If you are attending a large university, you will need to find a logical way to limit the size of the guide, or you will want to work with several other students in your class to gather all the information.

10. Make copies of the questionnaire that appears on the next page and use it to survey members of your class or students in your dormitory. As many of the questions ask for personal information, you will have to distribute and collect the questionnaires in some way that assures respondents of anonymity. When you have gathered the data, tabulate it, and analyze the data to see what conclusions you can draw from the data.

QUESTIONNAIRE

Personal Data:

    Sex: M   F   Age: _____

Academic Data:

    Years in this college: 1 2 3 4 5 or more

    Class rank   Freshman   Sophomore   Junior   Senior
                Graduate student   Other

    Major: _____ Minor: _____

    Credit hours completed: _____

    Hours carried this term or semester: _____

    Grade point average: _____

Financial Information:

    Dollar amount of scholarship income this year: _____

    Dollar amount of bank loans for this year: _____

    Dollar amount received (or expected)
    "from home" for this year's expenses: _____

    Dollar amount saved from summer employment this year: _____

    Dollar amount earned weekly during this term: _____

    Hours worked per week during this term: _____

Secondary Research

1. Investigate a publicly held company to determine if buying its stock is a good or a poor investment at this time. You will want to read the company's annual report and search for magazine and newspaper articles about the company itself. In addition, you will want to read articles about the industry of which the company is a part. You should also read investor service reports about the company and the industry.

2. Investigate a city or geographic region (your own or another part of the country) to determine if it would be a favorable place for you to begin your career after graduation. You will want to learn about such things as population trends, employment projections, cost of living, openings in your field, and the elusive "quality of life."

3. Investigate graduate schools that offer advanced degrees in your field of specialization. Where are they located? What does a program cost? What are entrance requirements? What scholarship aid is available? What employment can you expect after obtaining an advanced degree? Are some schools ranked as "better" than others? Will potential employers notice if your degree is from one of the "better" schools or not?

4. Investigate some of the emerging concepts and industries that may be growth industries for at least the remainder of the century. Some "buzz words" are

hydroponics
robotics
telecommuncations
videotext
fiber optics
laser technology
automated office

What will happen in each area? What jobs will open up? What jobs and technologies will the new products and technologies replace? How can you take advantage of the new industries and technologies?

5. What is nonverbal communication? How can it help or hinder you at work and in social situations?

6. Read about improving listening skills. Write a report explaining one of the following:

    a. Why listening skills are important

    b. How to improve listening skills

7. Investigate successful interviewing techniques. Here are some questions to start your thinking. How can a person make a good impression

in job interviews? How should an employee conduct himself or herself to get the most from an evaluation conference or goal-setting conference? How does an interviewer evaluate responses from the interviewee?

8. Investigate government job opportunities. Investigate at any or all levels of government — city, state, and federal. What positions are available? How do citizens find out about government job opportunities? How does one apply for government positions? What are the pay and promotion opportunities in government employment?

9. Explain a technical term or concept in language a lay person can understand. Here is a "starter" list of possibilities.

a. How does a diesel engine work?

b. How can a laser beam be used in surgery?

c. What is the difference between AC and DC current?

d. When should a user specify series and when parallel electrical wiring?

e. What does it mean to "be long" or "be short" in the stock market?

f. What are LIFO and FIFO? How do they affect financial statements?

g. What electronic processes make worldwide direct telephone dialing possible?

h. What makes instant replay possible on television?

10. Investigate some aspect of the history of your major field. You will need to severely limit your topic to keep the report a manageable size. Here are some suggestions to start your thinking.

a. How did entrepreneurs keep money records before the advent of double-entry bookkeeping?

b. When did Home Economics leave the home and enter the classroom?

c. How did alchemy become chemistry?

d. How have chemists contributed to modern technology?

e. What was the impact of printing in the first one hundred years that movable type was used?

f. What changes came to the world as a result of cheap, controllable electric energy?

g. How did people buy necessities and luxuries before the advent of modern wholesale and retail distribution systems?

h. When did radio or television cross the line between novelty and necessity? How did that change affect the marketing and entertainment industries?

i. Except for volume, has agriculture really changed in 2,000 years?

j. What were some early American efforts in crime prevention and justice?

k. What was the first American city to have "city water and city sewage"? How did these services create a need for licensed plumbers?

l. How did adding typewriters change business offices?

m. How did Harvey's or Lister's discoveries effect changes in human health care?

Chapter 15

Seeking Employment

To the Student:
     As you read chapter 15 and complete the exercises and special project, you will be asked to
        . . . identify four resume formats
        . . . select an appropriate format for your resume
        . . . write a resume
        . . . write a letter of application
        . . . write other letters about employment.

In the previous chapters of this book, you have been learning to write letters, memos, and reports which you will use in the world of work. In this chapter, you will learn something about the process of seeking employment so that you may put your organizing and writing skills to work in the business world. Seeking a career position is usually a more formal process than applying for the various part-time jobs you may have held while continuing your education. You may need to write a letter of application and other special letters. You will certainly need to prepare a resume.

PREPARING A RESUME

Gather Personal Data

Your resume is a statement about you as you are at a particular time. You want it to present the best and most pertinent information that fits on one (or at most two) pages. To learn which information to select, you must spend time analyzing yourself. Psychologists agree that self-analysis is one of the most difficult tasks for any person, so you will need a good way to get started. One method is to open a personal "Personnel File." Get four file folders and label them:

Education

Employment

Honors, Awards, and Recommendations

Interests and Hobbies

Now, collect data for the folders.

Education

List the names and addresses of schools and colleges you have attended. If you have attended seminars, workshops, or short courses, be sure to include them as well. If you have student transcripts or other evidence of attendance, put those in the folder. Add dates for each educational experience. List majors and minors and include a complete list of classes at each school if you do not have transcripts for this folder. List graduation dates and the full names of your degrees.

Exercise A   1. Read each of the following entries for an Education folder carefully. Explain what information is missing.

    A. Central High School, 1977-1981
        Curriculum: College Preparatory
        Graduation: June, 1981

B. Central Valley Community College
Mahoning, Pennsylvania
Major: Business Administration
Associate of Arts Degree: June, 1983

C. Wayne State University, 1980 –
Detroit, Michigan
Major: European History
Bachelor of Arts degree anticipated in June, 1985.

2. Gather the materials you need to complete your own Education folder in your personal "Personnel File."

Employment
Begin with your first paid employment and list the name, address, and telephone number of each employer, the nature of the employment, the beginning and ending wages, the dates of employment, the name of your immediate supervisor, and the reason for leaving that employment. If you received a promotion or were given special responsibilities, make note of those facts.

If you have had very little opportunity for paid employment, put in your employment substitutes. A job history tells an employer that you have demonstrated your responsibility to meet work obligations. You can prove the same sense of responsibility with other work or projects for which you were not paid. Have you managed a household? Have you participated regularly in church and community service activities? Have you offered your services as a tutor? Have you been in charge of a function or committee in a school or social club? Have you completed any unpaid internship or apprenticeship program? Have you been active in a neighborhood association? Have you worked in support of a political candidate? List any of these activities and include the name of the organization, its address, and the names, addresses, and telephone numbers of people who could recommend you for your unpaid work experience.

Exercise B   1. Read each of the following entries for an Employment folder carefully. Explain what information is missing.

A. Hobie's Hot Dogs, Summer, 1977
Cooked, cleaned up, served, balanced cash for 1 week

B. Assisted Dr. Marion Feldman with library research about left- and right-brain theories
University of California, Davis
Winter, 1982
Minimum student wage: $3.35

C. Paramount Manufacturing Company
344 West Highland Road
West Orange, NJ 07052
1980-82
Hourly worker on production line
Starting salary: $4.25
Ending salary: $5.31
Promoted to inspector for pipe fittings

2. Gather the materials you need to complete the Employment folder in your personal "Personnel File."

Honors, Awards, and Recommendations
Although most of these entries will not appear on the final resume, a complete list will help you in the process of self-analysis. Were you an "honor monitor" in third grade? If so, start the list there. Add awards for attendance, for scholarship, for public service, for athletics, for entries in the county fair, for community service. If you attained the rank of First Class Scout or were named "best salesperson of the month" when you delivered newspapers, put these facts on the list. Do you have any letters in a scrapbook that thank you for service or commend you for doing a job well? If so, put copies in this folder. Of course, if you have awards of merit or letters of recommendation from any employer, add them to the file.

Exercise C   1. Study the following list of honors and awards carefully. Then classify the items in the list into three categories using the following symbols:

S = item is useful for self-analysis only
M = item may interest a future employer
D = item will definitely interest a future employer

Winner, DAR essay contest in tenth grade
Named to all-state basketball team as a H.S. junior
Phi Beta Kappa
Elected captain of college cheerleading team
Member of winning team in the all-city bowling league
Second place, Voice of Democracy contest
Listed in Who's Who in American University Students
$25 winner for employee suggestion box, March, 1980
First place, all-state clarinet competition
Basic Education Opportunity Grant scholarship
National Merit scholarship
Football letter in high school
Honors college
Football letter in college
Volunteer of the Month (for Meals on Wheels)

Christmas bonus (Paramount Manufacturing Co.)
100% club for meeting sales goals (2 years)
High School Student Council President
Honorable mention, Kentucky all-state swim meet (diving)
College Student Council President
Mortar Board
Dean's list (1 semester)
Perfect attendance pin (1 year, high school)
Dean's list (4 semesters)
Second place, midwest regional college debate contest
All-state debate team (high school)

2. Gather the material you need to complete the Honors, Awards, and Recommendations folder in your personal "Personnel File."

Interests and Hobbies

Interests and hobbies indicate how you spend your resources when you expect no financial reward. For self-analysis purposes, you might do well to make two lists. The first list is interests and hobbies you no longer practice. Did you start an insect collection which was thrown away in the last housecleaning? Did you start an autograph collection, a stamp collection, a coin collection, or a poster collection that is no longer active? What kinds of clubs, athletic, or social organizations have you stopped attending?

Make a second list of your current interests or hobbies. List organizations of which you are a member and indicate whether you are really active in the organization or a "sometime attender." Did you hold office in an organization? Do you spend many hours reading? If so, list the last ten books you read. Do you jog or take part in other regular physical exercise? What kinds? Do you play an instrument or sing or act? Do you enjoy doing odd jobs and house repairs? Do you garden, cook, sew, paint? Do you ski, skate, or swim? Do you spend a good deal of time organizing or attending parties? Do you follow certain sports as a spectator and fan? In short, account for the hours you use to "have a good time."

Exercise D

1. Study the following list of interests and hobbies carefully. Then classify the items in the list into three categories using the following symbols:

   S = item is useful for self-analysis only
   M = item may interest a future employer
   D = item will definitely interest a future employer

   Sleeping
   Reading mysteries
   Reading the "100 Great Books"
   Hiking
   Reading Spanish literature
   Partying

Cooking
Trying new recipes
Running
Outdoor sports
Skiing
Ski patrol
Football
Stamp collecting
Coin collecting
Beer can collecting
Computer club
Chess club
Sailing club
Golf
Refinishing furniture
Dog training
City chorus
PTA
Listening to music
Playing trombone
Photography
Social secretary, Delta Delta Delta Sorority
Set design for little theatre
Treasurer, Alpha Gamma Mu Sorority
Chairperson, AAUW Book Sale

2. Some of the items in the list in question 1 could be turned into items of interest to a prospective employer if the writer seeks certain positions. Select some items from the list that would show useful skills if the writer were applying for each of the following positions:
Camp counselor
Newspaper reporter
Bookkeeper
Home economist
Physical education teacher
Bank trainee

3. Gather the material you need to complete the Interests and Hobbies folder in your personal "Personnel File."

Once you have established a "Personnel File," remember to keep adding to it. The U.S. Department of Commerce predicts that a typical person entering the job market for the first time in the 1980s will change careers (not merely change jobs or get promotions) five times during his or her working life. For each new job search, you will need an up-to-date resume, and the best way to have relevant information is to add new information to your "Personnel File" regularly.

Now you need to take a good long look at yourself. Too many people set out to look for a position without considering the kind of work they will most likely enjoy and therefore do well. Browse through the Education folder. Which classes did you enjoy? Why? Which classes did you like least? Why? Now look at your answers to the "Why?" question. If you did not like a class because of the "lousy teacher," ask yourself what will happen if the supervisor on your new job is like that teacher. Can you be productive in spite of a personality conflict? Did you like a class because "It was easy"? If so, how will you react if your new job is hard? Can you face personal intellectual challenge? What subjects did you most enjoy studying? Why? Remember to look at yourself for each answer. Stop thinking about the people in the class or the teacher or the text; think about your own interests and actions and reactions.

A trip through your Employment folder can be even more instructive. If you are like most people, you have had some jobs you liked, some to which you were neutral, and some that you disliked. Why? Try not to concentrate on individuals; think about the job itself. You probably liked at least some parts of every job. What were those pleasant aspects of the job? Why did you enjoy them? Did you like to work alone or with other people? Did you prefer the physical or mental parts of a job? Did you like detail work? Were you good at meeting the public? Why did you leave each job? Remembering each job you have held, what can you learn about yourself and the world of work?

Honors, awards, or recommendations always bring good feelings. When you look through this folder, try to relate these activities to the working world. What kinds of jobs can give you opportunities to shine as you did when you achieved these awards or recommendations? What qualities in yourself made you eligible for recommendation? How can you use these qualities in your working career?

Reviewing your interests and hobbies can be even more revealing. If your idea of a good time is listening to stereo while you read a good book, you probably won't be happy working as a sales representative who meets new people daily and must talk easily with them. Conversely, if your happiest hours are spent working with a committee to accomplish some civic or social goal, you probably will not be happy working alone as a computer programmer.

What if you discover that your happiest times are with other people, but your favorite courses are in the computer field? Don't despair; start an extensive investigation of positions available to persons with a good computer background. Some companies organize programming as a team function. Many companies need sales personnel who have a firm grasp of computer languages. Simply avoid applying for positions that require you to spend more time with machines than with people.

Once you have investigated yourself, you must try to match your strong points with the job market. Your college placement service or the local public library will have a collection of recent books that may help you interpret your findings. A list of some helpful books appears in a bibliography at the end of this chapter. Your college may have career counselors, or you may wish to consult a professional career consultant. You can broaden your knowledge of job titles by reading the *Occupational Handbook* or *Dictionary of Occupational Titles*. Time you spend investigating job opportunities and job responsibilities will not be wasted. If you can start your career in a position that matches your attitudes and aptitudes, you can expect to do well.

When you have narrowed your job search to certain kinds of positions, then you need to take time to investigate companies who hire such workers. Again, your college placement office or library can help you find information. Most colleges and many public libraries have a special collection of books about job seeking which can help you learn how to investigate particular companies and how to gain access to employment officers in those companies. Some of these books are in the bibliography at the end of this chapter.

When you have completed your self-analysis and have spent time researching the contemporary employment market, you are ready to write an effective resume. Your resume should show a potential employer that you have the qualities and talents the firm needs to accomplish its business goals. Selecting the best format for a resume will help to highlight your value to an employer.

Select a Format

No one has yet invented the perfect resume. Indeed, the resume that pleases one personnel office may be found wanting in another office in the same company. You can increase your chances of being well received by selecting a resume format that allows you to present yourself most clearly. You have four general types from which to choose.

The Chronological Resume
This format is the most common one for young college graduates. It focuses reader attention on job titles, duties performed on the job, and the dates of the job. A chronological resume is a good choice if you have a background of work experience that is appropriate for your age and pertinent to the position you are seeking.

This format also emphasizes your educational background by dates, degrees, and major and minor. If your academic background is one that would be expected in the field in which you seek work, a chronological resume is a good choice. Look at the example of a chronological resume prepared by Penny Huyck who has recently completed her college education. She is seeking employment in her major field and has "average" experience for a young person entering the job market.

PENNY HUYCK
301 N. Kendall
Kalamazoo, MI 49007
Telephone: (616) 345-6439

QUALIFIED BY
     Skills in communication, public speaking, writing and editing,
     leadership, production, research and evaluation, programming, using
     audio-visual equipment.

PROFESSIONAL OBJECTIVE - Public Relations

PROFESSIONAL EXPERIENCE
     1983 to Present   LAYOUT ARTIST, PROOFREADER, AND ACCOUNTING ASSISTANT
                          for the American Society of Agricultural Engineers.
                          Proofread and keylined technical transactions.
                          Developed editing, production, and accounting
                          skills.

     1983 Summer   PRODUCTION MANAGER of weekly newspaper. Managed
                          seven-person staff, editing, typesetting, and layout
                          of all materials. Developed communication, writing,
                          editing, leadership, and production skills.

     1983 Spring   RESEARCHER AND EDITOR for a Western Michigan
                          University English professor. Researched materials
                          and edited final copy of her book. Developed
                          research and editing skills.

     1983 Spring   RESEARCHED and participated in the design of a
                          Public Relations master's degree program for Western
                          Michigan University. Researched and planned with
                          the Public Relations Society of America, professors,
                          students, and Chairperson of the Communications
                          Department. Developed writing, editing, research,
                          evaluation, and programming skills.

     1982 Winter   LAB ASSISTANT, Western Michigan University Language
                          Lab. Operated multipurpose duplicator, 16mm
                          projector, cassette player, reel-to-reel player,
                          slide projector, and panel for 42 listening
                          stations. Coordinated faculty-student projects.
                          Accomplishment: offered supervisory position for
                          Fall 1983. Experienced with audio-visual equipment
                          and programming.

     1979 to 1980   ASSISTANT TEACHER, Sara Swickard Preschool, Western
                          Michigan University. Organized, developed new
                          teaching ideas, billed and budgeted, redesigned
                          facility. Developed communication and leadership
                          skills and patience.

Penny Huyck
Page 2

1975 to 1980	<u>YOUTH</u> <u>REPRESENTATIVE</u> AND <u>ASSISTANT</u> <u>DIRECTOR</u>, Straits Area Resort Ministry, St. Ignace and Mackinaw City, MI. Personnel Committee. Created learning environment in youth center, counseled youth, solved problems, designed projects involving community, advertised, wrote articles for newspapers, performed in musicals. Developed communication, public speaking, writing, leadership, and programming skills.

<u>EDUCATION</u> - Bachelor of Science, Cum Laude, Majors--English with writing emphasis, Communication, Western Michigan University, June, 1980.

Financed educational expenses through scholarships, above jobs, full-time work as assembly line worker, temporary manager of grocery store-gas station business, and cashier.

The Functional Resume

A functional resume emphasizes the skills you can transfer from one kind of position to another. If you were a successful crew chief at a construction site, you managed people. If you are now seeking employment as an office manager, you may use the functional resume to emphasize your management experience while minimizing your connection with the construction industry. Thus, this format is particularly useful if you are changing job fields. Because you include few names, dates, or places, it is also a good format to use if you are re-entering the job market after a long absence.

The functional resume requires lengthy self-analysis. Usually you will need to study some of the new books written about seeking new careers. These books will help you translate your experience into words that indicate universal skills. However, you should know that some personnel managers dislike the format because it can be used to mask a poor job record or lack of specific training. Study the example of a functional resume written by Ray Olan. This older man has recently returned to college and completed a degree in a field related to his previous employment but not identical with it. He is emphasizing his transferable (functional) skills which will be useful in any job category.

RAY M. OLAN
5139 Greenhill
Scranton, PA 18512
(717) 382-3202

OFFERING

Diverse background in business; accounting degree; outstanding scholastic and leadership record; proven organizational and managerial skills, extensive experience in manuscript proofreading and editing; cultural sensitivity; extensive world travel.

EDUCATION

Master of Business Administration (3.81 GPA) April, 1983
Temple University, Philadelphia, PA 15281
    Concentration: **Accounting**

Bachelor of Science, June, 1965
Villanova University, Philadelphia, PA 15257
    Major: **Computer Science**
    Minor: **Accounting**

ADMINISTRATION AND MANAGEMENT SKILLS

* Conceived, planned and coordinated complex program schedule for an extensive international awareness festival. Coordinated the efforts of a fourteen-person committee, including scheduling of all activities.

* Supervised staff and facilities for a nonprofit organization. Planned curriculum, ordered and distributed materials for small school.

* Supervised office and bookkeeping activities for manufacturing firm and department store.

WRITING, EDITING, AND COMMUNICATIONS SKILLS

* Experienced in preparation of manuscripts, from typing original copy and editing, to final proofreading of publisher page proofs. Demonstrated ability to work with fine detail.

* Created and edited newsletter for public school. Organized material, designed layout, typed final copy.

* Served as active executive board member of several community organizations. Facilitated reaching group goals through directed leadership.

* Used communication skills when demonstrating and instructing use of accounting machines. Able to communicate in speaking and writing-- clearly, concisely and effectively.

EXPERIENCE

Director, St. Paul's Day School. Designed and executed curriculum, ordered and distributed materials, supervised teachers, implemented programs, prepared financial budget and statements of tuition and fees. 1980 to present.

President, Board Member, Angling Road Parent Teacher Organization. President two terms. Created and edited PTO Newsletter. Chairperson, "Friends Around the World," an international awareness festival. Coordinated activities of board members, initiated new activities. 1976 to 1980.

Proofreader of manuscripts for university professor, including editing, preparation of tables and charts, and final typing. 1972 to present.

Demonstrator, Instructor, National Cash Register Company, New York City, New York. Responsibilities included internal wiring of accounting machines, construction of program bars, assisting clients with training employees, demonstrating use of accounting machines in showroom. 1971.

Bookkeeper, Kent Scott, Inc., Easton, Pennsylvania. Conducted all bookkeeping activities of manufacturing firm, including payroll, accounts receivable, accounts payable, general journal, to trial balance. Supervised small office staff. 1969-1971.

Bookkeeper, Siegel's Department Store, Easton, Pennsylvania. Conducted all bookkeeping activities for department store. Operated NCR billing machine. 1968.

PERSONAL BACKGROUND AND INTERESTS

Have lived in Pakistan for two years and have traveled extensively, including India, Iran, Turkey, Afghanistan, USSR, Japan, Taiwan, Poland and Western Europe. Interests include: gardening, reading, current events, camping, swimming. Highly motivated and self-directed, enjoy creative and challenging work experiences.

CREDENTIALS

Credentials including references are available from the Temple University Placement Office, Ellsworth Hall, Philadelphia, Pennsylvania 15281.

The Targeted Resume

This resume format resembles the functional resume because it emphasizes skills rather than history. It is a good choice if you have special talents or experience that cannot be shown in the two more common formats. If you use this format, you must be sure of the particular position you want. You can send the same targeted resume to six different TV stations, but you cannot send the same resume to a TV station and to an advertising agency.

The targeted resume begins by indicating a job title or specific position. Be sure that the company receiving your resume has a position such as the one you are seeking, or your resume will not receive a favorable review. After naming the position you seek, show your special talents or experience that will make you valuable in that position. Many young people who graduate with a degree in the liberal arts find the targeted resume a useful tool when they first seek to enter a professional field.

Jane Deere graduated from college with a major in biology. She had considerable unpaid experience in the arts and in audio-visual technology. She wanted employment in television, but she knew that if she used a standard chronological format, studio personnel would not read beyond the words *Major: Biology* when they could choose from so many new graduates who could list *Major: Television Production.* Nor did she have sufficient experience to prepare a lengthy functional resume, so she chose the targeted format.

```
                         JANE DEERE'S
          QUALIFICATIONS FOR WORK IN TELEVISION PRODUCTION

School Address:                    Home Address:
368 Harmon Hall                    1408 E. Hatch
Valparaiso University              Angola, IN 46703
Valparaiso, IN 46383               (219) 651-7472
(219) 392-0711


Education
     B.A. Valparaiso University (Indiana)
     Expected date of graduation:  June, 1983
     Course work related to communications:
          Basic Design               Film and Literature
          Theater Lighting           American Literature
          Audio Visual Media         Experimental Fiction
          Photography 1              Communications Tech.
          Photography 2              Individualized Study in
                                     Communications
     Junior Year Abroad:
          Institute for American Students, Aix-En-Provence, France


Work Experience
     1982 Valparaiso University Instructional Services
     Duties and Responsibilities:
          Designed graphics          Set up P.A. systems
          Worked with photography    Ran T.V. cameras
          Ran movie projectors       Directed T.V. programs
          Trained new staff          Worked with sound equipment
     K-80 Slide Show
     Produced a slide-tape presentation for Valparaiso University Freshman
     Orientation

     1981 Upjohn Company, DelRay, Florida
        Research Associate in cross pollination.  Supervised cross pollination
        project of cucumbers and tomatoes

     1978-1980 Long Lake Country Club, Angola, Indiana 46703.  Waitress

School Activities                  Special Interests and Hobbies
     Disc jockey (WVUD,            Water sports
       Valparaiso University Radio) Oriental cooking
     Film Society                  Insect collecting
     Yearbook
     Photography for public relations

References With Permission
     Ms. Lisa Franks                  Dr. C. Weston
     Director of Instructional        Major Advisor
        Services                      219 West Hall
     Valparaiso University            Valparaiso Univeristy
     Valparaiso, Indiana 46383        Valparaiso, Indiana 46383
     (219) 392-1101                   (219) 391-3827

              Dr. W. Stone, Project Director
              445 N.W. 11th Ave.
              Boca Raton, Florida 33432
```

Reprinted with permission.

The Qualifying Resume

This format is a rather recent development which combines elements of the chronological resume and the functional resume. The aim of the resume is to show the reader how education and experience have qualified the writer to hold a certain position. The resume usually begins with a broadly stated employment goal (rather than the specific statement used in a targeted resume format). Then education and experience appear in order of importance to the reader, but the marginal notes show how these translate into qualities that the prospective employer will want to see in any applicant.

The qualifying resume is a useful tool for any applicant, but it is particularly useful for young people who have valuable work experience and general education that are unusual for the position sought. Older candidates for employment can use this format to translate volunteer work to employable skills. Some personnel managers like to see this format because it proves that applicants have taken time to do a careful self-analysis before applying for a position. The qualifying resume in this chapter was prepared by John Daly, a young college graduate who could easily have used the chronological format. He thought that adding appropriate qualifying statements would show both his maturity and his serious intention to begin a business career.

JOHN L. DALY

PRESENT ADDRESS: 1618 Fraternity Village Drive, Kalamazoo, Michigan 49007 (616)
                    381-3630

PERMANENT ADDRESS: 2124 Davis Street, Wyandotte, Michigan 48192 (313) 284-7267

EDUCATION

WMU Business   Bachelor of Business Administration, Western Michigan University
School AACSB   Honors College, Kalamazoo, MI 49008. April 1982. GPA 3.50.
Accredited   Major: General Marketing
                        Minors: Business Communication/Administrative Services, and
                                 General Business

VALUABLE EXPERIENCE

Performed   Active SIFE (Students in Free Enterprise) member. Promoted free
Under   enterprise locally and nationally; performed for children's televi-
Pressure   sion; placed first in Regional Competition among 11 colleges.
                    (1980-81)

                    Sigma Chi Fraternity Treasurer. Handled $56,000 in income and dis-
                    bursements. Chaired Finance Committee. Controlled records. (1981)

Controlled   Vice-Chairman, WMU Student Budget Allocations Committee. Chosen
$160,000   from 50 people by student-organization leaders. Allocated monies to
Student Funds   all campus organizations. Ran hearings and debates. (1981-82)

WORK EXPERIENCE

Related   Salesperson, Regal Shoe Shop, Portage, MI. Duties included:
Work   stocked shelves; handled transactions; marked alterations; assisted
Experience   customers. (Summer 1981)

                    Salesperson, Sagebrush, Portage, MI. Attended 5-day training
                    school. Duties included: ran register; stocked shelves; marked
                    alterations; assisted customers. (Summer 1980)

Maintained   Manufacturing Laborer, Karmazin Products Corp., Wyandotte, MI.
Steady   Recognized for cooperation and adaptability. Duties included:
Employment   operated furnace conveyor; chain-lifted steel frames. (Summer 1979)

                    Other Jobs Held: Receptionist, Busboy, Dishwasher, Janitor.

ACTIVITIES AND HONORS

Continuous   Member: SBAC, SIFE, Marketing Club, WMU Development Program, Sigma
Involvement   Chi Fraternity, offices held: Pledge Class President, Secretary
Throughout   Finance Committee, Assistant Rush Chairman, Treasurer, Chairman
School   Finance Committee, Chapter Editor; Inter-Fraternity Representative.

                    WMU Honors Program; Phi Eta Sigma Honors Fraternity; WMU Academic
                    Scholarship Recipient; Dean's List; Order of Omega Greek Scholastic
                    Honorary.

CREDENTIALS

Helpful   Credentials including references are available from the University
Placement   Placement Service, Western Michigan University, Ellsworth Hall,
Staff   Kalamazoo, MI 49008, or by calling: (616) 383-1710.

Include Appropriate Information

These four sample resumes are not set forms to copy. They do represent some of the possibilities for organizing information when seeking employment. Inventive job seekers and professional career counselors create other layouts and combinations of information almost daily. You should select a format that seems to present you in the most favorable light. Then adapt the format to fit your own needs. Whatever format you choose, you should include certain standard information somewhere on the one or two pages you type.

Identification Information
Your name, address, and telephone number should be at the top of page 1 for easy reference. Be sure that the telephone number includes an area code and that your zip code appears in the address. Even if you are preparing your resume for the only major employer in a small town, these two touches show that you understand common business procedures.

College graduates who begin a job search in the final semester have a special problem. Many of them expect to move home or at least out of campus housing after graduation, but the resumes must show a current address and phone number. John Daly, for example, expected to move home after graduation unless he accepted employment elsewhere, so he listed two addresses. A more precise way to convey the same information is

Address until May 1, 1982
  1618 Fraternity Village Dr.
  Kalamazoo, MI 49007
  (616) 381-3630

Address after May 1, 1982
  2124 Davis Street
  Wyandotte, MI 48192
  (313) 284-7267

If you must prepare a resume when all you know is that you must move on a certain date, arrange for a friend or relative to take and forward messages for you. Be sure that this friend or relative will actually be at home to answer the telephone during most normal business hours. Here is one example of a way to show such an arrangement:

Address until May 1, 1982
  1618 Fraternity Village Dr.
  Kalamazoo, MI 49007
  (616) 381-3630

Messages after May 1, 1982
  Mr. Irving Small
  37 Oak Street
  Kalamazoo, MI 49008
  (616) 534-9999

If all your friends and relatives are away from the phone during the day, consider hiring an answering service for the duration of your job search.

Opening Statement
This part of the resume is optional. As you saw in the examples, some applicants used a "Qualified by" statement; another called that part of the

resume an "Offering" statement. Another used a "Job Objective" statement, and one person omitted this opening statement entirely.

If you wish to use the same resume to apply for a variety of positions, omit the opening statement. Obviously, you cannot send a resume that lists a "Job Objective" in the sales field to the personnel office of a hospital. By the same token, if you are "Qualified by" a strong theoretical and practical background in cost accounting, you would not send that resume to an employer specializing in tax accounting.

If you want to use either of these opening statements, here are some hints about writing them.

The "Offering" or "Qualified by" statement is only two or three lines long and acts like the topic sentence in a paragraph. It tells the reader highlights of the skills and experiences that will be mentioned in the resume. One difficulty with opening statements is that too many of them sound exactly alike. If you have something unusual to offer for a person of your age and experience, be sure to get that information in the opening statement. If you have almost exactly the same qualifications as others have, you might do better to concentrate on writing a descriptive "Job Objective" statement.

The "Job Objective" statement describes your job preference. It may be very specific if you use the targeted format, or it may be more general— describing a field in which you seek employment. Few workers start at the top, so most applicants who use a "Job Objective" statement indicate both the entry level position in the field and add a "leading to" clause in which they mention a job title that they hope to hold in five years or so. This statement indicates that the applicant seeks specific employment and is not interested in "just any job."

Education Information

If you have completed any classes beyond high school graduation, you will include information about your educational background somewhere in your resume. Where you place educational information depends on the resume format you select. Wherever you place the information, most personnel managers expect to see the following information:

Full name and address of the college or university

Degree(s) received or credit hours completed

Date of degree

Major and minor fields of study

Name and description of any special projects or publications

Special honors or a high grade point average

If you have attended workshops or completed other special training, they should be included in this section. If you attended more than one college or university or earned more than one degree, put the most recent university or degree at the top of the list as you can see in the resume prepared by Ray Olan.

Even this list of what personnel managers expect to see is not a rule. Jane Deere did not include her major or minor field of study because she did not want the personnel manager to have that information until she could explain her educational history in a face-to-face interview. Likewise, if you have only an average grade point instead of a superior one, omit that information. If you have no special projects or honors, simply omit the category.

If you have entered college, do not refer to your high school education in this section. Should you need to prepare a resume to help you find summer employment, use an education statement similar to this:

> 1983 — New York University   New York, NY 10114
>   Major: Computer Science
>   Anticipated graduation: January, 1987

Work Experience

Most employers expect even young people to have some paid or unpaid work experience, and they expect to see evidence of that experience in a resume. If you select the chronological format, list your work experience in reverse chronological order showing the most recent employment at the top of the list. Indicate the dates of employment by years only. List the name of the employing organization and its location (city and state are usually sufficient). Designate your job title. If the job had no specific title, pick one that describes the position. Summarize your job duties and responsibilities or special accomplishments.

Many college graduates have held several different jobs on the way through college. Usually only one or two of these can be related to the position the graduate now seeks. In such a case, the work experience section can be divided into two sections such as "Professional Experience" and "Other Work Experience." In the latter category, the writer merely lists the types of jobs held, such as "casual laborer, telephone receptionist, busperson, chauffeur." "Professional Experience" is not necessarily paid work experience. It can be internship or apprentice work; it can be volunteer experience; it can be full-time work or part-time work, but it must be clearly related to the kind of work you now seek. If the relationship is only functional ("managed," "advised," "reviewed," "administered"), then perhaps the information should be in a functional format.

If you select a nonchronological format, you have considerably more latitude about the way to show a prospective employer that you have had work experience that relates to the position you now seek. Showing a clear relationship between past employment and a new career field is not always easy, but it is usually possible. You just have to keep rearranging information until it shows you in the best possible light to a future employer.

Exercise E   Take the contents of the Employment folder in your personal "Personnel File" and arrange the information appropriately for each of the following resume formats:

    a. Chronological

    b. Functional

    c. Qualifying

Other Information

As you have seen in the sample resumes, this category of information varies from person to person. What is appropriate for one person is not appropriate for another. Consider your audience. Then plan to include those items that relate to the job but that do not fit easily under the headings *Education* or *Experience*. Find a way to highlight them in your resume.

A category for *Honors and Awards* can be used to show special merit. Do not list high school honors and awards. Do list awards that relate to employment. Sports awards are related to employment in physical education, in recreation services, and even in physical therapy, but they are not important for positions in accounting or engineering.

If you were a student member of a professional association such as the Data Processing Management Association and you seek employment in the data processing field, show your professionalism in a section called *Memberships*. If you were an officer in any student organization, you will want to use a *Memberships* category to show that you held responsibility in a student organization. Just a list of memberships does not convey much useful information to a prospective employer. You can use the space to better advantage to show other important information about yourself.

If you have special certification or knowledge, invent an appropriate category to show that information. Some examples of information that should appear on the resume are

    Ability to read or write a foreign language

    Journeyman status in a trade union

    Chauffeur's license

    Medical Assistant Certificate

    State certification in such fields as

        nursing

        physical or occupational therapy

        cosmetology

auto mechanics

Real estate broker's license

Certified Public Accountant

Notary Public

If you are willing to relocate or to travel, include that information if the position you seek might normally be one that would call for travel or reassignment. You may want to indicate when you will be available for employment. You may have other special information that will help to show that you are mature, responsible, and ready to do good work for a new employer; find a way to include it.

Do not fill up a page with trivia. Some people fill a category of *Interests and Hobbies* with "reading, music, and sports." Such information is of little use to a personnel manager. However, if your hobbies are "completing a collection of Tibetan coins" and "Mandarin-style Chinese cooking," you at least stand out as a person with unusual special interests. You must decide if those unusual interests will be considered an asset or a liability in your special job market before you include them.

References and Credentials

Whatever format you select for a resume, reserve the last section for reference and credential information. If you are using a college placement service to help in your job search, the college or university will usually prepare a special packet that includes your grades, letters of recommendation that you submit to them, and a list of references you have arranged for. When a prospective employer wants to consider your application, he or she can request your "credentials package" from the university. To show that you have the information prepared, you use a statement such as that shown at the end of John Daly's resume.

If you are sending your resume to many companies, the people who have agreed to act as your references will probably prefer that they be contacted only by companies that are seriously considering your application. Then you may use a statement that requires the company to contact you for reference information:

REFERENCES

References available upon request.

The company will understand that if they call or write you, you will send a sheet containing the names, addresses, and phone numbers of references.

The third alternative is simply to list at least three (and not more than five) people in the closing section of your resume. These people should be able to attest to your ability to work, your maturity, your sense of responsibility, and your attitude toward work. The best references are usually your supervisors from previous work experience. Another good reference is a college professor in your major field. The best professorial references are instructors you had for more than one class, those for whom you did some special research, or those who sponsored a campus organization for which you did special service. The professor must know you as more than a name and social security number if he or she is to be an effective reference. Do not list members of your family or your personal friends.

Be sure to contact people before you list their names as references. The best contact is a personal visit or a phone call, but you can write a letter asking permission. After you have completed the resume, you can help your references give a good account by sending each of them a copy of the resume and indicating the kind of position you are seeking.

For each reference, list a complete name with personal title (Ms., Mrs., Mr., or Dr.), a work title (Associate Professor, Foreman, Production Manager, or Office Manager), a complete business address, and a business phone number with area code and extension. Most personnel managers prefer that you also indicate your relationship to the person you list as a reference.

Exercise F   Think of at least five people you would like to list in the reference section of your resume. Collect the information you will need to list each person correctly.

Omit Inappropriate Information

Federal and state laws enacted in the last 10 to 15 years prohibit prospective employers from asking for certain kinds of information. Usually these laws apply to businesses of a certain size or businesses that have government contracts or that are regulated by the Interstate Commerce Commission. Personnel managers in the affected businesses prefer to receive resumes that contain no "illegal" information. Your college or university placement service, the public library, or state employment office can probably provide current information, but you can expect to find that the following items should not be included on your resume:

Age

Health

Physical characteristics (height, weight, sex)

Marital status

Dependents

Religion

Racial or ethnic information

A photograph
Financial information
Citizenship status

Produce a Finished Copy

Job seekers who plan to send resumes to many companies often have their resumes printed professionally. Printers specializing in resumes can be found near most colleges and universities. The least expensive resumes are those printed directly from the page you typed. If you ask for typesetting, the price will be higher. Or you may choose to type your own resume and duplicate as many copies as you need. If you use the targeted format, you may have to prepare an individual resume for each company to which you apply. Whether you do your own typing or ask for typesetting, you will need to type at least one copy of the resume. Because your resume is important, you will probably want to type several versions until you complete one that looks "best." Here are some guidelines.

1. *Limit your resume to one page.* For beginning job seekers, a one-page resume is sufficient. If you have a great deal of experience or many special factors to display, you may need two pages. If you have the resume printed, you may use the back and front of heavy paper, but if you type, use two sheets for a two-page resume. If you think you need more than two pages, you are including too much irrelevant material; remove some information.

2. *Leave at least a one-inch margin at the top and bottom and on both sides.* You may use larger margins, but not smaller ones.

3. *Plan your page to include empty space.* No one enjoys reading a full page of fine print—including a prospective employer. Use the empty space in such a way that as you pick up the resume, your eye is just naturally drawn to the facts in the resume that you believe are your strongest points.

4. *Be sure your resume contains only facts.* Do not indicate by your choice of verbs that you liked one job better than another. Be sure, too, that your facts are absolutely correct. You may omit giving information that you feel may hurt your chances for a position but do not stretch the truth or lie about your background.

5. *Use phrases rather than sentences.* A phrase writing style saves space and allows you to fill the resume with action verbs which will focus the reader's attention on your ability to accomplish job objectives.

6. *Write the phrases in parallel structure.* If you examine the examples in this chapter, you will see that all the writers used the past tense of verbs in every phrase.

7. *Be sure the final copy is error-free and typed with a carbon ribbon on a modern typewriter.* If you do not have access to such a typewriter, you can take your copy to a secretarial service for final typing.

If you elect to have a typeset resume, you may prepare copy on an ordinary typewriter, but be sure that the copy you take to the printer contains no errors. The printer will prepare a "proof copy" for you before completing your order. Read it carefully. You, not the printer, are responsible for accuracy.

8. *Aim for simplicity.* Extra color, binders, illustrations, and fancy paper or print style are all distracting to a reader. You want the reader to concentrate on the written material about you, not on the printer's work.

USING YOUR RESUME

Preparing a resume helps writers to get a mind set for seeking employment. Looking at life from an employer's point of view is very helpful in bringing the right kinds of answers to mind in interviews. However, the real value of a resume is that it serves as a personal emissary to an employer. If you have a personal interview scheduled, take a copy of your resume to the interview. You can hand it to the interviewer at the end of the interview "to remind you of me when you make a decision about filling the position we discussed." An interviewer will be impressed with your preparation and will appreciate having written evidence of your qualifications.

If you are seeking employment in a field that has professional associations and conventions, you can attend a convention and meet potential employers. Inquire about employment. If you learn that a firm might have an opening, get the correct name and address of the person who is in charge of hiring. Be sure to get the name and title of the person with whom you talked. You will be able to mention his or her name when you apply for a position. You can offer your resume to the person you meet "for your reference if the hiring officer contacts you." Sometimes the new acquaintance will take the resume, sometimes not; but you will have made an impression about your serious intention to seek employment.

If you have no way to make personal contacts in your field, one of the most common ways of getting a resume to a potential employer is to send the resume with a letter of application.

Exercise G   Make a list of ways you could make contact with a potential employer in your field.

WRITING A LETTER OF APPLICATION

Letters of application fall into two general categories—solicited and unsolicited. Research shows that the unsolicited letter is not very effective, but for young people entering the job market the first time, it is sometimes the only possibility. Both letters use a personal letter style such as you studied in chapter 4, but they include an Enclosure notation to show that the resume is enclosed. Both letters follow the same general pattern.

The first paragraph states your purpose: to obtain employment. The middle paragraph or paragraphs mention the highlights of your background which make you a good candidate for the position you seek. Do not repeat the resume, but rather try to make the prospective employer so interested in your qualifications that he or she will read the full resume. Always refer the reader to "the enclosed resume." The final paragraph requests a personal interview and gives data that will facilitate action.

Unsolicited Letters of Application

When you send an unsolicited letter of application, you are not answering an advertisement for employment, and you are usually writing to a company that does not employ anyone who is a friend or acquaintance of yours. Unless your application arrives the very day that an employment officer happens to have an opening for a person with your background, the chances of obtaining an interview with an unsolicited letter are slim.

However, you will often receive a rather standard reply which states that the company is not hiring just now but will keep your materials on file for a certain period of time. That form letter from the company can give you a good excuse to write again near the end of the holding period. The follow-up letter will have the advantage of being addressed to a person and will show that you have persistence. It may serve to rescue your original letter and resume from the files and put you back in the running for positions that might open soon.

You can increase your chances of being considered for employment by doing some intensive homework about the companies you intend to query with an unsolicited letter of application. The latest edition of the *College Placement Annual* is usually available in college placement offices. This book contains names and addresses of personnel officers of several hundred larger American companies. Further, other sections of the book indicate the kinds of help the company will probably hire during the year and locations of offices that may be hiring. Other sources of addresses and information are *Standard and Poor's Register, The Thomas Register*, and telephone directories. An unsolicited letter addressed to a specific person often has a greater chance for consideration than one addressed merely to "Personnel

Office." You can telephone companies and ask the switchboard operator for the name of a person to whom you should send an application. Or you may ask for the Personnel Office and ask the clerk who answers for the name and correct title of the person in charge of the department.

Each unsolicited letter of application must be individually and meticulously typed. If you can find a way to change the content of the first paragraph to tailor it to the particular company, do so. Even if you send the same letter to fifty firms, do not get the letter printed. Most secretarial services will set a fairly low rate for typing fifty copies of the same letter with a new address for each letter because the body of the letter will be on an automatic playback. Unless you are an expert typist, you should not try to type these letters which should be error free and placed on a good quality bond paper.

John Daly's letter to Oscar Levinson is an unsolicited letter of application. You can see that it could easily be sent to any of thousands of firms which might be hiring a person as a sales representative. As such letters go, it is a good one; but because it has to be so general, it will probably not appeal to many prospective employers.

2124 Davis Street
Wyandotte, MI 48192
May 2, 198-

Mr. Oscar Levinson
Vice President for Marketing
Barton Corporation
140 Industrial Way
St. Louis, MO 63104

Dear Mr. Levinson:

Will you please consider me for a position as sales representative for your company?

My education and experience have prepared me well for a position in sales. My college major in marketing provided me with both general and special knowledge of sales and related fields. As the enclosed resume shows, I also have practical retail sales experience. Further, my services as fraternity treasurer and as a member of the student budget committee required that I keep records and make decisions involving over $200,000 a year.

My classes in business communication have shown me the value of listening, speaking, and writing well. These skills were invaluable not only in the workplace, but also in representing student organizations and the University itself to the public.

Presiding over budget committee hearings required that I listen carefully and speak clearly. Preparing reports for SIFE and serving as fraternity chapter editor helped me polish my writing skills.

When you have studied the other qualifications on the enclosed resume and sent for my credentials, please let me know a convenient time when we can discuss the possibility of my joining your sales staff.

Sincerely,

John L. Daly

John L. Daly

Enclosure

A variation of the unsolicited letter of application that is sometimes more effective is one to a company that employs someone you know in a position of at least equivalent merit to the one you seek. Then you can open your letter by mentioning the person's name as John Daly did in his letter to S.M. Hedderson. If you can name a person already employed by the company, you demonstrate that you have some knowledge of the company and the working conditions. You will probably be considered ahead of a stranger if openings are available. If you attended conventions and workshops in your field and collected names, use them in the opening paragraph of an unsolicited letter of application.

2124 Davis Street
Wyandotte, MI 48192
May 16, 198-

Mr. S. M. Hedderson
Steelton Office Furnishings
12214 North Michigan Avenue
Chicago, IL 60637

Dear Mr. Hedderson:

At the office equipment show in Chicago last week, Pieter
VanderRoest, of your midwest staff, told me that you may
have an opening in the next training class for eastern sales
representatives. Please consider my application for any
such opening.

Marketing products and ideas is a challenge that I welcome.
Selling your expanding line of modular office landscaping
would give me an opportunity to put my training and experience to good use. As you read the enclosed resume, you will
see that I have had practical experience in retail sales at
two shops, and I have completed a business degree with a
major in marketing.

You will also see that my experience on the Budget Allocation
Committee has already given me an opportunity to learn one
often neglected sales skill--listening carefully. In addition
to listening skills, I can bring a keen attention to detail
and a practiced ability to speak convincingly to strangers.

When you have studied the qualifications on the enclosed resume and examined my credentials, please let me know a convenient time when we can discuss the possibility of my joining
the next sales class to learn to sell Steelton's modern line
of furniture and modular office landscaping.

Sincerely,

John L. Daly

John L. Daly

Enclosure

Solicited Letters of Application

You send a solicited letter of application if you are answering an advertisement or if you are writing at the request of a person in the company. As many positions are filled by word-of-mouth advertising, one of the best sources of leads for employment is currently employed people who know of vacancies. If you are fortunate enough to know a person who would like to hire you, you may still go through the entire hiring procedure beginning with a letter of application. In this case, the opening paragraph can be much more direct, as the following example shows.

> Joe Jones, Marketing Director, asked that I write you to arrange
> for an interview for the sales vacancy in his department.

Such an opening paragraph shows that both you and Joe Jones respect the personnel department's role in the hiring procedure, but it also practically guarantees that you will be on the interview list. Study Penny Huyck's letter to Ian Bartholomew. It is based on a personal invitation to apply for a particular position.

301 North Kendall
Kalamazoo, MI 49007
May 15, 198-

Mr. Ian Bartholomew
Personnel Director
Michigan Mutual Company
P.O. Box 118
Lansing, MI 48906

Dear Mr. Bartholomew:

Susan Spitzer, editor of your in-house employee publication, asked me to send my resume to you as a first step toward being considered for the new position which will be available on the M-Pact staff, beginning July 1.

Practical experience meeting deadlines has helped me sharpen my skills in all aspects of newspaper production; thus, I could immediately begin work on layout and keylining when M-Pact changes to an 8-page format.

Please read the enclosed resume and consider my qualifications to join the M-Pact staff. Then, please suggest a convenient time for an interview when I can show you and Ms. Spitzer samples of my work.

Sincerely,

Penny Huyck

Penny Huyck

Enclosure

Another solicited letter is one written in response to a help-wanted advertisement. Some ads are "blind" (they give a box number and no company name), while others list a company name and address.

COMMUNICATION ASSISTANT. Major corp. needs experienced writer, editor to meet weekly deadlines with quality copy. Prefer degree in English or communications. Write Box 10 Evening Herald, Ft. Wayne, IN 46802.

COMMUNICATION ASSISTANT. Carstairs Co. needs experienced writer, editor to meet weekly deadlines with quality copy. Prefer degree in English or communications. Send resume to 1324 West Garfield, Ft. Wayne, IN 46802.

If you answer an advertisement that lists the company name and address, take time to investigate the company before writing your letter. If you know something about the company's products and markets, you can better tailor your qualifications to the kind of job the company offers. Do start the letter with reference to the advertisement as Penny Huyck does when she writes to Carstairs Company.

301 North Kendall
Kalamazoo, MI 49007
June 1, 198-

Carstairs Company
1324 West Garfield
Ft. Wayne, IN 46802

Attention: Personnel Department

Gentlemen:

Please consider my application for the vacant position of
communications assistant at Carstairs Company as advertised
in the Evening Herald on Tuesday, June 1.

Affiliation with the American Society of Agricultural
Engineers gave me an opportunity to read many Carstairs
bulletins and taught me to rely on technical data you
supplied. You see that I have already acquired a broad
background in agricultural machinery.

In addition, successful newspaper experience has taught me
to meet deadlines regularly and calmly. Because of my
editing experience, you can expect quality copy each week.

After you have read the enclosed resume, call Mr. Calvin
Gretchner at (616) 323-0423 to verify my ability. Then,
if you would like to see writing samples, let me know a
convenient time when I may show you my portfolio.

Sincerely,

Penny Huyck

Penny Huyck

Enclosure

If the ad is blind, it will at least give a job title and some idea of the qualifications the company seeks. You must concentrate on showing how your background meets those qualifications. Again, the best opening for this letter is reference to the blind advertisement as shown in Penny Huyck's letter directed to "Personnel Office."

301 North Kendall
Kalamazoo, MI 49007
June 1, 198-

Personnel Office
Box 10
Evening Herald
Ft. Wayne, IN 46802

Gentlemen:

Please consider this letter an application for the position
of communications assistant which you listed in the Evening
Herald on Tuesday, June 1.

Successful newspaper experience has taught me to meet deadlines regularly and calmly, and I have had extra experience
in editing. Therefore, you can expect quality copy each
week. Furthermore, as you can see on the attached resume,
my education credentials are exactly those your ad specifies.

You may call Mr. George Benham of the Tri-County News at
(616) 383-1988 to verify my writing and production capabilities. If you would like to see writing samples, call me
at (616) 345-6439 to arrange a time when I may show you my
portfolio.

Sincerely,

Penny Huyck

Penny Huyck

Enclosure

Now that you have read the sample letters, you can see how information varies ever so slightly to meet specific needs of each situation. You can save time in the job seeking process if you start now to rough out some variations of letters which you can use to accompany your resume. If you are answering an ad, you will not have the luxury of time to write and rewrite a letter. Advance planning can assure that your letter will be among the first to arrive.

OTHER EMPLOYMENT LETTERS

Follow-up Letters

If your letter of application was successful, you will be invited to interview for a job. After the interview, you have one more letter to write. You should write it as soon as you get home from the interview and mail it the same evening if possible. This letter is called a follow-up letter. It often helps you secure a position that many applicants want. During your interview time, pay close attention to names and titles. As soon as you have been officially dismissed, write down names and titles of all those who spent time talking with you. If you have the slightest doubt about spelling or title, stop before you leave the building to ask a secretary or receptionist to confirm the name and title. Because people value their names, you can lose a position by sending a follow-up letter to a person whose name you have misspelled.

Send a follow-up letter to each person with whom you spent time alone. In each case, begin by thanking the person for taking time with you. Remind the reader of the day or date of the interview and the name of the position for which you were interviewed. Then be sure the rest of the letter is not the same for each person to whom you write.

The middle paragraph or paragraphs should show that you are very much interested in the position. If some aspect of the job is especially to your liking, say so. In some cases, you may have been asked for additional information. Provide the information either in this paragraph or mention it here and put the information on a separate enclosure.

In the final paragraph, make a direct statement about your interest in the position and ask the reader seriously to consider you for the position. Be explicit about your availability for further interviews and your willingness to send additional information.

Penny Huyck has written two versions of a follow-up letter. The first letter is one that Penny might write to indicate that she wants to be considered an active applicant for the position. The second letter is one Penny might write if she decided that she would probably not be satisfied and productive in the position. Even though she did not want the position, Penny still wrote a simple follow-up letter as a courtesy. The company can now set her application aside and concentrate on applicants who want the position.

301 North Kendall
Kalamazoo, MI 49007
May 25, 198-

Ms. Susan Spitzer
Editor, M-Pact
Michigan Mutual Company
P.O. Box 118
Lansing, MI 48906

Dear Ms. Spitzer:

Thank you for the time you spent on Tuesday morning showing me your production facilities and reviewing my writing portfolio.

I was pleased to see how well my experience has prepared me for the responsibilities that joining the M-Pact staff would entail.

Please consider me an active applicant for the new staff position. If I can provide further information or additional work samples, please call me at (616) 345-6439.

Sincerely,

Penny Huyck

Penny Huyck

```
                              301 North Kendall
                              Kalamazoo, MI 49007
                              May 25, 198-


Ms. Susan Spitzer
Editor, M-Pact
Michigan Mutual Company
P.O. Box 118
Lansing, MI 48906

Dear Ms. Spitzer:

Thank you for the time you spent on Tuesday morning
showing me your production facilities and explaining
the new staff position on the M-Pact staff.

Although I would enjoy doing layout and keylining in
such modern surroundings, I had hoped the position
would involve more writing.

Your needs will probably be best served by another
candidate at this time.  If a writing position be-
comes available, please consider me again.

                         Sincerely,

                         Penny Huyck
                         Penny Huyck
```

LETTER OF ACCEPTANCE

If your job campaign has been successful, you will receive a letter or phone call asking you to report for work on a certain date, at a certain place, and at a specified salary. If you receive a phone call and the time is very short, you do not need to write a letter, but if the reporting date is some time in the future, you should confirm the offer in writing. Certainly, if the company writes to you offering a position, you will accept (or reject) the position in writing. Penny Huyck's short letter to Susan Spitzer shows this final step in the job search process.

301 North Kendall
Kalamazoo, MI 49007
June 10, 198-

Miss Susan Spitzer
Editor, M-Pact
Michigan Mutual Company
P.O. Box 118
Lansing, MI 48906

Dear Ms. Spitzer:

I am happy to accept your offer to begin work on the
M-Pact staff on July 1, 198-, at an initial salary of
$16,000.

In the meantime, I will study the orientation materials
you sent and plan to report to the Personnel Office at
8:30 a.m. on July 1.

                        Sincerely,

                        Penny Huyck

                        Penny Huyck

Review A well planned job search begins with self-analysis which is followed by close examination of the current market for your job skills. When you have assembled data about yourself, select an appropriate resume format and prepare a one- or two-page resume that will show a prospective employer the talents you can bring to business. Then use personal contacts or write a letter of application to send your resume to employers who may be seeking employees with your talents. If your application results in an interview, be sure to send a follow-up letter thanking the company for talking with you. When your job search is complete, confirm your appointment by letter.

Special Project Prepare a resume and letter of application you could use to seek employment.

SELECTED BIBLIOGRAPHY

Biegelersen, J.I. *Job Resumes.* Rev. ed. New York: Grosset & Dunlap Publishers, 1982.

Bolles, Richard N. *The Quick Job-Hunting Map (Advanced Version).* Berkeley, CA: Ten Speed Press, 1979.

Bolles, Richard N. *The Quick Job-Hunting Map (Beginning Version).* Berkeley, CA: Ten Speed Press, 1979.

Bolles, Richard N. *Tea Leaves—A New Look at Resumes.* Berkeley, CA: Ten Speed Press, 1979.

Bolles, Richard N. *The Three Boxes of Life.* Berkeley, CA: Ten Speed Press, 1978.

Bolles, Richard N. *What Color Is Your Parachute?* Rev. ed. Berkeley, CA: Ten Speed Press, 1980.

Bolles, Richard N., and John Crystal. *Where Do I Go from Here with My Life?* Berkeley, CA: Ten Speed Press, 1980.

Cohen, Leonard. *Choosing to Work: An Action-Oriented Job Finding Book.* Reston, VA: Reston Publishing Company, 1979.

College Placement Annual. Bethlehem, PA: College Placement Council (published annually).

Djeddah, Eli. *Moving Up.* Rev. ed. Berkeley, CA: Ten Speed Press, 1978.

Eisen, Jeffrey. *Get the Right Job Now!* Philadelphia: J. B. Lippincott Company, 1978.

Feingold, S. Norman, and Glenda Ann Hansard-Winkler. *900,000 Plus Jobs Annually: Published Sources of Employment Listings.* Garrett Park, MD: Garrett Park Press, 1982.

Garrison, Clifford B., and others. *Finding a Job You Feel Good About.* Allen, TX: Argus Communications, 1977.

Gootnick, David. *Getting a Better Job.* New York: McGraw-Hill Book Company, 1978.

Heschong, Naomi H. *Get the Job You Want.* 3d. ed. Woodbury, NY: Barron's Educational Series, 1982.

Jackson, Tom. *Guerrilla Tactics in the Job Market.* New York: Bantam, 1978.

Lathrop, Richard. *Who's Hiring Who.* 3d. ed. Berkeley, CA: Ten Speed Press, 1977.

Medley, Anthony H. *Sweaty Palms: The Neglected Art of Being Interviewed.* Belmont, CA: Wadsworth, 1978.

Chapter 16

Additional Exercises and Cases

1. Write a single sentence to describe your audience and purpose if you were to write a message in each of the following situations:

a. You are to plan a speech for Vocational Education Day at your daughter's elementary school where you will explain your job as an accountant who works as an auditor for the Internal Revenue Service.

b. You must plan to describe your job as an accountant who is an auditor for the Internal Revenue Service to a grand jury which has been convened to investigate tax fraud.

c. Plan what to tell a friend who has won $3,000 in the state's lottery. He writes to ask your advice about how best to invest the money.

d. Plan a message to your parents who have offered to buy a used car for you if you give them a list of features you want in a car.

e. Plan a message to the instructor for this class who asks you to write a message explaining what you expect to learn from the class.

f. Plan a message to the instructor of this class who asks you to write a message explaining how you expect to benefit from attending this class.

2. Fill in the patient information on the insurance forms on pp. 447 and 448 for each of the following situations.

a. You have cut your hand at work. The cut required emergency treatment and stitches. You are covered by insurance in your name, and you ask the benefits be paid directly to the doctor who treated you.

b. You broke your wrist playing volleyball at the beach last summer. Your parents, who carry only this medical insurance, paid the bills and now want you to fill in the necessary information so that they may be reimbursed for that expense by the insurance company.

BENEFIT REQUEST FORM
TYPE OR PRINT

PATIENT INFORMATION (TO BE COMPLETED BY EMPLOYEE)

1. PATIENT'S NAME *(First name, middle initial, last name)*	2. PATIENT'S DATE OF BIRTH	3. EMPLOYEE'S NAME AND ADDRESS
FULL TIME STUDENT ☐ YES ☐ NO IF YES, WHERE		

4. PATIENT'S ADDRESS *(If different from employee)*	5. PATIENT'S SEX MALE ☐ FEMALE ☐	6. EMPLOYEE'S SOC. SEC. NO.
	7. PATIENT'S RELATIONSHIP TO INSURED SELF ☐ SPOUSE ☐ CHILD ☐ OTHER ☐	8. GROUP NAME *(e.g. employer)*

9. OTHER HEALTH INSURANCE COVERAGE ☐ Yes ☐ No If Yes, Enter Name of Policyholder and Plan Name and Address and Policy or Medical Assistance Number	10. WAS CONDITION RELATED TO: A. PATIENT'S EMPLOYMENT YES ☐ NO ☐ B. AN ACCIDENT YES ☐ NO ☐	11. IF AN ACCIDENT ☐ A.M. date _____ 19 ____ and time _____ ☐ P.M. description (how & where) _____

12. PATIENT'S OR AUTHORIZED PERSON'S SIGNATURE *I Authorize the Release of any Medical Information Necessary to Process this request.* SIGNED _____ DATE _____	13. *I AUTHORIZE PAYMENT OF MEDICAL BENEFITS TO UNDER-SIGNED PHYSICIAN OR SUPPLIER FOR SERVICE DESCRIBED BELOW.* SIGNED *(Employee or Authorized Person)*

PHYSICIAN OR SUPPLIER INFORMATION (TO BE COMPLETED BY PHYSICIAN AND RETURNED TO EMPLOYEE)

14. DATE OF:	ILLNESS (FIRST SYMPTOM) OR INJURY (ACCIDENT) OR PREGNANCY (LMP)	15. DATE FIRST CONSULTED YOU FOR THIS CONDITION	16. HAS PATIENT EVER HAD SAME OR SIMILAR SYMPTOMS? YES ☐ NO ☐

17. DATE PATIENT ABLE TO RETURN TO WORK	18. DATES OF TOTAL DISABILITY FROM	THROUGH	DATES OF PARTIAL DISABILITY FROM THROUGH

19. NAME OF REFERRING PHYSICIAN	20. FOR SERVICES RELATED TO HOSPITALIZATION GIVE HOSPITALIZATION DATES ADMITTED DISCHARGED

21. NAME & ADDRESS OF FACILITY WHERE SERVICES RENDERED *(If other than home or office)*	22. WAS LABORATORY WORK PERFORMED OUTSIDE YOUR OFFICE? YES ☐ NO ☐ CHARGES:

23. DIAGNOSIS OR NATURE OF ILLNESS OR INJURY. RELATE DIAGNOSIS TO PROCEDURE IN COLUMN D BY REFERENCE TO NUMBERS 1, 2, 3, ETC. OR DX CODE

1.
2.
3.
4.

24. A DATE OF SERVICE	B* PLACE OF SER-VICE	C FULLY DESCRIBE PROCEDURES, MEDICAL SERVICES OR SUPPLIES FURNISHED FOR EACH DATE GIVEN PROCEDURE CODE (IDENTIFY:) *(EXPLAIN UNUSUAL SERVICES OR CIRCUMSTANCES)*	D DIAGNOSIS CODE	E CHARGES	F

25. SIGNATURE OF PHYSICIAN OR SUPPLIER SIGNED _____ DATE _____ 32. YOUR PATIENT'S ACCOUNT NO.	26. 30. ENTER THE TAXPAYER IDENTI-FICATION NUMBER TO BE USED FOR 1099 REPORTING PURPOSES.	27. TOTAL CHARGE	28. AMOUNT PAID	29. BALANCE DUE
		31. PHYSICIAN'S OR SUPPLIER'S NAME, ADDRESS, ZIP CODE & TELEPHONE NO.		

* PLACE OF SERVICE CODES

1 - (IH) - INPATIENT HOSPITAL	4 - (H) - PATIENT'S HOME	7 - (NH) - NURSING HOME	O - (OL) - OTHER LOCATIONS
2 - (HO)- OUTPATIENT HOSPITAL	5 - DAY CARE FACILITY (PSY)	8 - (SNF)- SKILLED NURSING FACILITY	A - (IL) - INDEPENDENT LABORATORY
3 - (O) - DOCTOR'S OFFICE	6 - NIGHT CARE FACILITY (PSY)	9 - AMBULANCE	B - OTHER MEDICAL- SURGICAL FACILITY

APPROVED BY AMA COUNCIL ON MEDICAL SERVICE 6-74

*PLEASE USE CURRENT PROCEDURAL TERMINOLOGY CODES FOR SURGERY

Aetna Life and Casualty. Reprinted with permission.

BENEFIT REQUEST FORM
TYPE OR PRINT

PATIENT INFORMATION (TO BE COMPLETED BY EMPLOYEE)

1. PATIENT'S NAME *(First name, middle initial, last name)*	2. PATIENT'S DATE OF BIRTH	3. EMPLOYEE'S NAME AND ADDRESS

FULL TIME STUDENT
☐ YES   NO   IF YES, WHERE

4. PATIENT'S ADDRESS *(If different from employee)*	5. PATIENT'S SEX MALE FEMALE	6. EMPLOYEE'S SOC. SEC. NO.
	7. PATIENT'S RELATIONSHIP TO INSURED SELF SPOUSE CHILD OTHER	8. GROUP NAME *(e.g. employer)*

9. OTHER HEALTH INSURANCE COVERAGE ☐ Yes ☐ No If Yes, Enter Name of Policyholder and Plan Name and Address and Policy or Medical Assistance Number	10. WAS CONDITION RELATED TO: A. PATIENT'S EMPLOYMENT YES ☐ NO ☐ B. AN ACCIDENT YES ☐ NO ☐	11. IF AN ACCIDENT date _____ 19 ____ and time _____ description (how & where) _____ ☐ A.M. ☐ P.M.

12. PATIENT'S OR AUTHORIZED PERSON'S SIGNATURE *I Authorize the Release of any Medical Information Necessary to Process this request.* SIGNED DATE	13. *I AUTHORIZE PAYMENT OF MEDICAL BENEFITS TO UNDER- SIGNED PHYSICIAN OR SUPPLIER FOR SERVICE DESCRIBED BELOW.* SIGNED (Employee or Authorized Person)

PHYSICIAN OR SUPPLIER INFORMATION (TO BE COMPLETED BY PHYSICIAN AND RETURNED TO EMPLOYEE)

14. DATE OF:	15. DATE FIRST CONSULTED YOU FOR THIS CONDITION	16. HAS PATIENT EVER HAD SAME OR SIMILAR SYMPTOMS? YES ☐ NO ☐
ILLNESS (FIRST SYMPTOM) OR INJURY (ACCIDENT) OR PREGNANCY (LMP)		

17. DATE PATIENT ABLE TO RETURN TO WORK	18. DATES OF TOTAL DISABILITY FROM THROUGH	DATES OF PARTIAL DISABILITY FROM THROUGH

19. NAME OF REFERRING PHYSICIAN	20. FOR SERVICES RELATED TO HOSPITALIZATION GIVE HOSPITALIZATION DATES ADMITTED DISCHARGED

21. NAME & ADDRESS OF FACILITY WHERE SERVICES RENDERED *(If other than home or office)*	22. WAS LABORATORY WORK PERFORMED OUTSIDE YOUR OFFICE? YES ☐ NO CHARGES:

23. DIAGNOSIS OR NATURE OF ILLNESS OR INJURY. RELATE DIAGNOSIS TO PROCEDURE IN COLUMN D BY REFERENCE TO NUMBERS 1, 2, 3, ETC. OR DX CODE

1.
2.
3.
4.

24. A DATE OF SERVICE	B* PLACE OF SER- VICE	C FULLY DESCRIBE PROCEDURES, MEDICAL SERVICES OR SUPPLIES FURNISHED FOR EACH DATE GIVEN PROCEDURE CODE* (IDENTIFY:) *(EXPLAIN UNUSUAL SERVICES OR CIRCUMSTANCES)*	D DIAGNOSIS CODE	E CHARGES	F

25. SIGNATURE OF PHYSICIAN OR SUPPLIER SIGNED DATE	26. 30. ENTER THE TAXPAYER IDENTI- FICATION NUMBER TO BE USED FOR 1099 REPORTING PURPOSES.	27. TOTAL CHARGE	28. AMOUNT PAID	29. BALANCE DUE
32. YOUR PATIENT'S ACCOUNT NO.		31. PHYSICIAN'S OR SUPPLIER'S NAME, ADDRESS, ZIP CODE & TELEPHONE NO.		

* PLACE OF SERVICE CODES

1 - (IH) - INPATIENT HOSPITAL	4 - (H) - PATIENT'S HOME	7 - (NH) - NURSING HOME	O - (OL) - OTHER LOCATIONS
2 - (HO)- OUTPATIENT HOSPITAL	5 - DAY CARE FACILITY (PSY)	8 - (SNF)- SKILLED NURSING FACILITY	A - (IL) - INDEPENDENT LABORATORY
3 - (O) - DOCTOR'S OFFICE	6 - NIGHT CARE FACILITY (PSY)	9 - AMBULANCE	B - OTHER MEDICAL SURGICAL FACILITY

*PLEASE USE CURRENT PROCEDURAL TERMINOLOGY CODES FOR SURGERY

APPROVED BY AMA COUNCIL ON MEDICAL SERVICE 6-74

Reprinted with permission.

3. Mary and Martin Brown built the house located at 2333 Abbott Avenue in your city in 1965. They have paid off the mortgage and now want to sell the house for $70,000. They will list it exclusively with your realty firm. The house has city water and sewer, a gas furnace, gas hot water heater, and stove. The lot is 85' by 130' and has been extensively and attractively landscaped; the Browns have a large vegetable garden as well. Annual taxes on the house are $3,000. The Browns are willing to have the house shown on Tuesdays, Thursdays, and weekends, but ask that you phone them (354-8890) before bringing prospective buyers to the house. They have provided the sketch and blueprint shown below. Fill in the Uniform Listing Contract (p. 450) for this house.

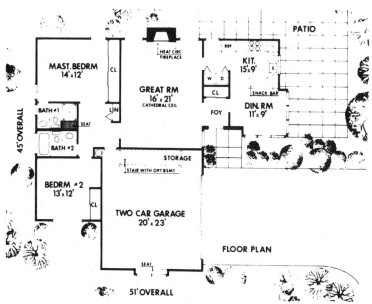

FLOOR PLAN

Reprinted with permission of Associated Press.

UNIFORM LISTING CONTRACT

	RESIDENTIAL			
	RES./ACRE	MLS AREA	PRICE	MLS NUMBER
	RES./COMM			
	LAKE			

ADDRESS _____

BETWEEN _____ AND _____ CITY/TWN _____

LAKE NAME _____ ROAD/LAKE FRONTAGE _____

EXTERIOR _____ GARAGE _____

	BASEMENT	LEVEL 1	LEVEL 2	LEVEL 3
APPROX. SQ. FT.				
NO. OF ROOMS				
NO. BEDROOMS				
BATHS/LAUNDRY				
FIREPLACES				

APPROX. LIV. AREA _____ LOT SIZE OR ACRES _____ ☐ WALK-OUT BASEMENT

☐ FORMAL DIN. RM. ☐ FAMILY ROOM ☐ RECREATION ROOM ☐ SWIM POOL

☐ WATER WELL ☐ CITY WATER ☐ WATER IN STREET ☐ GAS IN HOUSE

☐ SEPTIC SYSTEM ☐ CITY SEWER ☐ SEWER IN STREET ☐ GAS IN STREET

OWNER _____ PH _____

ADDRESS _____

SHOWING INSTR. _____

HEAT SYSTEM _____ COOLING SYSTEM _____

ENC. BAL. _____ WHERE _____ RATE _____

LEGAL DESCRIPT. _____

TERMS _____

APPROX. TAXES $ _____ FOR 19 _____ ZONE _____

REMARKS: _____

ASSESSMENTS $ _____ FOR _____

SCHOOL DIST. _____ APPROX. BLDG. AGE _____

BROKER _____ PH. _____

L/S _____ PH. _____

LST _____ TO _____ BROKERAGE _____ MIN. _____

THE DESCRIPTIVE MATTERS ABOVE ARE FOR OFFICE USE ONLY AND ARE NOT BE CONSTRUED AS REPRESENTATIONS.

Reprinted with permission.

450

4. Marta Charbenau is Director of Marketing for the Hariott Hotel in Anaheim, California. When she returns from an Alaskan vacation, the messages shown on pp. 454 to 458 are in her in-basket. Read them carefully and then complete the following exercises.

a. List the items in the order she should deal with them. Give reasons for the order you have chosen.

Order	Item	Reason
1		
2		
3		
4		
5		

b. Indicate the format she should use for each response she makes. Give reasons for your choices.

Item	Format	Reason
1		
2		
3		
4		
5		

c. Show the inside address or memo heading she will use for each written message.

Answer to Item	Address or heading
1	
2	
3	
4	
5	

d. Read each item closely. What facts you can infer about each person to whom she must respond?

Item	What the writer can infer about the reader
1	
2	

3

4

5

e. Indicate whether her answer should be planned directly or in-directly. Give a reason for your decision.

Item	Writing Plan	Reason
1		
2		
3		
4		
5		

U82-Code 1

The advertisers listed on the left will make additional
information available free as noted in their
advertisements in this issue. Circle below
the corresponding number of each company
you wish to know more about.

1	2	3	4	5	6	7	8	9
10	11	12	13	14	15	16	(17)	18
19	20	21	22	23	24	25	26	27
28	29	30	31	32	33	34	35	36
37	38	39	40	41	42	43	44	45
46	47	48	49	50	51	52	53	54
55	56	57	58	59	60	61	62	63
64	65	66	67	68				

Type or print clearly your name and address. Please
allow enough time for processing your requests.

Name **Karen Hughes**

*Title_____

*Company **Cartwrite travel**

Address **1697 Wilmot Street**

City **Mesa** State **AZ** Zip **85204**

This card is a tearout from a well known travel magazine. By circling the number 17, Karen
Hughes indicated she would like further information about the Hariott Hotel. Marta receives
about a dozen such cards a month which she answers with a form letter and a prepared envelope of the latest brochures and price lists.

6/18

Hope you froze in Alaska —
Here's the final copy for your new
brochure. If you get it back
by June 25, we can run before
our down week in July. Otherwise,
think August.

Pete the Printer

To Marta Charbenau

Date 6/15　　　Time 1:22

Ms. Marilyn Storms

OF Plasticorp

PHONE NO. 492-0135

Message: Can you book
a dinner for 100-125
on July 6 @ $10 each?
(were booked at Duke's
which burned)

Message Taken By: tl

Angels Fan Club

P.O. Box 2880

Los Angeles, CA 90053

June 12, 198-

Group Accommodations Director
Hariott Hotel
14 Acacia Drive
Anaheim, CA 92805

Dear Sir or Madam

Can you accommodate 150 Angels fans for a big baseball weekend beginning July 18 next year? I am writing to all the larger hotels in the area to ask about rates and facilities which we can offer West Coast fans.

Participants will check in during the afternoon of July 18, attend the game that night, and entertain themselves on Saturday until evening. Then we will want a banquet meal together before the bus leaves for the stadium.

On Sunday, some members of the team will sign autographs at our hotel during a Sunday baseball brunch. Most guests will check out before the twi-night double-header on the 20th.

We have reserved a block of 250 tickets, but some of the fans will be local and only come to brunch. Our tentative estimate for room bookings is 150 fans who will probably want double room accommodations.

What prices can you offer for rooms, banquet and brunch? Will fans receive a discount for other local attractions on Saturday?

We hope to start promoting this weekend during the end of this season, so please let me hear from you by July 15.

Yours truly

G Patterson

G. Patterson, President

Travelures

1734 North 18 Street
Ogden, Utah 84401

June 17, 198-

Manager
Hariott Hotel
14 Acacia Drive
Anaheim, CA 92805

Dear Sir:

Our organization has reservations for August 1-3 for a group
of 31, 15 double rooms and a single for the tour director. We
have brought a group this size each summer for the past nine years.

This year the bus did not fill, but rather than cancel the
tour, we want to bring the 20 clients who did sign up, but at the
regular price for a standard tour group.

Therefore, I am writing to ask that you amend the enclosed
contract to allow us to enjoy the rates for groups of 30 or more
even though we have fewer people on the tour.

Sincerely,

Gene Wicks

Gene Wicks

Enclosure

*Please handle this,
Marta. Unless we're
hurting, say NO.
B. Starkey*

458

5. Each member of a study committee in your office did research about a different copy machine. You inspected the New Blue Model 10. You are to report directly to the Office Manager, Tracy Martino, explaining what you found out about that particular copier. Use the information below to make your report.

 a. It copies ordinary photographs clearly.

 b. It produces two copies per second.

 c. It collates or sorts copies during a run.

 d. It copies on nonstandard size paper.

 e. It will copy on various weights of paper from 16 lb. to 40 lb.

 f. It copies on ordinary paper.

 g. It reduces copy up to 60% when required.

 h. It enlarges copy up to 40% when required.

 i. It copies from any color original.

 j. It automatically adjusts for extra-light or extra-dark original print.

6. A research firm recently surveyed 1,000 large companies to study their boards of directors. Here are some of the findings. Organize the information into a message that will be informative to the chairman of the board of directors of your small corporation. The chairman's name is Leslie Fortinbras.

Size of boards

5 members for companies with sales under $50 million a year

7 members for companies with sales between $100 million and $150 million a year

9 or 10 members for companies with sales between $500 million and $1 billion a year

13 to 15 members for companies with sales over $1 billion a year

Number of meetings a year

4 to 6 for board of 5 members

6 to 8 for boards of 7 members

8 to 10 for boards of 9 or 10 members

10 to 12 for boards of 13 to 15 members

Compensation for board members

The average compensation is $15,600 a year plus travel expenses and any special committee expenses.

Outside directors also get accident, medical, and life insurance.

All directors get liability insurance to protect them from individual stockholder suits.

Most directors' fees may be deferred until retirement if the directors choose.

Average hours of work for each board member

28 hours in preparation for meetings

45 hours in travel to and from board meetings

50 hours at board and committee meetings

Composition of boards

Large boards have four inside and nine outside members.

All companies are moving away from naming their own officers, lawyers, and bankers to boards.

Seventy-five percent of outside directors are retired corporate executives.

Seventy percent of boards have one woman or more serving on the board.

Outside directors usually retire at age 70.

Inside directors usually retire at age 68.

7. Here are some facts about the life of a business executive. Combine them into a message that would interest young people who are learning about careers.

a. Born in 1938 in Wichita, Kansas

b. 1950-58, worked in the family grocery store—beginning wage, 50 cents an hour; ending wage, 75 cents an hour

c. 1958, opened a pizza restaurant in partnership with his older brother

d. 1960, tried to expand but failed in Oklahoma City because the restaurant was started in a run-down building

e. 1960-65, opened other restaurants using uniform, new, attractive buildings

f. 1968, failed in eastern expansions because people in the East did not like the thin crust on his pizza

g. 1968-70, experimented with "regional" formulas for pizza to satisfy each part of the country

h. 1969, sold stock in the pizza chain to the general public and bought back 40% of the franchised stores

i. 1977, sold his chain of restaurants to a major company for $300 million of its stock and a position on the board of directors

8. Choose one aspect about the city in which you live, and write a unified, coherent paragraph for a small brochure your Chamber of Commerce is preparing. Be sure to support your general statements with facts and examples and to provide effective internal transitions.

9. Some scholarship applications require a "statement from the applicant." Write a different paragraph for each of the following situations.

a. Explain why you wish to attend college.

b. Explain why you wish to continue your college education.

c. Why do you wish to complete a major in (fill in your own major)?

d. How will receiving this scholarship improve your opportunity to study?

10. Many businesses and organizations are preparing fact sheets about themselves. Employees who travel carry a supply of the little cards and give them to customers and others who may inquire "What business are you in?" The cards can also be distributed inexpensively at trade shows and conventions. During the Bicentennial year, the government prepared a small card shown in Figure 16.1. Prepare two such cards for your college or university.

a. Use chronological order.

b. Use order of importance with the most important fact placed first on the card.

1776

BICENTENNIAL

1976

"The Second Century"
TWO HUNDRED YEARS
OF AMERICAN HISTORY

A NATION IS BORN . . .

1607	Jamestown Colony founded
1620	Mayflower pilgrims land at Plymouth, Mass.
1765-67	The Stamp Act and Townsend Acts impose new taxes inspiring colonial protest
1773	Boston Tea Party
1774	First Continental Congress meets
1775	Colonists and British Troops clash at Concord and Lexington
1776, July 4	Declaration of Independence adopted by Continental Congress
1781	Cornwallis surrenders at Yorktown
1783	The Treaty of Paris ends the American Revolution
1787	U.S. Constitution drafted by Constitutional Convention
1788	U.S. Constitution becomes effective
1791	Bill of Rights added to Constitution

A YOUNG NATION'S CHALLENGES . . .

1803	The Louisiana Purchase
1803-06	Lewis and Clark expedition
1812-14	War with Britain; "Star-Spangled Banner" written
1823	Monroe Doctrine establishes foreign policy in Western Hemisphere
1836	Mexicans besiege the Alamo
1846-48	War with Mexico
1849	Gold discovered in California
1857	Dred Scott Decision upholds slavery

THE WAR BETWEEN THE STATES . . .

1860	Southern states organize the Confederate States of America
1861	Confederacy fires on Ft. Sumter and Civil War begins
1861	Battle of Bull Run
1863	Battle of Gettysburg
1865	Lincoln assassinated; Andrew Johnson becomes president
1865	Gen. Robert E. Lee surrenders

EVENTS AFTER THE WAR . . .

1869	Trans-continental railroad completed
1876	Custer and his troops wiped out at Little Bighorn
1898	War with Spain begins
1901	McKinley assassinated; succeeded by "Teddy" Roosevelt
1906	Major earthquake in San Francisco
1914	Panama Canal completed

WORLD WAR I AND ITS AFTERMATH . . .

1914	World War I begins in Europe
1915	Germany sinks the "Lusitania" and U.S. enters the war
1918, Nov. 11	Armistice signed
1927	Lindbergh makes solo flight across Atlantic

THE DEPRESSION AND WORLD WAR II

1929	Stocks decline sharply and Stock Market crashes
1930	Banks close; unemployment reaches its peak
1932	Franklin D. Roosevelt initiates "New Deal" to fight Depression
1935	First Social Security Act passed
1940-41	German troops overrun Europe
1941, Dec. 7	Japan attacks Pearl Harbor, U.S. declares war on Japan, Germany, Italy
1944, June 6	D-Day: Allies invade Europe
1945	F. D. R. dies; H. S. Truman succeeds
1945	Germany surrenders
1945	Atomic bomb dropped on Japan; Japan surrenders
1946	First United Nations General Assembly session

AND MORE CURRENT . . .

1950	War begins in Korea
1952	First Hydrogen bomb test
1954	Supreme Court outlaws segregation
1959	Alaska and Hawaii become states
1961	First communications satellite "Telstar" put into orbit
1961	First U.S. manned space flight
1963, Nov. 22	J. F. Kennedy assassinated; L. B. Johnson becomes President
1965	Martin Luther King awarded Nobel Peace Prize
1968	Robert Kennedy and Martin Luther King assassinated
1969	Apollo 11; first man on the moon
1973	Satellite launched to Venus
1973	Watergate bombshell involves many top government officials
1974	President Nixon resigns; Gerald Ford becomes 38th President
1975	America prepares to celebrate its Bicentennial

Figure 16.1 Bicentennial Fact Sheet.

11. Some diversified companies are well known for one of their product lines. For instance, Pepsico is best known for Pepsi Cola. However, it makes other soft drinks, owns restaurant chains, manufactures sporting goods, and owns a truck line.

Get a copy of the annual report of another company as diversified as Pepsico. Prepare a small fact card that will show the various company interests and the volume of business in each division.

12. Rearrange these directions for changing a tire so that by following them, you can complete the process correctly.

    a. Place the spare wheel on the axle.

    b. Activate the warning flasher on the vehicle.

    c. Remove the jack from the vehicle.

    d. Place wheel chocks at the front and back of the wheel diagonally opposite the tire to be changed.

    e. Loosen (but do not remove) the wheel nuts by fitting the wheel nut wrench on each nut in turn and turning the wrench counterclockwise.

    f. Remove the wheel to be changed from the axle.

    g. Use the flat end of the wheel nut wrench to pry loose and remove the hubcap of the damaged wheel.

    h. Turn off flasher lights.

    i. Turn off engine.

    j. Park on a level surface if possible.

    k. Set out road flares 50 and 75 yards behind the vehicle.

    l. Set vehicle with manual transmission in reverse gear.

    m. Set the vehicle's hand brake to *on* position.

    n. Replace the jack in the vehicle.

    o. Remove the spare tire from the vehicle.

    p. Remove wheel chocks and replace them in the vehicle.

    q. Place the jack under a marked jack point nearest the tire to be removed.

    r. Place the damaged wheel in the vehicle.

    s. Insert the flat end of the wheel nut wrench in the jack socket to form a jack handle.

    t. Remove the nuts from the damaged wheel and place them in the hubcap.

    u. Replace the hubcap.

v. Move the jack handle alternately up and down to activate the jack and raise the vehicle so that the damaged wheel is clear of the ground.

w. Replace the wheel nuts and tighten each one slightly by turning the wheel nut wrench clockwise.

x. Extinguish the flares and replace them in the vehicle.

y. Use the wheel nut wrench to finish tightening all nuts.

z. Activate the jack to lower the vehicle to the ground.

13. You work for a company that manufactures small office hardware such as staplers, pencil sharpeners, and adjustable paper punches. Management wants to start exporting this line of supplies. Therefore, the instruction sheets that are packed with each item must be rewritten into four languages—French, Spanish, German, and Japanese. Management feels that if the company first simplifies its present direction sheet and includes more pictures, the translation process will be easier and the instructions clearer.

You have been asked to write instructions for the standard stapler. Your superior specified that you are to

a. use as many illustrations as possible

b. use the simplest language possible

c. describe the process of filling the stapler

d. describe using the stapler to attach notices to bulletin boards as well as to hold loose papers together.

14. Write specific procedures for employees to follow when they fill out a Service Call form (see Case 1, chapter 3). Here is a copy of the form.

SERVICE CALL

Date_____Time_____ A.M. ☐
                                            P.M. ☐

Name_____

Address_____

Service Address_____

Phone _____ Apt. No. _____

SERVICE WANTED:

☐ Install   ☐ Repair   ☐ Deliver   ☐ Pickup

☐ Contract   ☐ Complaint   ☐ Warranty   ☐ Estimate

COMMENTS: _____

_____

_____

Product_____ Make_____

Model_____ Serial No._____

BILLING:

☐ C.O.D.   ☐ Charge   ☐ Repeat   ☐ Guarantee

Promised for _____ Route _____

Serviceman_____ Taken by_____

TOPS NO. 4100

Reprinted with permission.

15. Write general procedures for employees to follow when they fill out a Service Call form.

16. Bring a standard form from your place of employment. Prepare both general and specific procedures for filling out the form correctly.

17. Rewrite the following recipe into specific step-by-step procedures. Simplify the technical language so that novice cooks who do not understand such terms as *dredge* or *fold* can bake the cake.

DARK CAKE

Ingredients:

1½ c. sugar	¼ t. salt
1 c. butter or substitute	3 eggs
1 t. baking soda	1 c. sour milk
½ c. cocoa	2 c. cake flour
½ c. chopped raisins	½ c. chopped nuts

Cream sugar and butter. Add egg yolks. Beat thoroughly. Sift and measure flour with baking soda and salt. Combine sifted dry ingredients and ½ c. sour milk with first mixture. Combine ½ c. sour milk with cocoa and heat in a double boiler until cocoa is melted. Cool. Add to cake batter. Add raisins, which have been dredged in 2 T. of flour, and nuts. Mix thoroughly. Fold in stiffly beaten egg whites. Pour into prepared layer cake pans and bake at 375° for about 25 minutes. Spread cooled cake with chocolate icing.

18. One of your goals in this class is to "improve writing." But each student in a class has different abilities and sometimes different goals as well. Define improvement as it pertains to your own writing. Set up a checklist that will help you to measure your improvement. You should be able to use the checklist to measure your improvement since the beginning of the course to the present time. The same checklist should also be able to provide information about the improvement you make during the remainder of the course.

a. Use the checklist to assess your work to date. Write a memo to your instructor summarizing your progress to date.

b. Use the checklist and the information in the memo to your instructor (Exercise 18a) to set specific goals for yourself for the remainder of the course. Write a memo to your instructor explaining your goals.

19. Coaches and players enjoy talking about a good season or a winning season. How did your college or university do last year? Define either "good" or "winning" and apply the definition to the combined sanctioned sports in your college. *Or,*

19a. Investigate the records of all the teams in a major city to assess how proud the citizens should be of "our sports teams." Don't forget that major cities now also field teams in such sports as soccer, women's basketball, and volleyball. *Or,*

19b. Using library resources, investigate the records of all teams in five major cities to determine which city could best claim it had a "winning year."

20. Study the printout that follows. Write a memo to the head of the personnel department, Mark Kelly, indicating whether the company has an "absentee problem."

ANNUAL ABSENCE SUMMARY

	PLANT A			PLANT B		
Day	Possible Workdays	Days Worked	Vacation Days	Possible Workdays	Days Worked	Vacation Days
Monday	4,700	3,680	320	7,050	6,270	480
Tuesday	5,200	5,055	120	7,800	7,540	200
Wednesday	5,200	5,000	120	7,800	7,580	200
Thursday	5,100	4,805	120	7,500	7,209	200
Friday	5,200	4,780	320	7,800	7,170	480

21. Five years ago your company bid for a government contract but lost because the company did not meet government requirements for affirmative action. Since then the company has been making changes to bring its hiring practices more in line with those of other firms. Study the information in the chart that follows and report to the Vice President for Governmental Affairs about the progress the company has made in five years in changing its employment practices.

EMPLOYEE STATISTICS

Job Category	Number of Males	Year	Number of Females	Minority Either Sex
Managerial	11	Current	2	1
	12	− 1	2	1
	13	− 2	2	2
	12	− 3	1	1
	12	− 4	0	1
Technical	25	Current	4	1
	28	− 1	2	1
	31	− 2	3	1
	25	− 3	1	1
	24	− 4	2	0
Fabrication	148	Current	56	26
	158	− 1	50	26
	175	− 2	55	27
	160	− 3	50	22
	167	− 4	48	21
Sales	10	Current	1	1
	10	− 1	0	0
	10	− 2	0	0
	12	− 3	0	0
	13	− 4	0	0
Office	2	Current	16	3
	2	− 1	15	3
	1	− 2	15	3
	1	− 3	14	2
	0	− 4	14	2

22. Here are three outlines that have errors such as lack of parallelism, poorly stated purpose statements and message plans, and format errors. Revise them to conform with the rules you studied in chapter 8.

OUTLINE 1

PURPOSE STATEMENT AND MESSAGE PLAN: Word processors are a valuable asset to today's businesses. Information systems such as word processors improve accuracy and appearance of written materials while increasing efficiency and decreasing costs.

    I. Word processors improve accuracy and appearance of written materials.

       A.   The original is typed into memory and all changes are made within memory.

       B.   Word processors can ease the problem of retyping large amounts of information.

  II.   Word processors can also increase efficiency.

       A.   Word processors can perform many tasks quickly.

       B.   Word processors encourage employees to specialize.

 III.   Finally, businesses can decrease their costs with word processors.

    A.   Word processor allows a fewer number of employees to perform all needed tasks.

    B.   Word processors can store large amounts of information in a very small disk. Thus, eliminating large, expensive filing cabinets.

CONCLUSION: The word processor's ability to accurately and efficiently process information while decreasing costs will be extremely valuable to many businesses.

OUTLINE 2

PURPOSE STATEMENT AND MESSAGE PLAN: I have selected William Lloyd as the person most suitable for the new office manager because he possesses needed qualities such as experience, his sales record, and good leadership.

    I.   Mr. Lloyd's 27 years are more than adequate for the position of branch manager.

        A.   He has worked as a salesman for the company for 27 years.

        B.   He has had his broker's license since 1962.

        C.   Plus, he has held two other realty sales jobs.

            1. Century Sales

            2. Will-Sell Realty

    II.   Mr. Lloyd's long years of experience have earned him a good record as a salesman.

        A.   He has made sales of $1 million annually for the past eight years.

        B.   Even with this amazing sales record, he still treats every sale as if he were the buyer.

    III.   One of the most important factors in choosing Mr. Lloyd as branch manager is his leadership capabilities.

        A.   He has been active in many social groups.

            1. Rotary Club

            2. School Board

            3. Church Choir

        B.   Colleagues often look to Mr. Lloyd and ask him for business and other advice.

CONCLUSION: Upon viewing the facts, I believe Mr. William Lloyd should be the new branch manager at Benson's new branch office.

OUTLINE 3

PURPOSE STATEMENT AND MESSAGE PLAN:
Computers entice young white collar felons to try their hands at
that most exciting new crime—computer crime. They are
tempted because the rewards are high, security is often lax, and
companies do not usually want to prosecute the perpetrators of
computer crimes.

I.   These white collar felons are fully aware of what they are
     doing and are usually young and educated.
     A.   Vandalism is among the top crimes involving the
          computer.
          1.   example of vandalism
          2.   costs time and money
     B.   Theft and fraud are the most common and costly
          crimes.
          1.   example of big-time theft
          2.   example of theft not involving money

II. Since these crimes are increasing, it is most important to
     have good security systems, but this is not an easy task to
     accomplish.
     A.   Types of security systems
     B.   Examples of security systems

III. For the criminals who happen to get caught, chances are
     that not a lot will happen to them.
     A.   Large companies do not want to prosecute.
          1.   lack of evidence
          2.   bad publicity

CONCLUSION: The criminal who is committing the
crime is becoming harder and harder to detect every day. The in-
telligence of the criminal mind figures out new, inventive ways
to commit the crime; court action and prevention of the crime
are steps still in the making.

23. The following two memos need subject lines and side headings.
Determine how the body should be broken into segments and provide appropriate side headings. Write a subject line that will attract the reader's attention as well as identify the subject of the message.

MEMO

TO: Chapter members

FROM: John Curran, Treasurer

SUBJECT:

DATE: December 1,198-

At the November 11 meeting, members approved (by a 190-43
vote) dues of six-tenths of one percent of total wages paid
during the year, January 1 - December 31. This assessment
will cover National dues, State Conference dues, and Chapter dues for the year. The enclosed card, Assessment for
Dues, is provided for you to compute the amount due the
Chapter for the first billing period, January 1 through
March 31. Use this form to determine the amount you owe.
If you have completed a form for National membership,
please complete the additional enclosed form. If you pre-
paid $25 last fall but have never filled out a membership
card, please do so now. Disregard any billing notice from
National. Please send me your check together with the Assessment for Dues card and a National application, if appropriate, in the envelope provided with this message.

Attachments: 3

MEMO

TO: Carter Hansen

FROM: Pieter Jacobsen, Analyst *PJ*

SUBJECT:

DATE: January 15, 198-

Some new developments have taken place in the silver market. The combination of these new facts with some market
fundamentals makes a strong case for a rapid rise in the
price of silver. Please consider the following facts. The
biggest buyers of silver such as makers of film will need
more silver as (a) the economy improves in industrialized
countries and (b) people in developing countries begin to
use small cameras. Manufacturers of many electronic and
electrical devices and equipment use silver for its high
conductivity. These manufacturers will be increasing their
need for silver as (a) the general economy improves and (b)
defense orders increase. During the last several years,
the world has seen a decrease in silver production. When
the price was under $5 an ounce, even the largest mines
furloughed workers. Furthermore, much silver is produced
as a by-product of mining for copper and zinc, and production of these metals has been extremely limited for several
years. Therefore, the most fundamental argument in favor
of a rising price for silver is that a fairly significant
gap exists between new mine production and annual use. In
some years, this gap has been met by recovering silver from
photographic darkrooms and melting coins and silver. Now,
however, it appears that the silver sources above the
ground will be depleted in a short time so the price must
rise to (a) encourage new production and (b) entice holders
to sell their silver hoards.

24. Outline the messages from problem 23.

25. The letters that follow this problem contain all the material necessary to convey a complete message, but the paragraphs are out of order.
Rearrange the paragraphs in a logical order.

Michigan Natural Areas

P.O. Box 1000
Livonia, MI 48151

May 16, 1983

Betty Rock, Chairperson
Natural Areas Conservancy
        of West Michigan, Inc.
P.O. Box 1415
Grand Rapids, MI 49501

Dear Betty:

Hope to meet you next week.

Dinner is at 5:30 at Denbo's Restaurant, 2001 28th Street, S. W. Gail's
program is scheduled for 7:00 p.m. They have a room for us, but you'll
be ordering from the menu so no reservation is required.

Can you or someone else in your group (the more, the merrier, of course)
come along too, so we can talk about ways the two organizations can cooperate.

On Wednesday, May 21, our Board is meeting for supper in Grand Rapids.
After supper, the new Executive Director for MNA, Gail Pettibone, will
bring a slide show. We hope to have a number of the members in the
Grand Rapids area come for dinner or at least for the slide show and to
meet Gail.

Thank you for the encouraging note last month.

Sincerely,

Barb

Barbara Haas, Secretary
Western Chapter

FIRST FEDERAL SAVINGS
And Loan Association Of Albany

(member FSLIC)

Eugene Kuhn, Jr.
President

21 W. Cherry
Albany, GA 31701
(912) 384-8896

November, 1983

Dear Customer:

I want to thank you for your support in making First Federal Savings of Albany a solid, growing institution. Without you, we could not be moving ahead with this exciting opportunity to expand our operations.

First Federal Savings of Dawson is located in Dawson, Georgia, about one hour north of Albany, and has been a solid part of that community for many years. Currently, the institution has three offices, one downtown and two branches. While First Federal Savings of Albany will keep its name, First Federal Savings of Dawson will add "a division of First Federal Savings and Loan of Albany" to its name in the future.

It is with a great deal of pleasure that I bring you news of our institution's continued growth and economic expansion. Recently, members of the Board of Directors of First Federal Savings of Albany and First Federal Savings of Dawson, Georgia, agreed in principle to merge. This merger represents a unique opportunity to strengthen both institutions, providing for extended service and greater convenience to you.

We realize how important the goodwill and loyalty of our customers is to us. Consequently, you may dial 367-8876 with any questions you may have. Additionally, I and other designated officers will be available to meet with you personally, and welcome the opportunity to do so.

Unlike many recent mergers that have taken place out of weakness, this merger is based on the strength and stability of two very secure financial institutions. When combined, our assets will rank us the eighth largest savings association in Georgia, with $569 million as of June 30, 1983. In addition, the increase in reserves will rank us fourth in the state with regard to net worth. It is the inherent soundness of our partnership that brought our two associations together.

Sincerely,

Eugene Kuhn, Jr.
President

EK:lc

474

26. Outline the messages from problem 25.

27. Supermarkets have always subsisted on lower profit margins (.8%) than other businesses such as department stores (4%). Therefore, grocers must have a very high turnover of stock to make a profit. They must attract shoppers with some special inducements and hope the shoppers will do all their shopping after taking advantage of the unusual bargain that brought them to the store in the first place. Here are a few of the strategies supermarkets use to attract customers.

a. Nonfood lines — clothing, appliances, and furniture

b. Specialty food lines — deli departments, international cheese shops, fresh fish counter

c. Special promotions — price promotions, housewares, bonus gifts for collected cash register tapes, free dinnerware

d. Generic goods — products with a lower government grading than national or private brands

e. Automated checkout — ways to speed up the checkout process

f. Super supermarket — huge stores providing higher sales per square foot

g. Bulk buying — allowing customers to buy in large quantities at a reduced price per pound or item

Study the grocery advertisements in a local newspaper. Select an advertisement that covers at least one full page and write a short report, using specific examples, to explain the marketing strategies one area supermarket uses to attract customers. You may find other strategies in addition to the ones suggested in this problem.

28. You are an independent financial consultant who has been asked to investigate the pension fund described in Case 1, chapter 11. Herman Hatcher, president of ABC Corporation, is considering making the plan available to his employees. You have completed the report (Case 1, chapter 11); now prepare a letter of transmittal without synopsis to accompany the report. The address for ABC Corporation is 1114 La Cienega, Inglewood, California 90301.

29. The situation is the same as in Case 28. However, this time prepare a letter of transmittal with synopsis.

30. Prepare an abstract of the information in Case 1, chapter 11.

31. Prepare an abstract of the information in Case 42, chapter 16.

32. You are an independent employment counselor. Dennis Mazzello is a client. He has brought you complete personal information and asks that you prepare an appropriate resume he can use to seek employment as a salesperson for one of the major paper companies. He wants the position to

be one in which he can gain experience as a stepping stone to a management position. Here is the information.

PERSONAL DATA

Address: 13567 Ten Mile Road
    Detroit, Michigan 48035
Telephone: (313) 743-9876
Born in Detroit, Michigan, on July 15, 1962.
Father emigrated from Milano in 1950. Now employed as sales manager for Italiano Foods, a specialty food importing concern.
Two younger brothers and a sister. Mother died last year in an auto accident.
Wears glasses. Left leg is ½" shorter than right leg due to surgery following a football injury.
Prefers to work in the Great Lakes area but willing to relocate if necessary to find employment.

EDUCATION

Bachelor of Science degree from Western Michigan University in Kalamazoo, Michigan 49008, awarded in August, 1983.
   Major: Printing Management
   Minor: Paper Science
   Grade Point Average: Overall — 2.8
           Major — 3.2
Diploma from St. Mary's High School in Warren, Michigan 48093, awarded in June, 1979.
Attended:
  Belton Elementary School, 1967-73
  368 Cordon Drive, Dearborn, Michigan 48091
  Central Middle School, 1973-75
  4869 Morton Street
  Warren, Michigan 48093

EMPLOYMENT

Worked counter and helped with cleanup at Herbie's Burgers, 457 Kellum Drive, East Detroit, Michigan 48079 in 1976 and 1977.
Sales and general help for Bernardo's Tire Store, 68990 Woodward Avenue, Royal Oak, Michigan 48088 in 1977, 1978, and 1979. Supervisor: Bernard Lorenz.
Construction and maintenance for Lord's Printing Company in Detroit, Michigan 48065 in the summers of 1979 and 1980 and helped with inventory during most Christmas breaks through-

out college. Helped to add camera and plate department in 1979. Had the offer to work there in summer of 1981 as well, but chose a position that offered more money.

Mechanic for Apollo Industries in Ecorse, Michigan 48077. Assistant in production of tool and die parts in summers of 1981 and 1982. Supervisor: Stan Olszewski.

Assistant in University Paper Pilot Plant as part-time employment (20 hours a week) during school in 1982 and 1983. Operated the coater, the paper machine, and calender stack. Did some testing. Various supervisors. Major advisor, Dr. Lewis Beckworth, may have work records.

Earned 75% of college expenses through employment in summer, Christmas, and spring breaks.

HONORS, AWARDS, AND RECOMMENDATIONS

High school honor roll, 4 times
Dean's list last semester of college
Two scholarships from the Paper Technology Foundation
Pell grant
Named to all-city team as defensive guard in 1978

INTERESTS AND HOBBIES

Three years of football at St. Mary's
Graphic Arts Society at WMU
Intramural sports at WMU included volleyball, bowling, and touch football
Treasurer for magazine sales at St. Mary's
Origami

REFERENCES AND CREDENTIALS

On file with Placement Bureau of Western Michigan University, Kalamazoo, Michigan 49008

33. For family reasons, Muriel Eisenberg, a licensed social worker with an ACSW Certificate, has moved to the area where you are an independent employment consultant. She is seeking employment as a social worker and wants your assistance in preparing a resume. You agree to help her and in an interview elicit the following information to work with.

Muriel Eisenberg was born and raised in Duluth, Minnesota, where she was graduated with a B.S. degree in 1970 from the College of St. Scholastica. Her dual majors were social casework and psychology. She obtained employment with the New York State Department of Mental Hygiene and moved to Rockland. There she was a caseworker for the Children's Unit. She also began her graduate study at the Graduate School of Social Services at Fordham University. She took courses in 1971 and 1972 but did not matriculate for a degree.

Then she transferred some credits and in 1973 enrolled in the University of Minnesota in Duluth, from which she was graduated in 1974 with a Master of Social Work degree. The program emphasized planning and policy making, program evaluation, and regional planning for social agencies. While at the university, Muriel completed two years of part-time field experience with the Minnesota Community Mental Health Board. She focused particularly on evaluation research, completing several instruments that were later adopted by the Northeast Regional Board.

While in Minnesota, she married George Eisenberg, and they again moved to New York. She returned to Rockland and was employed in the Community Services Unit. Her major responsibilities from 1974 to 1976 were developing halfway house and out-placement programs for the retarded. Toward this end, she wrote proposals, conducted community relations campaigns, supervised outpatients, and inspected local facilities in three counties. She also carried a normal caseload of children and adults in foster care. In 1976, she achieved ACSW certification.

In 1976, her husband's company transferred him to Nashville, Tennessee. She took two years off from the work force to start a family and began working again in 1978 as a clinical social worker for the Children's Center in the Zinmann Psychiatric Care Center in Belle Meade. Here she had direct responsibility for individual and family therapy and helped to develop group treatment plans. She completed case histories on incoming patients and planned with community agencies for after-care. When necessary, she worked with the courts to place children in special care facilities.

In 1980, she took leave to have a second child but remained active on the Clinical Care Evaluation Committee and the Regional Evaluation Board. When she returned to work in 1982, she continued with the work she had been doing since 1978 but also became chairperson of the Evaluation Committee.

In addition to her busy professional and personal life, Eisenberg has been an active volunteer for Senior Services and Meals on Wheels. She and her husband regularly attend temple services, and she tries to find time to participate in Hadassah activities. At least once a year, she makes time to attend seminars to keep up to date in her field. Some typical seminars are

A 10-hour seminar on Family Therapy conducted by the director of Acherman Institute (New York, New York)

A two-day workshop, "T.A. for Healthy Children," conducted by Sara Landers of Vanderbilt University

A week-long seminar on Reality Therapy conducted by David Glasser of University of Michigan

She has been a member of the National Association of Social Workers since 1972 and a member of the Association for Emotionally Disturbed Children since 1976.

She feels that her experience has prepared her particularly well to work with retarded and disturbed children in both a community and an institutional setting. Her husband does not expect further transfers for some time, and she would like a position that will allow her to work toward a supervisory position if she cannot start in supervision.

She has brought two excellent letters of recommendation. One is from Dr. Hiram Wellman, Zinmann Psychiatric Care Center, 4556 Nashville Boulevard, Belle Meade, and the other is from Judge Parker Lamb, District 5, County Court House, Nashville.

34. Dennis Mazzello (Case 32) has not been able to find any openings in his field. He asks you to write a general cover letter that he may adapt to send to each of the paper companies that have distribution in the Great Lakes area.

35. Proofread and improve these paragraphs from secondary research papers.

In the case concerning Social Security, Janet Blair thought
she would get away with it and not be caught. Janet made two mistakes. One of her accomplices, Stella M. Abrams who worked for
Social Security in Philadelphia, cashed stolen welfare checks through
the same account she had set up for depositing the checks. This is
where she made her mistake because the people named on the welfare
checks complained. When leading to the account, the Social
Security Administration discovered that no such beneficiaries
listed under the Social Security numbers on the checks existed.[16]
The second mistake occured when Stella Abrams deposited the Social
Security checks, and took money order. These money orders were
accidentally stolen and she filed a claim. The Secret Service
matched the name against a list of Social Security employees and
confronted her.[17]

---

[16]Thomas G. Donlan, "Social Security Scam," Barron's, 18 August
1980, p. 9.

[17]Donlan, p. 16.

Excerpt A.

For the criminals that get caught, chances are that they will
receive little or no punishment. Many cases do not even get to
court for various reasons. One being that the management of big
corporations refuse to prosecute, saying that it will be bad
publicity for the company. Another major reason for not prosecut-
ing is lack of evidence. However, other actions can be taken such
as firing the criminal. The white collar cases that do get to
court will most likely have lengthy and complicated trials. Those
found guilty get little or no sentencing because they have no previous criminal record. "A study of 82 white collar felons sentenced
in the District of Columbia found that of these, fifty percent
received light sentences or probation. About eighty percent received sentences ranging from one week to six months in prison,
about ten percent received sentences ranging from six months to
three years in prison, and only about twenty percent received sentences exceeding three years in prision."[7] Computer criminals get
around our laws as they stand now. "The computer felon not only
challenges our imagination but our system of justice as well."[8]

---

[7]August Bequia, Computer Crime (Lexington, MA: Heath and
Company, 1978), p. 5.

[8]Bequia, p. 6.

Excerpt B.

After the original recording is made, it is arranged in
different ways to make it sound better. The computer plays an
important role in this. There are basically two computer controlled
ways of rearranging a recording. The first is by the use of an
equalizer. This is an instument having one control for each
channel that emphasizes higher and lower frequencies.[4] An equalizer can also reduce background noise.[5] The use of a computer
instead of the human ear is that a computer can define even the
slightest variation in sound. This helps to make a recording
as near perfect as possible.

"Mixers are controls whose purpose is to mix various elements
of a program together."[6] Mixers differ from equalizers in that
they blend all the diffrerent tracks together instead of emphasizing
impulses on seperate tracks. Again the computer is important in
mixing. Not only can the computer distinguish between minute
sounds but it is also compacted into micro-components which take
up very little space.

---

[4]Norman H. Crowhurst, Audio Systems Handbook (Blue Ridge
Summit, PA: Tab Books, 1969), p. 31.

[5]Crowhurst, p. 31.

[6]Crowhurst, p. 41.

Excerpt C.

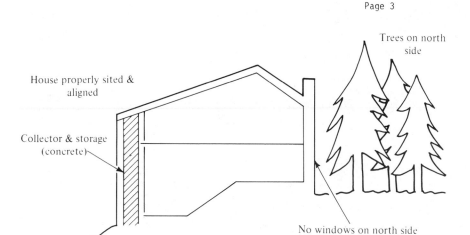

Trees on north side

House properly sited & aligned

Collector & storage (concrete)

No windows on north side

South ←———○———→ North

Figure 14.17 Passive Solar System (wall storage).[13]

The important element to consider in using this system is the building itself.[9] The design and materials used in building the house are very important, as the house itself will act as the collector and the storage for the heat collected. Therefore, this system is suitable to those people who are planning to build their houses. They can chose those materials that are produced to suit the passive solar heating system.[10] In addition, a proper planning of the building can prevent the house from overheating or underheating, and help heating

---

[9]Ralph Wolfe and Peter Clegg, Home Energy for the Eighties (Charlotte, VT: Garden Way Publishing, 1980), p. 48.

[10]David Wright and Barbara Wright, "The State and State of Mind of: The Passive Art," Solar Age Catalog (Harrisville, NH: Solar Vision, Inc., 1977), p. 26.

Excerpt D.

the house evenly.[11] The wall of the house can be an efficient heat collector; if it's built in the form of concrete. The windows are also the
other collectors that are common among the users of passive systems. If
glasses are used in them, the heat collected is much stronger as they absorb the heat directly.[12] The passive system is shown on page 3, figure
14-17.[13]

In this system, the concrete wall of the house will collect and act
as the storage for the heat needed in this system.[14] The warm air is
circulated by natural means, the warm air will force the cool air
through the outlets and window shutters. Sometimes a small fan may be
installed as to accelerate the circulation more effectively. On the
whole, the performance of this system is much dependant on the building
structure and the materials used in the construction of the house itself.

---

[11]Wolfe, P. 48.

[12]P. G. Down, Heating and Cooling Load Calculations (London: A.
Wheaton & Co., 1969), p. 146.

[13]Billy C. Langley, Comfort Heating, 2d ed. (Reston, VA: Reston
Publishing Co., Inc., 1978), p. 327.

[14]Langley, p. 328.

36. Use the computer resources in your library to compile a bibliography for one of the research topics listed at the end of chapter 14.

37. Prepare a paraphrase and a summary for each of the following paragraphs. Introduce each summary and prepare the bibliographic and note references for each paraphrase.

a. This paragraph is taken from Volume 53, number 6 of the *Wall Street Journal* published on Thursday, October 21, 1982, in Bowling Green, Ohio (Dow Jones & Company, Inc., publishers). The paragraph occurs on page 33 of Section A in a column called Viewpoint which is written by Hodding Carter III. The column headline is "Politics: A Game for Those Who Have Made It?" and it begins in the fourth column of newsprint on the page.

But the central point is that the high cost of running for office does matter, and it will matter more in coming years as costs continue to explode. First, big money is not usually contributed out of disinterested love of the democratic process. Second, insofar as candidates do not have to put themselves into political hock for the money they need to run, they are too often able to avoid it only by virtue of personal wealth. Third, the public in whose name this high-stakes game is played is increasingly cynical about the process. It does not seem purely coincidental that the long slide in voter participation coincides almost exactly with the escalation of campaign spending. Vastly larger amounts are spent each year to influence a steadily shrinking percentage of the electorate.

b. The following paragraph is taken from an article entitled "Mortar and Pestle" published in *Cuisine* in September, 1982, which is Volume 11, number 9 of the magazine. The article was written by Jennifer Brennan with photographs by Constance Hansen. The paragraph is from the first page of the article which appears on the following pages: 18, 22, and 23.

The ideal mortar should be manufactured from a material which does not retain the odors and oils from the more pungent ingredients. Suitable materials include nonporous acid-proof porcelain, brass, or a hard stone (for example, basalt or marble). A tough earthenware mortar also does a workmanlike job. Mortars of hardwood are fine for use within one important limitation: the wood retains odors, particularly from moist ingredients. Once garlic has been mashed in a wooden mortar, the vessel cannot be used for anything other than garlic-based mixtures; the memory indissolubly remains. Pestles are often of the same material as the mortar, though they can be made from anything that will withstand the jarring shocks of repeated blows (again, ceramic materials, brass, stone, and hardwoods are favorites).

c. The following paragraph was excerpted from a section called Follow-Through in the August 2, 1982, issue of *Forbes*, a bi-weekly magazine published by Forbes, Inc., in New York. The August 2 issue is Number 3 in Volume 130; the complete article appears on page 10 under the title, "The Diamond's Best Friend."

Last February, however, Australia's diamond diggers, a combine called the Ashton Joint Venture, signed an agreement in principle to channel their diamonds through De Beers. The deal, still to be formally ratified, will let De Beers handle all of Ashton's gem production, 10% of its total output. Of the remainder (semiprecious stones, industrial diamonds, etc.), De Beers will handle 75%. So much for the Australian threat. Russia, another major—and unpredictable—diamond producer, has also stayed in the fold. Soviet gem-quality stones (perhaps as much as 50% of the output of the Siberian mines) have long moved through De Beers via shadowy third parties. They still do. (Russia exports only gem diamonds; the rest it keeps.)

d. The next paragraph is from page 407 in chapter 33, "Planning Your Nutrition Program," of a book, *Let's Get Well*, which contains 580 pages. The author is Adelle Davis, and her publisher is Harcourt, Brace & World, Inc. of 757 Third Avenue, New York, NY 10017. The quotation is from the first edition of the book which was published in 1965.

Because malnutrition of years' standing often precedes the onset of any illness, digestion and absorption are usually below par and putrefactive bacteria thrive in the intestine. Sickness causes the digestion to become even more faulty. Simultaneously the need for body requirements skyrockets, and nutrients are often lost through vomiting, diarrhea, excessive fluid intake, and/or the use of diuretics. Furthermore, every cell in the body continuously needs nutrients, of which only a few can be stored. To escape this dilemma and to furnish an ever-flowing supply of nutrients, small frequent meals, preferably containing 25 percent of the calories as fat, are an essential part of every health-building program. These meals should supply only the amount of food that can be completely digested at one time.

38. Three students wrote letters seeking summer employment. Evaluate the strengths and weaknesses of each letter. Then write a memo to your instructor indicating which letter is most likely to draw favorable attention

from a company personnel department. Be sure to support your choice with evidence.

```
                                        18938 Audrey
                                        Warren, Michigan 48091
                                        March 2, 1983


        Personnel Director
        Cameron Construction Company
        9573 Sims Road
        Sterling Heights, MI 48089

        Dear Sir:

            With my experience in construction work, I think I could do a fine
        job for your company as a laborer this summer as you will need more help
        in the good weather.

            You will be able to use me in any of your areas of construction
        work.  I've had experience in Michigan Bell Telephone work:  laying pipe,
        squeeze boring, and doing clean-ups.  In addition, you'll find I can work
        well on a big construction site.  Last summer I worked at St. Johns
        Hospital in Detroit; I was the only laborer for our company at the site.
        I was in charge in finding and setting grades for sidewalks and drive-
        ways, as well as keeping up the maintenance on our machines.

            You will also like to know that I have my Laborer's Union Card and
        belong to Local 1119 in Sterling Heights.

            References are listed on the enclosed data sheet.  After you have
        contacted them about my personal traits and work abilities could you
        call me before April 21 to set up an appointment.  I will be home after
        April 21 and would like to discuss my qualifications for summer work at
        your company.  My home phone number is 547-3922 and my number here at
        school is (616) 383-0967.

                                        Cordially,

                                        W. Dennis

                                        Wesley Dennis


        Enclosure
```

567 Williams Hall
Michigan State University
East Lansing, Michigan 48823
March 15, 1983

Personnel Department
Zoological Gardens
5683 West 13 Mile Road
Royal Oak, Michigan 48073

Gentlemen:

    I was completely overjoyed to learn that your Animal Center hires
college students as animal caretakers over the summer. I would like to
submit an application for this position.

    During my employment at the Central Biological Lab, I learned how to
handle small laboratory animals such as rats, mice, gerbils, and hamsters.
I was also in charge of caring for the larger labatory animals such as
dogs, guinea pigs, rabbits, and primates. I am also familiar with water-
ing, feeding, and cleaning of animals and their cages. I am capable of
drawing blood by heart punctures in small animals and via the juggler
in the dog. I have also learned methods of restraining these animals.
I think you will find I am a capable and resourceful employee of many
talents.

    The enclosed data sheet has details of my educational background
and previous job experience.

    I will be in Royal Oak the first week of May and if it would be
convenient for you, I could drop by for an interview.

                                        Thank You,

                                        Lane Talbert

                                        Lane Talbert

Enclosure

168 West Hall
Detroit University
University Place
Detroit, MI 48230
March 1, 1983

Ms. Myrtle Lundquist
Personnel Director
Woods Motor Inn
Traverse City, MI 49684

Dear Ms. Lundquist

When you need a waiter who has three summer's experience taking orders,
recommending and serving wine, making salads and cooking dishes and
deserts at table side, please call me.

I have always had people-related jobs. Employment as a head bagger, as
a bell captain, as a banquet supervisor, as a resident advisor, and as
a waiter in your restaurant for three summers, all point this out. I am
currently a junior at U of D, studying business. This puts me in contact
with the type of people that frequent your organization the most--people
with college degrees.

The fact that I have worked for your organization for three summers is
indicative of my abilities, knowing your high standards. Because of this
experience, I should need minimal training this summer.

I will be getting out of school at about the same time the tourists start
coming, the end of May. Please examine the attached resume and call or
write to me to suggest a time when we could discuss the possibility of
putting my experience to work for you.

Yours truly

Evin P. Flude

Evin P. Flude

39. Many companies are using strictly structured interviews to insure that all hiring officers ask the same questions of all applicants at all branches of the company. Part of such an outline appears below. Outline the answers you would give to each element in the section entitled "Obtaining Relevant Information."

IV. Obtaining Relevant Information

  A. Education

    1. Degrees obtained or in process

      a. Course program — please describe
      b. Emphasis
      c. Special interests within course program
      d. Additional education

    2. Why chosen — why pursued

  B. Work experience

    1. Previous positions held (as applicable)

      a. Describe position
      b. Describe responsibilities, authorities
      c. Describe reporting relationships

    2. Special assignments, projects

      a. How obtained
      b. Why pursued
      c. Results

  C. Accomplishments within career

    1. Describe accomplishments
    2. How achieved
    3. Why achieved

  D. Career goals

    1. Describe short-term (1-2 years) and long-term (3-5 years) career goals
    2. How formulated
    3. Relationship to position
    4. Describe particular skills, abilities, interests you want to use and/or develop in future

40. Write messages about as many of the outlined answers in Case 39 as your instructor requests.

41. Use the information that follows to write a memo to Hannah Feldstein, Assistant Personnel Director, pointing out the changes that must be made in the company's application form which is printed after the list of anti-discrimination laws.

ANTI-DISCRIMINATION LAWS: WHAT YOU CAN — AND CAN'T ASK

Subject	What You Can Ask	What You Can't Ask
Race or color		Complexion or color of skin. Coloring.
Religion		Inquiry into an applicant's religious denomination, religious affiliations, church, parish, pastor, or religious holidays observed. An applicant may not be told, "This is a (Catholic, Protestant, or Jewish) organization."
National origin		Inquiry into applicant's lineage, ancestry, national origin, descent, parentage, or nationality. Nationality of applicant's parents or spouse. What is applicant's mother tongue?
Sex		A preemployment inquiry as to sex on an application form shall be unlawful.
Marital status		Are you married? Where does your spouse work? What are the ages of your children, if any?
Age	Are you between 18 and 65 years of age? If not, state your age.	How old are you? What is your date of birth?
Disability	Do you have any impairments, physical or mental, which would interfere with your ability to perform the job for which you have applied? If there are any positions or types of positions for which you should not be considered or job duties you cannot perform because of a physical handicap, please explain.	Do you have a disability? Have you ever been treated for any of the following diseases? (List diseases) Has any member of your family ever had any one of the following diseases? (List diseases)
Name	Have you ever worked for this company under a different name? Is any additional information relative to change of name, use of an assumed name, or nickname necessary to enable a check on your work record? If yes, explain.	Original name of an applicant whose name has been changed by court order or otherwise. Maiden name of a married woman. If you have ever worked under another name, state name and dates.
Address or duration of residence	Applicant's place of residence. How long a resident of this state or city?	
Birthplace		Birthplace of applicant. Birthplace of applicant's parents, spouse, or other close relatives.
Photograph		Requirement that an applicant affix a photograph to the employment form at any time before hiring, or at his option.
Citizenship	Are you a citizen of the United States? If not a citizen of the United States, does applicant intend to become a citizen of the United States? If you are not a United States citizen, have you the legal right to remain permanently in the United States? Requirement that applicants state whether they have ever been interned or arrested as an enemy alien.	Of what country are you a citizen? Whether an applicant is a naturalized or a native-born citizen; the date when the applicant acquired citizenship. Requirement that the applicant produce naturalization papers or first papers. Whether applicant's parents or spouse are naturalized or native-born citizens of the U.S. The date when such parents or spouse acquired citizenship.

ANTI-DISCRIMINATION LAWS: WHAT YOU CAN – AND CAN'T ASK (Continued)

Subject	What You Can Ask	What You Can't Ask
Language	Inquiry into languages applicant speaks and writes fluently. What foreign language do you read fluently? Write fluently? Speak fluently?	Inquiry into how applicant acquired ability to read, write, or speak a foreign language.
Education	Inquiry into the academic, vocational or professional education of an applicant and the public and private schools she has attended.	
Experience	Inquiry into work experience. Inquiry into countries applicant has visited.	
Character	Have you ever been convicted of any crime. If so, when, where, and disposition of offense?	Have you ever been arrested? (An employer's use of an individual's arrest record to deny employment would, in the absence of business necessity, constitute a violation of the human rights law.)
Relatives	Names of applicant's relatives already employed by this company.	Names and addresses, ages, number, or other information concerning applicant's children or other relatives not employed by the company.
Notice in case of emergency	Name and address of person to be notified in case of an accident or emergency.	
Military experience	Have you ever been a member of the armed services of the United States or in a state militia? If so, did your military experience have any relationship to the position for which you have applied?	Inquiry into an applicant's general military experience.
Organizations	Are you a member of any club, organization, etc. (exclude organizations, the name or character of which indicates the race, creed, color, or national origin of its members)?	List all clubs, societies, and lodges to which you belong.
References	Who suggested that you apply for a position here?	

CAUTION: Even questions that would ordinarily be lawful may, in some circumstances, be held to be evidence of unlawful discrimination—when you request information that's not job related and that has disproportionately burdensome effect on minority group members.

APPLICATION FOR EMPLOYMENT

MALE
FEMALE _____

HEIGHT _____ WEIGHT _____

COLOR
OF HAIR _____

COLOR
OF EYES _____

The use of this Blank does not indicate there are any positions open and no obligation is assumed by accepting this application.

DATE_____19____

Answer All Questions Carefully and Complete In Own Hand Writing.

OWN TELEPHONE NUMBER _____

NEARBY TELEPHONE NUMBER _____

NAME _____

PRINT FULL NAME AS IT APPEARS ON YOUR SOCIAL SECURITY CARD	LAST	FIRST	MIDDLE OR MAIDEN	SOCIAL SECURITY ACC'T NO.			

PRESENT ADDRESS			HOW LONG AT PRESENT ADDRESS	OWN HOME RENT OR BUYING	ROOM BOARD BATCH	LIVE WITH PARENTS

PREVIOUS ADDRESS		HOME ADDRESS			

WHERE BORN		DATE BIRTH	ALIEN OR CITIZEN	IF NATURALIZED GIVE DATE AND PLACE	

SINGLE MARRIED DIVORCED	SEPARATED WIDOWED WIDOW	HOW MANY PERSONS DO YOU SUPPORT	SONS	DAUGHTERS	OTHERS	DESCENT OR NATIONALITY

WIFE'S MAIDEN OR HUSBAND'S FIRST NAME	AGE	OCCUPATION	PLACE OF EMPLOYMENT	HOW LONG

HOW LONG HAVE YOU LIVED IN THIS COUNTY	HOW LONG HAVE YOU LIVED IN THIS STATE	WHERE DID YOU LIVE PRIOR TO THAT TIME	ADDRESS	CITY	STATE

PREVIOUS EMPLOYMENT—NAME LAST EIGHT EMPLOYERS INCLUDING SELF EMPLOYMENT

NAME		ADDRESS				RATE OF PAY
CLOCK NO.	KIND OF WORK		FROM	TO	REASON FOR LEAVING	

NAME		ADDRESS				RATE OF PAY
CLOCK NO.	KIND OF WORK		FROM	TO	REASON FOR LEAVING	

NAME		ADDRESS				RATE OF PAY
CLOCK NO.	KIND OF WORK		FROM	TO	REASON FOR LEAVING	

NAME		ADDRESS				RATE OF PAY
CLOCK NO.	KIND OF WORK		FROM	TO	REASON FOR LEAVING	

NAME		ADDRESS				RATE OF PAY
CLOCK NO.	KIND OF WORK		FROM	TO	REASON FOR LEAVING	

NAME		ADDRESS				RATE OF PAY
CLOCK NO.	KIND OF WORK		FROM	TO	REASON FOR LEAVING	

NAME		ADDRESS				RATE OF PAY
CLOCK NO.	KIND OF WORK		FROM	TO	REASON FOR LEAVING	

NAME		ADDRESS				RATE OF PAY
CLOCK NO.	KIND OF WORK		FROM	TO	REASON FOR LEAVING	

EDUCATION	NAME AND LOCATION OF SCHOOL	NO. OF YEARS ATTENDED	COURSE OF STUDY GENERAL	SPECIAL	DATE OF LEAVING MO. YR.
GRAMMAR SCHOOL					
HIGH SCHOOL					
NIGHT SCHOOL					
CORRESPONDENCE SCHOOL					
COLLEGE OR UNIVERSITY					

WHAT WERE YOUR ACTIVITIES IMMEDIATELY AFTER LEAVING SCHOOL?

I SERVED IN THE ARMED FORCES OF—NAME OF COUNTRY _____

DATE OF ENTRANCE	BRANCH OF SERVICE		RANK
DATE OF DISCHARGE	STATUS OF DISCHARGE		
ARE YOU NOW A MEMBER OF ANY MILITARY OR NAVAL ORGANIZATION?	IF SO NAME AND ADDRESS		

OVER

493

LIST ORGANIZATIONS TO WHICH YOU BELONG OTHER THAN LABOR UNIONS

_____

_____

_____

CHARACTER REFERENCE—GIVE NAMES AND ADDRESSES OF THREE PERSONS, NOT RELATIVES OR FORMER EMPLOYERS, WHO HAVE KNOWN YOU FOR THE PAST FIVE YEARS

1 _____

2 _____

3 _____

IF YOU HAVE WORKED HERE BEFORE PLEASE
GIVE DATES AND KIND OF WORK DONE

WILL ANYONE WORKING
HERE RECOMMEND YOU?

SPECIAL QUALIFICATIONS OR REASONS
WHY I WOULD LIKE TO WORK HERE

WHAT PHYSICAL
DEFECTS HAVE YOU

IN CASE OF ACCIDENT PLEASE NOTIFY	ADDRESS	TELEPHONE NUMBER
KIND OF WORK DESIRED		WAGES EXPECTED

I hereby authorize investigation of all statements contained on this application with no liability arising therefrom.
I declare that I am in good health, and have no injury or disease (except as stated herein) constitutional or otherwise.
If hired, I agree to have deducted from my earnings any advance on wages, loan or the cost of badge, tools or other equipment obtained and not returned by me on or before date of termination of service.
All of my answers to this application for employment are correct to the best of my knowledge.
I understand that any false statement will be sufficient reason for my dismissal.

DATE_____ WITNESS_____ SIGNED_____

DO NOT WRITE BELOW THIS LINE

_____

_____

_____

_____

_____

_____

_____

_____

_____

_____

_____

INTERVIEWED BY

42. You work in the production department of a national financial magazine. The editor has received a free-lance article which he wants to print, but he says to you, "This writer is in love with numbers. They are ALL written out. See what you can do to get some of the numbers out of the paragraphs and into some kind of visual that will leave an impression on our readers." Here is the article you are to revise and "liven up with visual enhancements."

HOW DOES YOUR SHELTER SHELTER?

Oil and gas tax shelter programs are not all created equal. Some have returned as much as 110% after tax to investors at the end of their term. Others have returned nothing at all. How do you tell which will do well and which won't before you become a limited partner?

One man has been working on the problem. After studying prospectuses of SEC-registered programs, he concluded that there are actually four basic types of programs. His study covers 500 partnerships put together by 64 sponsors before 1981.

All the sponsors were still in business and raised money in 1981. But the money raised from the public before 1981, some $2.5 billion, had been put to work and uncovered either gushers or dry holes. Although the oil and gas in successful wells may flow for another 20 years or more, the ultimate return on the investor's dollar can at least be projected. For the 500 partnerships studied, the results were disappointing. The average return was only 9.9%, down substantially from 12.8% only two years before.

If the general partner and the limited partners shared both nondeductible capital costs and deductible drilling costs, the limited partners' chances of a decent return were best. This partnership can be called a promoted interest structure. Sixty-six of the 500 partnerships used this structure and raised $232.4 million. Twenty-four percent of these will return over 20% to partners; only 6.4% will have no payout at all. Between these two extremes, 27.4% will enjoy a return of between 10% and 20%; while 42% will gain less than 10%.

The riskiest type of program to limited partners is one called functional allocation. In such programs, capital costs are paid by the general partner. Intangible or drilling or deductible costs are paid by the limited partners. Because investors can write off in the first year everything they put in, functional allocation is the most popular type of program. Of the 500 partnerships, 219 were of this type. While 21.6% of them can be expected to return over 20% to investors, 35.1% will have no payout at all. Even these figures may paint too rosy a picture. Among those returning over 20% are two big sponsors with more liberal payout terms and stronger financing. If these two programs were removed from the sample, the percent which returned over 20% would decline to 13%. Between the two extremes, 11.6% will return between 10% and 20% and 31.7% will return less than 10% of the total of $1462.8 million invested in functional allocation structures.

In the other two program structures, limited partners pay essentially all of the costs. The general partner pays 1%, but he gets that in a management fee. He doesn't have to reach in his pocket for any cash. In one structure called carried interest, the general partner shares in revenues from the first barrel produced. In the other structure, labeled reversionary interest, the sponsor doesn't begin to share in revenues until after the investor gets at least some money back.

Surprisingly, the carried interest structure turned out to be more favorable for investors than the reversionary interest structure. Of the 92 partnerships with a carried interest structure (capitalized at $344.4 million), 21.8% will return over 20%; 40% over 10%; 29.1% under 10%; and 8.6% nothing at all.

Of the 123 programs with a reversionary interest structure (capitalized at $425.5 million), 18% will return over 20%; 22.3% over 10%; 47.9% under 10%; and 11.8% nothing at all. Both these structures are used primarily by new sponsors who don't have much cash. The problem with reversionary interest is it gives sponsors an incentive to charge higher fees than they really should, since they don't get a stream of income as early as those with a carried interest structure.

How can you tell what kind of structure the deal you are considering has? It won't be labeled "functional allocation" or "carried interest" in the prospectus. Your broker might know, but he might not. The answer is to study carefully two particular sections which are in every prospectus. One is called 'Use of Proceeds' and the other, 'Allocation of Costs and Revenue.' These will tell you who is paying for what and who is getting what. Remember, you want to be sure the sponsor's interest is closely tied to your own—that you are really in it together.

43. The department in which you are taking your writing class is hosting the state convention of the Business and Technical Writing Association. Because the majority of people attending the convention are coming by car rather than by using public transportation, the host committee plans to provide a local map to direct conventioneers to the meetings which will be held at the university. Please provide the map and simple directions to reach the university or college from the main east-west and north-south highways. Be sure to use the easiest route to follow, even if it is a little longer. Be sure not to send drivers the wrong way down one-way streets.

44. You work in the Alumni Relations Department of Northern University. Your superior, Patricia Everard, has been asked by the president to investigate the admissions and dismissal policy of the university. Some alumni have indicated that the "scoop" is that Northern is an "easy-in-easy-out" school. In other words, the school accepts many more students than it intends to keep and then flunks out large numbers, keeping only the most desirable. Prepare a report that your superior can pass on to the president basing your observations on the facts below.

The university has a 4-point grading system. In order to graduate, students must have at least twice as many grade points as credit hours, essentially a C average. As a long-standing policy, any time students fall below a 2-point average, they are warned. If, during the next semester, they do not raise the average back to a 2-point level, they are dismissed. After a semester out of school, dismissed students can apply for readmission. Students who are readmitted have one semester to bring their grade point averages back to C.

In the fall, two years ago, the University had 7,140 entering freshmen. At the end of the fall semester, 607 were placed on warning, commonly called probation. At the end of the spring semester, 418 students were dismissed and 592 placed on warning of a freshman class that numbered 6,966 at the beginning of the semester.

The sophomore class numbered 5,460 that same fall and finished with 436 on probation and 327 dismissed. That spring, out of 5,041 sophomores, 302 were dismissed and an additional 403 were warned.

Of the 4,200 students who were juniors in the fall, 252 were dismissed and 336 were warned. For the spring, out of 3,888 who began, 233 were dismissed and another 311 placed on probation.

The figures for seniors were 3,150 enrolled for the fall semester with 252 placed on probation at the end and 189 dismissed. There were 3,949 enrolled, of which 176 were dismissed and 236 warned at the end of the spring semester.

Last year, the fall semester began with 7,820 freshmen, 5,980 sophomores, 4,612 juniors, and 3,444 seniors. The end of the semester found 647 freshmen warned. At the semester's end in the spring, 450 freshmen were dismissed and 638 placed on warning. The sophomores had 359 and 478 dismissed and on probation respectively at the end of the first semester; comparable figures were 336 and 448 for the second semester. The junior figures for the same period were 277 and 368; 261 and 347. The senior results were 206 and 191 dismissed; probations amounted to 275 and 256. The class distributions for the second semester were freshmen, 7,503; sophomores, 5,602; juniors, 4,343; and seniors, 3,196.

There were 315 readmitted students, of whom 138 were dismissed at the end of the fall semester two years ago. In the spring, 126 of 300 were dismissed. Comparable figures for last year were 148 out of 345 and 144 of 328.

45. Opening a franchised business is expensive. The average opening cost (exclusive of the cost of land and buildings) for several popular franchises is between $150,000 and $200,000. The parent companies supply various services to help the franchisee. They also inspect the premises regularly, provide training help, and in most cases share in advertising costs. The franchisee pays a one-time licensing fee and then a percentage of each month's gross sales to the parent company. The services vary from company to com-

pany, as do the fees. Consider the services and fees connected with the following three franchise operations after initial opening costs. Which one would you prefer to invest in if you met the basic financial requirements?

FRANCHISE A

Annual royalty of 3% of gross sales
Annual contribution of 2% of gross sales for shared advertising costs
Operate in a protected territory
Receive leads from national advertising
Ongoing sales and management training available
Ongoing management consultation available
Group insurance available
Discounts available for furniture and fixtures

FRANCHISE B

Annual royalty of 3% of gross sales paid monthly
Monthly contribution of ½ of 1% of gross sales for shared advertising costs
Receive regular updated materials to insert in the four company manuals issued during initial training
Receive regular monthly visits from quality inspectors from national organization
Cooperative purchasing of raw materials available

FRANCHISE C

Monthly lease of facilities for 1% of gross profits
No charge for national advertising
Receive continuing management guidance including regular financial statement analysis
Purchase all basic raw materials from parent company
Training materials available

46. Trekkies in Business is a new (fictitious) club for Star Trek fans majoring in business. The club operates on a very small budget. Thus, for its spring membership drive, the head of Trekkie publicity made, by hand, the poster below. Club members placed xeroxed copies of the poster on bulletin boards on campus.

Despite their publicity efforts, the Trekkies did not have an increase in membership. Some members blamed the head of publicity. They felt the membership drive poster was of such low quality that it discouraged, rather than encouraged, new membership.

Study the poster carefully. Then compose a message to the head of publicity suggesting specific reasons the poster failed to attract new members and recommending improvements.

YOU'RE INVITED

WHAT: A MEMBERSHIP "TEA"

Get to Know Us For All Trekkies
and What We Can   Enrolled In Business
Do for You!

We'll Provide Plenty of Cookies & Tea!

YOU'RE INVITED

WHEN: Tuesday
April 13

A Fun Time Open
to all Trekkies enrolled At 4:00
In Business -- Details
on New Membership
Requirements & Renewals.

APPROVED

OFFICE OF STUDENT ACTIVITIES

YOU'RE INVITED

WHERE: Room 141
East Hall

Trekkies In Business

47. Re-read the letter from Clare Lowrenson, Executive Director for FUN WITH FOODS (see Cases at the end of chapter 4). Then use the following information to compose an appropriate reply.

You talked briefly with the special events manager at the Nelson Hotel. She was adamant that the surcharges were necessary and that she could make no exceptions. You checked with two comparable hotels. One has already instituted special surcharges and the other expects to add such charges soon. However, neither of the other hotels' charges are as high as those at the Nelson. The Chamber's legal counsel read over the complaint letter and contract. He pointed out that a clause in Section XVI especially states that the hotel may add nominal surcharges for services to groups. You made an appointment with Gerhard Blum, the Nelson's manager, and asked him to read Lowrenson's letter. You also told him about the lower charges at two other hotels and pointed out that three weeks is very short notice for a nonprofit association to raise extra money to pay hotel bills. He finally agreed to cut the surcharges in half and to confirm that fact with the group.

48. Re-read the letter from Sue O'Ryan, president of IABC/Michigan (see Cases at the end of chapter 4). Then use the following information to compose an appropriate reply.

You can send a standard convention packet that lists all the facilities in the city which offer accommodations for meetings. The packet contains information about the city and a map which describes the locations of all listed facilities. Each facility is also represented by an informative sheet which shows the accommodations available, suggests a price range for common services such as the coffee service, and lists a contact person who can provide more information and accept reservations.

49. Re-read the letter from Lorna Edwards in chapter 4. Then use the following information to write an appropriate reply.

Three Chicago area stores carry Bann surgical supports. They are

Walton Drugs
1508 South Michigan Avenue
Evanston, IL 60202

Canaday's Hospital Supply
3218 Randolph Street
Chicago, IL 60601

Best Orthopedic Supply
14432 South 72 Avenue
Cicero, IL 60650

50. Re-read the letter to Marta Charbanau from Gene Wicks (see Case 4 in this chapter). Then use the following information to compose an appropriate answer.

The reservations manager indicates that the hotel is 80 percent booked for the dates that Wicks will be bringing his group. As August is the height of the tourist season, the hotel likes to keep space available for casual trade and late reservations. In short, the hotel is "not hurting," to use the manager's phrase.

51. Re-read the letter from the Angels Fan Club (see Case 4 in this chapter). Then use the following information to compose an answer.

You have a special packet which contains standard information for large groups. The hotel has rooms available, but to reserve as many as 75 rooms, the Club should sign a preliminary contract by July 1. You can easily accommodate up to 500 guests for brunch. Menu choices for all meals and package prices for both meals and rooms are part of the packet. Depending on the tour package the Club selects, other area attractions are available free or at a discount. Fans who are not reserving rooms may park at the hotel and join the others for meals. Fans who come for meals may leave their cars and join the group for charter bus service which the hotel can arrange.

Appendix A

Reviewing Fundamentals

The body of this text has been written to help you learn to organize your thoughts to convey a coherent, unified message to a reader who needs the information you have. But to be sure your message is clearly understood and accepted, you should follow standard rules for grammar and punctuation. This section of the text reviews some of these fundamentals which help to make meaning clear.

You may refer to Appendix A when you have a question about usage. Or you may read it carefully and complete the exercises to help you learn to write better sentences, to use punctuation accurately, and to handle numbers and capital letters consistently.

SENTENCE STRUCTURE

The sentence is the basic unit of thought in writing. Every sentence has a main clause, one that can stand alone to communicate effectively. When a main clause stands alone, it is often called a simple sentence. The word *simple* refers to the structure of the sentence, not to its length or to the idea it communicates. The following sentences are all simple sentences.

1. Depositors receive interest on their savings.
2. The Internal Revenue Service issued new regulations in July, 1983, to tax interest and dividends.
3. The new tax costs a great deal to collect and confuses many savers.
4. Low-income people and many elderly people depend on interest as a part of their income.
5. Who will educate the taxpayers about the new withholding tax?

These sentences differ in many ways. Some are long, and some are short. Sentences 1-4 are statements; the fifth sentence is a question. Sentence 4 has two subjects, called a compound subject. Sentence 3 has two main verbs, called a compound predicate. The five sentences have three common traits, however. First, each sentence expresses only one idea. Second, each sentence has an end marker, either a period or a question mark, which shows the reader when the idea ends. Third, each sentence is a main clause which can stand alone structurally.

Exercise A   Place end markers (periods or question marks) after each group of words that can stand alone as an idea.

Managers of banks and brokerage firms worried about preparing customers for the new withholding tax law the Internal Revenue Service prepared brochures, television and radio announcements, and mailings to provide information about the law many financial managers feared this information confused customers even further what could banks do to help their customers many banks appointed their own experts to explain the law to customers these experts tell customers what the law means they also inform customers of the choices for payment allowed by the law the experts warn customers of the penalty for trying to evade the law the new withholding tax has proven very difficult for banks and other financial institutions to administer.

Compound Sentences

In contrast to simple sentences which have only one idea in one main clause, compounds sentences convey two or more ideas in a single sentence. You can form compound sentences in two ways: (1) by using a coordinate conjunction (*and, or, nor, but, for, so, yet*) to join main clauses, or (2) by using a semicolon (;) to separate them.

Two rules govern the formation of all compound sentences. First, the main clauses you are joining to form one sentence must be closely related in meaning.

> Dewayne Witherspoon earned a degree in animal husbandry, but his ambition led him beyond the farm.

is an acceptable compound sentence because both main clauses are about what Dewayne Witherspoon wanted to do with his life.

> Dewayne Witherspoon earned a degree in animal husbandry; people of all ages like to play the card game Duo.

is not an acceptable compound sentence because the ideas in each main clause have no relationship.

Second, the ideas joined to form compound sentences must be equal in importance. The two main clauses, "Dewayne Witherspoon lives in Burlington, Wisconsin" and "Dewayne Witherspoon plans to market Duo internationally," should not be joined in a compound sentence because they are not equal in importance. Witherspoon's home town has little to do with the success of his card game.

When you form compound sentences with coordinate conjunctions, place a comma before the conjunction that joins the clauses.

> Dewayne Witherspoon marketed Duo on a wide scale, and it made him a rich man.

When you form compound sentences with a semicolon, remove the comma and coordinate conjunction and replace them with a semicolon.

> Dewayne Witherspoon marketed Duo on a wide scale; it made him a rich man.

Semicolons frequently appear in compound sentences in which adverbs such as *however, therefore, nevertheless, moreover, thus, otherwise, hence, consequently*, and *finally* begin the second clause:

> Dewayne Witherspoon earned a degree in animal husbandry; however, his ambition led him beyond the farm.

Notice that a comma follows the adverb that begins the second clause.

Exercise B   Use coordinate conjunctions (*and, or, nor, but, for, so, yet*) or a semicolon to join main clauses in the paragraph below. Remember to join clauses related in meaning.

> Dewayne Witherspoon's interest in marketing led him beyond the family farm. After high school, he earned a degree in animal husbandry. He joined the family farm near Burlington, Wisconsin. He could have remained a farmer for the rest of his life. He soon found he had ambition. This ambition wasn't satisfied on the farm. He was interested in buying and selling. He took a trip to Enid, Oklahoma. He played a card game called Duo. He liked playing the game. He found the owner of the rights to the game. He bought the rights. He and his sister formed a company to manufacture and market the game. They think Duo will surpass Monopoly in total sales within a decade. Witherspoon's venture has been very successful. He has kept an interest in the family farm.

In making compound sentences from these simple sentences, you probably found a number of correct ways to join main clauses together. The compound sentence is a useful tool because, by joining clauses, you can remove choppiness from your writing and show relationships between ideas. To use this tool correctly, remember to join only related ideas and only two or three at a time. Joining too many ideas together results in tedious, hard-to-follow sentences.

Complex Sentences

Complex sentences consist of one main clause and at least one subordinate clause. As you saw in Exercises A and B, each main clause could stand alone and had at least one subject and verb. Subordinate clauses cannot stand alone. They depend on a main clause to complete their meaning. They are joined to main clauses by two groups of words: (1) relative pronouns such as *who, whoever, whose, which, what, that* and (2) subordinate conjunctions such as *after, although, as, as if, as soon as, because, before, if, once, since, that, unless, until, when, whenever, where, wherever, and while*.

Complex sentences also relate ideas together. They are particularly useful in showing the relative degree of importance of two ideas in a sentence. Generally, the more important idea goes in the main clause of a complex sentence, the less important idea in the subordinate clause. For example, in a paragraph about the success of Asian Indians who have come to the United States to live, you might have these two ideas:

Ali Raza is now chief executive of a computer software firm.

Ali Raza worked his way through school as a farmhand.

Since the subject is *success*, the first idea is more important and goes in the main clause. The second idea is less important and forms the subordinate clause. The complex sentence that results when the two ideas are joined is

Ali Raza, who worked his way through school as a farmhand, is now chief executive of a computer software firm.

Each item in Exercise C (below) is a set of two simple sentences. When joined correctly, the simple sentences form a complex sentence. Because Exercise C asks you to use relative pronouns as conjunctions, the subordinate clause is called an adjective clause. This clause functions as an adjective. Therefore, you must place it next to the word it best relates to or explains in the main clause.

If the main idea is

The change in the immigration law benefited Asian Indians.

and the subordinate idea is

Asian Indians came to the United States in increasing numbers after 1965.

the subordinate clause relates to *Asian Indians*, the last words in the main clause. The resulting complex sentence is

The change in the immigration law benefited Asian Indians who came to the United States in increasing numbers after 1965.

If the main idea is

The amended immigration law benefited Asian Indians.

and the subordinate idea is

The law changed in 1965.

the resulting complex sentence is

The amended immigration law, which changed in 1965, benefited Asian Indians.

The subordinate clause relates to the word *law* in the main clause.

Because both of these subordinate clauses are adjective clauses, they may never begin a sentence. Adjective clauses always follow the word they relate to in the main clause. They may appear in the middle or at the end of the main clause, depending on where the word they relate to is.

Exercise C   Combine the main idea in Column A with the subordinate idea in Column B to form a complex sentence. Use relative pronouns to join the ideas together.

A Main Idea	B Subordinate Idea
1. Over 300,000 Asian Indians live in the United States.	Most Asian Indian immigrants have become U.S. citizens.
2. Asian Indians are members of one of the richest ethnic groups in America.	Most Asian Indians are well educated, professional people.
3. One Asian Indian immigrant owns 4,000 acres of California farmland.	The farm land costs as much $10,000 an acre.
4. Another Asian Indian immigrant runs a newspaper with a circulation of 8,500.	He graduated from Poona University in India as well as University of California.
5. Marriage ads are profitable to newspapers with large Asian Indian audiences.	Marriage ads emphasize education, employment, appearance, and age.

In Exercise D, you will use subordinate conjunctions to form complex sentences from two simple sentences. The subordinate clause that results is called an adverb clause. Adverb clauses are not tied to a particular word in the main clause as adjective clauses are. Adverb clauses may come before the main clause, in the middle of the main clause, or at the end of the main clause.

Exercise D   Combine the main idea in Column A with the subordinate idea in Column B to form a complex sentence. Use subordinate conjunctions to join ideas together.

A Main Idea	B Subordinate Idea
1. Portable heaters became popular in the United States.	Oil-producing countries raised the price of oil.
2. Oil-filled heaters are made of pressed steel rather than cast iron.	Some modern space heaters look like radiators found in older homes.

3. Many Europeans use oil-filled heaters as their only source of heat.

Houses in Europe sometimes lack central heating.

4. Kerosene heaters have also gained widespread use.

They were introduced from Japan in the mid-1970s.

5. Consumer protection agencies claim manufacturers could improve kerosene heaters.

Manufacturers could use some of the money spent on advertising on product safety.

Exercise E   Combine these simple sentences to form compound or complex sentences as appropriate. For variety, avoid combining all the sentences in the same way.

Employed Americans think benefits to unemployed workers are generous. Our employment benefits are skimpy compared to those in many European countries. In the Netherlands, unemployment benefits include state-subsidized housing, allowances for children, and free medical care. These benefits continue for two and a half years. In addition to other benefits, Emil Hoekstra has received nearly $200 a week for the last two years. He is an unemployed factory worker. Belgium's unemployment benefits are even better. They never run out. The lifestyles of Denmark's unemployed workers don't change very much. Their unemployment benefits give them 90 percent of their previous salaries. Jobless Americans don't usually consider taking vacations. Jobless people in Holland get vacation pay. Full-time students in many European countries also benefit. They receive special allowances for their children. Most unemployed workers in America find new jobs in three months. Unemployment benefits are too low to support them adequately. Unemployment benefits run out quickly. In France and England, less than half the unemployed workers find new jobs in three months. Unemployment benefits in these European countries last longer and offer more support than do such benefits in the United States.

PROBLEMS WITH SENTENCE STRUCTURE

Main clauses have two traits: they have subjects and verbs, and they can stand by themselves to express ideas. By understanding these traits, you can test each sentence you write to make sure that it is complete. In this way, you can avoid two major grammatical errors in sentence structure—fragments and run-on sentences.

Fragments

As the term indicates, fragments are only partially complete sentences. They look like sentences because they start with a capital letter and end with a period, but they lack a subject or a verb or sometimes both. They cannot stand by themselves to express ideas. By definition, all subordinate clauses are fragments because they depend on a main clause to complete ideas.

Exercise F   Join the fragments to main clauses to form complete sentences.

Main Clause	*Fragment*
1. Algoma College has trouble recruiting top high school athletes.	Prefer to enter schools with bigger sports programs.
2. Algoma's athletic facilities are old.	Are a weak recruiting tool.
3. Athletes from regional and state championship teams are impressed by modern sports palaces.	Algoma's older facilities carefully maintained.
4. Algoma College's sports program is not well known outside the immediate vicinity of the school.	Don't play in a conference.
5. Top athletes feel they would get little recognition.	If they decided to attend Algoma.

Present participial phrases, the first principle part of a verb plus *-ing*, are fragments when they stand alone. For example, "running for Congress" is a fragment because it does not express a complete idea. You can correct this kind of fragment by making it part of a complete sentence. You can use the phrase as a subject

Running for Congress is exhausting.

or as a predicate

Cal DeFazio is *running for Congress* from the Seventh District.

or as a modifier

Running for Congress, Cal DeFazio had to raise money for his campaign.

Exercise G   Use the following present participles as (a) subjects, (b) predicates, and (c) modifiers of complete sentences to describe De Fazio's actions during the campaign.

1. shaking hands with voters all day
2. eating rubbery chicken at political banquets
3. sleeping in different hotels every night
4. working 18 hours a day
5. never seeing his family

Past participial phrases are also fragments when they stand alone. Part participles are the third principle part of verbs. You can turn every past participial phrase, like "rejected by the voters," into a complete sentence by adding a subject:

DeFazio was *rejected by the voters.*

You can also use some past participial phrases as modifiers:

Rejected by the voters, DeFazio took a month's vacation.

Some past participial phrases, like "fought hard throughout the campaign," cannot be used as modifiers, however; they act only as part of the predicate of the sentence.

Exercise H   Use these past participial phrases in sentences as (a) parts of predicates and (b) modifiers to explain DeFazio's defeat in the election.

1. shaken by his loss
2. sunk in debt
3. fallen from favor
4. caught by his own ambition
5. driven to run for office in the next election

Infinitives are constructions made up of the preposition *to* plus a verb: *to go, to be, to witness, to capture.* Infinitives often form longer phrases like *to vacation in the mountains, to be close to nature at its best and most unspoiled, to witness natural wonders like the geysers of Yellowstone and the giant sequoias of Yosemite, to capture some of the splendor of nature on film.* Even though some of these phrases are long, they are fragments. They can go before verbs as subjects of complete sentences:

To vacation in the mountains became Shelly's goal after she saw the exhibition of Ansel Adams' photographs.

or after verbs as objects or complements:

After viewing Ansel Adams' photographs, Shelly longed *to vacation in the mountains.*

Exercise I   Use each infinitive phrase as (a) the subject or (b) the object or complement of a verb in a complete sentence.

1. to earn a moderate income
2. to spend money prudently
3. to develop a habit of saving a part of each paycheck
4. to look for investment opportunities by reading business magazines and newspapers
5. to develop a plan for investing money

Prepositional phrases, like infinitive phrases, are also fragments unless they are joined to a complete sentence. Here is a list of words often used as prepositions.

about	behind	in addition to	to
above	below	in spite of	toward
according to	by	instead of	under
after	during	into	until
against	except	on	up
at	for	out	upon
because of	from	through	with
before	in	throughout	

When prepositions are joined with other word groups, they form phrases. "During his 25-year career as a butcher" is a prepositional phrase. Because by itself it is a fragment, it must be part of another sentence.

During his 25-year career as a butcher, Rudy Balch worked for two different supermarkets.

"Instead of working for someone else" is also a fragment. It could be used in this complete sentence:

He decided to start his own butcher shop instead of working for someone else.

Exercise J   Write complete sentences in which you use each of these prepositional phrases to describe some of Balch's activities as he started his own business.

1. with $100,000 borrowed from the bank
2. against his accountant's advice
3. after advertising for clerks
4. behind the counter 12 hours a day
5. in spite of the predictions of his relatives

A final kind of fragment results from noun phrases. "Secretaries in large corporations" is such a phrase. It can be used anywhere a noun can be used in a sentence. Here are some examples.

> *Secretaries in large corporations* sometimes have opportunities for advancement.

> Good communications skills are required of *secretaries in large corporations.*

> The agency recruits *secretaries in large corporations* for management positions.

> Wilma Peterson and Betty Andrus are *secretaries in large corporations* in midtown Manhattan.

Exercise K   Write two different sentences that use the following noun phrases about secretaries in two different ways.

1. knowledge of the business
2. patience with fussy clients
3. ability to solve office problems
4. contributions to policy decisions
5. value to the executive

Run-on Sentences

Fragments are errors because they lack essential parts, subjects or predicates, to make them complete sentences. Run-on sentences are errors for the opposite reason. They are two or more complete sentences written as one sentence. Writers of run-on sentences fail to recognize where one complete sentence stops, and another begins. As you learned earlier, a period is the appropriate end marker for complete sentences that make statements. Omitting the period between complete sentences results in one kind of run-on sentence called a fused sentence:

> Habits and customs rather than written rules govern much of a worker's behavior informal rules are sometimes more powerful than formal rules.

Placing a comma between complete sentences produces another kind of run-on sentence called a comma splice:

> Habits and customs rather than written rules govern much of a worker's behavior, informal rules are sometimes more powerful than formal rules.

You can correct run-on sentences in a number of ways, some of which you have already studied. Here are some ways to correct run-on sentences.

Form separate sentences:

Habits and customs rather than written rules govern much of a worker's behavior. Informal rules are sometimes more powerful than formal rules.

Form a compound sentence:

Habits and customs rather than written rules govern much of a worker's behavior, for informal rules are sometimes more powerful than formal rules.

Form a complex sentence:

Because informal rules are sometimes more powerful than formal rules, habits and customs rather than written rules govern much of a worker's behavior.

Exercise L   Correct each of these run-on sentences by rewriting it as (a) separate sentences, (b) a compound sentence, and (c) a complex sentence.

1. Most offices have an unwritten dress code new employees have to learn it to survive.
2. Having a personal secretary is a sign of high rank, sharing a secretary indicates lower rank.
3. Uncarpeted floors are a sign of low status supervisors have carpeted offices.
4. Information represents power in large organizations, employees guard their sources of information carefully.
5. The keys to the executive washroom once symbolized power most employees had to use common facilities now top executives have private washrooms with showers.

SUBJECT—VERB AGREEMENT

Subjects and verbs must agree in number. If the subject of a sentence is singular, the verb must be singular. If the subject is plural, the verb must be plural. To help distinguish between singular and plural verbs, remember that a third person, singular verb in the present tense always ends in *s*.

Present Tense, Singular

First person:	I help
Second person:	you help
Third person:	he, she, it helps

Because a third person singular verb in the present tense ends in *s*, the verbs in the following examples agree with the singular subject *robot*.

> An industrial robot *helps* with dirty and dangerous jobs.
> An industrial robot *does* repetitive jobs.

By contrast, plural verbs do not end in *s*, as the following examples using plural subjects show.

> Robots *replace* humans in the workplace.
> Robots *work* around the clock without need for rest.

When the subject and verb are close to each other in the sentence, rules of agreement are easy to apply. When other words separate them, however, you must identify the subject to insure its agreement with the verb. In the sentence

> A leading manufacturer of computer components uses robots for boring jobs.

the subject is *manufacturer*. "Of computer components" is a prepositional phrase. You can remove it and still have a structurally complete sentence:

> A leading manufacturer uses robots for boring jobs.

The pronouns in the following list are often separated from the verb by prepositional phrases. These pronouns are always singular.

one	someone	nobody
anyone	somebody	each
anybody	everyone	either
anything	everybody	neither

When these words are subjects of sentences, they take singular verbs. In the following example, "Each of the robots does the work of several human workers," remove the prepositional phrase "of the robots," and you can see clearly that the singular subject *each* requires the singular verb *does*.

As you learned earlier, many sentences have compound subjects; that is, two or more subjects. When these subjects are joined by *and*, they are plural and take a plural verb. Here is an example.

> The Unitron *line* of medium technology robots and the Dectron *line* of high technology robots *include* units with 20,000-pound load capacity.

The word *and* acts like a plus sign between subjects. It makes two singular subjects plural. If you substitute phrases like *as well as, along with*, or *together with* for *and*, you have one subject and a prepositional phrase. Do not mistake the object of the preposition for a subject. Study the following example and explanation carefully.

> The Unitron *line* of medium technology robots as well as the Dectron line of high technology robots *includes* units with 20,000-pound load capacity.

"As well as the Dectron line of high technology robots" is a prepositional phrase. It can be removed from the sentence and therefore does not help to determine the number of the verb.

When *or* or *nor* (as well as *either . . . or, neither . . . nor*) join two subjects, the verb takes the number of the subject closer to it.

> Either an automated conveyer system or *robots lower* costs of manufacturing.

The plural subject *robots* is closer to the verb than the singular subject *system*. Therefore, the verb must be plural. If the subjects were reversed, the singular subject *system* would be closer to the verb. The verb would have to be singular *lowers*.

A final rule about subject-verb agreement to be aware of concerns verb-antecedent agreement in complex sentences. When a clause begins with a relative pronoun (*who, whoever, whose, which, what, that*), the relative pronoun is the subject of the clause. A relative pronoun has the same number as its antecedent which is the word it refers to in the main clause. In the following sentence, the verb-antecedent agreement is clear.

> Industrial robots which perform flawlessly have revolutionized Japanese industry.

Which, the subject of the subordinate clause, clearly refers to the plural word *robots*. Thus, *which* requires the plural verb *perform*. In some complex sentences, several words or phrases may separate the relative pronoun from its antecedent as the following sentence shows.

> The UFW is only one of the labor organizations which fears loss of jobs through increased use of robots.

As you can see in this sentence, the verb in the subordinate clause is the singular *fears*. It agrees with *one* rather than with *organizations*, the word immediately in front of it.

Exercise M Select the verb that agrees in number with the subject. Cross out any word groups that come between the subject and verb.

1. One use for medium technology and high technology robots (is, are) on factory assembly lines.

2. More than most U.S. companies, General Electric (has, have) committed itself to the use of robots.

3. New technology (allows, allow) faster replacement of human workers by robots.

4. Robots, in spite of their promise of higher productivity, (has, have) only begun to catch on in American industry.

5. Highly optimistic forecasts for increased use of the robot (has, have) been made by robot manufacturers.

6. Each of these products (costs, cost) more than most manufacturers care to pay.

7. Higher productivity and excellent performance (makes, make) robots desirable future additions to the workplace.

8. Manipulators operated by humans or a computer (controls, control) most robot operations.

9. The industrial robot, looking nothing like those that (stars, star) in movies, (has, have) become increasingly more versatile.

10. A robot controlled by skilled human managers (completes, complete) dangerous work quickly and cheaply.

PUNCTUATION

In the first part of this section, you reviewed the use of periods and question marks. These punctuation marks are called end markers because they let the reader know where sentences stop. Now you will review internal punctuation marks such as commas, semicolons, colons, apostrophes, and quotation marks. Used properly, these punctuation marks clarify meaning within the boundaries of sentences.

Commas

Commas have five common uses:

1. to divide main clauses in compound sentences

2. to separate introductory elements from the main clause

3. to set off interrupters

4. to separate items in a series

5. to separate elements in geographical names, addresses, and dates.

Here are some guidelines and examples to show you how to use commas in sentences.

1. Place a comma before the coordinate conjunction (*and, or, nor, but, for, so, yet*) that joins main clauses in compound sentences. Review the structure of compound sentences before you start.

School lunches provide nutritious meals, and they help to absorb surplus food.

(A comma appears before *and* because *and* joins two main clauses.)

School lunches provide nutritious meals and help to absorb surplus food.

(No comma appears before *and* because the verb *help* does not have its own subject.)

2. Place a comma after introductory elements: (a) words, (b) phrases, or (c) clauses, which come before the main clause.

   a. However, many children are ineligible for school lunch programs.

   b. According to government figures, more parents can pay for their children's lunches than now do so.

   c. Although most people don't realize it, all school lunch programs receive some form of government aid.

3. Use commas to separate interrupters from the main structure of the sentence.

Food for Children Center, an antihunger group, protests cuts in government support.

Such groups, which review various food programs, claim that some poor children have been excluded from lunch programs.

The government maintains that genuinely poor children still receive free lunches, as a high official recently pointed out.

4. Use commas to separate items in a series including the item that comes before the conjunction.

Schools must serve specified portions of meat or meat substitutes, vegetables, and bread or bread substitutes to qualify for government aid.

Student leaders, food directors, and school administrators have joined forces to solve the problem of wasted food.

They have tried to develop more appetizing meals, to improve cafeteria surroundings, and to involve parents in the programs.

5. Use commas to separate elements in geographical names, addresses, and dates. Notice the commas after (a) county-state, (b) city-state, and (c) month-year combinations when they occur in the middle of sentences.

   a. Schools in St. Louis County, Minnesota, have developed a successful lunch program.

   b. For example, Whitman High School in Duluth, Minnesota, has made its cafeteria resemble a fast-food restaurant.

c. The food director at Whitman started the program on September 1, 1982, to cut waste.

People interested in Whitman's program can visit the school or write to its food director at 1849 Paul Bunyan Road, Duluth, MN 55807.

(Notice that no comma appears between the state name and zip code.)

Exercise N   Punctuate the following sentences with commas.

1. At the end of World War II the government-funded school lunch program began.

2. Supporters of the program intended it to provide nutritious lunches for rich middle-class and poor children.

3. Every school gets a subsidy for its lunch program but many schools do not meet federal nutrition standards.

4. School lunches are often deficient in nutrients like iron thiamin magnesium and vitamin C.

5. Some school lunches especially those served in fast-food style cafeterias also have vitamin A deficiencies.

6. A few schools offer a choice of conventional cooked lunches fast-food lunches and salad lunches.

7. Students usually drink the milk served with lunch but they waste the vegetables.

8. Parents in Ralston Kansas got involved in school lunch program planning.

9. When federal funds were cut they feared that local taxes would rise.

10. On May 8 1982 concerned citizens met at the District Administration Building 69 McCormick Road Ralston and formed a committee to oversee the lunch program.

11. The committee whose members represented all sections of Wheeler County Kansas expected to find mismanagement and waste.

12. To their surprise they found a well run program.

13. They invited Jean Olsen director of food services to join the committee.

14. The lunch program was well run yet students complained about it.

15. With student help the committee planned a new menu.

16. The new menu which contained many of the students' favorite foods greatly reduced the complaints.

17. The students prefer cheeseburgers with onions pickles and lettuce to baked fish and mashed potatoes.

18. Some parents however feared the school was serving only junk food.

19. These parents were invited to lunch at the cafeteria and they were convinced that meals were nutritious.

20. The only real loser was the Snack Shack in nearby Revere Kansas.

Semicolons

The semicolon (;) has two major functions. First, as you have already learned, it may be used to separate clauses in compound sentences and often does so when the second clause begins with an adverb. A few adverbs which often begin clauses are *however, therefore, nevertheless, thus, moreover, otherwise, hence, consequently*, and *finally*. This example of simple sentences will remind you how to form a compound sentence using a semicolon.

> Ed Kolcavage wanted to go to college. However, he didn't have enough money.

The semicolon replaces the period after *college*.

> Ed Kolcavage wanted to go to college; however, he didn't have enough money.

Second, the semicolon may separate items in a series when the item is already punctuated by a comma.

> Kolcavage got scholarship applications from Algoma College, the school he wanted to attend; the UFW, his mother's trade union; and The Alliance, a social organization to which his family belonged.

If commas alone separated the items, the sentence would read

> Kolcavage got scholarship applications from Algoma College, the school he wanted to attend, the UFW, his mother's trade union, and The Alliance, a social organization to which his family belonged.

The semicolons in the series help make meaning clear.

Exercise O   Punctuate the following sentences with semicolons and commas.

1. Ed Kolcavage's parents encouraged him to go to college moreover they promised to help him with expenses.

2. The high school guidance counselor told Kolcavage about federal assistance programs such as Pell grants state assistance programs available to

residents and college assistance programs including work/study programs.

3. The counselor also told him to apply early otherwise he might not be eligible to start school in the fall.

4. Because banks process state loans for college Kolcavage got a list of three banks to visit in his home town: First Federal 115 West Fourth Street Citizens State Bank 27 East Main Street and CNB Bank 1005 Woodrow Drive.

5. He tried for a month to get a summer job finally Ace Construction hired him as a laborer.

Colons

Colons (:) separate lists and series from the rest of the sentence.

> Algoma College offers three kinds of student assistance: scholarships, loans, and jobs.

Placement of the colon is important. It should not come directly after the verb. In the sentence

> Algoma College offers: scholarships, loans, and jobs.

the colon is not needed. The sentence reads perfectly well without it.

> Algoma College offers scholarships, loans, and jobs.

Exercise P   Place colons only where needed in the following sentences. Use commas or semicolons to separate items in series.

1. Algoma College offers three different kinds of work/study jobs maintenance assistant library aide and kitchen aide.

2. Algoma College's merit scholarships are based on high school grades class standing demonstrated talent and activities record.

3. Many private scholarships are available from a variety of sources corporations service organizations community organizations family foundations veterans' groups and trade unions.

4. Kolcavage also learned of three other aid programs Supplemental Educational Opportunity Grants which do not need to be repaid National Direct Student Loans which charge 5 percent interest and the Algoma College Loan Plan which charges 12 percent interest.

5. Kolcavage's high school counselor advised him to have a copy of his parents' latest tax return ready to file for aid early and to fill out aid forms carefully.

Apostrophes

Apostrophes signal the possessive case of nouns.

1. To form the singular possessive, add *'s* to singular nouns and indefinite pronouns.

Singular Possessive

Nouns	*Indefinite Pronouns*
one worker's salary	anybody's pay
a company's profits	somebody's ideas
a week's pay	nobody's fault
one year's experience	

2. To form the plural possessive, place an apostrophe after the plural form of nouns.

Plural Possessive

Two workers' salaries
Many companies' profits
Four weeks' pay
Seven years' experience

3. A few nouns like *woman, man*, and *child* form plurals irregularly. Place the apostrophe before the *s* in each of these words to show possession.

Singular Possessive	*Plural Possessive*
A woman's salary	Women's salaries
A man's job	Men's jobs
The child's school	The children's school

Apostrophes also show where letters have been left out of words to form contractions. To form the contraction *doesn't*, for example, the words *does* and *not* are written as one word, *doesnot*. Then the *o* is removed, and an apostrophe is inserted in its place to show where the *o* was.

Exercise Q   Use apostrophes to mark possessives and to show where letters have been left out of contractions.

1. White collar workers jobs are in jeopardy.

2. Female executives ability to cope with loss of a position often doesnt match male executives.

3. A lack of understanding about "how to play the game" rather than incompetence often causes a womans failure.

4. According to a Chicago psychologists assessment, these women feel they didnt really fit in the organization in the first place.

5. Whether female or male, all employees egos are crushed by layoffs.

6. Layoffs sometimes result from an organizations decision to eliminate a department.

7. The department heads job is the first to go.

8. Aggressive job searches wont turn up a similar position quickly, even with an employment consultants advice.

9. Several years experience isnt a guarantee of immediate success in the job market.

10. Switching fields is among ones options in looking for work.

Quotation Marks and Underlining

Quotation marks indicate you have used another person's exact words. Such quotations are called direct quotations. Direct quotations vary in length. Some are complete sentences, while others are only a few words. Study the examples that follow.

1. When asked to describe how he felt about losing his job, Phil Edgar said, "I still wake up at night thinking about it."

2. "A real shock" was Maxine Schultz's response. "I couldn't believe it happened to me," Schultz added.

In the first example, notice the comma after *said*. Always place a comma after introductions to quotations like *Phil Edgar said, he responded*, and *she answered*. Notice also that the period that ends the sentence is inside the quotation marks. In the second example, the phrase *a real shock* has no punctuation except the quotation marks because it is fully integrated into the sentence. The comma that ends the quotation *I couldn't believe it happened to me* is inside the quotation marks.

Other items generally placed in quotation marks are titles of chapters or other specific sections of books as well as titles of magazine, journal, and newspaper articles.

Underlining in a written or typed report functions in the same way as italics in printed material. Some items such as book titles and the names of magazines, journals, and newspapers are always underlined. The names of television programs and movies are underlined because they would appear in italics in print. Finally, words or letters when referred to as words or letters are also underlined, as the following example shows.

To make the word *company* plural, change the *y* to *i* and add *es*.

Exercise R Place quotation marks around direct quotations and underline as appropriate.

1. Robert Missigman refused a lower position at lower pay because as he stated to his employment counselor I couldn't afford to support a family on less money.

2. Missigman read the employment ads in the New York Times and even bought a copy of Dress for Success.

3. At first I answered every ad and sent out 25 letters and resumes a week. I didn't have any luck Missigman recalls and staying home seemed easier.

4. Bob Missigman's response to joblessness is typical notes employment counselor Henry Babik. Babik writes in his article Response Patterns of the Unemployed The unemployed become depressed and insecure and lose their early drive to find a new job.

5. With the help and support of his counselor, Missigman eventually found a new job. He says about his period of unemployment I can describe it in one word, awful, with a capital A.

Hyphenation

Hyphens are useful for three purposes. First, they show divisions of words at the end of lines. If you cannot avoid dividing a word at the end of a line, consult a dictionary to find out where you may divide it. A dictionary separates words into syllables to show you where to hyphenate. For example, the word *enterprise* is divided into three syllables, *en/ter/prise.* Thus, to divide it, you can place a hyphen after *en* or *enter.* Never guess at the division of words and never hyphenate one-syllable words or unpronounced syllables at the ends of words.

Exercise S Place a diagonal line at each place the dictionary shows hyphenation is allowed in the following words.

1. personal	6. diminished
2. wealth	7. industry
3. experience	8. suburbs
4. insurance	9. distribution
5. choice	10. enviable

A second use of hyphens is to join phrases of two or more words that form a single unit when they modify a noun. For example, the words *hard fought* form a single unit requiring a hyphen when they modify *battle* in the sentence

Hank Smith waged a hard-fought battle to get an education.

They do not need a hyphen when they stand alone.

His battle to get an education was hard fought.

A third use of hyphens is with numbers from 21 to 99 when the numbers are spelled out.

He'll be twenty-one on Friday.
We're celebrating his twenty-first birthday on Saturday.

Exercise T   Place hyphens where needed in the following sentences.

1. Algoma College experienced a one fourth decrease in enrollments last year.
2. It decided to admit high risk students like Hank Smith.
3. Smith's father had a low level, low paying job with Ressler, Inc.; his mother, incapacitated by arthritis, was in an adult care facility.
4. Smith financed his education with a long term government loan and a scholarship that was tax exempt.
5. He also found a part time job because his school work only allowed him to work part time.

Capitalization

No complete set of rules for capitalization has ever been developed, but a few guidelines will you help you to understand when to capitalize.

1. Capitalize the first word of every sentence.
2. Capitalize the first and every main word (not prepositions or the word *and*) of titles.
3. Capitalize names of (a) people, (b) places, (c) organizations, (d) days and months, (e) regions, (f) religions, (g) languages, and (h) races and nationalities.

    a. Cynthia Harris Winslow, William P. McShane, Jr.
    b. Kingston, Luzerne County, Pennsylvania, U.S.A., Toronto, Ontario, Canada, Europe
    c. Veterans of Foreign Wars, Rotary Club, United Negro College Fund, Boy Scouts, Republic Steel, Federal Bureau of Investigation
    d. Friday, November 12
    e. the North, the South, the Midwest, the Orient
    f. Anglican, Baptist, Buddhist, Jewish, Methodist, Moslem, Roman Catholic
    g. Chinese, English, French, Urdu, Swahili

h. American, Arab, Black, Aryan

3. Capitalize titles when they are part of a name.

Governor Jesse Rydell	but	Jesse Rydell, the governor
Professor J.T. Dove	but	J.T. Dove, a professor
Sturgis High School	but	a high school in Sturgis
Dr. Marie Halston	but	Marie Halston, a doctor
Aunt Mary	but	Mary Engle, my aunt

4. Do not capitalize (a) directions, (b) seasons, (c) nonessential parts of names

   a. north, south, east, west, north of Los Angeles, south of Washington, D.C.

   b. spring, summer, fall, winter

   c. Concorde supersonic jet, Italian sausage, Kodak film, Remington rifle, Mississippi delta

Exercise U   Capitalize where necessary in the following paragraph.

hank smith's first semester at algoma college held many surprises for him. he started school on september 5, a typical fall day in northern iowa, but that was all that was typical about his first week of school. breakfast was usually leftover hostess cupcakes and a bottle of sugar-free dr. pepper. smith then walked to his anthropology class. His professor, dr. lester lansdowne, usually kept the class late. Thus, after anthropology, hank had to hurry along westminster drive to his next class, french literature. his last class on monday was math 101. When it was over, hank jumped into his chevy pickup, stopped at mcdonald's for a cheeseburger, and drove to brandstatler's, a company specializing in paper products. four hours of packing boxes made walsh cafeteria's food look good even though the "real" german potato salad and "authentic" mexican enchiladas weren't much like the originals. finally, hank was off to the library to finish oliver twist and to prepare for tuesday's classes. the photography club met on tuesday, too, he remembered. He got a lot of good advice at pella high school, he thought, but nobody told him college would pack a month's work into a single week.

Numbers

A few guidelines will help you to decide when to spell out numbers and when to use figures in your writing.

1. Single-digit numbers (one to nine) are often spelled out.

   Hank Smith took four courses his first semester.

2. Multi-digit numbers (10 and over) are usually written as figures.

   Smith averaged 25 hours of work every week. He packed 1,500 boxes a week.

3. Consistency is desirable when both single- and multi-digit numbers appear together.

   He worked three hours Monday, four hours Tuesday through Thursday, and ten hours Friday and Saturday.

   or

   He worked 3 hours Monday, 4 hours Tuesday through Thursday, and 10 hours Friday and Saturday.

4. Figures are always used in (a) dates, (b) addresses, (c) money, (d) identification, and (e) statistics.

   a. January 15, 1944; 1970-1980

   b. 120 Forest Drive (Apt. 4-D)

   c. $20; $20.50; $.50 or 50 cents; $2 million; $15 billion

   d. Public Act 1717; Size 14; 78 × 14 tires; chapter 5; pp. 169-176

   e. 50 percent; 3.2 grade point average; 0.15 inch of rain; 3.15 earned run average; 3-2 odds; 2:1 ratio

5. If a number is the first item in a sentence, it must be written in words.

   Twenty-five people attended the meeting.

   If the number is large, revise the sentence to avoid writing it in words.

   A crowd of 7,250 people filled the hall.

   not

   Seven thousand two hundred and fifty people filled the hall.

Exercise V   Revise the following paragraph to demonstrate correct use of numbers.

The Fastclean Company was founded on February first one thousand nine hundred and thirty nine by two brothers who believed that good service could also be fast service. For twenty dollars a month, they rented Apartment One-D at two thousand seventeen North Arlington and opened the first one-hour cleaning store in Butte, Montana. During February, they served only forty-two customers, earning a net profit of two dollars and eighteen cents. But these customers were pleased. Each one told one or two friends. By the beginning of summer, business had increased over five hundred percent. The brothers never looked back. They opened new stores at the rate of one a year during the difficult war years and stepped up the pace to as many as ten a month in the early nineteen fifties. But even amid success, hard times hit the original shop. In nineteen eighty one, Lemuel Karstairs filed for Chapter Eleven bankruptcy.

Appendix B

Writing
with Style

Two paragraphs may contain the same information. Both may be grammatically correct. Yet one sounds better than the other. Which of the following paragraphs do you think is more readable?

Paragraph 1	*Paragraph 2*

It has come to my attention that Greg Krum and Scott Stewart have applied for the assistant manager job at Frantz's Steak House. It is my decision to hire Krum rather than Stewart because Krum seems to have the qualities to work in a restaurant. First, there is the work record of both applicants. Krum worked for Giammona's Restaurant part time for two years as a busser and waiter. He was also employed by Starr Oil and Heating cleaning furnaces during the summer. Stewart was employed as a dishwasher at Hilltop Lodge. This is his only work experience. Second is the matter of the applicants' responsibility. Krum was the advertising manager of his high school yearbook and newspaper. In this type of situation, he had to meet the public due to the fact that he had to sell advertising and collect the money for it. Krum is also involved with the youth group at his church as a member of the finance committee. Nothing is mentioned on Stewart's application about outside activities. In a restaurant type of situation, Krum is definitely the right man for the job. He has more restaurant experience than Stewart, and he seems more self-motivated, active, and responsible. Stewart doesn't seem to have much get-up-and-go.

Greg Krum rather than Scott Stewart is the better choice for the assistant manager job at Frantz's Steak House. Krum has a better work record than Stewart. Krum bussed and waited tables part time for two years at Giammona's Restaurant. He also cleaned furnaces during the summer for Starr Oil and Heating. Stewart, on the other hand, worked part time for six months as a dishwasher at Hilltop Lodge. Krum's outside activities show his sense of responsibility. As the advertising manager of his high school newspaper and yearbook, he met the public through sales of advertising. He also serves on the finance committee of his church's youth group. Stewart doesn't mention outside activities on his application. Because of Krum's previous restaurant experience and his demonstration of responsibility in outside activities, I've selected him rather than Stewart as assistant manager.

Although both paragraphs contain the same information, the second paragraph is concise and readable while the first paragraph is long and wordy. The guidelines in this chapter center on removing wordiness from writing. Following them should help you produce paragraphs more like the second example than the first one. One word of caution, however, before you begin: Ignoring any of these guidelines is preferable to writing an awkward sentence.

Subject Delayers

Subject delayers, also called expletives, replace the real subject of a sentence. The most common subject delayer is *there* plus any part of the verb *to be* (*is, are, was, were, be, been*). Here is a sentence that begins with a subject delayer.

> There are many outdoor summer activities featuring entertainment, music, and good food in the city.

There are replaces *activities* in the first or subject position and pushes *activities* to a less significant middle position in the sentence. Removing *there are* puts *activities* back into the first part of the sentence.

> Many outdoor summer activities featuring entertainment, music, and good food take place in the city.

Exercise A   Rewrite the following paragraph to remove subject delayers.

> Many outdoor summer activities complete with entertainment, music, and good food take place in the city. First, there is what is known as CityFest, the largest festival in the city. This festival has entertainment, food, drinks, games and, best of all, a remarkable mixture of people from every part of town. Second, there are outdoor music festivals which feature many kinds of music. For example, there was a jazz festival last summer at which outstanding musicians such as Herbie Hancock and Grover Washington, Jr., appeared. Finally, there is "Taste of the City," an activity at which some of the city's most popular restaurants sell food. Last summer, there were Armando's Famous Tamales, Angelo's Pizza, and Aunt Mary's Hot Pastries at the "Taste." A sample of these delicious treats cost only $.75 each. There can't be a better way to spend a summer in the city than to participate in these inexpensive and entertaining events.

Broad References

Like other pronouns, *it* and *this* (as well as *that, these,* and *those*) should have clear antecedents, specific words to which they refer. In the following example, *it* is used correctly.

> The outcome of a football game is sometimes in doubt until the final seconds. It depends upon skill, luck, and a host of other factors.

It refers directly to *outcome. Outcome* can replace *it* in the second sentence.

> The outcome depends upon skill, luck, and a host of other factors.

In the next example, *this* does not refer clearly to any word in the first sentence.

> Effective communication helps to determine the success of an enterprise. This is true in organizations as different as oil companies and professional football teams.

This refers to an idea, rather than to a specific word in the first sentence. Neither *effective communication* nor any other word in the sentence can replace *this*. Removing *this* altogether by combining the sentences or supplying a noun for *this* to modify clarifies the meaning of the sentence.

> Effective communication helps to determine the success of organizations as different as oil companies and professional football teams.

> Effective communication helps to determine the success of an enterprise. This principle is true in organizations as different as oil companies and professional football teams.

Exercise B   Rewrite the following sentences to remove broad references.

1. Personnel in large organizations are like members of a team. It is necessary for all the team members to understand the organization's philosophy.

2. Like a football coach, the manager communicates the organization's philosophy to team members. This is one of the manager's chief duties.

3. The coach of a professional football team sets a chief goal of winning the Super Bowl and then develops objectives for each player. That is the formula that leads to success.

4. Team members also discuss personal goals with the manager in one-to-one interviews. This motivates team members to higher achievement while it benefits the organization.

5. Personnel decisions are easier to make when communications are open. It is often possible to agree on goals that fulfill both organizational and personal needs.

Passive Voice

Verbs have two voices, active and passive. In the active voice, the subject of the sentence acts.

> Midwest Farm Insurance encourages employees to continue their education.
> Ellen Lasko took two courses at Marshall Community College.
> These courses counted toward an associate's degree.

In the passive voice, the actor is in a part of the sentence other than the subject or is absent altogether.

> Employees are encouraged to continue their education.
> Two courses were taken by Ellen Lasko.
> These courses are counted toward an associate's degree.

Verb phrases in the passive voice are easy to recognize. Look for any part of the verb *to be* (*is, are, was, were, be, been*) plus a past participle. Past participles are the third principle part of verbs given in the dictionary. The following chart shows the difference between active and passive verbs in all the tenses.

Tense	Active Voice	Passive Voice
Present	Ellen *takes* a course	A course *is taken*
Past	Ellen *took* a course	A course *was taken* or *taken was* a course
Future	Ellen *will take* a course	A course *will be taken*
Present Perfect	Ellen *has taken* a course	A course *has been taken*
Past Perfect	Ellen *had taken* a course	A course *had been taken*
Future Perfect	Ellen *will have taken* a course	A course *will have been taken*

As you can see, passive verbs are wordier than the corresponding active verbs. Further, sentences with passive verbs are indirect and sometimes unclear. Thus, sentences with active verbs generally produce better writing than those with passive verbs.

Here are three ways to change passive voice to active.

1. Make the actor the subject of the sentence.

    Passive: The rules of grammar *have been studied* by Ellen.
    Active: Ellen *has studied* the rules of grammar.

    Sometimes you have to supply the actor.

    Passive: Ellen *was taught* the difference between active and
                passive verbs.
    Active: Professor Greene *taught* Ellen the difference be-
                tween active and passive verbs.

2. Replace a passive verb with a different verb in the active voice.

    Passive: Ellen *was gifted* with a natural flair for writing.
    Active: Ellen *had* a natural flair for writing.

3. Remove either part of the *to be* verb or the past participle.

    Passive: Marshall Community College *is located* in
                Brighton County.
    Active: Marshall Community College *is* in Brighton
                County.

Exercise C   Underline the passive verbs in the following sentences. Then rewrite the sentences in active voice.

1. Ellen was sent to a private school when she was thirteen.
2. Her education was furthered at Davidson College of Business.
3. She was then employed in the Claims Department of Midwest Farm Insurance.
4. Situated on the third floor of the SIB Building is the Claims Department.
5. Ellen took a refresher course in math which was offered by the Data Control Institute.
6. Advantage was also taken of Midwest's policy of employee skill development.
7. Paid for by the company is one-half her tuition for job-related courses.
8. She has also been given released time to attend a course in the morning.
9. Disciplined study habits are demanded of a student who also works full time.
10. If she is promoted by the time her degree is earned, it is felt the effort was worthwhile.

Biased Language

Organizations as well as individuals express their attitudes through words. When these words are biased in any way, they imply biased actions. Thus, to show that they are not biased toward either sex, organizations avoid biased language in favor of neutral, unbiased language.

Equal treatment of both sexes means using unbiased terminology in job descriptions.

Biased	*Unbiased*
businessman, businesswoman	business person, executive
salesman, chairman, chairlady, chairwoman	salesperson, sales representative, chair, chairperson
foreman	manager, supervisor
stewardess, steward	flight attendant
male nurse	nurse
woman doctor	doctor
workman	worker, laborer, employee
cleaning woman, cleaning lady	cleaner, housekeeper

Equal treatment also means avoiding "man-words."

Biased	*Unbiased*
manmade	synthetic, artificial
manpower	human energy, workforce
primitive man	primitive people
manhood	adulthood
a man's work	work

Equal treatment also means avoiding use of the pronoun *he* to refer to members of both sexes. For example, a statement like

A consumer wants his money's worth when he buys a product.

is biased because women are consumers also. The phrases *he or she* (*he/she*), *his or hers* (*his/hers*), and *him or her* (*him/her*) may be substituted for masculine pronouns *he, his*, and *him*. Such substitution may, however, produce an awkward sentence.

A consumer wants *his or her* money's worth when *he or she* buys a product.

To avoid this kind of awkwardness, use plural pronouns (*they, their, them*) rather than singular.

Consumers want *their* money's worth when *they* buy a product.

Exercise D   Rewrite the following paragraph to remove biased language.

> Changes in the workplace since our forefathers' time have improved life both on and off the job. No longer does a workman spend 50 hours a week at a factory, for labor-saving devices have reduced the manpower needed to turn out a product. Thus, although the workman spends less time on the job, he is actually more productive. The businessman has time now for involvement in community activities. For example, he can participate in community activities that directly affect the quality of his life and that of his family. Often, because of his professional expertise, he can become chairman of a civic committee. But a man doesn't have to be an important executive to contribute. The mailman, the factory foreman, the cameraman at the local television station each can bring his particular knowledge and ability to the solution of local problems. This kind of manpower focused on particular problems usually results in efficient and inexpensive solutions. In fact, many small towns have a gentleman's agreement by which the town council takes no action until the town fathers study an issue. Only freedom from the 10-hour work day permits this kind of civic involvement.

Pronoun Shifts

Pronouns have both person and number.

	Singular	*Plural*
First Person:	I, my, mine, me	we, our, ours, us
Second Person:	you, your, yours, you	you, your, yours, you
Third Person:	he, she, it his, hers, its him, her, it	they, their, theirs, them

Indefinite pronouns such as *one, everybody*, and *nobody* are always third person as are all nouns.

First person pronouns are subjective. Speakers and writers use them to tell personal experiences or stories. Second person pronouns directly address the reader. They are useful for giving directions. Third person pronouns are objective. They are used to talk about someone or something other than the speaker or writer.

Writers create confusion when they shift without purpose from one person to another and from singular to plural and vice versa. The following sentences show shifts in number as well as in person of pronouns.

> A consumer wants their money's worth when they buy a product. You have to compare prices carefully to make sure you are getting a bargain.
>
> For example, I always check the price of the generic product and the store brand. You would be surprised at how often the generic's price is higher.

To correct these examples, aim for consistency in number and person of the pronouns.

> Consumers want their money's worth when they buy a product. They have to compare prices carefully to make sure they are getting a bargain.
>
> For example, they should always check the price of the generic product and the store brand. They would be surprised at how often the generic's price is higher.

Exercise F   Rewrite the following paragraph to make it consistent in person and number.

> Students can usually solve the financial problems they face in college. Students have many reasons for financial difficulties. For example, room and board, tuition, and books cost several hundred dollars a semester. Further, a student can spend between $20-$30 a week on social activities. Finally, students often fail to budget their money wisely. However, most students can find a solution to his or her financial problem. First, you can become a resident adviser and have your room and board paid for by the school. The second solution is to apply for financial aid so that the school helps to pay for your education. Third, if a person budgets his money, he or she will learn to spend wisely. A fourth solution is to get a part-time job so that you are making money throughout the semester. Although financial problems often occur, I have found ways to solve them. I plan to work during the summer and save money for the next school year. Another route students can take is to apply for a scholarship. Sometimes you can have your whole education paid for by the

college or some other group. When a student has severe financial difficulties, he should attend a college near his home to alleviate room and board and transportation expenses. All of us face financial difficulties while in college, but we can overcome them if we plan ahead.

Parallelism

Elements of a sentence performing the same function should be alike in structure. When elements are alike, they are said to be parallel. Parallel structure improves readability by insuring consistency and by clarifying relationships among parts of a sentence.

1. Nouns

> Poor: Eunice Simmons is an efficient worker, a good parent, and excels in photography.

> Good: Eunice Simmons is an efficient worker, a good parent, and an excellent photographer.

2. Adjectives

> Poor: Her pictures are clear, sharp, and artistically composed.

> Good: Her pictures are clear, sharp, and artistic.

3. Phrases

> Poor: To lead a full personal life and contributions to the community were her goals.

> Good: To lead a full personal life and to contribute to the community were her goals.

4. Verbs

> Poor: She joined the Photography Club and was running for City Council.

> Good: She joined the Photography Club and ran for City Council.

Exercise G   Rewrite the following paragraph to improve parallelism.

Some career counselors begin by giving clients a battery of standardized tests to measure their abilities, aptitudes, things they like to do, personal values, and personalities. With this information in hand, counselors can begin to match clients and career opportunities. Clients who score high in math and scientific areas may be encouraged to inquire about openings for engineers, mechanical trades, and the new computer technology. Others who like group activities and make high verbal ability scores could look into the need for teachers of various kinds or some kind of social work. Counselors encourage their clients to pursue their special interests even in the face of discouraging outlooks in some traditional professions. Private day care centers and training programs in business and industry need teachers even when public schools have declining enrollments or are laying off teachers. Tool and die makers need the same abilities and need to know some of the same facts as people in engineering. Every career is a ladder with rungs. Young people who want to be happy in their work and a success must first choose the right ladder to climb and then to be looking for the right rung to reach.

Index